TEXAS DISTRICT & COUNTY ATTORNEYS ASSOCIATION

# DWI INVESTIGATION & PROSECUTION

*(2016 edition)*

*by*

**RICHARD ALPERT**

**Texas District & County Attorneys Association**
505 W. 12th St., Suite 100, Austin, Texas 78701
(512) 474-2436 Fax (512) 478-4112
www.tdcaa.com
books@tdcaa.com

## TDCAA Staff




ISBN 978-1-934973-88-2




## Texas District & County Attorneys Association

*The Texas District & County Attorneys Association provides training and technical assistance to more than 5,000 state prosecutors and their staff members through regular training seminars and conferences. It hosts the largest annual gathering of prosecutors in the nation, provides technical assistance to the law enforcement community, and serves as a legislative resource in criminal law matters.*

*The Texas District & County Attorneys Association is committed to service and invites input from its members regarding better ways to serve the offices it represents and the people of the State of Texas.*

## Caveat

This book is intended to be a guide and is intended to provide accurate and current information about criminal law. It is, however, sold with the intention that TDCAA is not engaged in rendering legal or other professional advice. Each reader must be responsible for his or her own legal research. Because lawyers must be responsible for their own research and because the law is constantly changing, Richard Alpert, TDCAA and its employees do not warrant, either expressly or impliedly, that the information in this volume has not been subject to change, amendment, reversal, or revision.

Additionally, this guidebook is not a definitive collection of field operations directives; therefore, a peace officer confronted with a question of law should consult his/her available counsel (whether the city attorney, police advisor, or the local district or county attorney's office). Officers must abide by policies and procedures of their own departments, notwithstanding advice that may appear in the book to run counter to those policies or procedures.

# Acknowledgments

There are a number of people I would like to thank, without whose help and support this book would not be possible. To Tim Curry, the longtime former Tarrant County District Attorney, for giving me a job 29 years ago and for supporting my commitment to training and to vigorously prosecuting drunk drivers. To Tanya Dohoney for serving as my appellate guru and for helping ensure the DWI cases prosecuted by our Misdemeanor Section withstand the rigors of appellate review. To Clay Abbott for his encouragement, his contributions to this book, and the good work he does spreading the gospel of DWI enforcement throughout this state. To all the staff at TDCAA, but especially Rob Kepple, Erik Nielsen, Judy Bellsnyder, Ashlee Myers and Manda Helmick for making all of the DWI-related training I have done outside my office as painless and comfortable as possible. To Diane Beckham, my editor extraordinaire, without whom this book would never have happened. For her editing, encouragement, and patience I am forever grateful. To the misdemeanor attorneys I have had the pleasure of working with over the last decade whose talent continues to amaze and inspire me. To my secretaries, Shirley Little and Jane Scribner, whom I credit for keeping my DWI Case Law Update and the slew of papers that serve as the foundation for this book, current, manageable and readable. To Warren Diepraam and Jimmy Angelino for sharing their ideas and strategies for trying these cases. To M.A.D.D. for keeping the spotlight on the problem of drunk driving, especially to Susan Bragg and Bill Lewis for their very vocal support of my efforts. To Max Courtney, Mark Fondren, Dr. Maurice Dennis, Dr. Sue Howe, and Dr. Robert Johnson for their expert advice and assistance which has brought me to the brink of (almost) understanding the science behind breath and blood testing and the many ways and levels at which alcohol effects one's ability to safely operate a motor vehicle. To my fellow Tarrant County prosecutor Riley Shaw for sharing his expertise by writing a long-needed chapter on Juvenile DWI for this edition. To Sgt. Neal Maranto for sharing his insights from 20+ years of making DWI arrests that have consistently withstood the rigors of cross-examination in the courtrooms of Tarrant County. To Anna Summersett for her assistance reviewing this volume to ensure its advice is current and for her many suggestions that have been incorporated into this edition. To my wife Karen and my children, Rachel, Sarah and Joshua, who have always been so forgiving of me the times my training and travels and weekend writing episodes have taken me away from them and their needs.

**Richard Alpert**
*September 2015*

## About the Author

Richard Alpert is one of TDCAA's most-requested speakers and teachers, and for very good reason. His intoxication manslaughter and DWI trainings have guided new (and experienced) prosecutors through the law and strategy of these difficult cases. He has donated countless hours of time to all of TDCAA's efforts, as chair of the training committee, a frequent legislative resource, and now, as a two-time author of this book and *Intoxication Manslaughter*. His invaluable contributions to making blood search warrants a statewide tool were recognized when TDCAA named him a co-recipient of the State Bar Prosecutor of the Year in 2009.

Richard's teaching materials for DWI and Intoxication Manslaughter cases have long been used all over the state. He's an irreplaceable resource for any prosecutor or officer—no matter what their experience level—in helping to achieve just results for victims and their families in these very difficult cases. No matter what your set of facts, Richard has a great idea for how to turn them to an advantage. In 2007, he turned tragic cases into beneficial new law by helping to pass tougher penalties for intoxication manslaughter and assault cases when a police officer, fire fighter, or EMS worker is the victim.

Richard has been a prosecutor with the Tarrant County Criminal District Attorney's Office since 1987 and chief of the misdemeanor division for 19 years. He has been recognized for his accomplishments by receiving the MADD National President's Award for Outstanding Prosecutor in 2007 (the same year he was featured as a *Texas Monthly* "Super Lawyer" and a *Texas Lawyer* "Go-To Prosecutor"). Richard has twice won the C. Chris Marshall Distinguished Faculty Award from TDCAA, the National Traffic Safety Award from the National Association of Prosecutor Coordinators, and the Joe Encinia Memorial Award from Metroplex M.A.D.D.

I'm so grateful to Richard for his friendship, his compassion for his victims and passion for his career, his great ideas, his enthusiasm, his willingness to jump in to yet another TDCAA time-consuming project, and for always taking our phone calls when we have "just one more" intoxication crime question. I can't thank him enough for his incredibly quick turnaround and responsiveness to many pesky editor questions. I'm just glad that we haven't yet run out of subjects for Richard to write about—his knowledge is limitless.

**Diane Beckham**
*September 2015*

# PREFACE

Once upon a time, driving while intoxicated was viewed as little more than a traffic ticket, as evidenced by its negligible range of punishment—a range that was minimal and whose boundaries were rarely tested. Even when intoxicated driving resulted in death, the crime was simply called an "accident," and the killer got a slap on the wrist, paid a fine, kept his license, and drove away to drink and drive and perhaps kill another innocent victim.

The offense of DWI takes or ruins the life of more citizens than any other crime. Like some contagious virus, it has spread to every city in this country. DWI has killed more than twice as many Americans in the 1900s than had died in every war this country fought since its creation. DWI is a crime that chooses the sex, age, and number of its victims at random.

The fact that DWI has evolved from its early perception as a minor crime to its current level of prominence is due in large part to the efforts of MADD. (I won't even bother to state the meaning behind the letters because anyone who bothers to open this book know what they stand for.) Since MADD's inception in 1982, drunk-driving deaths have declined markedly. During the late 1960s and early 1970s, more than 50,000 people lost their lives each year on our nation's public roads—more than half of those deaths involved an alcohol-impaired driver. According to NHTSA national statistics, in 2009, an estimated 9,813 people died in drunk driving crashes involving a driver with an illegal BAC (.08 or greater). These deaths constitute 32 percent of the 30,797 total traffic fatalities in 2009. In comparison, there were 1,960 more deaths in 2008, but the percentage of those intoxicated drivers involved in fatal crashes only declined by .04 percent. The state with the largest number of traffic fatalities was Texas, with 3,071 killed. Of that number, 1,235—or 40 percent—had a BAC of .08 or above. As bad as those numbers are, there is no state that has done more than Texas to fight this battle, with law changes and innovative practices that expand the ability of law enforcement to obtain the evidence needed to hold these dangerous drivers accountable.

There are a multitude of reasons why the offense was once considered no big deal. In my heart I feel that one of those reasons is the difficulty that comes with trying to prove the commission of that offense. The goal of this book is to serve as an aid to those prosecutors who face the charge in trial daily; to help them overcome the difficulties inherent in attempting to prove an offense that, at its core, is based upon an "opinion."

Most DWI cases do not involve "falling-down drunks" who stumble from their cars and give breath samples that register at over twice the legal limit. Instead, most cases—if they include bad driving from the defendant at all—involve a driver weaving within a lane, and police stops during which a defendant performs, at most, three field tests whose methods are often hard to follow and whose scoring is an easy target for defense cross-examination. DWI prosecutors will most likely be trying cases where as long as two hours has passed between when the suspect was driving and when he appears on a videotape at the station house. On that tape the suspect does not sway, does not slur his speech and wants to talk to an attorney before he decides to give a breath sample (rather than admit that he won't give a breath or blood sample because he knows the result will convict him).

The difficulty of trying these cases is exacerbated because they seem to rise and fall on an "opinion" by an officer, an "educated guess" that the law has been broken by this citizen who, unfortunately, reminds every juror of their father, mother, sister, brother or themselves. In my 10 years as chief of the misdemeanor division in Tarrant County, I have seen young prosecutors with less than a month of experience march into court with facts as weak as these—or worse—and defeat seasoned defense attorneys whose practice is filled with clients accused of heinous capital crimes. I'd like to think my advice and my study of this crime and the laws that define it has helped prosecutors find the tools to pull off such victories. In this book, I hope to pass on those tactics and advice that have come from trying to help young attorneys overcome the obstacles inherent in trying such cases and to show juries the path to understanding that the crime they have heard about in trial—even though it may have taken less than a day to present—is not a minor offense.

This book provides suggestions on ways to pick a jury, give an opening statement, and present officer and scientific testimony. It cover tactics for cross-examining the criminal defendant and defense experts. It suggests ways to sum up the importance of the crime and the strength of your case to a jury. It presents arguments that have convinced jurors to send first offenders, whose commission of this offense has resulted in the death of another person, to prison.

Not all of the suggestions in this book were invented by me. Like all good prosecutors, I have watched others and stolen the best they could offer. But some of the suggestions in this book are of my own creation. Beyond reading this book, you are invited to do what I have invited prosecutors in and out of my office to do for more than a decade: Call or e-mail me with your questions and problems (**ralpert@tarrantcounty.com**).

The ultimate goal is to ensure that you are equipped for trial so that when your judge asks you, "What says the State?" you can respond with words and actions that will leave no doubt to that judge, the defense, and the jurors that you are, in every sense of the word, "Ready."

# Dedication

In memory of my father, Robert M. Alpert, who had a passion for helping others, a moral base that never wavered, a firm belief in justice, and who instilled in his children a belief that all things are possible; and to my mother, Abby Alpert, who shared his passion and keeps it alive.

## Other Books by TDCAA

Traffic Stops (2016)
Criminal Laws of Texas (2015)
Legislative Update (2015)
Penal Laws of Texas (2015)
Code of Criminal Procedure (2015)
Texas Crimes (2015)
Confessions (2015)
Penal Code & Code of Criminal Procedure ebooks (2015)
Offense Report Manual (2015)
Charging Manual (2015)
Transportation Code Crimes & License Suspensions (2015)
Case Preparation for Investigators (2015)
Investigating & Prosecuting Child Sexual Abuse (2015)
Warrantless Search & Seizure (2015)
Punishment & Probation (2014)
Warrants Manual for Arrest, Search & Seizure (2014)
Expunction & Nondisclosure (2014)
Predicates (2014)
Prosecutor Trial Notebook (2014)
Guide to Asset Seizure and Forfeiture (2014)
Intoxication Manslaughter (2014)
Family Violence Investigation & Prosecution (2012)
Family Violence Resource Notebook (2011)
Offense Report Manual (2011)
Conflicts of Interest (2010)
The Perfect Plea (2010)
State's Appellate Manual (2010)
Predicate Questions Manual (2010)
Juveniles (2010)
*Brady* Duties & the Pretrial Disclosure of Evidence (2009)
Victim Assistance Manual (2007)
Legal Ethics & Texas Criminal Law (2006)
HIPAA for Prosecutors (2006)
Mental Defenses (2005)
Future Danger (2004)
Capital Writs (2002)
Guide to Report Writing (1998)
Grand Jury Handbooks

## Website Resources

Check out TDCAA's website at **www.tdcaa.com** for further information on traffic stops, including:

- updates on TDCAA publications, including all code books
- a DWI Resources page, which includes Richard Alpert's DWI caselaw summary and up-to-date information on how to implement new U.S. Supreme Court cases, including *McNeely*
- discussions in the user forums on traffic stops
- recent Court of Criminal Appeals and U.S. Supreme Court decisions

*For more information or to place an order, call or write:*

Texas District & County Attorneys Association
**505 W. 12th St., Suite 100, Austin, Texas 78701**
**(512) 474-2436 Fax (512) 478-4112**
**books@tdcaa.com**

# Contents

## Forms & Trial Aids Included on CD-Rom:

**37 Tex Admin Code 19** ***(breath test regulations)***

**Agreed Motion for release of portion of blood evidence to defense**

**Blood Search Warrants** ***(sample warrants)***

**Bond Condition Pleadings & Order**

**Breath Alcohol Testing Regulations** ***(DPS manual)***

**Case Law Update June 2015**

**Case Synopsis: Response to Attacks on Blood Search Warrants**

**Expert Witness Transcripts**

- Dennis and Wimbish transcripts (Fowler)
- Hilburn transcript (Fowler case)
- Wimbish transcript (Mallard case)

**Field Sobriety Tests Review**

**HGN Demonstration** ***(video)***

**Interlock Bond Pleadings & Order**

**Law Enforcement Witness Information Form**

**Medical Screening Evaluation**

**NHTSA Official SFST Student Manual**

**Order for Release of Portion of Blood Sample to Defense**

**Sample Jury Charges**

- DWI Breath Test Refusal
- DWI Charge with Blood
- DWI Charge with Evidence of .08 Intoxication
- DWI Charge with Evidence of Drugs
- DWI Punishment—Jail Time Only
- DWI Punishment—Probation

**Search Warrant to obtain hospital-drawn blood sample**

**Studies: Blood Draw/Testing**

- Additional Blood Draw/Testing Studies
    - Goldfinger & Schaber: A Comparison of Blood Alcohol Concentration Using Non-Alcohol and Alcohol-Containing Skin Antiseptics
    - Zittel & Hardin: Comparison of Blood Ethanol Concentrations in Samples Simultaneously Collected into Expired and Unexpired Venipuncture Tubes
    - Winek & Paul: Effect of Short-Term Storage Conditions on Alcohol Concentrations in Blood from Living Human Subjects
    - Anderson, et al.: The Effects of Storage on the Accuracy of Blood Alcohol Readings
    - Glover: The Effect of Heat on Blood Samples Containing Alcohol
    - Chang & Kollman: The Effect of Temperature on the Formation of Ethanol by *Candida Albicans* in Blood
    - Barnhill, Herbert & Wells: Comparison of Hospital Laboratory Serum Alcohol Levels Obtained by an Enzymatic Method with Whole Blood Levels Forensically Determined by Gas Chromatography
- Fiorentino Study: Validation of Sobriety Tests for the Marine Environment

**Suggested Charging Language**

CHAPTER

1

# Making the Stop

Justifying the stop in a DWI case is invariably the first area of concern for prosecutors and officers. A police officer must have had reasonable suspicion that later leads to probable cause to make the arrest. Because DWIs are almost exclusively the product of warrantless arrests, Chapter 1 examines the basics of warrantless stops, then focuses on the fact patterns that commonly arise and the legal theories that justify further detention and arrest.

## Basics of Warrantless Stops

Most traffic stops involve warrantless arrests. Typically, an officer will encounter a potentially intoxicated driver either on the road or after the driver has hit something—another car, a tree, or a utility pole. The law does not require an officer to get a warrant to proceed further in these situations, but every officer and prosecutor should understand the legal significance of different types of encounters with citizens.

There are two different types of seizures of an individual:

- temporary detention; and
- arrest.[1]

Once a suspect has been seized without a warrant, the seizure can then be characterized as either a temporary detention or an arrest. A temporary detention requires a showing of reasonable suspicion; an arrest requires a greater showing of probable cause.

Temporary detentions for the purpose of investigation are more commonly called *Terry* stops.[2] Courts evaluate the reasonableness of a temporary detention in terms of the totality of the circumstances.[3]

Factors that justify an initial *Terry* stop may escalate into probable cause justifying an arrest. Probable cause is created when facts and circumstances within the officer's knowledge, and about which he had reasonably trustworthy information, cause a reasonable person to believe that an offense has been (or is being) committed.[4]

The concept of "custody" goes along with an arrest. A person is considered "in custody" only if a reasonable person would believe his freedom of movement is restrained to the degree associated with a formal arrest.[5] If a suspect is in custody, officers must give him *Miranda* warnings before he can be interrogated.[6]

#### *Voluntary Encounters*

Voluntary encounters do not implicate Fourth Amendment protections. An officer can approach an individual on the street or in another public place and ask questions without any legal justification.[7] A request for permission to search does not automatically turn an encounter into a seizure or impact the voluntariness of the suspect's cooperation.[8] Only when a police officer verbally or nonverbally conveys to the suspect that his compliance is required does a consensual encounter become a detention.[9]

---

1 See Diane Beckham, *Traffic Stops* (TDCAA © 2016) and *Warrantless Search & Seizure* (TDCAA © 2015) for further information on the law regarding arrest, search and seizure without a warrant.

2 *Terry v. Ohio*, 392 U.S. 1, 20 L.Ed.2d 889, 88 S.Ct. 1868 (1968).

3 *Woods v. State*, 956 S.W.2d 33 (Tex. Crim. App. 1997).

4 *Carroll v. U.S.*, 267 U.S. 132, 45 S.Ct. 280, 69 L.Ed.2d 543 (1925); *Texas v. Brown*, 460 U.S. 730, 103 S.Ct. 1535, 75 L.Ed.2d 502 (1983).

5 *Stansbury v. California*, 511 U.S. 318, 114 S.Ct. 1526, 128 L.Ed.2d 293 (1994); *Dowthitt v. State*, 931 S.W.2d 244, 254 (Tex. Crim. App. 1996) (adopting *Stansbury*). For more information on custodial interrogation, see Diane Beckham, *Warrantless Search & Seizure* (TDCAA © 2015).

6 *Miranda v. Arizona*, 384 U.S. 436, 86 S.Ct. 1602, 16 L.Ed.2d 694 (1966).

7 *U.S. v. Drayton*, 536 U.S. 194, 122 S.Ct. 2105, 153 L.Ed.2d 242 (2002); *State v. Bryant*, 161 S.W.3d 758 (Tex. App. — Fort Worth 2005); *State v. Woodard*, 341 S.W.3d 404 (Tex. Crim. App. 2011).

8 *Hunter v. State*, 955 S.W.2d 102 (Tex. Crim. App. 1997).

9 *Hunter*, 955 S.W.2d 102.

## DETENTIONS

In most instances a police officer's encounter with a DWI suspect begins after the officer sees the suspect's vehicle in motion. The most common misstatement one hears is that there needs to be probable cause for such stops. If that were the case, the majority of stops would be illegal.

The standard for these stops—called temporary investigative detentions—is lower than probable cause and the burden more easily met.

### The Law

An officer is permitted to make a temporary investigative detention of a defendant if the officer has a reasonable suspicion that some activity out of the ordinary is or has occurred, some suggestion to connect the detainee with the unusual activity, and some indication that the activity is related to crime. The reasonable suspicion required does not rise to the level of probable cause such as is required to justify a warrantless arrest or search. Thus, whether the officer had probable cause to stop the vehicle was irrelevant, since he did not need probable cause to do so; rather, he needed only a reasonable suspicion based upon articulable facts.[10]

In other words, the law requires an officer who observes a vehicle in motion to allow that vehicle to remain in motion until the officer observes an articulable basis for interrupting its motion. The emphasis on "articulable" speaks to the fact that an officer's hunch or feeling that something was afoot without further description is not enough.

Although reasonable suspicion is hard to boil down into a simple set of rules, courts have formulated some helpful principles:

- The suspect's conduct does not have to be unlawful.[11]
- The officer's reasonable suspicion must be based on facts he knew at the time of the stop, not on knowledge he acquires later.[12]
- The totality of all information can be considered in determining whether a particular officer's actions were reasonable.[13]
- The defendant's actions do not have to be viewed in a vacuum, and a court cannot dissect each action to decide that each one, alone, appears purely innocent.[14]

Also note that a proper stop can, with the passage of time, become unreasonable and that the officer must have some observable and articulable basis for any further detention, including a request that the driver exit the vehicle and perform field sobriety tests.

---

10 *Stone v. State*, 685 S.W.2d 791 (Tex. App. — Fort Worth 1985), *aff'd*, 703 S.W.2d 652 (Tex. Crim. App. 1986); *Brown v. Texas*, 443 U.S. 47, 51, 99 S.Ct. 2637, 61 L.Ed.2d 357 (1979).

11 *U.S. v. Sokolow*, 490 U.S. 1, 7, 109 S.Ct. 1581, 104 L.Ed.2d 1 (1989); *Derichsweiler v. State*, 348 S.W.3d 906 (Tex. Crim. App. 2011), *cert. denied*, 132 S.Ct. 150 (2011).

12 *Terry v. Ohio*, 392 U.S. 1, 21-22 (1968); *Davis v. State*, 947 S.W.2d 240, 243 (Tex. Crim. App. 1997); *Andrews v. State*, 79 S.W.3d 649 (Tex. App. — Waco 2002, pet. ref'd) (stop not justified when officer pulled over defendant: (1) at early morning hour; (2) leaving a place that served alcohol; (3) pulling to side of road for no apparent reason; (4) vomiting by passenger; (5) due to over-consumption of alcohol—but officer didn't know two of these facts until after the stop).

13 *Porter v. State*, 969 S.W.2d 60 (Tex. App. — Austin 1998, pet. ref'd).

14 *Woods v. State*, 956 S.W.2d 33, 38 (Tex. Crim. App. 1997).

## THEORIES FOR STOPPING A DEFENDANT

***Traffic Violations***

An officer's observation of a traffic violation will always justify a temporary investigative detention. Some of the more common examples would be: speeding, running a stop sign or traffic signal, failing to signal a lane change, or failing to dim lights. [**See a list of common Transportation Code traveling violations at Table 1-1.**]

It will be well worth your time and effort to read the Transportation Code sections relating to traffic violations. Many of the regulations are very broadly worded and will therefore apply to a number of regularly observable traffic violations.

Whether the officer correctly identifies the legal basis for the stop will not matter.[15] The officer should try to note as many details as possible in support of the decision to make a stop. In many instances, the facts described in a suppression hearing give rise to reasons for the stop that had not occurred to the officer or were not the primary basis for the stop at the time.[16] Prosecutors should always do an independent comparison of the facts of a case with the code to see if there are any alternative reasons for the officer's stop.

While the officer's observations do not have to be sufficient by themselves to establish the traffic offense, the officer should be clear on the elements of the law that constitute a traffic offense. For instance, Transportation Code §502.409 forbids "obscured" front or rear license plates, but this statute may not justify stopping a vehicle with out-of-state license plates and an "obscured" front plate from a state that only requires rear plates.[17]

Although the U.S. Supreme Court recently ruled that an objectively reasonable mistake of law by an officer does not violate the 4th Amendment, Texas' more stringent good faith exception in CCP art. 38.23 probably requires exclusion of similary obtained evidence.[18] The good faith exception in art. 38.23 is limited to an officer's reliance on probable cause. But evidence seized in Texas after an officer's reasonable mistake of law may be admissible through the attenuation doctrine, for instance, if the officer discovers a valid warrant during the traffic stop. Regardless, the best advice is for officers to be clear on the elements of an offense before pulling a driver over on that basis.

Other driving behaviors that fall short of a criminal or traffic violation may still provide a sufficient basis for a traffic stop.[19] The activity need only be "out of the ordinary" and "related to a crime."[20] For instance, the officer may have seen the car rapidly accelerate from a stopped position coupled perhaps with spinning tires.[21]

Many members of the public believe that an intoxicated driver will always demonstrate some bad driving. This is a naive point of view. Many very intoxicated but experienced drinkers are able to drive their vehicles relatively well until they have to react to something. A stop may be based on violations of vehicle registration laws or having an expired

---

15 *Whren v. U.S.*, 517 U.S. 806, 116 S.Ct. 1769, 135 L.Ed.2d 89 (1996); *Ohio v. Robinette*, 519 U.S. 33, 117 S.Ct. 417, 136 L.Ed.2d 347 (1996); *O'Hara v. State*, 27 S.W.3d 548 (Tex. Crim. App. 2000); *Crittenden v. State*, 899 S.W.2d 668 (Tex. Crim. App. 1995); *Garcia v. State*, 827 S.W.2d 937 (Tex. Crim. App. 1992); *Reed v. State*, 308 S.W.3d 417 (Tex. App. — Fort Worth 2010); *Kessler v. State*, 2010 WL 1137047 (Tex. App. — Fort Worth 2010, pet. ref'd) (not desig. for pub.).

16 *Id.*; see also *State v. Mercado*, 972 S.W.2d 75 (Tex. Crim. App. 1998); *State v. Wood*, 828 S.W.2d 471 (Tex. App. — El Paso 1992, no pet.).

17 *U.S. v. Granado*, 302 F.3d 421 (5th Cir. 2002); see also *Mahaffey v. State*, 364 S.W.3d 908 (Tex. Crim. App. 2012) (no reasonable suspicion for stop when no signal required by Transportation Code §545.104(a) for two lanes merging into one).

18 *Heien v. North Carolina*, 135 S.Ct. 530 (2014) (officer's reasonable mistake of interpretation of traffic law could still justify a warrantless traffic stop); *U.S. v. Alvarado-Zarza*, 782 F.3d 246 (5th Cir. 2015); see also *State v. Mazuca*, 375 S.W.3d 294 (Tex. Crim. App. 2012) (officer's conduct was not flagrant and he discovered a valid warrant during the traffic stop).

19 See *Zervos v. State*, 15 S.W.3d 146, 152 (Tex. App. — Texarkana 2000, pet. ref'd); but see *Corbin v. State*, 85 S.W.3d 272 (Tex. Crim. App. 2002) (reversal on DWI based on failure to meet community caretaking exception, but officer also testified that the defendant committed the offense of failure to maintain single lane under Tex. Trans. Code §545.060) (Cochran, J. concurring) (The officer "stated that he stopped appellant for committing an offense: failure to maintain a single lane. This is not community caretaking; this is crime investigation"); see also *U.S. v. Lopez-Valdez*, 178 F.3d 282, 288 (5th Cir. 1999) (trooper's incorrect belief that a driver had violated state traffic laws is insufficient to justify a vehicle stop).

20 *Stone v. State*, 685 S.W.2d 791 (Tex. App. — Fort Worth 1985), *aff'd*, 703 S.W.2d 652 (Tex. Crim. App. 1986).

21 *Bice v. State*, 17 S.W.3d 354 (Tex. App. — Houston [1st Dist.] 2000, no pet.); *Collins v. State*, 829 S.W.2d 894 (Tex. App. — Dallas 1992, no pet.); *Harris v. State*, 713 S.W.2d 773 (Tex. App. — Houston [1st Dist.] 1986, no pet.).

**TABLE 1-1: Common Traffic Violations**

| Offense | Transportation Code § | Penalty |
|---|---|---|
| Unsafe passing to the left | §545.053 | $1-200 |
| Passing in a "no passing" zone | §545.055 | $1-200 |
| Unsafe passing to the right | §545.057 | $1-200 |
| Driving on improved shoulder | §545.058 | $1-200 |
| Failing to drive in a single lane | §545.060 | $1-200 |
| Following another car too closely | §545.062 | $1-200 |
| Passing a school bus | §545.066 | $500-1,250; Class A (serious bodily injury) or state jail felony (w/prior) |
| Improper turn at intersection | §545.101 | $1-200 |
| Unsafe turning | §545.102, -.103 | $1-200 |
| Improper use/failure to use turn signal | §545.104 | $1-200 |
| Failure to signal stop; sudden stop | §545.105 | $1-200 |
| Improper stop/failure to stop at intersection | §545.151 | $1-200 |
| Failure to yield right of way at intersection | §545.153 | $1-200 |
| Failure to or improper yield to emerg. vehicle | §545.156 | $1-200 |
| Passing authorized emergency vehicle or tow truck | §545.157 | $1-200; $1-500 (property damage); Class B (bodily injury) |
| Driving around railroad crossing gate | §545.251 | $50-200 |
| Disobeying traffic sign at railroad crossing | §545.252 | $50-200 |
| Improper stopping or parking (usually in an intersection) | §545.302 | $1-200 |
| Driving at unsafe speed | §545.351 | $1-200 |
| Driving over speed limits | §545.352 | $1-200 |
| Driving too slowly | §545.363 | $1-200 |
| Reckless driving | §545.401 | $0-200 and/or 0-30 days |
| Moving a parked vehicle unsafely | §545.402 | $1-200 |
| Driving through a safety zone | §545.403 | $1-200 |
| Driving child without safety seat | §545.412 | $25-250 |
| Failure to wear seat belt | §545.413 | $25-50; $100-200 |
| Transporting child in bed of pickup | §545.414 | $25-200 |
| Transporting child on boat or watercraft drawn by vehicle | §545.4145 | $1-200 |
| Improper backing of vehicle | §545.415 | $1-200 |
| Riding double on a single passenger motorcycle | §545.416 | $100-200 |
| Driving with view obstructed | §545.417 | $1-200 |
| Racing (includes "peeling out") | §545.420 | Range from Class B to 2nd degree |
| Fleeing (or attempting to flee) police officer | §545.421 | Class B; Class A if done recklessly |
| Driving through driveway parking lot | §545.422 | $1-200 |
| Moving unsafe vehicle equipment | §547.004 | $1-200 |
| Driving without lights on | §547.302 | $1-200 |
| Driving without taillamp emitting plainly visible red light | §547.322 | $1-200 |
| Driving with windows tinted too darkly | §547.613 | $1-200; $1-1,000 if in business |
| Failure to display inspection sticker | §548.602 | $1-200 |
| Displaying fictitious inspection sticker | §548.603 | Class B–2nd degree |
| Operating vehicle in dangerous mechanical condition | §548.604 | $0-200 |
| Failure to stop & render aid | §550.021 | 0-5 years and/or $0-5,000 (BI); 3rd degree felony (SBI or death) |
| Failure to stop & render aid (damage to vehicle) | §550.022 | Class C or B |
| Striking unattended vehicle | §550.024 | Class C or B |
| Striking structure/fixture/highway landscaping | §550.025 | Class C or B |

inspection sticker. An equipment failure—such as a broken tail light or driving on a tireless metal wheel—can likewise be a violation of the law that supports a traffic stop. To hold that an officer has to wait until bad driving occurs would be a terrible rule that would put others at great risk. Addressing these thoughts or biases will be discussed in **Chapter 7: Jury Selection.**

### WEAVING WITHIN THE LANE

Many DWI cases begin with an officer seeing the driver weaving on the road. Weaving as justification for a stop has generated a tremendous amount of litigation; therefore, it is important for officers and prosecutors to have a clear understanding of the courts' positions on weaving.[22] While no clear-cut rule has emerged yet, a few guidelines can be gleaned from the cases:

- Weaving within a single lane is not as good a reason for a traffic stop as weaving into another lane.[23] The offense of "failure to maintain a single lane" in Transportation Code §545.060 has two elements: (1) failing to drive within a single lane; (2) when it is unsafe to do so. (Officers should be prepared to testify as to the safety risk in all appropriate cases.)
- Little or no other traffic on the road makes it less likely that the officer can justify a stop based on unsafe driving. If the driver's failure to drive within a single marked lane is the sole basis for the traffic stop, the evidence must show that the driving was unsafe, considering all of the circumstances, to justify a detention.[24]

---

22 See, e.g., *Fox v. State*, 900 S.W.2d 345 (Tex. App. — Fort Worth 1995), *pet. dism'd*, 930 S.W.2d 607 (Tex. Crim. App. 1996) (weaving in lane and low speed together justified temporary detention even though neither act is unlawful); *Glover v. State*, 870 S.W.2d 198 (Tex. App. — Fort Worth 1994, pet. ref'd) (officer had reasonable suspicion justifying temporary detention of driver based on radio broadcast of information that EMS technician had seen white Corvette with particular license plate number weaving); but cf. *State v Arriaga*, 5 S.W.3d 804 (Tex. App. — San Antonio 1999, pet. ref'd) (drifting in own lane not enough).

23 *Held v. State*, 948 S.W.2d 45 (Tex. App. — Houston [14th Dist.] 1997, pet. ref'd) (weaving randomly across three lanes of traffic is sufficient for reasonable suspicion that driver may be intoxicated. "irrelevant that the actual weaving may or may not be criminal in and of itself"); *Raffaelli v. State*, 881 S.W.2d 714 (Tex. App. — Texarkana 1994, pet. ref'd); *Townsend v. State*, 813 S.W.2d 181, 185 (Tex. App. — Houston [14th Dist.] 1991, pet. ref'd) ("An officer's observation of a driver weaving back and forth across several lanes of traffic is sufficient to give rise to a reasonable suspicion that the driver may be intoxicated"); *State v. Houghton*, No. 02-11-00375-CR, 2012 WL 5258731 (Tex. App. — Fort Worth 2012) (not designated for publication) (weaving within a single lane and then crossing white stripe that marked boundary of left-turn lane insufficient to justify stop without testimony that the movements were done in an "unsafe manner"); cf. *State v. Arriaga*, 5 S.W.3d 804, 807 (Tex. App. — San Antonio 1999, pet. ref'd) (weaving within the driver's own lane does not give rise to reasonable suspicion — officer said he could not remember the number of times he saw the defendant drift; officer didn't testify about the weaving being erratic, unsafe, or tends to indicate intoxication or other criminal activity, time of night, location of the stop); *State v. Tarvin*, 972 S.W.2d 910, 912 (Tex. App. — Waco 1998, pet. ref'd) (weaving within single lane).

24 *Corbin v. State*, 85 S.W.3d 272 (Tex. Crim. App. 2002) (community caretaking exception did not justify stop where defendant drove 20 feet outside the line before returning to his lane of traffic and drove 52 mph in a 65 mph zone: "Given the frequency with which the average driver occasionally strays over the side stripe of the road, we have difficulty even characterizing this behavior as distress"); *Hernandez v. State*, 983 S.W.2d 867, 870 (Tex. App. — Austin 1998, pet. ref'd) (single instance of drifting across traffic lane, little traffic on road and defendant never caused a dangerous or unsafe condition for other motorists: "We cannot turn a blind eye to common sense and experience. There are myriad reasons why the wheels of a vehicle might drift slightly across a lane marker a single time").

- Fluctuating speed plus weaving can equal reasonable suspicion for a traffic stop.[25]
- Speeding while weaving constitutes a traffic offense for which the officer can pull the driver over.[26]

Examples of additional details that may support a "weaving" stop would include:

- a description that the vehicle just pulled out of a bar around closing time;
- some indication that the weaving was part of more erratic driving behavior or was unsafe; or
- other vehicles taking evasive action to avoid the vehicle.

**TIP**

If a driver's weaving on the road presents a danger to others, it will justify a stop. The more evidence that other drivers were affected by the defendant's driving, the more likely the court will uphold the stop.

It helps if the officer is able to describe other traffic affected by the weaving, but that is not always necessary.[27] Jurors will be able to relate to descriptions about other vehicles taking evasive action: What would a reasonable driver do if she observed a vehicle nearby weaving back and forth within its lane? Common sense would tell us that we don't want to be driving around that vehicle and would take steps to avoid it. Of course, the law does not require that the officer wait till a wreck occurs to pull someone over, but it is always helpful to have an officer detail the unsafe driving when appropriate.

### PRETEXT STOPS

No discussion of warrantless arrest would be complete without mentioning pretext stops. One example of this kind of stop is where an officer watches a person leave a known drug house, follows the vehicle until the driver speeds or commits an otherwise minor traffic violation, then stops the car in the hopes that the temporary detention will lead to observation of a greater offense that would justify a search or arrest of the suspect. The fact that the officer might have other reasons for stopping a vehicle other than a traffic violation—even if the officer purposely followed a vehicle to wait for an observable traffic violation—will not invalidate the stop.[28] In the context of DWI, pretext stops do not happen that often, but one could certainly imagine a scenario where an officer pulls over a person for some other legitimate reason and then finds evidence of the driver's intoxication. That's no problem in Texas. So long as an objective basis for such stops exists, the fact that the officer had another, pretextual reason will not invalidate the traffic stop.

---

25 *Dowler v. State*, 44 S.W.3d 666 (Tex. App. — Austin 2001, pet. ref'd); *Fox v. State*, 900 S.W.2d 345 (Tex. App. — Fort Worth 1995), *pet. dism'd, improv. granted*, 930 S.W.2d 607 (Tex. Crim. App. 1996) (fluctuating speed at least four times, weaving within its lane were sufficient for investigative detention).

26 *Taylor v. State*, 916 S.W.2d 680 (Tex. App. — Waco 1996, pet. ref'd) (weaving, speeding, driving in unsafe manner sufficient to justify investigative detention); *Raffaelli v. State*, 881 S.W.2d 714, 716 (Tex. App. — Texarkana 1994, pet. ref'd) (reasonable suspicion when officers saw the defendant weaving within his own lane and driving at "high" rate of speed); *Oliphant v. State*, 764 S.W.2d 858 (Tex. App. — Corpus Christi 1989, pet. ref'd).

27 See, e.g., *Gajewski v. State*, 944 S.W.2d 450 (Tex. App. — Houston [14th Dist.] 1997, no pet.); *Hernandez v. State*, 983 S.W.2d 867 (Tex. App. — Austin 1998, pet. ref'd).

28 *Arkansas v. Sullivan*, 532 U.S. 769, 121 S.Ct. 1876, 149 L.Ed.2d 994 (2001); *Whren v. U.S.*, 517 U.S. 806, 116 S.Ct. 1769, 135 L.Ed.2d 89 (1996); *Ohio v. Robinette*, 519 U.S. 33, 117 S.Ct. 417, 136 L.Ed.2d 347 (1996); *O'Hara v. State*, 27 S.W.3d 548 (Tex. Crim. App. 2000); *Crittenden v. State*, 899 S.W.2d 668 (Tex. Crim. App. 1995) (pretext stops are valid so long as objective basis for stop exists).

#### COMMUNITY CARETAKING

An emerging justification for stops, particularly in the DWI context, is community caretaking. If you have watched any TV in your life you know that one role of the police officer is to protect and serve the community. DWI is a dangerous crime with life-threatening implications. Beyond seeking out criminals, officers have an obligation to come to the aid of citizens who appear to be in distress. From that concept we have a body of case law concerning what is known as the "community caretaking" function of police officers.

The Court of Criminal Appeals first addressed this issue in 1998 in *Hulit v. State*,[29] in which an officer saw a lone individual in a running vehicle, on the roadway, slumped over the steering wheel. The officer never stated that he believed a crime was being committed. Instead, he said he wanted to make sure the driver was OK. The officer knocked on the driver's windshield, and when the driver quickly tried to leave, the officer determined the driver was intoxicated and arrested him for DWI.

Since that time the Court has provided more detailed guidance as to what factors are relevant to a determination of when community caretaking provides sufficient basis for a traffic stop:

1. the nature and level of distress exhibited by the individual;
2. the location of the individual;
3. whether the individual was alone and/or had access to assistance independent of that offered by the officer; and
4. to what extent the individual, if not assisted, presented a danger to himself or others.[30]

These four factors combined with the totality of the circumstances available to the officer are the framework through which the question, "Would a reasonable person believe the individual is in need of help?" will be answered.[31] Once again, sufficient details and a good articulation of the officer's concerns will mean the difference between a valid and invalid stop.

#### CITIZEN CALLS

The boom of the cellular phone business has made citizen calls to police an ever-increasing basis for investigative stops. One problem inherent in police patrols detecting intoxicated drivers is that both parties are in motion. Given the limited number of patrol officers and the vast amount of roadway they are expected to cover, it is often just a matter of luck that an intoxicated driver and a patrol officer meet at all. The citizen with a cell phone helps increase the odds of detection.

Here is a common example of such a stop:

> At 2:35 a.m. dispatch received call from concerned citizen that a brown pickup truck, license # UTV-765, was observed weaving across several lanes of traffic on Hwy 820 heading in a westerly direction. The citizen is in a red Honda Civic and is following the brown pick-up truck.

---

29 *Hulit v. State*, 982 S.W.2d 431 (Tex. Crim. App. 1998).

30 *Wright v. State*, 7 S.W.3d 148 (Tex. Crim. App. 1999), *rev'd on remand*, 18 S.W.3d 245 (Tex. App. — Austin 2000, pet. ref'd); *Gonzales v. State*, 369 S.W.3d 851 (Tex. Crim. App. 2012).

31 See, e.g., *Wright v. State*, 7 S.W.3d 148 (Tex. Crim. App. 1999), *rev'd on remand*, 18 S.W.3d 245 (Tex. App. — Austin 2000, pet. ref'd) (exception can apply to driver or passenger); *Andrews v. State*, 79 S.W.3d 649 (Tex. App. — Waco 2002, pet. ref'd); *Chilman v. State*, 22 S.W.3d 50 (Tex. App. — Houston [14th Dist.] 2000, pet. ref'd); *Cunningham v. State*, 966 S.W.2d 811 (Tex. App. — Beaumont 1998, no pet.).

The patrol officer typically will be dispatched to the location. Often, he will see not only a vehicle matching the description but also the concerned citizen's car behind the suspects. If the officer observes further suspicious driving independent of that reported to him by the dispatcher or phoned in by a citizen, the legal basis for the stop will be clear and difficult to challenge.[32]

The legality of the stop is not as clear in those cases where the officer stops the vehicle with no independent basis beyond the bad driving reported by the citizen. The good news for prosecutors is that there is ample case authority to support these stops.[33] A reporting citizen who is not a criminal informant is presumed to be credible. The identified citizen has more credibility then the unidentified informant.

The test that can be derived from the courts in these cases is: Did the reporting citizen place himself in a position where he could be held accountable for his intervention?[34] It does not matter that the officer did not actually know the identity (name) of the citizen so long as the manner in which the citizen gave the information exposed her identity to discovery. The prosecutor must develop the details from the patrol officer or dispatch on how they could have confirmed the identity of the caller. In this age of Caller-ID, the ability to call anyone—let alone the police—without exposing your identity to discovery is very unlikely.

The defendant will frequently object to admission of details of the police broadcast on which the officer made his decision to stop the defendant. This evidence, however, is admissible.[35] This information is not hearsay, because it is not offered for the truth of the matter asserted but to show how and why the defendant's vehicle was initially identified and followed.

The prosecutor may also overcome this objection by arguing an exception to the hearsay rule, including: (1) excited utterance; (2) present sense impression; (3) business record; or (4) public records exception.[36] The information also might not be considered hearsay if it is not offered for the truth of the matter asserted.

## STOPS OUTSIDE JURISDICTION

### CCP Art 14.03. Authority of Peace Officers

(d) A peace officer who is outside his jurisdiction may arrest, without warrant, a person who commits an offense within the officer's presence or view, if the offense is a felony, a violation of Title 9, Chapter 42, Penal Code, a breach of the peace, or an offense under Section 49.02 (public intoxication), Penal Code....

---

[32] *Navarette v. California*, 134 S.Ct. 1683 (2014); *Alabama v. White*, 496 U.S. 325, 110 S.Ct. 2412, 110 L.Ed.2d 301 (1990); *Stewart v. State*, 22 S.W.3d 646, 650 (Tex. App. — Austin 2000, pet. ref'd); *Hime v. State*, 998 S.W.2d 893, 895-96 (Tex. App. — Houston [14th Dist.] 1999, pet. ref'd) (DWI tip, erratic driving).

[33] See, e.g., *Brother v. State*, 166 S.W.3d 255 (Tex. Crim. App. 2005), *cert. denied*, 546 U.S. 1150 (2006); *Ferguson v. State*, 573 S.W.2d 516 (Tex. Crim. App. 1978); *State v. Stolte*, 991 S.W.2d 336 (Tex. App. — Fort Worth 1999, no pet.); *State v. Sailo*, 910 S.W.2d 184 (Tex. App. — Fort Worth 1995, pet. ref'd); *State v. Adkins*, 829 S.W.2d 900 (Tex. App. — Fort Worth 1992, pet. ref'd); *Albert v. State*, 659 S.W.2d 41 (Tex. App. — Houston [14th Dist.] 1983, pet. ref'd).

[34] *Hawes v. State*, 125 S.W.3d 535 (Tex. App. — Houston [1st Dist.] 2002, no pet.) (tow truck driver following suspicious driver in his own readily traceable vehicle); *Vanderhorst v. State*, 52 S.W.3d 237 (Tex. App. — Eastland 2001, no pet.); *State v. Fudge*, 42 S.W.3d 226 (Tex. App. — Austin 2001, no pet.) (stop found to be legal when officer's sole basis for the stop was details of bad driving provided to him by a cab driver in a face-to-face encounter; distinguishing *Florida v. J.L.*, 529 U.S. 266, 120 S.Ct. 1375, 146 L.Ed.2d 254 (2000)); *Hime v. State*, 998 S.W.2d 893 (Tex. App. — Houston [14th Dist.] 1999, pet. ref'd).

[35] *Kimball v. State*, 24 S.W.3d 555 (Tex. App. — Waco 2000, no pet.).

[36] *McDuff v. State*, No. 08-10-00104-CR, 2011 WL 1849540 (Tex. App. — El Paso, Aug. 24, 2011, pet. ref'd) (not for publication).

(g)(1) A peace officer listed in Subdivision (1), (2), or (5), Article 2.12, who is licensed under Chapter 1701, Occupations Code, and is outside of the officer's jurisdiction may arrest without a warrant a person who commits any offense within the officer's presence or view, other than a violation of Subtitle C, Title 7, Transportation Code.

(2) A peace officer listed in Subdivision (3), Article 2.12, who is licensed under Chapter 1701, Occupations Code, and is outside of the officer's jurisdiction may arrest without a warrant a person who commits any offense within the officer's presence or view, except that an officer described in this subdivision who is outside of that officer's jurisdiction may arrest a person for a violation of Subtitle C, Title 7, Transportation Code, only if the offense is committed in the county or counties in which the municipality employing the peace officer is located.

(3) A peace officer making an arrest under this subsection shall as soon as practicable after making the arrest notify a law enforcement agency having jurisdiction where the arrest was made. The law enforcement agency shall then take custody of:

(A) the person committing the offense and take the person before a magistrate in compliance with Article 14.06; and

(B) any property seized during or after the arrest as if the property had been seized by a peace officer of that law enforcement agency.

**TIP**

Hot pursuit can justify a municipal police officer's stop outside her jurisdiction if the pursuit began in the officer's jurisdiction.

---

The first question that must be answered is: What constitutes an officer's jurisdiction? In general, officers' authority to make warrantless arrests is limited to their geographic jurisdiction under common law and Code of Criminal Procedure Chapter 14. Not all officers have statewide authority to make warrantless arrests for any offense committed in their presence, particularly traffic offenses.

Effectively eliminating a Court of Criminal Appeals decision to the contrary,[37] a 2005 amendment to Article 14.03(g)[38] expanded municipal police officers' jurisdiction beyond the city limits. These officers may now make warrantless traffic stops anywhere within any counties in which the municipality resides and are no longer limited to the municipality's geographic jurisdiction. The legislation does not change the court's jurisdiction; therefore, a citation must be filed in the proper court.

Officers may make a warrantless traffic arrest outside of their jurisdiction only if they are:

1. in hot pursuit,[39] or
2. participating in the arrest with an officer who has geographic jurisdiction.[40]

Arrests may still be made for offenses that constitute a breach of the peace, such as DWI.[41] Offenses committed before Sept. 1, 2005, are still controlled by caselaw limiting a municipal officer to making traffic arrests (for offenses that are not a breach of the peace) to the geographic jurisdiction of the municipality.[42]

---

[37] *State v. Kurtz,* 152 S.W.3d 72 (Tex. Crim. App. 2004).

[38] HB 915 and SB 907, 79th R.S., effective Sept. 1, 2005.

[39] *Yeager v. State,* 104 S.W.3d 103 (Tex. Crim. App. 2003).

[40] *Armendariz v. State,* 123 S.W.3d 401 (Tex. Crim. App. 2003) (citing *Astran v. State,* 799 S.W.2d 761 (Tex. Crim. App. 1990)); *Lewis v. State,* 15 S.W.3d 250, 255 (Tex. App. — Texarkana 2000, no pet.) (arrest made by officers of another county is lawful if an officer of the county in which the arrest was made was present).

[41] TEX. CODE CRIM. PROC. art. 14.01(a); *Reichaert,* 830 S.W.2d at 351, distinguishing *Romo v. State,* 577 S.W.2d 251 (Tex. Crim. App. 1979) (DWI is breach of peace; running a red light and speeding are not).

[42] *Kurtz,* 152 S.W.3d 72; *Angel v. State,* 740 S.W.2d 727, 736 (Tex. Crim. App. 1987), superceded by statute, TEX. CODE CRIM. PRO. art. 14.03(g) (expanding a peace officer's jurisdiction beyond the city limits of which he is employed but expressly limiting the expansion to arrests for offenses other than traffic offenses); *Reichaert v. State,* 830 S.W.2d 348, 350 (Tex. App. — San Antonio 1992, pet. ref'd); TEX. CODE CRIM. PROC. art. 2.13.

An officer may make arrests outside of his jurisdiction if the suspect committed the offense in the officer's view, and the city officer then notifies an appropriate local officer.[43] Though Article 14.03 specifies that the officer should notify the arresting agency within that jurisdiction, violation of this provision will not necessarily lead to suppression of the stop.[44] Another way police departments can solve the geographic jurisdiction problem is to contract with neighboring agencies to extend their investigative authority under Local Government Code §362.002(b).[45] The arresting officer should be prepared to testify about such an agreement.

Perhaps the easiest violation to rely upon for a stop outside of the officer's jurisdiction is "breach of the peace," typically a justification used in an accident situation.[46] [**Breaches of the peace are discussed in further detail later in this chapter under the heading "Accidents."**]

## Warrants as a Basis

Officers regularly run license plates of vehicles they observe in an effort to detect stolen vehicles or individuals who may have outstanding warrants. Receiving confirmation of a warrant over a police broadcast will provide a sufficient basis for an investigative stop. The key will be what the broadcasting party relied upon. A copy of the warrant in the file is also very helpful.

Because most DWI cases involve the officer observing the suspect driving prior to arrest, an outstanding warrant for the defendant will typically not come into play. An outstanding warrant can be helpful in some situations in which the officer never actually observes the defendant driving. For instance, an officer may arrive at the scene of an accident and discover that the driver has outstanding warrants. The warrant justifies an arrest, but during the course of the arrest, the officer may have the opportunity to observe behavior that also supports investigating the potential DWI.

## Roadblocks

Many other states have used roadblocks and sobriety checkpoints in the battle against DWI. Not Texas, however. Stopping all cars at a particular place to further a law enforcement goal may be reasonable, depending on the specificity and importance of governmental interest at stake and the uniformity of the policy setting up the particular roadblock. At a minimum, the U.S. and Texas Constitutions require that police act reasonably when they set up a roadblock and stop drivers without a warrant, probable cause, or even individualized suspicion.[47]

In 1989, the Court of Criminal Appeals held that suspicionless stops pursuant to a roadblock were always violations of the federal constitution.[48] The following year,

---

43 See, e.g., *Preston v. State*, 983 S.W.2d 24 (Tex. App. — Tyler 1998, no pet.).

44 *Bachick v. State*, 30 S.W.3d 549 (Tex. App. — Fort Worth 2000, pet. ref'd) (failure to notify arresting agency within that jurisdiction did not warrant suppression of evidence); see also *Preston v. State*, 983 S.W.2d 24 (Tex. App. — Tyler 1998, no pet.); *Romo v. State*, 577 S.W.2d 251 (Tex. Crim. App. 1979).

45 See *Chavez v. State*, 9 S.W.3d 817, 819 (Tex. Crim. App. 2000); *Dominguez v. State*, 924 S.W.2d 950, 955-56 (Tex. App. — El Paso 1996, no pet.).

46 See Tables 1-2 and 1-3, later in this chapter, for a list of offenses that constitute a breach of the peace or have been found not to be a breach of the peace.

47 U.S. CONST. amend. IV; TEX. CONST. art. I, §9.

48 *Higbie v. State*, 780 S.W.2d 228 (Tex. Crim. App. 1989).

however, the U.S. Supreme Court ruled to the contrary,[49] and the Court of Criminal Appeals reversed itself.[50] But the Texas court stopped far short of authorizing roadblocks, ruling that roadblocks will not get a judicial green light until the Legislature expressly gives police statewide authority to set them up.[51]

In general, stopping a car at a checkpoint is a seizure.[52] A "visible police presence" where the traffic keeps moving until officers spot a violation is not a roadblock.[53]

The reasonableness of a seizure at a vehicle checkpoint depends upon a balancing of: (1) the gravity of the public concerns served by the checkpoint; (2) the degree to which the checkpoint effectively addresses those concerns; and (3) the severity of the intrusion upon individual liberty.[54]

## SOBRIETY CHECKPOINTS

According to the U.S. Supreme Court, roadblock stops established to identify intoxicated drivers are not inherently unreasonable.[55]

In evaluating DWI roadblocks, courts must balance the public interest in the roadblock against the individual driver's right to privacy in light of three factors: (1) the state's interest in preventing accidents caused by drunk drivers; (2) the effectiveness of a DWI roadblock in preventing these accidents; and (3) the level of intrusion on an individual's right to privacy that is caused by the roadblock.[56]

The Court of Criminal Appeals has interpreted U.S. Supreme Court caselaw on roadblocks to require statewide authorization and policy guidance—legislative approval, in other words—which Texas currently does not have.[57] The court noted that the roadblock program upheld in *Sitz*, which involved a DWI task force established by the Michigan legislature and operating under the direction of the *Michigan Department of State Police*, "demonstrate[s] the proper practice to follow in order to establish a constitutionally viable set of guidelines for DWI roadblocks."[58]

In 2000, the Supreme Court reaffirmed its position that roadblocks, if properly

---

49 *Michigan Dep't of State Police v. Sitz*, 496 U.S. 444, 448-49, 110 S.Ct. 2481, 110 L.Ed.2d 412 (1990).

50 *King v. State*, 800 S.W.2d 528 (Tex. Crim. App. 1990).

51 *Holt v. State*, 887 S.W.2d 16, 18 (Tex. Crim. App. 1994).

52 *U.S. v. Martinez-Fuerte*, 428 U.S. 543, 556, 96 S.Ct. 3074, 49 L.Ed.2d 1116 (1976); *State v. Sanchez*, 856 S.W.2d 166, 168 (Tex. Crim. App. 1993) (plurality op.) (roadblock search is "suspicionless search").

53 *State v. Skiles*, 938 S.W.2d 447 (Tex. Crim. App. 1997).

54 *Sitz*, 496 U.S. at 448-49, overruling *Higbie v. State*, 780 S.W.2d 228 (Tex. Crim. App. 1989); *Brown v. Texas*, 443 U.S. 47, 50-51, 99 S.Ct. 2637, 61 L.Ed.2d 357 (1979); *Schenekl v. State*, 30 S.W.3d 412 (Tex. Crim. App. 2000).

55 *Sitz*, 496 U.S. at 455; see also *State v. Wagner*, 810 S.W.2d 207 (Tex. Crim. App. 1991); *King v. State*, 800 S.W.2d 528 (Tex. Crim. App. 1990); but cf. *State v. Van Natta*, 805 S.W.2d 40 (Tex. App. — Fort Worth 1991), *pet. ref'd*, 811 S.W.2d 608 (Tex. Crim. App. 1991) (holding roadblock unconstitutional despite *Sitz* on theory that State must still offer evidence of effectiveness of roadblock); *King v. State*, 816 S.W.2d 447 (Tex. App. — Dallas 1991, pet. ref'd) (on remand) (Texas roadblock effectively limited to license checks authorized by Transportation Code); *State v. Hubacek*, 840 S.W.2d 751 (Tex. App. — Fort Worth 1992, pet. ref'd) (officers can ask for insurance papers at roadblock, but it may not be subterfuge for DWI arrests; state constitution only requrires reasonableness standard).

56 *Brown v. Texas*, 443 U.S. 47, 99 S.Ct. 2637, 61 L.Ed.2d 357 (1979); *Holt*, 887 S.W.2d at 18.

57 *Holt*, 887 S.W.2d at 19 ("We believe that the Supreme Court implicitly makes it a requirement that for any DWI checkpoint program to pass constitutional muster, it must at a basic minimum be authorized by a statewide policy emanating from a politically accountable government body").

58 *Holt*, 887 S.W.2d at 18-19.

established and justified by public interest, can dispense with the requirement for individualized suspicion.[59] Until the Texas Legislature acts, however, it is unlikely that the Court of Criminal Appeals will give carte blanche to arrests resulting from DWI roadblocks.

## Crashes & Warrantless Arrests

An officer who observes a suspect driving a vehicle and committing a traffic violation is witnessing an offense in his presence within the meaning of CCP art. 14.01. An officer who has not seen the defendant driving—for instance, comes across the suspect at a crash scene—must have some other authority for an arrest without a warrant.

**Art 14.03 Authority of Peace Officers**

(a) Any peace officer may arrest, without warrant:

(1) persons found in suspicious places and under circumstances which reasonably show that such persons have been guilty of some felony, violation of Title 9, Chapter 42, Penal Code, breach of the peace, or offense under Section 49.02, Penal Code, or threaten, or are about to commit some offense against the laws....

### PLACING THE DEFENDANT BEHIND THE WHEEL

"Wheeling" the defendant is important for prosecutors as an evidentiary issue in proving the elements of "driving" or "operating" in a DWI case.

It does not take a lot of evidence to "wheel" the defendant. Simply seeing the defendant behind the wheel of the car can be enough. If the only reasonable inference is that a person drove the car (for instance, if there are no other passengers), the prosecution does not need a witness saying that she saw the defendant driving the car. His confession may also be enough.[60] In *Peddicord v. State*,[61] the court held that the defendant's statement that he was the driver, together with a witness' statement that he saw the defendant in the driver's seat within two minutes of the accident, was sufficient for any rational trier of fact to find beyond a reasonable doubt that the defendant was the driver.

If the defense cites cases that were handed down before 1991 that suggest more evidence is needed, you should note that the standard of review applied to those cases is different than the standard of review applied today. Those older opinions were reviewed under the "reasonable hypothesis" standard, where all other reasonable hypotheses in circumstantial evidence cases had to be ruled out to sustain a conviction. The Court of Criminal Appeals in *Geesa v. State*,[62] overruled this construct and held that the same legal sufficiency analysis applies to circumstantial evidence cases and direct evidence

---

59 *City of Indianapolis v. Edmond*, 531 U.S. 32, 121 S.Ct. 447, 148 L.Ed.2d 333 (2000).

60 *Zavala v. State*, 89 S.W.3d 134 (Tex. App. — Corpus Christi 2002, no pet.); *Kerr v. State*, 921 S.W.2d 498, 501 (Tex. App. — Fort Worth 1996, no pet.) (evidence sufficient to prove operation of car when witness heard a car slide off the road and immediately saw defendant get out of the car alone); *Folk v. State*, 797 S.W.2d 141 (Tex. App. — Austin 1990, pet. ref'd); *Dickson v. State*, 642 S.W.2d 185, 189 (Tex. App. — Houston [14th Dist.] 1982, pet. ref'd) (evidence sufficient to prove defendant was driving when witness saw him exiting the driver's side of a stolen van immediately after it came to a stop); see also *Fruechte v. State*, 316 S.W.2d 418, 419 (Tex. Crim. App. 1958) (defendant found in driver's seat of a damaged car not far from accident sufficiently corroborated him as the driver).

61 942 S.W.2d 100, 106 (Tex. App. — Amarillo 1997, no pet.).

62 820 S.W.2d 154 (Tex. Crim. App. 1991).

cases. An appellate court is no longer required to rule out all reasonable hypotheses, but instead must simply ask whether, after viewing the evidence in the light most favorable to the state, any rational trier of fact could have found the essential elements of the crime beyond a reasonable doubt. Under this new construct, it is much easier to prove circumstantially that a particular defendant was operating a motor vehicle.

Officers should always check for seatbelt injuries and steering wheel injuries at the scene of an accident. Be sure to do this with passengers as well so they cannot later claim that they were driving. In serious accident cases, officers may want to consider blood, fiber, and trace evidence from the car (or windshield, etc.) to corroborate driving facts.

## CRASH SCENES

**TIP**

A wonderful resource for officers and prosecutors on crash reconstruction by expert John Kwasnoski, professor emeritus of forensic physics at Western New England College in Massachusetts is available free online in Adobe PDF format. Get the 40-page booklet, *Crash Reconstruction Basics for Prosecutors: Targeting Hardcore Impaired Drivers,* from **www.ndaa.org/pdf/crash_reconstruction_basics.pdf**

An officer faces two potential problems in a crash case: (1) justifying the arrest (usually based on breach of the peace, public intoxication, or under the suspicious place exception to the warrant requirement); and (2) compiling enough evidence to place the defendant behind the wheel. A crash scene is a "suspicious place," and the crash itself clearly constitutes a "breach of the peace," thereby supporting the warrantless arrest.[63]

In determining whether the scene of an accident could qualify as a "suspicious place" that would justify a warrantless arrest, courts have pointed out that any place may become suspicious for purposes of justifying a warrantless arrest based on probable cause, when an individual at the location and the accompanying circumstances call for immediate action or detention by police.[64]

Other examples of behavior that would justify a warrantless arrest for a breach of the peace include: driving the wrong way down a highway,[65] striking another car, or striking a tree. A mere traffic offense will generally not constitute a breach of the peace.[66] **[For more information about crash investigations, see *Intoxication Manslaughter* by Richard Alpert (TDCAA © 2013).]**

---

63 See, e.g., *Cooper v. State*, 961 S.W.2d 229 (Tex. App. — Houston [1st Dist.] 1997, pet. ref'd) (accident in bar parking lot).

64 *Dyar v. State*, 125 S.W.3d 460 (Tex. Crim. App. 2003); *Lewis v. State*, 412 S.W.3d 794 (Tex. App. — Amarillo 2013, no pet.) (crash scene qualified as suspicious place when defendant voluntarily returned to the scene, admitted to being hit-and-run driver, admitted that she had too much to drink, and only 30-60 minutes had elapsed between crash and defendant's return to scene).

65 *Ruiz v. State*, 907 S.W.2d 600 (Tex. App. — Corpus Christi 1995, no pet.).

66 *Reichaert v. State*, 830 S.W.2d 348 (Tex. App. — San Antonio 1992, pet. ref'd).

## TABLE 1-2: Crimes That Are a "Breach of the Peace"

**(1) DWI** — *Cooper v. State*, 961 S.W.2d 229 (Tex. App. — Houston [1st Dist.] 1997, pet. ref'd); *Romo v. State*, 577 S.W.2d 251 (Tex. Crim. App. 1979); *McGuire v. State*, 847 S.W.2d 684 (Tex. App. — Houston [1st Dist.] 1993, no pet.) (authorizing citizen's arrest following DWI and failure to stop after accident);

**(2) Public intoxication** — *Heck v. State*, 507 S.W.2d 737 (Tex. Crim. App. 1974); *State v. Nailor*, 949 S.W.2d 357 (Tex. App. — San Antonio 1997, no pet.); *Trent v. State*, 925 S.W.2d 130 (Tex. App. — Waco 1996, no pet.);

**(3) Dangerous driving, speeding, swerving and running into other cars** — *Lopez v. State*, 936 S.W.2d 332 (Tex. App. — San Antonio 1996, no pet.); *Ruiz v. State*, 907 S.W.2d 600 (Tex. App. — Corpus Christi 1995, no pet.);

**(4) Suspected shoplifter throwing a clothes rack at a security guard** — *Mungia v. State*, 911 S.W.2d 164 (Tex. App. — Corpus Christi 1995, no pet.);

**(5) Carrying a handgun** — *Turner v. State*, 901 S.W.2d 767 (Tex. App. — Houston [14th Dist.] 1995, pet. ref'd) (citizen's arrest);

**(6) Throwing a beer bottle** — *Knot v. State*, 853 S.W.2d 802 (Tex. App. — Amarillo 1993, no pet.) (at another citizen in response to question about purse-snatching); *Head v. State*, 96 S.W.2d 981, 982 (1936) (at police car)

**(7) Fighting** — *McGuire v. State*, 847 S.W.2d 684 (Tex. App. — Houston [1st Dist.] 1993, no pet.); *Woods v. State*, 213 S.W.2d 685 (Tex. Crim. App. 1948) (assault in a crowd);

**(8) Failing to stop and give information after a wreck** — *Crowley v. State*, 842 S.W.2d 701 (Tex. App. — Houston [1st Dist.] 1992, pet. ref'd);

**(9) "Extending the middle finger** of [the defendant's] right hand" to a school principal during graduation — *Estes v. State*, 660 S.W.2d 873, 875 (Tex. App. — Fort Worth 1983, pet. ref'd);

**(10) Indecent exposure** —*Romine v. State*, 336 S.W.2d 181, 183 (Tex. Crim. App. 1960);

**(11) Criminal trespass** —*Dunn v. State*, 979 S.W.2d 403, 409 (Tex. App. — Amarillo 1998, pet. ref'd);

**(12) Theft** —*Andrade v. State*, 6 S.W.3d 584 (Tex. App. — Houston [14th Dist.] 1999, pet. ref'd).

## TABLE 1-3: Crimes That Present No "Breach"

**(1) Obscene gestures** ("shooting the bird") and honking a car horn — *State v. Rivenburgh*, 933 S.W.2d 698 (Tex. App. — San Antonio 1996, no pet.) (under Penal Code §42.01);

**(2) Speeding and running a red light** — *Perkins v. State*, 812 S.W.2d 326 (Tex. Crim. App. 1991); and

**(3) Violation of traffic regulations** — *Reichaert v. State*, 830 S.W.2d 348 (Tex. App. — San Antonio 1992, pet. ref'd); *Woods v. State*, 213 S.W.2d 685, 687 (1948) (driving overweight truck); *Perkins v. State*, 812 S.W.2d 326, 329, n. 4 (Tex. Crim. App. 1991) (running red light).

## PUBLIC INTOXICATION

An officer who makes contact with an intoxicated suspect outside of his vehicle may also rely upon Penal Code §49.02 (public intoxication) to support the arrest. A defendant commits public intoxication when he is found in a public place and in such an intoxicated state that he is a danger to himself or others. Tying the defendant to earlier driving that caused a collision will provide sufficient evidence that the driver's intoxication rose to the requisite level of danger.

If an officer has probable cause to arrest a person in his presence for public intoxication, the officer may make the arrest without a warrant, even if a warrantless arrest for DWI would be invalid at that point.[67] The officer may even label the arrest as one for driving while intoxicated.

But in this situation, will the implied consent law apply? Surprisingly, yes. The implied consent law does not require that the offense for which the officer arrests a defendant be driving while intoxicated.[68]

**Transportation Code §724.011. Consent to Taking of Specimen**

(a) If a person is arrested for an offense arising out of acts alleged to have been committed while the person was operating a motor vehicle in a public place, or a watercraft, while intoxicated, or an offense under Section 106.041, Alcoholic Beverage Code, the person is deemed to have consented, subject to this chapter, to submit to the taking of one or more specimens of the person's breath or blood for analysis to determine the alcohol concentration or the presence in the person's body of a controlled substance, drug, dangerous drug, or other substance....

Both public intoxication and breaches of the peace will constitute "offense(s) arising out of acts alleged to have been committed while the person was operating a motor vehicle."[69] Therefore the implied consent law applies, and an officer can properly read the warnings to a suspect and hold him accountable for the consequences of his agreement or refusal to give a specimen.

---

[67] See, e.g., *Warrick v. State*, 634 S.W.2d 707 (Tex. Crim. App. 1982).

[68] TEX. TRANS. CODE §724.011(a); *Chilman v. State*, 22 S.W.3d 50 (Tex. App. — Houston [14th Dist.] 2000, no pet.); *Arnold v. State*, 971 S.W.2d 588 (Tex. App. — Dallas 1998, no pet.); *Elliot v. State*, 908 S.W.2d 590 (Tex. App. — Austin 1995, pet. ref'd).

[69] *Chilman v. State*, 22 S.W.3d 50 (Tex. App. — Houston [14th Dist.] 2000, pet. ref'd); *Arnold v. State*, 971 S.W.2d 588 (Tex. App. — Dallas 1998, no pet.); *Elliot v. State*, 908 S.W.2d 590 (Tex. App. — Austin 1995, pet. ref'd).

CHAPTER

2

# Defendant in Custody

Once an officer has pulled the defendant over, what activities can the officer perform to elevate reasonable suspicion to probable cause? Chapter 2 discusses permissible activities during the stop and ways an officer can go about obtaining evidence that will corroborate the ultimate decision to arrest—or, what I like to call "how long and how far."

The two questions answered in this inquiry are: (1) How long can an officer detain a suspect before an investigatory stop must become either an arrest or an illegal detention? and (2) How far can a suspect be removed from the inside and area of his vehicle, and how far may an officer intrude into that vehicle prior to making the decision to arrest?

## Activities During the Stop

Once a suspect has been seized without a warrant (in a DWI context, this generally means the officer has pulled over the driver), the seizure can then be characterized as either a temporary detention or an arrest. A temporary detention requires a showing of reasonable suspicion; an arrest requires a greater showing of probable cause.

Factors that justify an initial stop may escalate into probable cause justifying an arrest. The concept of "custody" goes along with an arrest. A person is considered "in custody" only if a reasonable person would believe his freedom of movement is restrained to the degree associated with a formal arrest.[1] If a suspect is in custody, officers must give him *Miranda* warnings before he can be interrogated.[2]

> **TIP**
>
> Officers should document and detail:
> (1) reasons for the stop;
> (2) observable signs of intoxication;
> (3) defendant's responses to questions'
> (4) facts that elevate reasonable suspicion for the detention to probable cause for the arrest.

### DETENTIONS

Reasonable suspicion to justify pulling over a driver means that an officer, based on objective facts, has reason to believe that a specific person is involved in some criminal activity.[3] A search or detention that begins reasonably can become unreasonable if officers exceed what is necessary to accomplish the investigation that initially justifies the search.[4]

There is no simple test for deciding when a stop has exceeded the boundaries of a temporary detention,[5] but two of the most commonly disapproved actions involve moving the suspect too far or detaining the suspect for too long.[6]

Before a suspect has been arrested, the rules regarding custodial interrogation found in *Miranda* and Code of Criminal Procedure Article 38.22 do not apply, and therefore, the officer can ask the suspect questions without having to give warnings.

During a routine traffic stop, an officer may:

- ask the driver to get out of the car;[7]
- detain the driver in order to check for outstanding warrants;[8]
- ask for information about license, vehicle ownership, registration, insurance, the driver's destination and why he is going there.[9]

---

1 *Stansbury v. California*, 511 U.S. 318, 114 S.Ct. 1526, 128 L.Ed.2d 293 (1994); *Dowthitt v. State*, 931 S.W.2d 244, 254 (Tex. Crim. App. 1996) (adopting *Stansbury*). For more information on custodial interrogation, see Alan Curry, *Confessions* (TDCAA © 2015).

2 *Miranda v. Arizona*, 384 U.S. 436, 86 S.Ct. 1602, 16 L.Ed.2d 694 (1966); see also *Missouri v. Siebert*, 542 U.S. 600, 124 S.Ct. 2601, 159 L.Ed.2d 643 (2004) (striking down departmental policy where officers question first, then give *Miranda* warnings to suspects).

3 *Brown v. Texas*, 443 U.S. 47, 51, 99 S.Ct. 2637, 61 L.Ed.2d 357 (1979).

4 *Davis v. State*, 947 S.W.2d 240, 243 (Tex. Crim. App. 1997).

5 *Florida v. Royer*, 460 U.S. 491, 103 S.Ct. 1319, 75 L.Ed.2d 229 (1983).

6 For more information on permissible length and activities during detentions, see Diane Beckham, *Warrantless Search & Seizure* (TDCAA © 2015), ch. 1.

7 *Pennsylvania v. Mimms*, 434 U.S. 106, 98 S.Ct. 330, 54 L.Ed.2d 331 (1977).

8 *Davis v. State*, 947 S.W.2d 240, 245 n. 6 (Tex. Crim. App. 1997).

9 *Mohmed v. State*, 977 S.W.2d 624 (Tex. App. — Fort Worth 1998, pet. ref'd).

A conscientious police officer will also use those first minutes of contact with a suspect to ask questions such as:

- Where have you been?
- Where are you going?
- Have you been drinking?
- How many drinks have you had?
- When was your last drink?

Even if an officer has articulable reasons at this point to believe that a suspect is intoxicated, he can still question the suspect without warning him of his rights.[10] The fact that the investigation has focused on the suspect driving the car does not transform it into a custodial situation.[11]

Once the officer has run the warrant check, written any ticket, and returned the driver's license and other documentation, the initial purpose of the stop has ended, and a detention after that point may—but doesn't necessarily—become unreasonable.[12]

### DEVELOPING PROBABLE CAUSE

After a potential DWI stop, one of the first things an officer may notice is the odor of an alcoholic beverage. Many defense lawyers will jump all over an officer that says he smelled "alcohol" rather than "an alcoholic beverage" because they believe alcohol is odorless. I also held that mistaken belief until a lecturer demonstrated that alcohol does indeed have an odor.

Whether a driver who smells of alcohol admits to drinking or lies and says he has not been drinking (in contradiction of that odor), the officer legally can ask the suspect to exit the vehicle. Officers should take careful note of the driver's actions when he exits the vehicle. Many things that a suspect does can be signs of impairment from alcohol and may help an officer develop probable cause that the suspect was driving while intoxicated. Examples of some things commonly noted include:

- having trouble finding his drivers license or proof of insurance;
- slurring his speech;[13]
- having red or bloodshot eyes;[14]
- unsteady balance;
- using the car to steady himself; and
- being slow to respond to questions or requests.[15]

## ARREST, *MIRANDA*, & INTERROGATION

Though the TV-watching public believes that suspects can never be asked questions that may incriminate them, that belief is incorrect. So long as the suspect is being

---

10 *Lewis v. State*, 72 S.W.3d 704 (Tex. App. — Fort Worth 2002, pet. ref'd).

11 *State v. Stevenson*, 958 S.W.2d 824 (Tex. Crim. App. 1997).

12 *U.S. v. Dortch*, 199 F.3d 193, 200 (5th Cir. 1999); *U.S. v. Shabazz*, 993 F.2d 431, 437 (5th Cir. 1993).

13 *Fontenot v. State*, 486 S.W.2d 941 (Tex. Crim. App. 1972).

14 *Miffleton v. State*, 728 S.W.2d 880 (Tex. App. — Austin 1987), *aff'd*, 777 S.W.2d 76 (Tex. Crim. App. 1989).

15 See, e.g., *Texas Dep't of Public Safety v. Walter*, 979 S.W.2d 22 (Tex. App. — Houston [14th Dist.] 1998, no pet.).

detained but is not yet under arrest, the officer is free to ask questions and the suspect is free to answer those questions to his detriment and without benefit of warning until he is placed under arrest.

At some point in a DWI stop, an officer will develop enough evidence to establish probable cause and justify arresting the suspect. Once the officer has reached that critical point in the encounter, any further statements by the suspect will be suppressed unless the officer gives *Miranda* warnings and the suspect waives those rights.

So when do *Miranda* warnings need to be given? After a suspect is placed in custody and before interrogation begins. Placing handcuffs on a suspect after FSTs may transform the investigative stop into an arrest[16] but that is not an absolute rule.[17]

While the officer is investigating—before the detention has escalated into an arrest —the suspected intoxicated driver is not in custody. The magic words, "You are under arrest," are not the only things that may trigger a court's finding that the defendant was actually in the officer's custody. Restraint of a suspect's freedom of movement to the degree associated with formal arrest, even without using the word "arrest," can also equal "custody."[18] However, minor shows of restraint necessary to complete a preliminary investigation (such as taking the suspect's key or directing him not to leave his vehicle), do not necessarily rise to the level of restraint necessary to effectuate an arrest.[19]

Without restraint, however, it is rarely necessary or even wise for an officer to give warnings at the scene or before the suspect arrives at the station. My advice to officers is to save the *Miranda* warnings until the end of the officer's contact with the suspect. That means that before those warning are given, the suspect should be transported to the station, read the DIC-24, asked for a breath or blood sample, and asked to perform FSTs again for a stationhouse videotape. [**See a discussion about field sobriety tests later in this chapter. See a sample DIC-24 form in Chapter 3.**]

In deciding whether a defendant is in custody in DWI cases, some courts have focused on whether or not the officer has asked the defendant to perform field sobriety tests (FSTs) before asking questions. If the questioning happens before the FSTs are done, the questions and answers likely will be admissible,[20] but if questions follow a request to perform FSTs, the courts are more likely to find the investigation has become custodial. But the intermediate courts of appeals are far from unanimous on this point, with some courts finding that even answers to questions that follow FSTs will be admissible.[21]

An officer must do two things when *Miranda* is given to ensure that the questions and answers that follow the warnings are admissible:

1. Read the warnings accurately and completely. Even minor variances in the wording can render the defendant's answers inadmissible.[22] The best approach is to always read the warnings directly from a card so there is no danger of mistake.
2. Get the suspect to acknowledge that he understands his rights and wants to waive them. Too many times an officer simply reads the warnings and then goes right into the questions, as if relying on the assumption that a suspect who knows his rights and speaks is waiving those rights. No such presumption exists.

Remember, a defendant has an absolute right to *voluntarily* incriminate himself. The defendant's rights have been violated only when an officer *compels* him to do so. Additionally, a defendant may incriminate himself by remaining silent pre-arrest, and a prosecutor's subsequent comments on this silence do not violate the Fifth Amendment.[23]

---

16 *Alford v. State,* 22 S.W.3d 669 (Tex. App. — Fort Worth 2000, pet. ref'd).

17 *Rhodes v. State,* 945 S.W.2d 115, 118 (Tex. Crim. App. 1997); *State v. Moore,* 25 S.W.3d 383, 387 (Tex. App. — Austin 2000, no pet.); *Gordon v. State,* 4 S.W.3d 32, 37 (Tex. App. — El Paso 1999, no pet.); *Nargi v. State,* 895 S.W.2d 820 (Tex. App. — Houston [14th Dist.] 1995), *pet. dism'd improv. granted,* 922 S.W.2d 180 (Tex. Crim. App. 1996).

18 *Stansbury v. California,* 511 U.S. 318, 114 S.Ct. 1526, 128 L.Ed.2d 293 (1994); *Dowthitt v. State,* 931 S.W.2d 244, 254 (Tex. Crim. App. 1996) (adopting *Stansbury*).

19 See, e.g., *State v. Whittington,* 401 S.W.3d 263 (Tex. App. — San Antonio 2013, no pet.).

20 *State v. Waldrop,* 7 S.W.3d 836 (Tex. App. — Austin 1999, no pet.).

21 *Hutto v. State,* 977 S.W.2d 855 (Tex. App. — Houston [14th Dist.] 1998, no pet.).

22 *State v. Subke,* 918 S.W.2d 11 (Tex. App. — Dallas 1995, pet. ref'd); see also *U.S. v. Patane,* 542 U.S. 630, 124 S.Ct. 2620, 159 L.Ed.2d 667 (2004) (officer must give complete warning even if suspect says he knows his rights).

23 *Salinas v. Texas,* 133 S.Ct. 2174 (2013) (defendant's silence during voluntary, non-custodial interrogation was admissible because defendant did not invoke his privilege against self-incrimination, so non-verbal conduct accompanying that silence was admissible).

Some of the most incriminating comments are often made on the ride to the stationhouse after the suspect has been arrested. With no questioning or prompting by the officer, a suspect will often admit he is guilty and beg for mercy; make derogatory comments about the officer's race or sex; or question whether the officer's parents were married at the time of his birth. These unsolicited comments are admissible regardless of warnings.

Texas has an oral confessions law—Code of Criminal Procedure art. 38.22—that requires all statements by a defendant to be written or recorded if the defendant is: (1) in custody, and (2) subject to interrogation. Both elements, custody and interrogation, must be met before the requirements of art. 38.22 apply.[24]

The smart officer will have a tape recorder with him or turn any camera in the squad car on the suspect to record these statements, which can later show a clear loss of normal mental faculties. A suspect does not need to be warned that he is being taped.[25]

## Field Sobriety Tests

There is nothing magical about observing signs of intoxication. At some point, most of us have made a routine determination that someone around us is intoxicated. You can tell by observing the way the person walks, talks, reacts, and speaks. Most field sobriety tests highlight coordination, balance, and dexterity, all of which diminish as a person becomes more intoxicated.

A refusal to do FSTs can help provide probable cause to arrest a person for DWI.[26] But police officers have historically used certain tests to confirm their suspicions. I will divide those field sobriety tests into two categories: standardized and non-standardized.

### STANDARDIZED TESTS

Horizontal gaze nystagmus (HGN), "one leg stand," and "walk & turn" are standardized field sobriety tests, a designation that essentially means these three were determined to be accurate evaluators of blood alcohol content in a series of studies that began in the 1970s in California.[27] Other tests to determine potential intoxication can still be valid; they simply are not "standardized."

Most of the current case law controversy involves the standardized tests.[28] Having standardized DWI tests on which officers can be trained has been helpful, but there has been one unfortunate consequence of the emphasis on the statistic that the standardized tests have been proven to be 78 to 90 percent reliable if administered correctly. From the phrasing of that statistic, defense attorneys make the argument that the tests should not be admissible at all if they were not done exactly as the training model suggests.

Many defense attorneys have tied their defense to the hope that the officer did not administer these tests correctly. But that hope springs from the illogical leap that the tests—in whatever form—can only assist an officer in forming his opinion on intoxication if they are done "by the book." Variations on how the tests were performed have not always resulted in the test results being excluded.[29]

Two of the tests—the walk and turn and the one leg stand—merely involve observation of the suspect's bodily functions. Even if the tests are not administered correctly, a suspect's inability to follow directions, walk a line, and hold his balance can be evidence of his intoxication. That said, it is important that officers administer the tests correctly and document their findings to minimize the possibility of defense attack.

---

24 *Rhode Island v. Innis*, 446 U.S. 291 (1980); *Jones v. State*, 795 S.W.2d 171 (Tex. Crim. App. 1990). For more information on confessions, see *Confessions* by Alan Curry (TDCAA © 2015).

25 *Meyer v. State*, 78 S.W.3d 505 (Tex. App. — Austin 2002, pet. ref'd).

26 *Lonsdale v. State*, 2006 WL 2480342 (Tex. App. — El Paso 2006, pet. ref'd); *Maxwell v. State*, 253 S.W.3d 309 (Tex. App. — Fort Worth 2008, pet. ref'd).

27 See "Development of a Standardized Field Sobriety Test," NHTSA, Nov. 2001, found at **www.nhtsa.dot.gov/people/injury/alcohol/SFST**.

28 See, e.g., *Youens v. State*, 988 S.W.2d 404 (Tex. App. — Houston [1st Dist.] 1999, no pet.); *Hunt v. State*, 848 S.W.2d 764 (Tex. App. — Corpus Christi 1993, no pet.) (HGN test results admissible as qualitative, but not quantitative, evidence of intoxication); see also *Emerson v. State*, 880 S.W.2d 759 (Tex. Crim. App. 1994) (HGN is a scientific test based on the scientific principle that a relationship exists between alcohol consumption and HGN).

29 *Compton v. State*, 120 S.W.3d 375 (Tex. App. — Texarkana 2003, pet. ref'd); *Leverett v. State*, 2007 WL 1054140 (Tex. App. — Dallas 2007, no pet.).

Because of defense lawyers' focus on correct administration of the FSTs, officers must write detailed notes during the tests, especially about the clues that might show the suspect did not perform the test correctly. For instance, if an officer later testifies that he observed two clues showing the test was not performed correctly but cannot recall which clues these were, it diminishes the impact of that testimony considerably.

The FSTs are "divided attention" tests, meaning that they measure a person's ability to concentrate on more than one task at the same time. Divided attention tests are designed to evaluate mental and physical abilities a person needs to drive a car safely. Intoxicated people have trouble focusing on two things at once—including information processing, memory, balance, clear vision, and coordination. In other words, can the defendant: (1) listen to instructions; (2) process and follow the instructions; and (3) carry out what is asked of them.

While an officer's ability to administer field sobriety tests correctly is important, the failure to do so does not make those tests irrelevant. What difference does it make if the officer had the suspect take seven steps instead of nine, if the suspect stepped off the line twice in the first four steps? Even if the instructions given to the suspect are incorrect, the suspect's inability to follow them can be a sign of intoxication.

### HGN TESTS[30]

The horizontal gaze nystagmus (or HGN) test is considered by many officers to be the most effective tool to determine the amount of alcohol in a driver's system.[31] "Nystagmus" is a term used to describe a bouncing eye motion. Although there are several types of nystagmus, alcohol causes two types: alcohol gaze nystagmus, which includes HGN, and positional alcohol nystagmus. The officer must administer the test in a way that ensures the suspect's eyes can be clearly seen—either in a well-lit area or by using a flashlight to illuminate the suspect's face. The suspect should not face toward the blinking lights of a police cruiser or passing cars, which may cause optokinetic nystagmus. While removing eyeglasses makes it easier for the officer to observe eye movement, neither glasses nor contact lenses affect the HGN test results.[32]

HGN tests basically call for an officer to observe an involuntary jerking of the eyes as the suspect gazes to the side. The officer observes such things as tracking of the defendant's eyes and the size of the pupils. While nystagmus is a naturally occurring phenomenon, alcohol and some other drugs will enhance nystagmus so that it can be seen with the naked eye.

An officer is typically looking for three "clues" per eye that would show enhanced nystagmus and therefore indicate a 77 percent chance that the blood alcohol concentration (BAC) is greater than 0.08.[33] These clues are: lack of smooth pursuit, distinct and sustained nystagmus at maximum deviation, and onset of nystagmus prior to 45 degrees. There is a maximum score of six clues, or three per eye. Four or more clues indicate a BAC of greater than 0.08. **[A video showing how HGN tests work is included on the CD-Rom as "HGN Demonstrations. Additional resources are available on the TDCAA website under the DWI Resources tab.]**

Use of the HGN test has been endorsed by the highest criminal court in Texas. After over a decade of hit-and-miss admissibility, the Court of Criminal Appeals took judicial notice of the reliability of the test in *Emerson v State*.[34] The case includes a nice summary of the history of the test's development. Recently, defense lawyers have begun to argue that the HGN test must meet the *Kelly*[35] standards but the Court of Criminal Appeals has never endorsed that position.

An officer does not need to be an ophthalmologist to perform an HGN test.[36] Some courts have held that an officer

---

30 Descriptions of the three standardized tests are taken from "Standardized Field Sobriety Testing & Drug Recognition Experts for Prosecutors," published by the Texas Dep't of Transportation Law Enforcement & Security Training Division, Texas Engineering Extension Service, the Texas A&M University System. For more information, call the program at (409) 845-6391.

31 "Development of a Standardized Field Sobriety Test," National Highway Traffic Safety Administration, November 2001, found at **www.nhtsa.dot.gov/people/injury/alcohol/SFST.**

32 Footnote 40 from the HGN brochure. See **www.nhtsa.dot.gov** for more information.

33 "Colorado Validation Study of the SFST Battery," Marcelline Burns & Ellen Anderson (Nov. 1995 final report) (when all three tests used, officers were accurate 93 percent of the time in determining BACs at or above 0.08); "A Florida Validation Study of the SFST Battery," Marcelline Burns & Teresa Dioquino (1997) (when all three tests used, officers accurate 95 percent); "Validation of the SFST Battery at BACs below 0.10 Percent," Jack Stuster & Marcelline Burns (August 1998) (91 percent accuracy when all three tests used; HGN test found to be 88 percent accurate, walk & turn 79 percent accurate; one-leg stand test found to be 83 percent accurate).

34 880 S.W.2d 759 (Tex. Crim. App. 1994); see also *Gullatt v. State*, 74 S.W.3d 880 (Tex. App. — Waco 2002, no pet.). Other states have followed suit. See, e.g., *State v. Hullinger*, 649 N.W.2d 253 (S.D. 2002).

35 *Kerr v. State*, 921 S.W.2d 498 (Tex. App. — Fort Worth 1996, no pet.) (*Emerson* does not require that an officer have "practitioner certification" before his testimony on HGN is admissible. Such determination is to be covered by T.R.Evid. 702); *Smith v. State*, 65 S.W.3d 332 (Tex. App. — Waco 2001, no pet.) (certification from a training course will suffice); *Ellis v. State,* 86 S.W.3d 759 (Tex. App. — Waco 2002, pet. ref'd) (some certification is required for officer to testify).

36 *Emerson v. State*, 880 S.W.2d 759 (Tex. Crim. App. 1994); *Anderson v. State*, 866 S.W.2d 685 (Tex. App. — Houston [1st Dist.] 1993, pet. ref'd); *Finley v. State*, 809 S.W.2d 909 (Tex. App. — Houston [14th Dist.] 1991, pet. ref'd).

need not even have certification to be able to administer the test accurately.[37] What the officer witness cannot do is testify that there is a direct correlation between the failure of the test and a correlation to a particular blood alcohol level.[38] That's not much of a loss—the officer can still testify that, in his opinion, the suspect's failure of the HGN test is proof of intoxication. However, an officer may testify to this correlation if the defense opens the door by leaving a false impression with the jury that invites the other side to respond.[39]

The reliability and correlation variables are more commonly introduced by the defense attorney in his attempt to impeach the police officer. Police officers should be familiar with the FSTs and should have training in the proper way to administer them, not because they will not otherwise be admissible, but rather as a part of the professionalism we should expect from police officers. It may be helpful for the prosecutor to offer a video of eyes with and without nystagmus.[40]

#### *SFST Practitioner Certification*

One line of attack against the admissibility of the SFSTs commonly used by the defense is to argue the officer is not qualified to testify about the tests unless the officer has "practitioner certification." This attack is easily dealt with as it is based upon a flawed argument and a repealed rule.

TCOLE rules (specifically, §221.9 SFST Proficiency) used to refer to "practitioner certification." That rule provided an SFST certificate was valid for two years, after which the applicant would have to requalify. **This section was repealed on July 14, 2011.** The reason for the repeal is that TCOLE determined that this material was taught in the basic peace officer course; therefore, there was no need to have a proficiency certificate available. So officers that have attended (and passed) the 24-hour DWI Detection/SFST course at any time are considered certified to perform the SFSTs and testify in court about SFSTs and their results. There is no other requirement for updates, re-testing, etc.

Even before its repeal, there was case law supporting the proposition that an officer did not need practitioner certification before his testimony on HGN would be admissible. While there is case law stating that "practitioner certification" signified an officer was qualified,[41] numerous cases have held that the determination of his qualifications would be determined by T.R.Evid. 702.[42] Furthermore, the fact that an officer's practitioner certification had lapsed did not prevent that officer from testifying about HGN.[43]

### A SCIENTIFIC RESPONSE TO HGN CHALLENGES

The field sobriety test most commonly excluded for errors in administration is the HGN test. Though it is true that there are at times minor errors in the way those tests are administered and performed, those errors do not always call for exclusion of the test results. Recognizing this, many appellate courts have held that without some evidence to show that a minor error altered the results' reliability, the results should still be admissible.[44]

It is crucial to be familiar with the studies that support the tests, because some of those studies speak directly to the question of the impact of variations on reliability. One such study, "The Robustness of the Horizontal Gaze Nystagmus Test," was written by Dr. Marcelline Burns in 2007. The study looked at the impact such variations as moving the stimulus too fast or holding the stimulus too close to the subject had on the reliability. It also examined the question of whether the test results were a reliable indicator that a person was at or above .08 and the question of whether the sub-

---

37 See, e.g., *Anderson v. State,* 866 S.W.2d 685 (Tex. App. — Houston [1st Dist.] 1993, pet. ref'd); *Ellis v. State,* 86 S.W.3d 759 (Tex. App. — Waco 2002, pet. ref'd).

38 *Smith v. State,* 65 S.W.3d 332 (Tex. App. — Waco 2001, no pet.); *Webster v. State,* 26 S.W.3d 717 (Tex. App. — Waco 2000, pet. ref'd) (error harmless after instruction to disregard testimony about percentage chance that suspect had a BAC over 0.10); *Youens v. State,* 988 S.W.2d 404 (Tex. App. — Houston [1st Dist.] 1999, no pet.).

39 *Jordy v. State,* 413 S.W.3d 227 (Tex. App. — Fort Worth 2013, no pet.) (defendant opened door to testimony about HGN correlations to blood-alcohol content of 0.10 or higher by asking State's expert about HGN correlation to loss of normal use of mental or physical faculties).

40 See *Hartsock v. State,* 322 S.W.3d 775 (Tex. App. — Fort Worth 2010, no pet.).

41 *Smith v. State,* 65 S.W.3d 332 (Tex. App. — Waco 2001, no pet.).

42 *Price v. State,* 2006 WL 1707955 (Tex. App. — Austin 2006, pet. denied) (not desig. for pub.); *Burkhart v. State,* 2003 WL 2199896 (Tex. App. — Dallas 2003, no pet.) (not desig. for pub.); *Kerr v. State,* 921 S.W.2d 498 (Tex. App. — Fort Worth 1996, no pet.).

43 *Liles v. State,* 2009 WL 3152174 (Tex. App. — Houston [1st Dist.] 2009, no pet.) (not desig. for pub.).

44 *Leverett v. State,* 2007 WL 1054140 (Tex. App. — Dallas 2007, no pet.) (small variations in the HGN test did not render its results inadmissble); *Taylor v. State,* No. 03-03-00624-CR, 2006 WL 1649037 (Tex. App. — Austin 2006, pet. ref'd) (not desig. for pub.) (no correlation shown between HGN test variations and reliability); *Reynolds v. State,* 163 S.W.3d 808 (Tex. App. — Amarillo 2005), *aff'd on other grounds,* 204 S.W.3d 386 (Tex. Crim. App. 2006); *Compton v. State,* 120 S.W.3d 375 (Tex. App. — Houston [1st Dist.] 2003, pet. ref'd) (minor variations in time taken to administer HGN test did not warrant its exclusion).

ject's position made a difference. All of the above variations have, for years, been argued by the defense as a basis for excluding HGN test results.

Dr. Burns' findings told a very different story. According to the study, moving the stimulus too fast may result in false negative errors. In other words, going too fast at best may result in an officer missing some clues. Holding the stimulus too close actually increased the number of clues correctly observed. Finally the position of the subject—standing, sitting, or lying down—had no significant effect on the test. [**Dr. Burns' complete study is available on the CD-Rom that accompanies this book.**] A well-prepared prosecutor will make sure his expert is familiar with this study and will use it to impeach defense experts attacks on the HGN test and its results.

#### WALK & TURN

The walk & turn test is another divided attention psychophysical test. Psychophysical means using the mind and body at the same time. So a "divided attention psychophysical test" requires a suspect to use his mind to process information that is being given to him and his body to execute the instructions.

In a walk and turn test, an officer will have the suspect assume a heel-toe stance, hold his arms down at his sides, and tell him not to begin the exercise until instructed to do so. The officer will instruct the suspect to take nine heel-to-toe steps, turn around the line with several small steps, and return with nine heel-to-toe steps.

There are eight validated clues of impairment for the walk and turn test. Two clues apply while the suspect is standing heel-to-toe and listening to the instructions:

- cannot keep balance
- starts too soon

The other six validated clues apply during the walking stage of the test:

- stops walking
- steps off the line
- takes the wrong number of steps
- misses heel-to-toe
- uses arms to balance
- turns improperly

Two or more clues indicate a 68 percent likelihood that the BAC is greater than 0.10.[45]

#### ONE LEG STAND

The one leg stand is another divided attention psychophysical test, in which the officer requires the suspect to stand on one leg. The suspect extends the other leg in a stiff-legged manner, with the foot held approximately six inches above the ground and with the toe pointed forward. The suspect must stare at the elevated foot and count out loud starting from 1001 until the officer tells the suspect to stop.

There are four validated clues of impairment identified with the one leg stand:

1. sways while balancing
2. uses arms to balance
3. hopping
4. puts foot down

Two or more clues indicate a 68 percent likelihood that the BAC is greater than 0.10.

### NON-STANDARDIZED TESTS

Any test other than the three standardized tests—HGN, "one leg stand" or "walk and turn"—is considered a non-standardized test. Some common ones include:

- the Rhomberg test (also known as the stationary balance test, where the officer asks a driver to stand still with her heels together, put her head back, and close her eyes, watching to see if the driver can keep her balance);
- the finger count test (the driver touches the tip of each finger in succession to the tip of her thumb, up and back, while counting to four and then backwards from four to one);

---

45 Percentages for likelihoods regarding FST results discussed in this section are based on a study sponsored by the National Highway Traffic Safety Administration and conducted by Southern California Research Institute.

- counting backwards (the driver counts out loud a set of numbers in reverse order, starting with a random number, such as 543 and ending with another random number, such as 501); and
- alphabet (the driver recites a portion of the alphabet, often starting with a specific letter, like F, and ending with a specific letter, like T).

All these tests are appropriate measures of intoxication and should be administered at the scene. The fact that scientists have not tied these other tests to the per se definition of intoxication does not mean they cannot be probative of whether a person has lost the normal use of his mental or physical faculties. Some of these non-standardized tests may make more sense to administer for drivers who are elderly or disabled and might not be able to perform standardized tests, such as the one-leg stand.

## FST REVIEW

There is more to say about HGN and the other FSTs, but Warren Diepraam has done a stellar job of discussing the use of and response to attacks on these tests in his "Field Sobriety Test Review," which can be found on the TDCAA website in the "DWI Resources" section. Highlights of this paper are reproduced here. See the website for further discussion.

### DEFINITION OF NYSTAGMUS

#### *Horizontal Gaze Nystagmus*

Nystagmus is a jerking of the eye or a bouncing eye motion caused by multiple factors. It is displayed in either pendular form where the eye oscillates equally in two directions or jerk form where the eye moves slowly away from a fixated point and then rapidly corrects by a fast movement or saccade. Horizontal Gaze Nystagmus (HGN) is a form of jerk nystagmus where the saccadic movement is towards the direction of the gaze. HGN is an involuntary motion that is not controlled by the subject.

Only 2 things cause HGN: DIP drugs (depressants such as alcohol, xanax, valium, etc., Inhalants, and PCP), and serious brain stem injury.

### CATEGORIES OF NYSTAGMUS

#### *Vestibular*

**Rotational:** Nystagmus occurs when an individual is spun around rapidly causing the fluid in the inner ear to be disturbed. This cannot happen at roadside. It only occurs while a person is spinning.

**Post Rotational:** Nystagmus is present when an individual stops spinning because the fluid in the inner ear remains disturbed for a period of time. This type of nystagmus only lasts for a few seconds, is more prevalent in one eye, and would not be present for entire duration of HGN test.

**Caloric:** Nystagmus is caused by movement of inner ear fluid due to a difference in temperature of the fluid between the left and right ear. This occurs by putting warm water in one ear and cold water in the other. This is not a roadside practice of law enforcement.

#### *Positional Alcohol*

Nystagmus occurs when a foreign fluid, such as alcohol, alters the specific gravity of the blood in unequal concentrations in the blood and the vestibular system. If the subjects head is uneven and they have this fluid inequity, this type of nystagmus may occur. For this reason, the head is held straight (note that the person can be standing, seated, or supine for the HGN test).

> **PAN I:** occurs when the alcohol concentration in the blood is greater than in the inner ear fluid. *PAN I occurs when BAC is increasing.*
>
> **PAN II:** occurs when the alcohol concentration in the inner ear fluid is greater than in the blood stream. *PAN II occurs when BAC is decreasing.*

You will ALMOST NEVER see Positional Alcohol Nystagmus in the field. The only way you will is if the defendant is lying down on a backboard and you turn his head to the side. The action of turning the head will induce Positional Alcohol Nystagmus.

Nystagmus (which should be distinguished from gaze nystagmus) can also result from neural activity. **For examples of this and more information about FSTs, see "Field Sobriety Tests Review" on the CD-Rom accompanying this book.**

### DEFENSE ATTACKS

One way to minimize avenues of defense attack on SFSTs is to make sure officers are following the guidelines recommended by NHTSA when administering the tests. Officers should be familiar with the NHTSA manual, because defense lawyers will be, and they are likely to have a copy of the manual with them in court.

A growing number of experts—some former police officers or trainers of officers—have left government employment and now work for defense attorneys. For a fee, they will come into court, listen to testimony of a police officer, review the defendant's performance on video, and tell the jurors that they should not rely on the FSTs. The two arguments will be: (1) the tests are rigged and unreliable, and no one can perform them adequately; or (2) the tests are reliable, when they are done correctly, but the officer did not administer them correctly in this case.

These experts will, for instance, note if an officer didn't tell the defendant that if he stepped off the line, one point would be taken away from his score on the walk & turn test. This expert will contend that your officer administered all of the tests incorrectly. For this reason, it is very important that both officers and prosecutors have the latest copy of the SFST training manual and know how the tests are supposed to be done.

As with other experts, explore with these defense experts where they got their training, and how long since they made a DWI arrest (if ever). Once you realize a particular expert will be a defense witness, make every effort to talk to other prosecutors who may have encountered them. Check the TDCAA website (**www.tdcaa.com**) for the expert's name (and a prosecutor contact name), or post a question about the expert on the user forum at the TDCAA website. And call the author to see whether he has transcripts on the former officer expert that will be used in your case.

In many instances, even well-trained officers—because of the circumstances under which they must give these tests—can't do them exactly like the book says. Defense experts will try to say any variance from protocol for these tests means they're worthless. The prosecutor needs to be prepared to argue that tests are merely a tool. Anything the officer asks the defendant to do to demonstrate his mental or physical faculties provides information about whether that defendant is intoxicated.

The SFSTs come with certain percentages by which they're supposed to be reliable. Those percentages are what might be affected by the test not being administered correctly—not the overall value of the SFSTs in indicating whether the defendant was intoxicated.

Another attack may be that the officer coerced the defendant into performing field sobriety tests. An officer's threat to take a suspect to jail if he continued to refuse to perform field sobriety tests will not result in exclusion of those test results.[46]

## Officer's Search & Report

Once a defendant has been arrested, officers may obtain valuable information vital to a later prosecution both through a search incident to arrest and in impounding the defendant's vehicle. The defendant himself can be a good source of evidence. Start with the car and things that logically would be in the car, including:

***Open Containers***

Besides noting any containers in the car, record the bar code number on the bottom of the can ("born-on date") so prosecutors can find out where and when the can was distributed. This may be used to rebut a defendant's statements at trial.

***Evidence on the Body***

Blood and hair evidence can be used to place a defendant behind the wheel or rebut a statement that he is a passenger. Check for seat belt bruises, airbag abrasions on the face, injuries tied to specific vehicle damage, brake impressions on the sole of shoes, knee injuries on the driver (or a broken femur), and wrist injuries from grasping the steering wheel.

***Car Condition***

Take photos to document contentious issues. If a defendant's tires are damaged from hitting the curb, officers should take pictures or film the damage with the in-car camera. Look for windshield star cracks, fingerprints, blood spatter. Check the settings of the seat and rearview mirror—do they indicate a small or large person was driving? Is this consistent with the defendant being the driver?

***Inspection Stickers***

If the defendant was involved in a wreck and he later tries to claim mechanical problems caused it, having information from the inspection sticker may provide a lead on when the car was last inspected and who performed the inspection. This may help rebut any claim that the car was not in good working order at the time of the wreck.

---

46 *Oguntope v. State,* 177 S.W.3d 435 (Tex. App. — Houston [1st Dist.] 2005, no pet.).

***Food***

Any food or discarded containers could be important in trying to recreate the defendant's whereabouts that day.

***Toll Tags***

If the defendant has a toll tag on his car, prosecutors might be able to track whether the vehicle passed through a toll booth at a certain time. This information is likely obtainable through subpoena if not given freely by the toll tag company.

***Cell Phones***

Once you know cell phone number, subpoenas can be issued to find out who a defendant spoke to that evening and the location of the call. Look at the list of numbers dialed and calls received on the cell phone, as well as the list of phone numbers. The friends listed in the defendant's cell phone directory could be witnesses as to the defendant's activities that day, or his drinking or driving habits.

***Title of the Car***

Evidence of vehicle registration papers found in the car can provide some evidence of who was operating the vehicle.

***From the Defendant***

Hand stamps could indicate clubs at which the defendant has been drinking. Credit card receipts in the defendant's wallet or pocket can help track her movements that evening as well as indicate the number of alcoholic beverages the defendant purchased. In areas with dry counties, the defendant may have cards in her wallet that reflect memberships in clubs where alcohol is served. Information in a car or wallet may also indicate whether the defendant is taking any medication or suffers any physical disabilities. As part of an inventory of the defendant's property, the officer can make a xerox copy of everything in the defendant's wallet. Paycheck stubs or other paperwork in the car may indicate where the defendant is employed.

Details included by officers in their reports about the impounding process can help prosecutors later tie the defendant to the vehicle. For instance, officers should note from whom they got the car keys to give to the tow truck driver. Also, to help in wheeling the defendant, note which towing company picked up the vehicle, the name of the tow truck driver, and who the towing company believed owned the vehicle, and to whom the vehicle was later released.

***Insurance Information***

If the defendant was involved in an accident, prosecutors can obtain information the defendant and any other driver give to their insurance companies. Information about the defendant's carrier may be in the car or in the defendant's wallet. Officers should be sure to reference the insurance information in their accident reports. Later, insurance companies and their records of the defendant's driving can be fertile ground. A court or grand jury subpoena has provided me with everything from photographs of the damage, pictures of the scene, even audio recordings of the defendant or his passengers admitting the defendant was intoxicated. Insurance reports will also contain the defendant's recitation of what happened to cause the accident.

You may face resistance from the insurance company in your attempts to obtain these records. Their efforts to impede you will likely fail.[47] What follows are some of the arguments and the proper legal response to defeat those arguments.

As a starting point, remember the party opposing the production of these files has the burden of proof. This was the holding in *Humphreys v. Caldwell*,[48] where the court held that it was proper to order production of claims adjustor files as those files did not contain attorney mental processes.

One argument is that the records are protected by the attorney-client privilege from T.R.Evid. 504(b). The defendant will assert that the privilege extends to an insured's communication to its insurer concerning potential liability covered by the policy, and, thus, protects communications by the defendant contained in the claim file. This argument will fail for a number of reasons. First, there is not usually an attorney-client relationship between an insurance company and its insured. The defendant would have to demonstrate that at the time of the communications, the insurance company was the defendant's counsel or a representative of their counsel. This type of relationship is unlikely to be found in your average insurance claim.

Another common argument is that the work-product privilege protects the claim file. The work product privilege protects documents prepared by attorneys or their agents in anticipation of litigation that contain the attorneys' mental processes, conclusions, or legal theories.[49] In rejecting one argument that a report was prepared in "anticipation of liti-

47 See, e.g., *In re Ford Motor Co.*, 988 S.W.2d 714 (Tex. 1998).

48 *Humphreys v. Caldwell*, 888 S.W.2d 469 (Tex. 1994).

49 *Humphreys*, 888 S.W.2d at 471; *National Tank Co. v. Brotherton*, 851 S.W.2d 193, 200 (Tex. 1993) (post-accident investigation).

gation," the court in *National Tank Co. v. Brotherton* held that the "litigation" must be more than merely the abstract possibility or unwarranted fear that there will be litigation. Furthermore, notes taken by attorneys during conversation with fact witnesses are not protected. "Neutral recitation of facts" are not protected work product.[50] So for this argument to hold up, the defendant would have to show that the file was prepared at the direction of or for the use of an attorney. Once again this is unlikely to be the case.

The investigative or party communication privilege protects only those communications made during or in anticipation of the *particular suit* in which the privilege is asserted.[51] So unless there is evidence that the claims file or report was prepared in connection with or in preparation of a law suit this privilege will not apply.

The consulting expert privilege protects the identity, mental impressions, and opinions of an expert who has been informally consulted or who has been retained in anticipation of litigation or preparation for trial if the expert will not be called to testify at trial and no testifying expert has reviewed the consulting expert's conclusions.[52] Unless the defendant can show the individuals who investigated the claim were hired as consulting experts this privilege will not apply.

### Officer's Perspective: The Arrest Decision

*by Neal Maranto, Traffic Sergeant, North Richland Hills PD*

The decision to arrest is based upon everything an officer sees from the first moment he spots the suspect vehicle to the point he has offered the last sobriety test he is going to offer.

At this point the officer weighs the evidence and makes the decision to arrest the suspect or let him go. our investigation at the minimum should be focused on building a wall of probable cause. Brick by brick, through your observations and questions, you gather pieces of fact that go together to establish probable cause. Rarely will the "wall" be solid. Invariably, there will be missing bricks that are missing. Not every intoxicated person slurs her speech or staggers. These "bricks" may be missing, but the wall may still stand. Be prepared to explain to the jury how not every intoxicated person shows every possible clue of intoxication.

When you first observe a vehicle whose driver you suspect may be intoxicated, view the facts in an unbiased manner. Let the facts develop as they will. View the facts for what they are. You, obviously, cannot create traffic violations, they will happen or they will not. Likewise, you cannot cause a person to have slurred speech. She either has it or does not. However, the fact is once you have conducted your investigation and made the decision to arrest, you have become a biased witness. You, through your investigation, have come to believe the suspect is intoxicated. Otherwise, you would not have arrested him.

Through careful questioning and your testimony at the far end, it is common for an officer to actually construct a wall of proof beyond reasonable doubt. By asking more in-depth questions than simply, "How much have you had to drink?" you ultimately paint a much more vivid picture for the jury.

## WITNESSES

Another tremendous source of information are witnesses and passengers who were at the scene. Be sure to record witnesses' names, addresses, phone numbers and drivers license numbers in the offense reports so your prosecutor may contact them. Officers should talk to any passengers on the scene and ask them questions such as:

- Where were you coming from?
- How much did the defendant drink?
- Were you watching the defendant all the time or paying very close attention?
- How did you pay for the drinks?
- What did you think about the defendant's driving?
- Is the defendant typically a good driver? An unsafe driver?

---

50 *Leede Oil & Gas Inc. v. McCorkle*, 789 S.W.2d 686 (Tex. App. — Houston [1st Dist] 1990) (orig. proceeding).

51 Tex.R.Civ.P. 166b(3)(d); *Republic Ins. Co. v. Davis*, 856 S.W.2d 158, 164-65 (Tex. 1993); *Turbodyne Corp. v. Heard*, 720 S.W.2d 802, 804 (Tex. 1986) (documents prepared by insurance co. were connected with settlement of its claim and not in "anticipation of litigation" and were not protected), *overruled on other grounds by Walker v. Packer*, 827 S.W.2d 833 (Tex. 1992).

52 Tex.R.Civ.P. 166b(3)(b).

### THE BOOKING PROCESS

When a defendant is booked into jail after an arrest, jail personnel compile a medical intake form. This form indicates, among other things, whether the defendant appeared to be intoxicated when he was booked, the defendant's answer when jail personnel ask him whether he is intoxicated, and other potentially relevant medical information. [**A sample medical intake form is included as Appendix 2-1.**] Prosecutors can also obtain a copy of the jail's property inventory for the defendant.

In every case, make it a habit to check the defendant's property at the jail. You never know what you might find. Officers should specifically look for cash or credit receipts that show recent alcohol purchases.

## Video

The next logical source for potential evidence is videotape. There are three ways police might capture some of the defendant's actions on video: (1) with a camera in the patrol car; (2) at the stationhouse; or (3) through surreptitious taping while the defendant is sitting in the patrol car or somewhere at the jail. With the advent of racial profiling statutes, cameras in patrol cars have become more widely used.

### CAMERAS IN PATROL CARS

There is no requirement that law enforcement videotape DWI arrests, and it is proper to object should any defense attorney state otherwise.[53] Although an opinion from the Texas Attorney General states certain counties are required to obtain and maintain video equipment, the opinion does not require all law enforcement vehicles to be equipped with records nor that each law enforcement encounter with the public be videotaped.[54]

From patrol cars, officers might obtain recordings in two ways: (1) taping field sobriety tests performed in front of the car; or (2) turning the video camera around to tape conversations when the defendant is sitting in the patrol car. Traditionally, we think of cameras in patrol cars being used to tape the stop. More and more, officers are using in-car video to tape what the defendant says inside the car. Recordings made in the back of a patrol car are admissible because the defendant has no reasonable expectation of privacy there.[55]

In *Meyer v. State*, the officer placed the defendant in the back of his patrol car after arresting him for DWI. As the defendant sat there, with the doors closed and windows shut, he made statements that the car's videotaping equipment caught. (The opinion does not give details about the monologue, other than to say that it was an "acrimonious tirade profanely blaming his wife and the two officers for his plight.") The court found the statements admissible.

A field sobriety test videotaped by an officer from a camera mounted on his dashboard will also be admissible.[56] Destruction of an on-scene video does not support suppression of a subsequent station video.[57]

The absence of sound on a DWI video will not affect its admissibility.[58] Tapes may contain otherwise objectionable items and should always be carefully reviewed before trial. It is always a good practice to edit those inadmissible statements out of the tape prior to trial.

### STATIONHOUSE VIDEOS

More likely what officers and prosecutors will encounter are videotapes made at the stationhouse.

#### *Waivers & Warnings*

Although Code of Criminal Procedure Article 38.22 used to require officers to warn defendants that they were about to be videotaped, that portion of the law was repealed. Officers no longer need to warn defendants that they are being taped.

Tactically, when you inform a defendant that he is being taped can make a big difference. If the officer delays telling the defendant that he is being taped, you might be able to see a big difference in how the defendant behaves before and after

53 *Rodriguez v. State*, No. 04-12-00528-CR, 2013 WL 5656194 (Tex. App. — San Antonio 2013, pet. dism'd) (not for publication).

54 Tex. AG Opin. GA-0731 (2009).

55 *Meyer v. State*, 78 S.W.3d 505 (Tex. App. — Austin 2002, pet. ref'd); Op. Tex. Att'y Gen. JC-0208 (2000).

56 *Poulos v. State*, 799 S.W.2d 769 (Tex. App. — Houston [1st Dist.] 1990, no pet.) (videotape not testimonial in nature, and showing it did not violate the defendant's 5th Amendment rights).

57 *Higginbotham v. State*, 416 S.W.3d 921 (Tex. App. — Houston [1st Dist.] 2013, no pet.) (destroyed video would not have affected outcome).

58 *Aguirre v. State*, 948 S.W.2d 377 (Tex. App. — Houston [14th Dist.] 1997, pet. ref'd).

he finds out he is being taped. Pre-arrest, the defendant typically isn't as much on his guard. After arrest, the defendant may be attempting to mask his intoxication to appear in the best possible light later when the video is shown to a jury.

Note that an officer's failure to obtain an explicit waiver of rights from the defendant can be a problem. This can happen if the officer reads the warnings to the defendant, asks whether the defendant understands the warnings, but then skips the question of whether the defendant agrees to waive his rights. Failure to get the defendant's explicit waiver may or may not result in any later statements being inadmissible.[59]

#### *Uncooperative Defendants*

Some DWI defendants—through attitude, coaching, or as a result of previous intoxication-related arrests—make a variety of unhelpful responses on video. But even seemingly exculpatory responses can be turned into good information supporting intoxication for a jury.

Commonly, defendants will refuse to coooperate or say that they want to talk to their attorney first. At this point, officers should note the difference between verbal and physical incrimination. A defendant's right not to incriminate himself extends only to verbal incrimination—not physical incrimination. An officer still can, and should, make note of the defendant's behavior indicating intoxication, even after the defendant has invoked his right to an attorney. Posture, how the defendant is anchoring his feet (for instance, standing wide apart to help balance himself), or putting his hand on some object to stabilize himself can all indicate intoxication.

A jury needs to understand—and the prosecutor must discuss—the fact that a person does not have a right to refuse FSTs. A defendant has no right to talk to an attorney before deciding whether to perform FSTs or give a sample of breath.[60] Prosecutors should think about the implications of refusing to take a breath test or perform field sobriety tests before talking to an attorney. There's very little that one would expect an attorney could tell a person suspected of DWI, unless the attorney happened to be drinking with the defendant that night. What would we expect an attorney to tell a client suspected of DWI? That if he has had too much to drink, he should decline all tests.

Another common response is for a defendant to feign misunderstanding of the situation. Officers ask defendants, after reading the statutory warnings to them, "Do you understand what I've just read to you?" Note, however, that the statute contains no requirement that the defendant answer "yes" before the officer can proceed to the next step. The law is aimed at intoxicated people, whose reasoning powers are impaired. If the law required all defendants to understand the warnings before officers could proceed, it would require that the defendant sober up before the officer could read him the warning. Instead, the law is designed to let the suspect know that there are consequences to his behavior. There is no requirement that the defendant actually understand the warnings.

Officers should also note whether the defendant reads along with the warnings as the officer reads them. What is the defendant's facial expression as the officer is reading the warnings? Is the defendant following along, or are his eyes glazed over and not following along with the written warnings as the officer reads?

A hostile officer on the videotape is another potential issue prosecutors will need to handle. Occasionally, a tape will show a defendant who appears from his introduction to be friendly and treat the officer with respect, yet the officer's demeanor makes clear that he's upset with defendant. Many officers have been hit, for instance, with a stream of racial slurs all the way driving to the stationhouse, only to have the defendant turn into a polite and professional Eddie Haskell once they reach the stationhouse. Officers need to document any past words or exchanges that explain this. If not documented, officer needs to tell you about this.

Other defendants will respond that they do not understand the warnings or will refuse to respond at all. Rather than allow the defendant to control the pace of the proceedings by stalling, officers should take control by responding, "I'm going to ask you one more time to give a sample, and any response other than affirmative I'm going to take as a refusal."

The prosecutor must be in a position to explain this game to the jury. Every minute a defendant delays the decision whether to give the sample is another minute that he's sobering up with alcohol dissipating from his system. Prosecutors must help the jury see this tactic as a game, in which the defendant cloaks his delay tactics in faux reasonableness, claiming rights that he does not have.

---

59 Tex. Code Crim. Proc. art. 38.22, §§2 & 3; see also *Davis v. U.S.*, 512 U.S. 452, 114 S.Ct. 2350, 129 L.Ed.2d 362 (1994); *Rocha v. State*, 16 S.W.3d 1 (Tex. Crim. App. 2000) (recorded statements need not contain express verbal statement that defendant waives his rights); *Barefield v. State*, 784 S.W.2d 38 (Tex. Crim. App. 1989) (totality of the circumstances governs admissibility of statements), overruled on other grounds by *Zimmerman v. State*, 860 S.W.2d 89 (Tex. Crim. App. 1993); *Stone v. State*, 612 S.W.2d 542 (Tex. Crim. App. 1981).

60 *Forte v. State*, 759 S.W.2d 128 (Tex. Crim. App. 1988) (breath tests); *McCambridge v. State*, 778 S.W.2d 70 (Tex. Crim. App. 1989); *Jones v. State*, 795 S.W.2d 171 (Tex. Crim. App. 1990) (FSTs).

Use a defendant's refusal to cooperate with tests on videotape to rebut the defense argument that the only evidence the state has of intoxication is the officer's subjective observation. Argue that the videotape was the defendant's single opportunity to be in front of an objective observer—the video camera—and the defendant refused to do it. The video tape is the law's way to give the defendant the chance to rebut the officer's impression that the defendant is intoxicated. Same with breath tests: The breath test is the defendant's chance to take an objective instrument and prove the officer wrong. The fact that the defendant refused to perform FSTs on video (or submit a breath sample) rebuts the idea that he was not intoxicated.

Some defendants feign ignorance as to why they've been arrested. If you take them at their word, you can't get much better evidence of intoxication than someone who doesn't understand what they've been arrested for after being told multiple times by the officer what's going on. Prosecutors should discuss this issue with officer pretrial. In this situation, while the officer is testifying about what is going on in the videotape, stop the tape, let officer explain how many times he told the defendant what he was being arrested for and what made him pull defendant over in the first place.

---

## Officer's Perspective: Sobriety Test Refusals

*by Neal Maranto, Traffic Sergeant, North Richland Hills PD*

Occasionally, officers encounter persons who will perform no field sobriety tests at all. In my experience, the people who refuse tend to be those who have previously been arrested for DWI. I have found that, in general, persons who refuse do so in a polite, apologetic manner. "I'm very sorry officer, but I have to refuse to do your tests." It is important for us to remain focused on our goal, which is proving our case to a jury and not losing our patience with the suspect.

Frequently, the suspect will tell you he would like to participate, but was told by an attorney, family member or friend to never participate. While this may be true, it tends to absolve the suspect of responsibility for not participating. Bring the focus back on him and explain what you want to do and why you deem it necessary to test him. When confronted with a person who is a total refusal, offer every test possible and make the suspect refuse each one.

I stopped a suspect who refused sobriety tests. I offered every test possible and the driver kept coming up with incredible reasons why he could not perform each test. When offered HGN, the suspect said his vision was so poor he could not see the dashboard. He said he could not see the stimulus at all. I later filed a MAB review so he was called in to DPS for a vision test.

I then offered each individual sobriety test. He refused the alphabet test, claiming he had never graduated kindergarten, although he had earlier told me that he owned three businesses.

At the end I offered him a portable breath test. I concluded by asking him if there was any test he could think of that would help me evaluate him and he said there was not. I ultimately did arrest him. Do not assume that because a person says he is refusing that he will not do anything. Get a suspect to say no to each test. Leave nothing to chance. If a suspect says they "cannot do" a test, do not assume he is refusing. Ask why not. The suspect may tell you about an injury that would affect his ability to do the test, or he may tell you he is too drunk to do it.

### *Time Delays*

The most significant problem with stationhouse videos is the time delay between stop and taping, particularly in counties where officers have no in-car video. Besides having to explain the delay to the jury, officers and prosecutors also need to realize that the more time that passes between arrest and stationhouse taping, the more time the defendant's body has to process the alcohol. Count on the defense to attack your rendition of how impaired the defendant appears at the scene compared to his behavior on the stationhouse video.

If the defendant is stopped at midnight, arrested at 12:20 a.m., but doesn't make it to the stationhouse on video until 2:30 a.m., chances are your jury will want to know the reason for the delay. If the officer has in-car video, that might explain what happened between arrest and the stationhouse video. If not, look to the officer's log for an explanation for the delay. Was the officer waiting on the tow truck? Or was there a long line for the intoxilyzer machine? Discussing the long line at the machine is another subtle way of reminding the jury what a significant problem DWI is.

### *Reviewing Videos*

If a prosecutor works in a county where officers routinely record stationhouse interviews, the prosecutor needs to visit the taping room to be able to keep the events on the videotapes in context. Reviewing will help put any defense attacks of the video in context for the jury. Physically examine the room where the videotapes are made. Camera angles can affect the ability of officers to observe, for instance, the defendant weaving while standing. An overhead camera won't be able to catch this as well as one situated lower. Prosecutors need to be aware of this and must be able to explain this phenomenon and prepare the officer.

If more than one officer administered FSTs to the defendant the night of the stop (for instance, one on the roadside and another one at the stationhouse), prosecutors should ask whether the officers explained and administered the tests in the same way. Prepare your officers to explain any discrepancies in the administration of the test, because defense lawyers will surely question them.

#### *Larger Counties*

The statute dealing with videotaping DWI suspects by officers in larger counties is not found in Penal Code chapter 49 or anywhere in the Transportation Code. Two important features of this law are: (1) It doesn't require videotaping. It only requires larger counties to purchase and maintain video equipment; and (2) It was never codified as a statute, either as part of the former DWI laws in Article 6701*l* of the Texas Civil Statutes or the newer DWI provisions in Chapter 49 of the Penal Code.

In 1983, the Legislature passed a bill that had the videotaping language in it, but the bill didn't tie the video provisions to any other law, such as Article 6701*l*. So the provision is effective, but it has only had a session law-type cite, and not a statutory cite. The videotape provision has never been codified or brought into the Penal Code. You can cite it as Acts 1983, ch. 303, §24. That section states:

> (a) Each county with a population of 25,000 or more according to the most recent federal census shall purchase and maintain electronic devices capable of visually recording a person arrested within the county for an offense under Article 6701*l*-1, Revised Statutes, or Subdivision (2), Subsection (a), Section 19.05, Penal Code.
>
> (b) The sheriff of the county shall determine upon approval by the county commissioners court the number of devices necessary to ensure that a peace officer arresting a defendant for an offense listed in Subsection (a) of this section may visually record the defendant's appearance within a reasonable time after the arrest.
>
> (c) The fact that an arresting officer or other person acting on behalf of the state failed to visually record a person arrested for an offense listed in Subsection (a) of this section is admissible at the trial of the offense if the offense occurred in a county required to purchase and maintain electronic devices under this section.

---

### Officer's Perspective: On-Scene Post-Arrest Evidence

*by Neal Maranto, Traffic Sergeant, North Richland Hills PD*

After the arrest is made and the suspect secured in the back seat, switch the camera and microphone to the in-car position. While most people know that police cars carry cameras that capture what happens in front of the vehicle, most do not know that these same systems can capture what happens in the back seat. Make sure the audio is recording as well.

Many times, suspects who were unaware of the presence of the recording devices have made incriminating statements. These statements are considered res gestae as long as you are not asking questions to cause the responses. In the eyes of the court, the suspect has no right to privacy in the rear of the police car.

Even if the suspect does not utter excited outbursts, frequently, there are repetitious questions that are asked of the arresting officer, such as, "Why did you stop me?" and "What am I charged with?" This can be excellent evidence of the short-term memory problems associated with alcohol intoxication.

## OPERATOR QUALIFICATIONS

No special training on the use of video equipment is necessary if the operator has basic knowledge of operating procedures or instructions.[61] Later in trial, the prosecutor will have to lay a predicate for admission of the video, and T.R.Evid. 901 addresses the proper predicate.[62] The fact that the machine was operating properly can be inferred from evidence and testimony by the operator or by someone else.[63]

---

61 *Clark v. State*, 728 S.W.2d 484 (Tex. App. — Fort Worth), *vacated and remanded on other grounds*, 753 S.W.2d 371 (Tex. Crim. App. 1987), *on remand*, 781 S.W.2d 954 (Tex. App. — Fort Worth 1989, no pet.); *Holland v. State*, 622 S.W.2d 904 (Tex. App. — Fort Worth 1981, no pet.).

62 *Leos v. State*, 883 S.W.2d 209 (Tex. Crim. App. 1994).

63 *Roy v. State*, 608 S.W.2d 645 (Tex. Crim. App. [panel op.] 1980); *Sims v. State*, 735 S.W.2d 913 (Tex. App. — Dallas 1987, pet. ref'd).

## TESTIMONIAL VS. NON-TESTIMONIAL ACTS

In the courtroom, some of the most common DWI issues litigated day to day are what portions of the video will be admissible, largely determined by whether the defendant invoked her right to counsel. Generally, from that point forward, all things the defendant said in response to interrogation will be inadmissible, and only non-testimonial things will be admissible. The following portions of a DWI defendant's videotape may be admitted:

1. visual depictions of field sobriety tests;[64]
2. verbal field sobriety tests—such as reciting parts of the alphabet or counting;[65]
3. audio portion of video when police questioning is the type normally incident to arrest and custody and is not reasonably likely to elicit testimony;[66]
4. refusal to perform field sobriety tests;[67]
5. the video portions after the audio is suppressed;[68]
6. a defendant's request for counsel during a refusal to take a breath test;[69]
7. video portions even if the audio did not record;[70] and
8. the video portion of field sobriety tests after *Miranda* is invoked;[71]

---

64 *Townsend v. State*, 813 S.W.2d 181 (Tex. App. — Houston [14th Dist.] 1991, pet. ref'd) (visual depictions of a sobriety test are not testimonial — evidence such as a person's voice, demeanor, or physical characteristics is outside the scope of protection against self-incrimination).

65 *Gassaway v. State*, 957 S.W.2d 48 (Tex. Crim. App. 1997) (reciting and counting not testimonial).

66 *Pennsylvania v. Muniz*, 496 U.S. 582, 110 S.Ct. 2638, 110 L.Ed.2d 528 (1990); *Jones v. State*, 795 S.W.2d 171 (Tex. Crim. App. 1990); *Mathieu v. State*, 992 S.W.2d 725 (Tex. App. — Houston [1st Dist.] 1999, no pet.) (officer's request that suspect perform sobriety tests and directions on how to do the tests do not constitute interrogation, nor do questions about a suspect's understanding of his rights); *Dawkins v. State*, 822 S.W.2d 668 (Tex. App. — Waco 1991), *pet. ref'd*, 825 S.W.2d 709 (Tex. Crim. App. 1992).

67 *Raffaelli v. State*, 881 S.W.2d 714 (Tex. App. — Texarkana 1994, pet. ref'd) (no distinction between allowing jury to hear about refusal to do FSTs or breath test refusals); *Dawkins v. State*, 822 S.W.2d 668 (Tex. App. — Waco 1991), *pet. ref'd*, 825 S.W.2d 709 (Tex. Crim. App. 1992); *Barraza v. State*, 733 S.W.2d 379, 381 (Tex. App. — Corpus Christi 1987), *aff'd*, 790 S.W.2d 654 (Tex. Crim. App. 1990).

68 *Huffman v. State*, 746 S.W.2d 212 (Tex. Crim. App. 1988); *Fierro v. State*, 969 S.W.2d 51 (Tex. App. — Austin 1998, no pet.).

69 *Griffith v. State*, 55 S.W.3d 598 (Tex. Crim. App. 2001); *Halbrook v. State*, 31 S.W.3d 301 (Tex. App. — Fort Worth 2000, pet. ref'd); *Ex parte Jamail*, 904 S.W.2d 862 (Tex. App. — Houston [1st Dist.] 1995, pet. ref'd).

70 *Burke v. State*, 930 S.W.2d 230 (Tex. App. — Houston [14th Dist.] 1996, pet. ref'd); see also *Aguirre v. State*, 948 S.W.2d 377 (Tex. App. — Houston [14th Dist.] 1997, pet. ref'd) (DWI video with no sound is admissible).

71 *Jones v. State*, 795 S.W.2d 171 (Tex. Crim. App. 1990).

The following parts of a DWI defendant's videotape can be suppressed:

1. invocation of the right to counsel;[72]
2. invocation of the right to terminate the interview;[73]
3. objected-to extraneous offenses.[74]

## ABSENCE OF VIDEOTAPE

The absence of a videotape in a DWI case is not grounds for acquittal.[75] A defendant is not entitled to a jury instruction on the state's failure to videotape the defendant.[76] To support a motion to dismiss based on destruction of a video, the defendant must show that the destruction was in bad faith.[77]

## UNAVAILABLE OFFICER

In some cases, the officer/witness who was in the room with the defendant will not be available to testify at trial. Texas courts have allowed admission of at least the video portion of the tape under what the federal courts have called the "silent witness" rule.[78] The key is whether there is sufficient evidence to enable a reasonable juror to conclude that the videotape is what the State claims it to be. A showing of how the tape is loaded and that the machine was working should suffice.

---

[72] *Hardie v. State*, 807 S.W.2d 319 (Tex. Crim. App. 1991).

[73] *Cooper v. State*, 961 S.W.2d 229 (Tex. App. — Houston [1st Dist.] 1997, no pet.).

[74] *Johnson v. State*, 747 S.W.2d 451 (Tex. App. — Houston [14th Dist.] 1988, pet. ref'd) (extraneous offenses mentioned by defendant or police on tape must be objected to at the time the tape is offered or the defendant has not preserved error).

[75] *Williams v. State*, 946 S.W.2d 886 (Tex. App. — Waco 1997, no pet.); *Irion v. State*, 703 S.W.2d 362 (Tex. App. — Austin 1986, no pet.).

[76] *Logan v. State*, 757 S.W.2d 160 (Tex. App. — San Antonio 1988, no pet.).

[77] *Gamboa v. State*, 774 S.W.2d 111 (Tex. App. — Fort Worth 1989, pet. ref'd).

[78] *Reavis v. State*, 84 S.W.3d 716 (Tex. App. — Fort Worth 2002, no pet.); *Page v. State*, 125 S.W.3d 640 (Tex. App. — Houston [1st Dist.] 2003, pet. ref'd).

# Appendix 2-1: Medical Screening Evaluation

## MEDICAL SCREENING EVALUATION

MEDICAL STAFF RECOMMENDATION (Check one only)

_____ Inmate medically cleared for general population and full duties
_____ Inmate medically cleared for general population and limited duties
_____ Inmate medically cleared for open medical housing
_____ Inmate medically requires medical single cell
_____ Inmate medically requires hospital floor housing
_____ Inmate medically requires infirmary housing
_____ Inmate medically requires negative air cell housing

Additional medically necessary inmate needs (Check if required)
Lower Bunk _____ No Stairs _____ Other (explain) _____

Signature of Reviewing Nurse: _____

### CLASSIFICATION PROFILE

1. Do you have diabetes? Yes No
2. Have you ever had a seizure? Yes No
3. Have you ever been in counseling for drug abuse, alcoholism or mental or emotional problems? Yes No
4. Do you or have you consumed alcohol? Yes No
5. How much do you drink, and how often? _____
6. When did you begin to drink? _____
7. Do you or have you used drugs? Yes No
8. How often was the use of drugs? _____
9. Do you have a history of psychiatric disorder? Yes No
10. Have you received mental health treatment? Yes No
    If yes, when? _____ where? _____ Dr.? _____
11. Would you like to see a mental health worker? Yes No
12. Is this your first arrest as an adult or juvenile? Yes No
    If no, when was your first arrest? _____
13. Were you ever arrested as a juvenile? Yes No
    If yes, when? _____ where? _____ why? _____
14. Did you ever spend time in a juvenile institution? Yes No
    If yes, did you have any problems there? Yes No
15. When was your first time in jail? _____ How old were you? _____
16. How many times have you been in jail? _____ Did you have any problems there? Yes No
17. Have you ever served prison time? Yes No
    If yes, when? _____ where? _____ why? _____
    If yes, did you have any problems there? _____
18. Are you or have you been a member or associate of a street gang, prison gang, or extremist organization? Yes No
    If yes, which? _____
19. Have you ever or been charged with escape, attempted escape, AWOL, or walk away? Yes No
20. Are you homosexual? Yes No
    If yes, can you house in general population? Yes No
21. Do you have any enemies in this jail? Yes No
    If yes, who? _____
22. Have you had any problems with another race? Yes No
    If yes, which race? _____
23. What is the highest grade you completed in school? _____
24. Do you have a high school diploma or a GED? Yes No
25. Would you like to work towards a GED while you are here? Yes No
26. Have you been employed or attending school 6 months prior to arrest? Yes No
27. Have you resided at the same address 1 year prior to arrest? Yes No
28. Would you like to request participation in an inmate work program while you are here? Yes No

I hereby certify that in consideration for any medical services rendered in good faith on my behalf, I shall hold Tarrant County, the Tarrant County Sheriff's Department, and any agents or employees thereof, harmless for any continuation or worsening of my pre-existing health condition(s).

INMATE'S SIGNATURE: _____ DATE: _____

INTERVIEWING DEPUTY: _____ DATE: _____

CFMT-22 GPC 1615 REV. 07-00

## RECEIVING SCREENING FORM

NAME ______________________ SEX ____ D.O.B. __________ DATE/TIME __________

### QUESTIONS ASKED BY RECEIVING OFFICER

1. Has inmate been involved in an automobile accident within the last 12 hours? Y N
2. Has inmate been involved in a physical confrontation within the last 12 hours? Y N

** If inmate answered YES to either question 1 or 2, contact Screening Nurse.

### RECEIVING OFFICER'S VISUAL OPINION

1. Is the inmate conscious? Y N
2. Does the new inmate have obvious pain or bleeding or other symptoms suggesting need for Emergency Service? Y N
3. Are there visible signs of trauma or illness requiring immediate Emergency or Doctor's care? Y N
4. Is there obvious fever, swollen lymph nodes, yellowing of the eyes or other evidence of infection which might spread through the jail? Y N
5. Is the skin in good condition and free from lice and crabs? Y N
6. Does the inmate appear to be under the influence of alcohol? Y N
7. Does the inmate appear to be under the influence of barbiturates, heroin, or any other drugs? Y N
8. Are there any visible signs of alcohol/drug withdrawal symptoms? Describe in remarks. Y N
9. Does the inmate's behavior suggest the risk of assault to staff or other inmates? Y N
10. Is the inmate carrying medicine or does the inmate report being on medicine which should be continuously given or available? Y N

### RECEIVING OFFICER SCREENING GUIDELINES FOR MENTAL DISABILITY / SUICIDE RISK

Transporting officer believes inmate may be suicidal. * Y N

QUESTIONNAIRE

1. "Do you know where you are?" Y N
2. "What is today's date? What year is it?" Answered correctly Y N
3. "Sometimes people tell me they hear noises or voices that other people don't seem to hear. What about you? Y N
   b. If yes, ask for an explanation, "What do you hear?"______________
4. "Have you attempted suicide previously?" (check wrist and neck for scars) Y N
   b. If yes, ask when and how ______________
5. "Are you thinking of harming yourself now?" * Y N
6. "Have you ever been so down/depressed that you couldn't do anything for more than a week? Y N
   b. "Do you feel this way now?" Y N
7. "When not on drugs or drinking, have you gone for days without sleep or feeling very energetic?" Y N
8. "Have you experienced a recent death of a close friend or family member? Y N
9. "Have you received MHMR Services or other mental health services? Y N
   b. If yes, ask where and when ______________
10. "Have you ever participated in special education programs?" Y N

### RECEIVING OFFICER'S OBSERVATION

1. Inmate talks or acts in a strange manner. Y N
2. Inmate is preoccupied or appears unusually confused. Y N
3. Inmate talks very rapidly or appears to be in an unusually good mood. Y N
4. Inmate believes he/she is someone else such as God, famous person or fictional figure. Y N
5. Inmate has very limited native vocabulary. Y N
6. Inmate struggles with words to express his/herself. Y N
7. Does the inmate seem extremely sad, apathetic, helpless, or hopeless? * Y N
8. Inmate is very worried about major problems other than legal situations (i.e.: financial, family, medical condition, fear of losing job, etc.). * Y N
9. Inmate holds position of respect in the community (professional, public official, and/or alleged crime is shocking in nature). * Y N
10. Inmate is apparently under the influence of alcohol or drugs. * Y N

COMMENTS: ______________________

ANY ONE OF QUESTIONS WITH AN ASTERISK (*), CHECKED (Y), OR AN INAPPROPRIATE RESPONSE INDICATES ADDITIONAL EVALUATION RECOMMENDED. NOTIFY SUPERVISOR IMMEDIATELY.

RECEIVING OFFICER'S SIGNATURE AND I.D. NUMBER ______________________

**The Tarrant County Jail does not discriminate on the basis of disability in the admission or access to, or treatment or employment in its programs or activities. Lt. Meyer has been designated to coordinate compliance with the non-discrimination requirements contained in Section 35.107 of the Department of Justice regulations. Information concerning the provisions of the Americans with Disabilities Act, and the rights provided thereunder, is available from the ADA coordinator. By signing below I acknowledge that I have been advised of this information during the intake process.**

INMATE'S SIGNATURE ______________________

CFMT-22 GPC 1615 REV. 07/00

CHAPTER

3

# Blood & Breath Evidence

Once an officer has arrested the defendant for DWI, the next step is asking the defendant to take a breath or blood test. Whether the defendant refuses to give a sample or consents, prosecutors and officers must have a basic understanding of the means of testing for the presence and quantity of alcohol in either breath or blood and how to address common defense challenges to both forms of testing.

# Statutory Requirements for Breath Tests

## IMPLIED CONSENT LAW & WARNINGS

Texas' implied consent law requires drivers suspected of DWI to submit a sample of breath or blood for testing.[1] While every Texas driver has already given consent simply by getting behind the wheel of the car and driving on public roadways, the law gives every driver the physical ability to refuse to comply. The consequence of refusal is a longer license suspension under Transportation Code §§724.011 and 724.035.[2] [**See more on license suspensions in Chapter 4.**]

**Transportation Code §724.011. Consent to Taking of Specimen**

(a) If a person is arrested for an offense arising out of acts alleged to have been committed while the person was operating a motor vehicle in a public place, or a watercraft, while intoxicated, or an offense under Section 106.041, Alcoholic Beverage Code, the person is deemed to have consented, subject to this chapter, to submit to the taking of one or more specimens of the person's breath or blood for analysis to determine the alcohol concentration or the presence in the person's body of a controlled substance, drug, dangerous drug, or other substance.

(b) A person arrested for an offense described by Subsection (a) may consent to submit to the taking of any other type of specimen to determine the person's alcohol concentration.

### DIC-23 & DIC-24 WARNINGS

The DIC warning states, "If you give [a] specimen and analysis shows that you have an alcohol concentration of 0.08 or more, your license, permit or privilege to operate a motor vehicle will be suspended...."[3] [**See a sample DIC-24 form at the end of this chapter.**] This warning is not defective even though it does not state that the defendant must have an alcohol concentration of 0.08 "at the time of driving."[4] The legislature did not intend to require a test to show that the defendant was impaired at the time of driving for a license suspension. The warning statute does not—and should not—contain the wording "at the time of driving" because it does not pertain to whether the defendant was driving while intoxicated.[5] A person arrested for DWI need not understand he can refuse before he provides a valid sample.[6]

The Spanish-language version of the warning is not required to track the statutory language verbatim as long as it substantially complies with the statutory warning.[7] All law enforcement agencies should have someone translate the warning forms into Spanish as well as audiotape a recording of someone reading the warnings. A subscription service provided by AT&T will translate any writing into any language. You can set up an account with AT&T by calling the translation line at 1-800-874-9426. AT&T will give your agency a client ID number and an extension.

It is not coercive to tell a DWI suspect that a warrant will be obtained if he refuses to provide a blood specimen.[8] The officer who reads the DIC-24 warnings and requests a sample does not have to be the arresting officer.[9] Although an officer should be the person giving the warnings, the fact that a civilian (in this case, a breath test operator) gives the warn-

1 TEX. TRANS. CODE ch. 724; *Rodriguez v. State*, 631 S.W.2d 515 (Tex. Crim. App. 1982) (statutory presumption of consent to breath test).

2 TEX. TRANS. CODE §§724.011 and 724.035.

3 See TEX. TRANS. CODE §724.015.

4 *Texas Dep't of Public Safety v. Benoit*, 994 S.W.2d 212 (Tex. App. — Corpus Christi 1999, pet. denied); *McClain v. State*, 984 S.W.2d 700 (Tex. App. — Texarkana 1998, pet. ref'd); *Shirley v. Texas Dep't of Public Safety*, 974 S.W.2d 321 (Tex. App. — San Antonio 1998, no pet.).

5 *Texas Dep't of Public Safety v. Butler*, 960 S.W.2d 375 (Tex. App. — Houston [14th Dist.] 1998, no pet.); see also *Moore v. State*, 981 S.W.2d 701 (Tex. App. — Houston [1st Dist.] 1998, pet. ref'd).

6 *State v. Roades*, No. 07-11-00077-CR (Tex. App. — Amarillo, Dec. 12, 2012, no pet.) (not for publication) (although State must show evidence warnings were provided prior to a breath test refusal, §724.015 does not require proof of warnings as a predicate to introduction of voluntary breath test).

7 *Gonzalez v. State*, 967 S.W.2d 457 (Tex. App. — Fort Worth 1998, no pet.) (different words in Spanish that substantially complied with the wording of the DIC-24 did not require exclusion of the defendant's consent to give a sample); see also *Montoya v. State*, No. 02-11-00315-CR (Tex. App. — Fort Worth, July 11, 2012, no pet.) (not for publication) (failure to translate a Spanish audio tape of the DIC-24 warning into English during trial was harmless error).

8 *Crofton v. State*, No. 06-12-00143-CR (Tex. App. — Texarkana 2013, pet. ref'd) (not for publication) (without evidence that suspect unintelligent about his rights or subjected to physical punishment, detention was lengthy, or questioning repetitive, consent was voluntary).

9 *Texas Dep't of Public Safety v. Walter*, 979 S.W.2d 22 (Tex. App. — Houston [14th Dist.] 1998); *McBride v. State*, 946 S.W.2d 100 (Tex. App. — Texarkana 1997, pet. ref'd) (not necessary for same officer to ask for breath or blood sample and also observe driver, arrest driver, transport driver or inform driver of consequences to refusal to take test).

ing does not make the defendant's refusal to take the test inadmissible.[10] The defendant must show a causal connection between his refusal to give a breath specimen and the fact that a civilian gave the warning.

The rule that DIC-24 warnings be given in writing does not apply to a case where a breath test was given. This rule only affects the admissibility of breath test refusals.[11] A failure to give the warnings in writing is not necessarily fatal—giving only oral and not written warnings to a defendant will not always make the test result inadmissible.[12]

The timing of an arrest in relation to giving the DIC-24 warnings is flexible; an arrest does not have to come before the warnings are read.[13] The requirement that the DIC-24 notice be given in writing is satisfied by making a written copy available to the suspect—for instance, by leaving a copy with a hospital nurse to give to the hospitalized defendant the next day.[14]

#### COMMERCIAL LICENSES

Courts have split over whether officers also need to tell drivers with commercial licenses about the consequences of a license suspension. The Waco court of appeals has ruled that the failure to warn a driver about the consequences under both Transportation Code chapter 724 (for non-commercial drivers) and chapter 522 (for commercial licenses) made the defendant's refusal to give a specimen involuntary.[15]

Fort Worth's court of appeals, however, has ruled that §724.015 does not distinguish between commercial and non-commercial vehicles, so it applies to all vehicles. The fact that different consequences are authorized by more than one applicable statute does not reduce the notice given to the defendant of the consequences provided for each.[16] The Fort Worth court noted the contrary holding in *Thomas* and declined to follow it.

### CONSEQUENCES OF COMPLYING WITH TEST REQUESTS

Although officers are safest when they stick with the wording of the warnings in the statute, courts will look at the totality of the circumstances in deciding whether extra warnings made a suspect's consent to testing involuntary.[17] In *Fienan v. State*, the Court of Criminal Appeals overruled *Erdman v. State*, which had held that telling a suspect anything outside the information contained in the DIC-24 warning about the consequences of giving or refusing a sample would be viewed as coercive and lead to exclusion of the evidence.[18]

### BREATH VS. BLOOD OPTIONS

Although the implied consent statutes discuss options of using breath or blood tests, the statutes do not give the suspect the right to choose one type of test or the other.[19] A police officer arresting a suspect for DWI is entitled to choose between asking the suspect to take a breath test or a blood test. The officer need not track the language of Transportation Code §724.012 and ask the defendant to take a breath or blood test.[20]

---

10 *Harrison v. State*, 766 S.W.2d 600 (Tex. App. — Fort Worth 1989, pet. ref'd); *Jessup v. State,* 935 S.W.2d 508 (Tex. App. — Houston [14th Dist.] 1996, pet. ref'd).

11 *Nebes v. State*, 743 S.W.2d 729 (Tex. App. — Houston [1st Dist.] 1987, no pet.).

12 *Lane v. State*, 951 S.W.2d 242 (Tex. App. — Austin 1997, no pet.); *Schaum v. State*, 833 S.W.2d 644 (Tex. App. — Dallas 1992, no pet.); *O'Keefe v. State*, 981 S.W.2d 872 (Tex. App. — Houston [1st Dist.] 1998, no pet.) (no harm shown where defendant was not giving DIC-24 statutory warnings in writing until after refusal); *Rowland v. State*, 983 S.W.2d 58 (Tex. App. — Houston [1st Dist.] 1998, pet. ref'd); *Jessup v. State*, 935 S.W.2d 508 (Tex. App. — Houston [14th Dist.] 1996, pet. ref'd).

13 *Nottingham v. State*, 908 S.W.2d 585 (Tex. App. — Austin 1995, no pet.).

14 *Texas Dep't of Public Safety v. Latimer*, 939 S.W.2d 240 (Tex. App. — Austin 1997, no pet.).

15 *Texas Dep't of Public Safety v. Thomas*, 985 S.W.2d 567 (Tex. App. — Waco 1998, no pet.) (giving only Chapter 724 warnings insufficient when driver also held commercial license). Also note the subsequent adoption of TEX. TRANSP. CODE §522.103, which requires a statutory warning regarding the effect a refusal will have on a commercial driver's license only when the defendant is stopped driving a commercial vehicle.

16 *Texas Dep't of Public Safety v. McGlaun*, 51 S.W.3d 776 (Tex. App. — Fort Worth 2001, pet. denied).

17 *Fienen v. State*, 390 S.W.3d 328 (Tex. Crim. App. 2012) (overruling *Erdman v. State*, 861 S.W.3d 890 (Tex. Crim. App. 1993)).

18 *Fienen*, 390 S.W.3d at 334.

19 *Aguirre v. State*, 948 S.W.2d 377 (Tex. App. — Houston [14th Dist.] 1997, pet. ref'd) (statute does not give suspect the right to blood test instead of breath test); *Drapkin v. State*, 781 S.W.2d 710 (Tex. App. — Texarkana 1989), *rev'd*, 175 S.W.3d 795 (Tex. Crim. App. 2005).

20 *State v. Neel*, 808 S.W.2d 575 (Tex. App. — Tyler 1991, no pet.).

An officer does not have to give *Miranda* warnings to a suspect before asking for a breath sample.[21] A suspect does not have the right to counsel before deciding whether to give a sample.[22] An invocation of the suspect's right to an attorney will not later exclude evidence of a refusal to take a breath test.[23] Commonly, a defendant will say, "I'm not refusing to give a sample—I just want to talk to my attorney." Officers should simply tell the defendant that he has no right to consult an attorney before deciding whether to consent to giving a sample. If the defendant sticks to this response, the officer must tell the defendant that he will document his response as a refusal. When this type of refusal is an issue at trial, the prosecutor should spend some time in voir dire on the limits of the 5th Amendment right to counsel.

After a suspect has provided a breath sample, the law does not require that the breath ampules be preserved.[24]

Texas courts have upheld the use of various field sobriety tests, including Passive Alcohol Sensors, as an indicator of intoxication but not as evidence to establish quantitative alcohol concentration.[25]

## Intoxilyzer 5000

Excerpted from paper by Max Courtney, Forensic Consultant Services, Fort Worth
Reprinted with permission

Analysis of breath samples for alcohol concentration have been done since the 1950s. The amount of alcohol in a person's breath can be accurately determined, with an acceptable level of specificity.

#### *Blood-Breath Correlations*

Initially, the various intoxicated-driver statutes spoke in terms of a blood alcohol concentration. Early research found a correlation between blood alcohol concentration and breath alcohol concentration. The widely published value was a 2100:1 ratio; that is, equal quantities of alcohol would be found in 1 mL of blood and 2100 mL of alveolar (deep-lung) breath. Subsequent research found (1) that the ratio is but an average, with individual variations, and (2) that the 2100:1 ratio generally under-represents the blood alcohol concentration when predicted by a breath alcohol analysis. In other words, one might use the ratio to predict a blood alcohol concentration of 0.18, based upon the breath test, when in actuality it might be 0.19 or higher. One blood-breath correlation study reported that breath alcohol results were lower than the corresponding blood alcohol results in 98 percent of the persons tested.

#### *Breath Alcohol Testing*

Evidentiary breath alcohol testing for the traffic law enforcement utilizes instruments that determine the alcohol concentration in the breath of a subject. Some use principles of spectroscopy, while others utilize gas chromatography. All instrumentation used in the United States measures grams of alcohol per 210 liters of breath.

#### *Alcohol Testing with the Intoxilyzer*

Texas uses the Intoxilyzer Texas Model 5000 Breath Analyzer for evidentiary breath alcohol testing. This instrument operates on the principles of infrared spectroscopy. There are currently two slightly different versions in use, the 66 option and the 68 option. Both go through the same sequence of steps to complete a breath alcohol analysis.

---

21 *Parks v. State*, 666 S.W.2d 597 (Tex. App. — Houston [1st Dist.] 1984, no pet.).

22 *Forte v. State*, 759 S.W.2d 128 (Tex. Crim. App. 1988); *McCambridge v. State*, 778 S.W.2d 70 (Tex. Crim. App. 1989); *De Mangin v. State*, 700 S.W.2d 329 (Tex. App. — Houston [1st Dist.] 1985), *aff'd*, 787 S.W.2d 956 (Tex. Crim. App. 1990).

23 *Jamail v. State*, 787 S.W.2d 380 (Tex. Crim. App. 1990) (mixing request for breath sample with warnings during custodial interrogation such that defendant perceived he had the right to consult an attorney will not negate the ability to show at trial the defendant's refusal to give a sample); *Garner v. State*, 779 S.W.2d 498 (Tex. App. — Fort Worth 1989), *pet. ref'd*, 785 S.W.2d 158 (Tex. Crim. App. 1990).

24 *Turpin v. State*, 606 S.W.2d 907 (Tex. Crim. App. 1980) (defendant's inability to obtain blood test within two hours did not make breath test results inadmissible).

25 *Fernandez v. State*, 915 S.W.2d 572, 576 (Tex. App. — San Antonio 1996, no pet.); *Fowler v. State*, 2007 WL 2315971 (Tex. App. — San Antonio 2007, pet. ref'd) (not desig. for pub.).

Underlying the method are the principles of spectroscopy. Specifically, the Beer-Lambert Law that, for a given substance, light of specific wavelengths will be absorbed in an amount that is proportional to the concentration of the substance. Higher concentrations will absorb proportionally more of the light. As more light is absorbed by the sample, the intensity of the light beam passing through the sample is diminished.

**Figure 3-1** is a schematic diagram of the Intoxilyzer 5000. Its operation can be broken down into four areas; the computer signals, the passage of the breath specimen through the system, the passage of light through the sample chamber, and the passage of the electronic signal from the photodetector through the circuitry.

The subject blows through a mouthpiece that has a baffle system to prevent liquid or solid matter from passing into the sample chamber. The breath specimen passes through a breath tube that is heated to prevent condensation of moisture. When the subject is blowing with sufficient pressure, a pressure switch closes, and a tone sounds. The instrument will accept a breath specimen as valid if the subject maintains the minimum pressure continuously for at least five seconds, and if the alcohol concentration is changing by no more than 0.01 per second at the conclusion of the specimen delivery. If these conditions are not met, an invalid test results.

A projection lamp provides the light that passes through the sample chamber. It consists of white light (all colors) and infrared light (heat energy). The light is focused into and out of the sample chamber by a pair of Fresnel lenses, and then passes through a rotating filter wheel. The wheel has a pin hole and three wavelength-specific filters. The light finally hits the photodetector in pulses of white light and the three individual wavelengths. The photodetector responds to the light hitting it by issuing an electrical pulse whose voltage is proportional to the intensity of the light pulse.

The signals from the three infrared wavelengths are analyzed separately by an electronic processor. One signal is used for quantitative analysis. The instrument compares the voltage from the photodetector at the conclusion of the subjects specimen delivery with the voltage stored prior to the breath specimen. The voltage difference is then translated into an alcohol concentration, expressed in grams per 210 liters, by comparing the voltage difference to the voltage differences produced with samples of known alcohol concentrations during the calibration procedure. The instrument also compares the voltages from two different wavelengths to see if the voltage-ratio pattern is consistent with that of ethanol. The instrument actually is calibrated to exclude acetone.

There are numerous "fail-safe" features designed to test the accuracy and to increase the validity of the test. An initial diagnostic check tests the ROM chips, RAM chip, the signal on the electric processor, the sample chamber temperature, the real-time-clock chip, the printer, and three electronic calibration points corresponding to alcohol concentrations of 0.100, 0.200, and 0.300. If all tests pass, the instrument continues with the testing sequence.

In the course of the test, the instrument continues to check against unfavorable conditions that could affect the test. It analyzes the contents of the sample chamber after each air blank to ensure that nothing remains that would absorb the light. It monitors the surrounding for radio frequencies that could theoretically affect the reading. It monitors the integrity of the processor signal. The instrument also conducts a reference analysis on a solution with known alcohol concentration as a calibration check, requiring that the result be within 0.010 of the predicted value. Finally the instrument compares the results of the two subject specimens and requires that the two results, to be valid, differ by no more than 0.020.

If any improper testing condition or environmental source of error is detected, the instrument invalidates the test. If a test is invalidated, the instrument will not print any test results. Rather, "INVALID TEST" will appear on the test record, along with the reason for the invalidation. A test record is said to be "VALID" if it has no invalidation messages, if the results are clearly printed, if all blank results are 0.000, and if it was signed by the operator. Conversely, the test record is "INVALID" if one of those four conditions is not met.

**Figure 3-1: Intoxilyzer Diagram for Use During Intoxilyzer Operator's Testimony**

PARTS, CONTROLS AND INDICATORS OF THE INTOXILYZER 5000

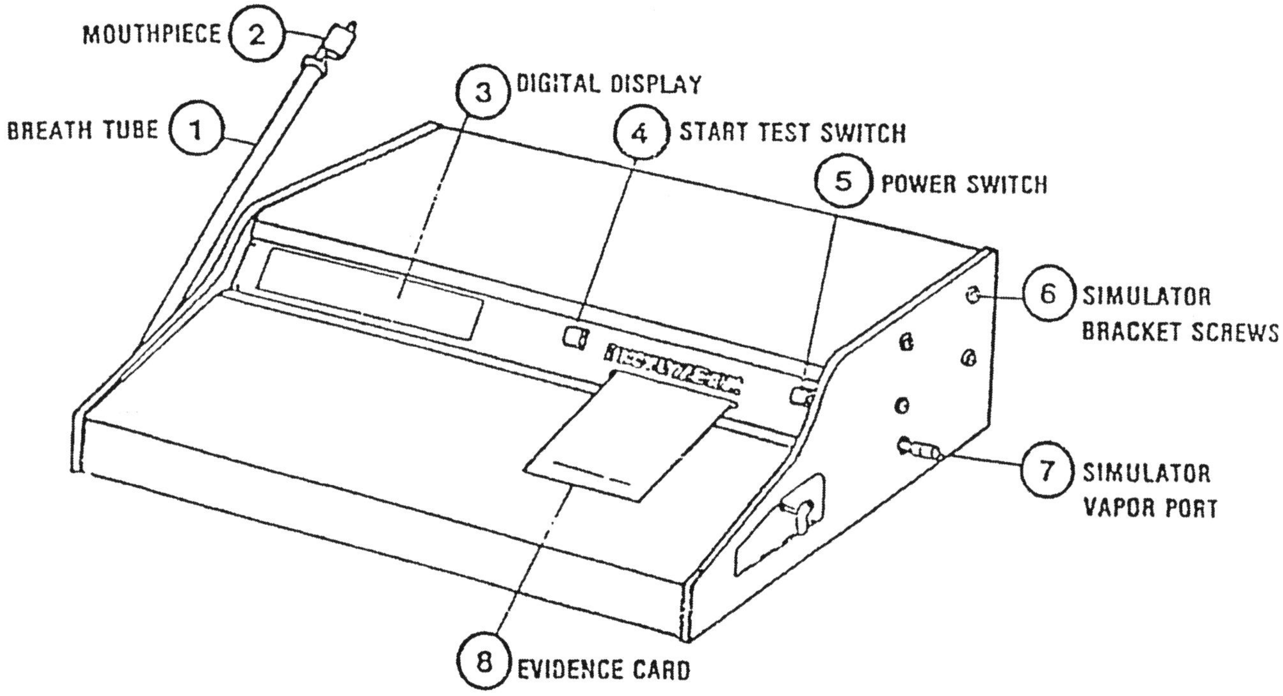


Finally, a breath alcohol test also must be administered according to the rules established by the Texas Department of Public Safety. A certified operator must conduct the test on a certified instrument used in a certified testing program that is under the supervision of a certified Technical Supervisor.

An operator is not required to be in the same room with a DWI suspect continuously for the 15-minute waiting period.[26] If a defendant raises a fact issue about the 15-minute waiting period requirement, he is entitled to an instruction that the jury disregard the test if it believes or has a reasonable doubt as to whether the State complied with the 15-minute observation requirement.[27]

The approved methodology requires two additional things of the operator that are not reflected on the test record. An operator must remain in the presence of the subject for at least 15 minutes prior to the test and must exercise reasonable care that the subject places nothing in the mouth. The operator also must use a fresh, disposable mouthpiece for each breath specimen tested.

[26] *McIntyre v. State*, No. 01-11-00821-CR (Tex. App. — Houston [1st Dist.] 2012, pet. ref'd) (not for publication) (presence can be actual or constructive; operator remaining within sight or call or at hand is sufficient).

[27] *State v. Atkinson*, 923 S.W.2d 287 (Tex. Crim. App. 1996).

Figure 3-2: Diagram of Intoxilyzer 5000

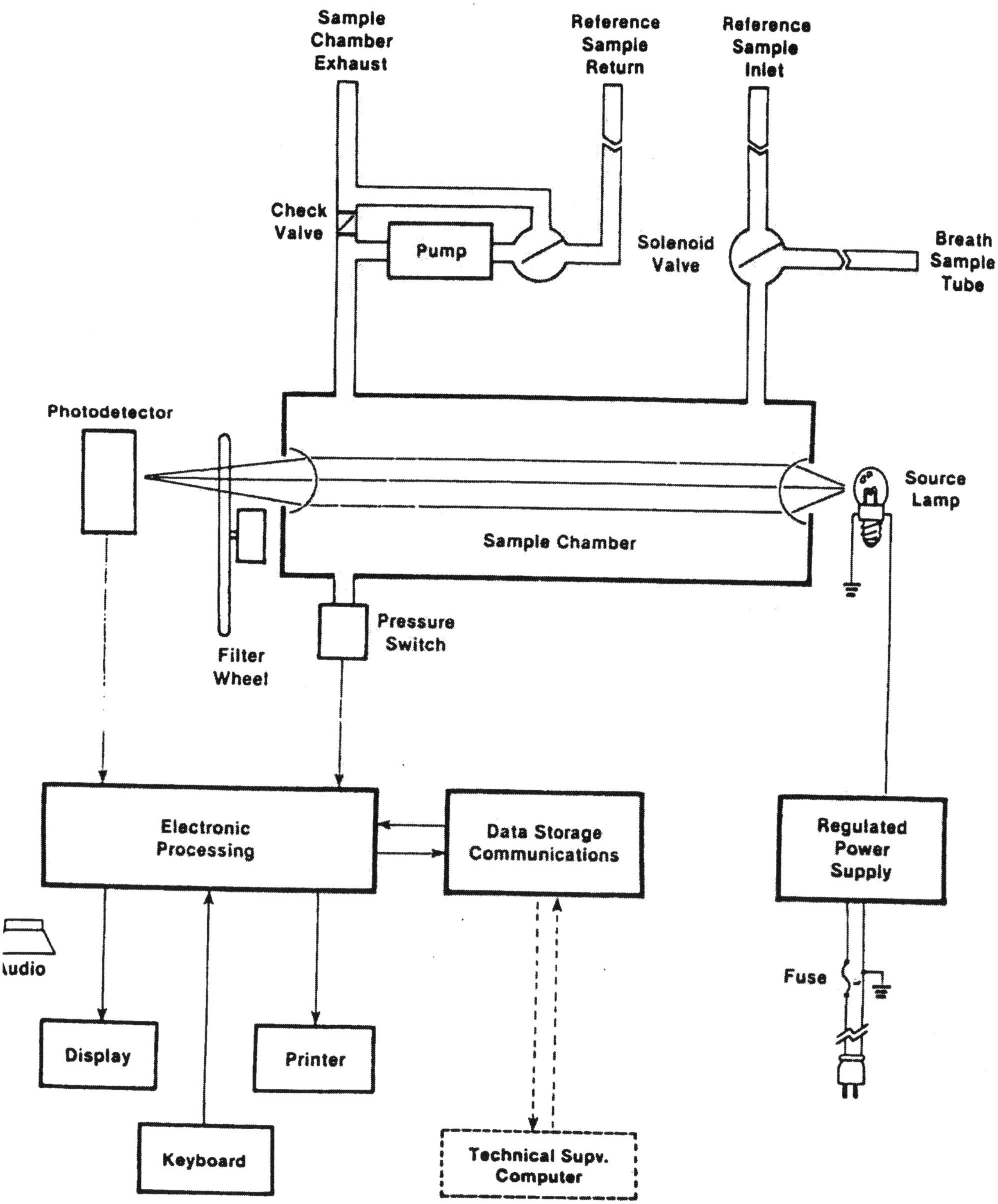


SCHEMATIC DIAGRAM OF THE INTOXILYZER 5000

## Breath Tests as Evidence

Courts have long held breath testing science to be admissible.[28] The application of that science is what will be subject to attack by the defense, including questions about:

- Who was operating the instrument?
- Was the testing done properly?

### ADMISSIBILITY

The *Kelly*[29] test for admission of scientific evidence under T.R.EVID. 702 applies to breath tests.[30] The three prongs required by *Kelly* are:

1. the underlying scientific theory must be valid;
2. the technique applying the theory must be valid; and
3. the technique must have been properly applied on the occasion in question.

The Court of Criminal Appeals has ruled that the first two prongs of *Kelly* are met by the Transportation Code,[31] although that opinion was later withdrawn and the appeal permanently abated on the death of the defendant.

> Harmonizing the Transportation Code and Rule 702, we hold that when evidence of alcohol concentration as shown by the results of analysis of breath specimens taken at the request or order of a peace officer is offered in the trial of a DWI offense, (1) the underlying scientific theory has been determined by the legislature to be valid; (2) the technique applying the theory has been determined by the legislature to be valid when the specimen was taken and analyzed by individuals who were certified by, and were using the methods approved by the rules of, the Department of Public Safety; and (3) the trial court must determine whether the technique was properly applied, in accordance with the department's rules on the occasion in question.[32]

A breath test result is not considered hearsay, because the computer—rather than a human—conducts the test itself.[33]

### BREATH TEST PREDICATE

To admit breath test results, the state must show:

1. proper use of reference sample;
2. existence of periodic supervision over the instrument and operation by one who understands the scientific theory of the instrument;
3. proof of result of test by witness or witnesses qualified to translate and interpret the result so as to eliminate hearsay.[34]

Testimony of an Intoxilyzer operator and a technical supervisor that an instrument was periodically tested to make sure it was working properly; that a test sample run before the defendant's Intoxilyzer tests demonstrated the machine was working

---

28 See, e.g., *Stevenson v. State,* 895 S.W.2d 694, 696 (Tex. Crim. App. 1995).

29 *Kelly v. State*, 824 S.W.2d 568 (Tex. Crim. App. 1992).

30 *Hartman v. State*, 946 S.W.2d 60 (Tex. Crim. App. 1997).

31 *Henderson v. State*, 14 S.W.3d 409 (Tex. App. — Austin 2000, no pet.); see also *Kirby v. State,* No. 12-01-080-CR, 2002 Tex. App. LEXIS 4028 (Tex. App. — Tyler May 31, 2002) (not for pub.).

32 *Henderson,* 14 S.W.3d at 412.

33 *Smith v. State*, 866 S.W.2d 731 (Tex. App. — Houston [14th Dist.] 1993, no pet.); but see *Stevenson v. State*, 895 S.W.2d 694 (Tex. Crim. App. 1995), *on remand*, 920 S.W.2d 342 (Tex. App. — Dallas 1996, no pet.) (questioning 5-4 whether, when Intoxilyzer operator did not testify, test results were hearsay. On remand, the Dallas court of appeals found that a breath test slip could not be considered "hearsay" and affirmed the original holding).

34 *Kercho v. State*, 948 S.W.2d 34, 37 (Tex. App. — Houston [14th Dist.] 1997, pet. ref'd).

properly; that the operator had been trained in the operation of the machine; and that the technical supervisor (who testified about the theory of the test) was certified by DPS, was sufficient predicate to admit the results of the Intoxilyzer test.[35] The operator and technical supervisor each perform a different function and will answer different questions.

### INTOXILYZER OPERATOR

The main goal for a prosecutor in questioning an intoxilyzer operator is to show how simple the instrument is to operate. The intoxilyzer operator shouldn't attempt to explain the science behind the breath test instruments, but instead should simply discuss the steps of the process. Analogously, the person who rotates your car's tires doesn't have to understand the nature of hardening rubber—just the proper steps to make sure that the tire stays on the wheel. **[See sample questions for intoxilyzer operators in Chapter 8.]**

The defense will often try to turn the operator into the expert they're not. Out of ego, sometimes, an operator on the witness stand will help them with this. It might be embarrassing to them to admit they don't understand the science behind the instruments. If the prosecutor is not careful, the intoxilyzer operator can turn into someone who inadvertently will impeach and contradict the real scientist, whose testimony will come later. It should be further noted that the intoxilyzer operator need not understand the science behind the instrument. All that is required is that the operator be certified and able to testify that the proper protocol for administering the breath test was followed.[36]

Although it's not always possible to bring the actual Intoxilyzer instrument into court, the prosecutor can bring a blown-up photograph of the instrument panel. This photograph can be used as an exhibit for demonstrative purposes for the operator to explain how the instrument operates. Have the operator identify the different parts of the instrument and take the jury step by step into what the operator did with the defendant. This will accomplish two things: (1) demonstrate that the operator is very competent in what they do, and (2) show that the instrument is not very complicated, and any juror likely could operate it.

### TECHNICAL SUPERVISOR & INSTRUMENT CERTIFICATION

An important area to cover in direct examination of the technical supervisor is to set out the safeguards in the intoxilyzer instruments and to vouch for the maintenance records for that particular instrument. The technical supervisor will also be able to give an opinion as to the defendant's intoxication and talk about retrograde extrapolation, if the relevant factors are known about the defendant.

Before trial, the prosecutor should talk to the technical supervisor. The technical supervisor needs to bring certification records to court and answer questions that establish that the instrument was working properly on the day the defendant submitted a breath sample. **[See predicate questions for technical supervisors in Chapter 8.]**

Certification and maintenance records of breath test machines are admissible under T.R.EVID. 803(6) to show that the Intoxilyzer machine used to test the defendant's alcohol concentration was working properly.[37] When a police agency substitutes one approved brand of breath testing equipment for another, the department need not reapply for certification of the entire breath testing program.[38]

A new technical supervisor can lay the predicate for old tests by relying on the previous supervisor's record as a basis for his opinion that the breath test machine was working properly.[39] **[See sample questions for technical supervisors in Chapter 8.]** This testimony does not violate a defendant's right to confrontation as long as the new technical supervisor does not testify that he prepared or created the report that was created by his predecessor and does not certify a report based on the machine's results.[40]

---

35 *Kercho*, 948 S.W.2d at 37.

36 *Reynolds v. State*, 204 S.W.3d 386 (Tex. Crim. App. 2006).

37 *Ponce v. State*, 828 S.W.2d 50 (Tex. App. — Houston [1st Dist.] 1991, pet. ref'd).

38 *State v. Krager*, 810 S.W.2d 450 (Tex. App. — San Antonio 1991, pet. ref'd).

39 *Henderson v. State*, 14 S.W.3d 409 (Tex. App. — Austin 2000, no pet.).

40 *Beard v. State*, 421 S.W.3d 676 (Tex. App. — Waco 2013, pet. ref'd) (neither tests nor results were testimonial).

## Defense Attacks on Breath Test Instruments

> **TIP**
>
> The state can impeach defense experts with circumstances of their prior testimony. For an interesting example of this, see *Sparks v. State,* 943 S.W.2d 513 (Tex. App. — Fort Worth 1997, pet. ref'd), where prosecutors pointed out that an in-court experiment with the Intoxilyzer 5000 demonstrated that, contrary to an expert's opinion, certain foods, chewing gum, and medication did not affect the test results.

Possibly the most important part of this process is learning about the expert. Has the person ever worked in breath alcohol or blood alcohol testing? Has the person had alcohol articles published in the scientific literature? Can the expert support the testimony with the publications of others? Does this person testify for the prosecution, as well? Does the person truly understand the theory and operation of the Intoxilyzer? Is the testimony consistent from trial to trial, over several years? If the answer is "no" to one or more of these, you're probably well on your way into the cross examination. If the expert has discovered phenomena that truly can affect the accuracy or validity of a breath test, surely those facts should be shared through publication in the scientific journals. After cross examination the prosecutor then must decide if rebuttal testimony is required by the State's expert to rehabilitate the case.

The basic line of defense strategy regarding the breath test instrument is its accuracy. The defense will question whether the Intoxilyzer is a machine or instrument and try to argue that the machine is prone to make mistakes. Typically, the defense will try to overstate the margin of error. Be familiar with the Intoxilyzer's acceptable range of margin of error. (And if you're not good at math, make sure to have someone sitting at counsel table who is.)

Most of the lines of attack are potential things that could go wrong with the instrument, and this kind of testimony is very speculative. Their argument: They have no way of knowing whether those things occurred in your case or not. [**See Table 3-1 for more information on common defense attacks on breath tests.**]

At this point, the predicate you established with your breath test operator will be critical. This will rebut the defense testimony by showing that when the instrument does malfunction, the result is that a test slip is not printed. The state's position should not be that the instruments never malfunction, but instead that it did not malfunction in this defendant's case.

Explore the defense expert's contact and knowledge with the model of instrument used in your case. Some experts have been around so long, they may have done tests on the older instruments but not the model on which your test was performed. This lack of familiarity may disqualify them from testifying on your instrument.

At a pretrial Rule 705(b) hearing, ask the defense expert what her opinion is about the instrument used in your case—in part to ensure she will not be testifying beyond her area of expertise. Also note that some defense lawyers will try to turn their Intoxilyzer expert into an expert on videotapes and FSTs, and it is important to establish their lack of qualification for this testimony as early as possible. [**See more on Rule 705(b) hearings in Chapter 4, "Pretrial Issues."**]

## TABLE 3-1: Attacks on Breath Tests

Excerpted from paper by Max Courtney, Forensic Consultant Services, Fort Worth
Reprinted with Permission

***Breath Temperature***

**Q:** Doesn't the Intoxilyzer make some assumptions about the person's breath temperature?

**A:** No. The Intoxilyzer is calibrated, and the calibration is checked, with vapor samples from solutions of known alcohol concentration that are heated to 34 +/- 0.2° C. Temperatures of subjects are not measured in the breath testing procedure. The 34° temperature is a reflection of the average temperature of human breath as it leaves the mouth. By comparison, the average sublingual body temperature is 37°C. Indeed, the breath does cool as it leaves the mouth, to an average of 34°, so this value is the best figure to use.

**Q:** What if a person has a fever or a higher body temperature? Will the breath be hotter? If so, will this affect the breath test result?

**A:** In fact, a higher body temperature will cause a higher breath alcohol result. A 3°F fever will increase the result by about 10%, so that a score of 0.100 would be read as 0.110 instead. Does the instrument, then, assume a breath temperature of 34°C? No, the instrument does not make assumptions. The statute states that a person whose alcohol concentration is 0.100 or greater is intoxicated, without regard to the temperature of the person. If this seems unfair, one should consider whether a person with a 3° fever, who is ill and debilitated, will be even more susceptible to the intoxicating effects of alcohol. Also, any effect of body temperature significant only in borderline cases. The 3° fever that is very significant in a borderline case would raise a 0.200 score to 0.220! Obviously both scores are well above 0.100.

***Residual Alcohol***

**Q:** If the person burps within 15 minutes of taking a breath test, will the results be affected?

**A:** Probably not. Residual alcohol is alcohol in the mouth cavity that is not in equilibrium with the body. If a person rinses the mouth with alcohol and then spits out the rinse, alcohol will remain in the mouth cavity for several minutes. Drinking an alcoholic beverage will produce residual alcohol, as will regurgitation or reflux if alcohol remains in the stomach. Without safeguards, this residual alcohol could cause an erroneously high result; the Intoxilyzer has two such safeguards. The instrument has a slope detector, which actually is a logic program that requires that the alcohol concentration essentially level off at the end of specimen delivery (changing by no more than 0.01 per second). Residual alcohol evaporates quickly so that the alcohol concentration would tend to rise rapidly and then fall rapidly, without ever leveling. Also, the instrument requires that the two breath specimens agree within 0.020 for a valid test. Residual alcohol tends to cause one score to be significantly higher than the other. While not perfect, the use of these two safeguards tends to exclude residual alcohol. Certainly no significant effect will be seen in anything but a borderline case. Good agreement between the two subject results virtually eliminates any influence of residual alcohol. As the two scores get farther apart, the probability of residual alcohol's contribution increases. The 0.020 agreement requirement will exclude residual alcohol in most cases. There is no significant additional effect in persons with partial or full dentures. The passage of a "burp" prior to the test, consisting of only gases from the stomach, does not affect the test result, since the gaseous alcohol is dissipated with the next breath and cannot be sustained long enough to satisfy the specimen delivery time requirement.

***Specimen Duration***

**Q:** Isn't it true that, the longer one blows, the higher the alcohol concentration reads?

**A:** Not exactly. The Intoxilyzer records the alcohol concentration of the breath at the last point of its delivery. While a subject continues to blow into the instrument, the breath comes from deeper and deeper in the lungs. The alcohol concentration of the breath continues to rise as the subject blows, rapidly at first and then slowly. If a subject provides, with equal breath pressure, a 6-second specimen and then a 12-second specimen, the longer delivery probably will result in a somewhat higher alcohol concentration. What is happening, of course, is that the breath alcohol concentration is getting closer and closer to the alveolar breath alcohol concentration. If residual alcohol is ruled out, then the higher result should be a more reliable indicator of the intoxication of the subject.

**Q:** Why do we record the alcohol concentration at the termination of the delivery, when it is at its highest level?

**A:** The statutes empower the Texas Department of Public Safety to establish rules for testing breath specimens; the Departments Regulations state that the breath specimen should be essentially alveolar in composition. Longer specimen delivery more closely approaches true alveolar composition of alcohol in the breath.

***Interfering Substances***

**Q:** Aren't there thousands of substances in human breath besides alcohol that will read on the Intoxilyzer?

**A:** No. It is true that virtually any organic substance (of approximately 3 million known substances) will absorb light of wavelengths used by the Intoxilyzer. The specificity of the method relies on three things: (1) a substance must be sufficiently volatile for it to be present in breath; (2) most volatile organic substances are toxic to humans in any significant concentration; (3) most volatile organic substances found in the body would trigger the "INTERFERENT" response in the Intoxtlyzer. Acetaldehyde can be found in trace quantities in human breath of drinking subjects. But an acetaldehyde concentration that would register a significant Intoxilyzer result would kill the subject. Acetone is found in a person in a state of ketosis, but any significant concentration will trip the "INTER-

FERENT" response. Low concentrations of methanol will not trigger the "INTERFERENT" response, but any significant concentration will induce permanent blindness or death. As long as a deprivation period is observed, there just really isn't anything other substance that would cause a significant error in an Intoxilyzer test.

***Intoxilyzer Warranty***

**Q:** Isn't it true that the manufacturer of the Intoxilyzer does not warrant that it will read alcohol accurately?

**A:** No. The Intoxilyzer manufacturer includes a "STATEMENT OF WARRANTY" inside the shipping box when an intoxilyzer is delivered. Until recently, this statement included some standard disclaimers (see Figure 5); the language has since been modified (see Figure 6). All intoxilyzers used for evidentiary testing in Texas were purchased under the specific terms of a contract between the manufacturer and the Texas Department of Public Safety. The contract includes a bid sheet from the manufacturer whereon they warrant that the instrument is capable of many things, including accurately analyzing alcohol (see Figure 7).

***Computer Program***

**Q:** Isn't it true that the manufacturer of the Intoxilyzer has some secret computer program that runs the instrument?

**A:** Yes. The ROM chips in the Intoxilyzer contain computer programs that run the tests and that store the test data. The programs are proprietary trade secrets and, as such, are not available to the public, nor to the Texas Breath Alcohol Testing Program. While the specific source codes to the programs are not known, the chips have been used in the 66 series Instruments for nearly five years, and the performance of the instrument has been evaluated continuously, with no "glitches" having been found. Perhaps a CMI programmer, in a diabolical scheme, decided to write in a secret loop that results in the doubling of the alcohol concentration score for any person named I.B. Client, d.o.b. 4-14-71. Or perhaps the "black box" attack is meaningless from a scientific standpoint.

***Contamination from Condensation***

**Q:** Does the condensation of the subject's breath inside the mouthpiece cause errors in the breath test?

**A:** No.

**Q:** What happens if contaminants are not effectively purged from the Intoxilyzer, the breath tube, or the mouthpiece? Will the score be affected?

**A:** Each measurement in the Intoxilyzer is preceded by a purge cycle. During this cycle, a pump draws room air through the mouthpiece, through the breath tube, and through the tubing and sample chamber inside the instrument. At the conclusion of the pump cycle, the instrument analyzes the sample chamber contents to see if anything remains that absorbs light. A positive finding will trigger the instruments "AMBIENT FAIL" response.

**Q:** What errors are introduced by condensation of the subject's breath on the inside of the mouthpiece?

**A:** Any alcohol on this condensate will be in equilibium with the subject's breath, so that its re-evaporation would also be at equilibrium. No error is introduced. One can note that condensation usually forms in the tubing connecting the reference analysis device to the instrument. Time after time, the instrument correctly analyzes this reference solution without high results from the condensation of alcohol in the tubing.

***Finiteness of Sample Size***

**Q:** Isn't the amount of alcohol that is actually measured so small that it is microscopic?

**A:** Yes. 210 liters is a large volume, approximately the size of a 55-gallon drum. A breath test result of 0.10 means that the amount of alcohol in the breath was the same as if 2 drops of alcohol were evaporated and allowed to fill that drum. The sample chamber of the lntoxilyzer is small, less than 3 fluid ounces.

**Q:** How much alcohol, then, is really being measured?

**A:** At the moment of measurement, there is approximately 0.00004 gram of alcohol in the sample chamber for a breath test specimen of 0.100.

**Q:** Can the Intoxilyzer really measure such small quantities accurately?

**A:** Many Intoxilyzers use a 0.100 reference analysis solution. The amount of alcohol in the sample chamber at the moment of that measurement also is 0.00004 gram, yet the instrument measures those samples repeatedly and almost always reports the result within 0.010 of the predicted value. The sensitivity of the Intoxilyzer is adequate for the measurement of minute quantities of alcohol in human breath.

***Individual Differences***

**Q:** Is it true that two persons of identical weight and identical alcohol elimination rate can drink the same amount of alcohol during the same time period and yet get different results on a breath test?

**A:** Yes.

**Q:** Can the results differ by as much as 50%?

**A:** Yes. Individual differences are observed. The differences can be as much as 50% or even greater! If one person scores a 0.010, and the other a 0.015, the difference is 50%. Differences in people do cause some differences in results. All are intoxicated if their alcohol concentration is 0.080 or greater. All are, per se, intoxicated if their alcohol concentration is 0.100 or greater.

***Comparison of Breath Test and Video***

**Q:** If a person performed perfectly on a videotaped sobriety evaluation and yet scored 0.18 on a breath test, would it cause you to question the accuracy of the breath test?

**A:** No. Individuals differ widely in their tolerance to alcohol. A person innately has a "natural" tolerance because of physical and physiological factors, and this varies from person to person. "Acquired" tolerance develops as a result of repeated exposure to alcohol, and it can develop within a few weeks. Intoxication means that a person has a measurable loss in the normal use of their mental and physical faculties. The increased time that would be required to note an emergency road condition and brake or change lanes often cannot be demonstrated by a person counting backward or standing on one leg. A person's ability to steer out of a skid generally cannot be demonstrated by the walk-and-turn or touching the nose. Videotapes may demonstrate "drunkenness" but they often cannot document subtle symptoms of intoxication that are, nevertheless, crucial in driving.

***Comparison of Field Evaluation and Video***

**Q:** Could a person show extreme signs of intoxication at the time of arrest and yet look nearly perfect on the video 45 minutes later?

**A:** Possibly. The degree of intoxication will change with time. One explanation of seeming improvement is adaptation. After a person's alcohol concentration stabilizes, the body becomes accustomed to this degree of impairment, so that the outward signs may lessen. If the time passage is longer, the Mellanby effect may be a factor. This phenomenon compares intoxication at a given level during the absorption and elimination phases after the alcohol concentration was considerably higher. Stress tolerance, a temporary sobering effect that may be caused by adrenaline secretions, also may enhance performance during a video evaluation.

***Blood-Breath Correlations***

**Q:** Does the Intoxilyzer assume a certain blood:breath ratio in the subject?

**A:** No. The Intoxilyzer measures alcohol concentration in the breath of a subject, in grams per 210 liters. No assumptions are made, and no formulae are used in a computation. The instrument simply is calibrated until a vapor with 0.100 gram of alcohol per 210 liters reads 0.100. Persons may assume, at their own risk, what a breath alcohol concentration means about blood alcohol. The statute deems a person with 0.100 gram of alcohol per 210 liters of breath intoxicated. Further, years of research have provided direct correlation between breath alcohol concentration and impairment. This research deems a person with 0.100 gram of alcohol per 210 liters of breath intoxicated. One can assume whatever they will about blood:breath ratios; conclusions as to the intoxication of a person require no assumptions if the breath alcohol concentration is 0.100 or greater. One common defense strategy on this point has been to point out that the manufacturer insists that the instrument reads "blood alcohol" according to the 2100:1 ratio. The manufacturer has filed an affidavit of explanation on this matter (see Figure 8).

***Radio Frequency Interference***

**Q:** Can a radio transmitter near the Intoxilyzer cause an erroneous reading?

**A:** No. The Intoxilyzer 5000 has a radio frequency antenna in the breath tube. If at any time during the test the instrument detects radio waves in the testing environment, the test is invalidated. The antenna is located outside of the metal case, while the electronic circuits that could be affected are inside.

***Intoxication at Time of Driving***

**Q:** Can the Intoxilyzer determine the alcohol concentration of a person 45 minutes, prior to the breath test, which showed an alcohol concentration of 0.110?

**A:** No. The Intoxilyzer measures only the person's alcohol concentration at the time of the test. Certainly, an Intoxilyzer result of 0.14 offers some scientific corroboration of the intoxication that was apparent to the arresting officer at the time of the offense. Without strong testimony from the arresting officer, a breath test case probably is doomed.

# Blood Tests

## ISSUES AND REQUIREMENTS

The conditions under which a blood sample can be drawn from a suspect in a criminal case are controlled by the Transportation Code sections cited below. Those conditions have changed over time and are less burdensome than they once were. Effective August 26, 1991, a prosecutor no longer needs to call someone to testify that the place where the blood was drawn had been inspected on a periodic basis by an agency of the state or county in which the sample was taken. (I mention this clearly outdated principle because I still come across defense attorneys who claim it is still the law.)

### SAMPLES DRAWN AT THE REQUEST OF LAW ENFORCEMENT

**Important note:** This section continues to address our state's implied-consent statute in Transportation Code §724.017 as a viable provision in light of *Missouri v. McNeely*. See the discussion of the *McNeely* case and its ramifications beginning on the next page.

If the blood sample is drawn at the request of law enforcement (as opposed to a sample drawn at a hospital for medical purposes or pursuant to a search warrant), the state must prove that the provisions of Transportation Code §724.017 were followed.[1] Namely, this requires proof that the sample was taken: (1) at the request or order of a peace officer under Chapter 724; (2) by a physician, qualified technician, registered professional nurse, licensed vocational nurse, or authorized emergency medical technician; (3) in a sanitary place.

Before 2013, Transportation Code §724.017(c) excluded "emergency medical services personnel" from the definition of "qualified technician," but two significant changes in 2013 have all but eliminated that exclusion. First, the Court of Criminal Appeals ruled that simply holding an EMT license did not disqualify a phlebotomist from making a valid blood draw. In *Krause v. State*, the court concluded that an ER employee who held an EMT-I license was functioning as a phlebotomist when she drew the defendant's blood in a hospital and the blood test results were therefore admissible.[41]

Second, effective Sept. 1, 2013, the legislature amended §724.017 to remove the EMS exclusion, replacing it with language provising that a "licensed or certified emergency medical technician-intermediate or emergency medical technician-paramedic" is qualified to draw blood upon an officer's request, with certain conditions. For results of any draw to be admissible, it must meet certain predicates. First, the medical director for the agency employing the technician (defined in Transportation Code §724.017(c)) must authorize its employees to conduct law enforcement blood draws and, in doing so, draft a protocol for this purpose. Second, the protocol may allow the emergency services personnel, on an individual basis, to refuse to comply with a requested law enforcement draw.

### COMPELLING A BLOOD SAMPLE

The circumstances under which a person can be compelled against their wishes to give a specimen of their blood are set out in Transportation Code §724.012 (formerly located in Art. 6701*l*-5 §3(I)).

#### Transportation Code §724.012. Taking of Specimen

(a) One or more specimens of a person's breath or blood may be taken if the person is arrested and at the request of a peace officer having reasonable grounds to believe the person:

(1) while intoxicated was operating a motor vehicle in a public place, or a watercraft; or

(2) was in violation of Section 106.041, Alcoholic Beverage Code.

(b) A peace officer shall require the taking of a specimen of the person's breath or blood under any of the following circumstances if the officer arrests the person for an offense under Chapter 49, Penal Code, involving the operation of a motor vehicle or a watercraft and the person refuses the officer's request to submit to the taking of a specimen voluntarily:

(1) the person was the operator of a motor vehicle or a watercraft involved in an accident that the officer reasonably believes occurred as a result of the offense and at the time of the arrest, the officer reasonably believes that as a direct result of the accident:

(A) any individual has died or will die;

(B) an individual other than the person has suffered serious bodily injury; or

(C) an individual other than the person has suffered bodily injury and been transported to a hospital or other medical facility for medical treatment;

(2) the offense for which the officer arrests the person is an offense under Section 49.045, Penal Code; or

(3) at the time of the arrest, the officer possesses or receives reliable information from a credible source that the person:

(A) has been previously convicted of or placed on community supervision for an offense under Section 49.045, 49.07, or 49.08, Penal Code, or an offense under the laws of another state containing elements substantially similar to the elements of an offense under those sections; or

(B) on two or more occasions, has been previously convicted of or placed on community supervision for an offense under Section 49.04, 49.05, 49.06, or 49.065, Penal Code, or an offense under the laws of another state containing elements substantially similar to the elements of an offense under those sections.

(c) The peace officer shall designate the type of specimen to be taken.

(d) In this section, "bodily injury" and "serious bodily injury" have the meanings assigned by Section 1.07, Penal Code.

#### *(1) Intoxication Offense*

The key point here is that the officer must have placed the person under arrest prior to requiring a mandatory blood sam-

[41] *Krause v. State*, 405 S.W.3d 82 (Tex. Crim. App. 2013) (rejecting conclusion in *State v. Laird*, 38 S.W.3d 707 (Tex. App. — Austin 2000, pet. ref'd) that paramedics fell outside the "qualified technician" category as "dicta" and distinguishing *Laird* by noting that the blood draw did not comply with "sanitary place" requirement because it occurred on a fire station floor).

ple. If the officer did not explicitly do so, you may get some help from *Nottingham v. State*.[42] Another important point to keep in mind is that the arrest may be for any offense under Chapter 49, including public intoxication.[43]

The circumstances of a crash and an odor of alcohol, without field sobriety tests or slurred speech, can provide an officer with a sufficient basis for believing the defendant was intoxicated at the time of the crash.[44]

#### *(2) Operating the Vehicle*

This is an important area to discuss with your officer before she testifies. Most are prepared to testify to their basis for believing the person was operating a motor vehicle but have not thought about the second requirement that the "accident ... occurred as a result of the offense"—in short, that the accident was caused by the defendant's driving while intoxicated. The officer should be prepared to list everything she observed or was told by other witnesses that supported the "reasonable belief" that: (1) the defendant was intoxicated, and (2) that the intoxication caused the accident. Ask your officer who caused the accident. (The answer should be the defendant). Then ask the officer to justify that with as many specifics as possible. Remember the defendant does not have to be the sole cause of the accident or the death of the injured party under Penal Code §6.04. The officer making the request for blood may base his belief that there is probable cause to arrest on the collective knowledge of all officers working the scene.[45]

#### *(3) Death or Serious Bodily Injury*

The injured party need not actually be dead for this section to apply. If the officer can articulate that based on what he observed at the scene, the injured party appeared to suffer serious bodily injury or be in critical condition. Any comments made by EMS personnel at the scene about the condition of the injured victim will be admissible on this issue.

#### *(4) Refusing to Provide Specimen*

The officer should inform the defendant orally and in writing of the consequences of a refusal just as they would do in a DWI case. The failure to give the warnings may not affect the admissibility of the mandatory specimen. The only piece of evidence that is not admissible if the warnings are not given is evidence of the refusal.[46]

### MANDATORY BLOOD SAMPLES

The Transportation Code provides for mandatory samples where intoxication is the suspected cause of a crash resulting in bodily injury or death, the defendant has committed DWI with a child passenger, or the defendant has committed prior intoxication offenses. An officer must have a reasonable belief that alcohol caused the crash before taking a mandatory sample.[47] The continued viability of this statute has been questioned by the Supreme Court's 2013 holding in *Missouri v. McNeely* that the inevitable dissipation of alcohol in blood alone does not constitute an automatic exigency to support a non-consensual, warrantless blood test during a DWI investigation.[48] The Court did note, however, that depending on the totality of the circumstances in a particular case, an exigency may develop. Otherwise, a warrant is required.

Rather than declare all mandatory blood draw statutes unconstitutional or conclude that exigent circumstances can never exist to justify a warrantless blood draw in a DWI case, the *McNeely* case simply concluded that there were no exigent circumstances shown in that particular case. The opinion upholds the decision in *Schmerber v. California*,[49] that metabolism of alcohol alone does not create an exigency, but a crash, a child passenger, high intoxication arrest numbers or any other complicating factor when added to metabolism might create an exigency, especially if officers are unable to get a judicial review (via a warrant) in a reasonable amount of time.

The Court of Criminal Appeals later declined to extend the automobile exception, special needs exception, or search incident exception to encompass warrantless blood draws.[50] Three months later, however, the Court granted a motion for rehearing in that case, leaving a final answer to the question up in the air.

---

42 *Nottingham v. State*, 908 S.W.2d 585 (Tex. App. — Austin 1995, no pet.).

43 *Porter v. State*, 969 S.W.2d 60 (Tex. App. — Austin 1998, pet. ref'd).

44 *Gowans v. State*, 995 S.W.2d 787 (Tex. App. — Houston [1st Dist.] 1999, pet. ref'd).

45 *Porter v. State*, 969 S.W.2d 60 (Tex. App. — Austin 1998, pet. ref'd); *Mitchell v. State*, 821 S.W.2d 420 (Tex. App. — Austin 1991, pet ref'd).

46 *Nebes v. State*, 743 S.W.2d 729 (Tex. App. — Houston [1st Dist.] 1987, no pet.).

47 *Badgett v. State*, 42 S.W.3d 136 (Tex. Crim. App. 2001).

48 *Missouri v. McNeely*, 133 S.Ct. 1552 (2013).

49 *Schmerber v. California*, 384 U.S. 757 (1966); see also *Huff v. State*, No. 04-13-891-CR (Tex. App. — San Antonio April 8, 2015) (the fact that a department's normal operating procedure does not involve seeking a warrant is not an exigent circumstance).

50 *State v. Villarreal*, No. PD-0306-14 (Tex. Crim. App. Nov. 26, 2014), *reh'g granted*, 2015 Tex. Crim. App. LEXIS 201 (Tex. Crim. App. Feb. 25, 2015).

The most conservative approach in addressing *McNeely* and *Villarreal* would be to get a search warrant whenever possible, even in mandatory blood draw situations. If an officer cannot get a blood search warrant in a reasonable amount of time, the officer should be prepared to explain why he was unable to get a warrant, note any additional factors creating an exigency, and proceed to take blood without a warrant under the Texas statute.

### WAYS AROUND THE MANDATORY BLOOD REQUIREMENTS

What if the officer failed to comply with the statute's requirements and you can't get a blood test under the procedure set out above? The statute only applies to samples drawn for the purpose described under this article.

#### *Medical Samples*

If the sample was drawn under standard medical procedures by the hospital to help diagnose or treat a person, that sample will be admissible if you show a proper chain of custody. If law enforcement was not involved in the decision to draw the blood sample, the requirements of Transportation Code §724.012 (formerly Article 6701*l*-5) are inapplicable, as are constitutional prohibitions against unreasonable search and seizures.[51] Prosecutors may use a grand jury subpoena to obtain hospital records that contain blood test results and these results/records are not privileged.[52] Another advantage of offering the hospital-drawn sample, even if you have a mandatory sample, is that it can help render problems with the mandatory sample harmless.[53]

Even if you are not relying on a hospital-drawn blood sample, it is a good idea to have a grand jury subpoena issued for any and all medical records of the defendant for the duration of his hospital stay, including a request for the results of any lab tests performed. This could come in handy if you later find the nurse or officer you need are unidentifiable or unreachable at the date of trial. It is not unusual for the nurse who drew the officer's sample to be different from the nurse or technician who drew the hospital's sample. You should explicitly include in your subpoena a request for the name(s) of the person(s) who drew and tested the blood sample.

#### *Consent*

If the defendant consents to a blood draw, there is ample authority that he has waived the statutory requirements.[54] If the person is incapable of giving consent or refusing to give a sample, remember that under the implied consent law in Transportation Code §724.014, he will be deemed to have consented if he is unconscious, dead or otherwise incapable of refusal, so long as he has been placed under arrest.

**Transportation Code §724.014. Person Incapable of Refusal**

(a) A person who is dead, unconscious, or otherwise incapable of refusal is considered not to have withdrawn the consent provided by Section 724.011.

(b) If the person is dead, a specimen may be taken by:

(1) the county medical examiner or the examiner's designated agent; or

(2) a licensed mortician or a person authorized under Section 724.016 or 724.017 if there is not a county medical examiner for the county.

(c) If the person is alive but is incapable of refusal, a specimen may be taken by a person authorized under Section 724.016 or 724.017.

#### *Exigent Circumstances*

Exigent circumstances—the fact that alcohol in the blood will dissipate quickly—also will justify the taking of a blood specimen in non-arrest situations. In *Aliff v. State*,[55] the defendant was seriously injured in a crash that left another motorist dead. After the defendant was transported to the hospital, the officer requested that a sample be drawn even though the defendant did not give his consent and was not under arrest at the time. In upholding admission of the blood specimen, the court held that the statute requiring the consent of a suspect before blood is taken only applies to situations where there has been an arrest. The court further held that taking the blood specimen did not violate the Fourth

---

51 *State v. Hardy*, 963 S.W.2d 516 (Tex. Crim. App. 1997); *Weaver v. State*, 721 S.W.2d 495 (Tex. App. — Houston [1st Dist.] 1986, pet. ref'd); *Vargas v. State*, 542 S.W.2d 151, 153 (Tex. Crim. App. 1976); *Hayes v. State*, 634 S.W.2d 359, 362 (Tex. App. — Amarillo 1982, no pet.); *Clark v. State*, 933 S.W.2d 332 (Tex. App. — Corpus Christi 1996, no pet.).

52 *State v. Hardy*, 963 S.W.2d 516 (Tex. Crim. App. 1997).

53 *Weaver*, 721 S.W.2d 495 (any error in the admission of the State compelled sample was rendered harmless because defendant's intoxication was shown with the medical sample).

54 See, e.g., *Bennett v. State*, 723 S.W.2d 359 (Tex. App. — Fort Worth 1987, no pet.).

55 *Aliff v. State*, 627 S.W.2d 166 (Tex. Crim. App. 1982).

Amendment. Taking a blood sample is a simple procedure and is very unintrusive, the court decided, analogizing it to scraping dried blood off of a suspect's fingernails.[56]

Even though officers had not actually arrested the defendant when his blood sample was taken, the court ruled the blood results were admissible because the officers had probable cause to arrest the suspect for involuntary manslaughter (a crime that now would be labelled intoxication manslaughter).

In *Pesina v. State*,[57] the court applied the same reasoning to a DWI charge where there was a collision and once again "exigency" supported taking a blood specimen without the suspect's consent.

### BLOOD SEARCH WARRANTS

The state can use a search warrant to obtain a blood specimen.[58] The Court of Criminal Appeals has ruled that the existence of the implied consent law does not preclude law enforcement drawing a suspect's blood under a search warrant. The Court pointed out that to interpret the implied consent statute otherwise would give DWI suspects more protection than other suspects. **[See sample forms for the affidavit, warrant, and return at the end of this chapter.]** A search warrant issued to take the suspect's blood is an evidentiary search warrant under CCP art. 18.02(a)(10).

The increase in use of warrants to obtain blood samples in all DWI-related offenses has resulted in an increased demand for magistrates to be available to review these warrants. Many jurisdictions have used electronic means (e.g. fax machines or emails) to transmit the applications for warrants without having to appear in court. Both the Court of Criminal Appeals and Texas legislature have more formally approved this process.[59]

Code of Criminal Procedure Article 18.01(j) states that any magistrate who is an attorney may issue search warrants under Article 18.02(a)(10) to collect blood specimens from people who are arrested under §§49.04–49.08 and refuse to submit to a breath or blood alcohol test. As such, it has additional statutory requirements. An exception exists for some small counties.[60]

Special circumstances are also required for second warrants for the same suspect's blood.[61] Finally, the affidavit must allege probable cause that a particular person committed an offense and that the evidence to be seized constitutes evidence of the offense.[62] In DWI cases this information is not difficult to articulate but remains essential. Blood warrants are also unique in that the evidence sought metabolizes and dissipates over time. To ensure the evidence sought is still relevant, a blood search warrant should include some understanding of the passing of time.[63]

The blood warrant also differs from more common search warrants in that it must identify the person to be searched instead of the location or place to be searched. Special care should be taken to specifically identify and describe the suspect.[64] Code of Criminal Procedure art. 18.08 also permits an officer executing a search warrant to "call to his aid any number of citizens ... who shall be bound to aid in the execution of the same." To execute the blood warrant requires the officer to find qualified help; to assist in that quest, the forms at the end of this chapter include a directive from the magistrate ordering medical personnel to assist as the law requires. **[See also "DWI Search Warrant Challenges" on the CD-Rom for summaries of those cases needed to defeat defense search warrant challenges.]**

## Blood Evidence

To introduce blood results, the state must show: (1) a proper chain of custody, and (2) that the blood tested was the same as the blood drawn from the defendant. The state cannot rely solely on medical records to prove a blood test result.[65]

---

56 See *Cupp v. Murphy*. 412 U.S. 291, 93 S.Ct. 2000, 36 L.Ed.2d 900 (1973).

57 *Pesina v. State*, 676 S.W.2d 122 (Tex. Crim. App. 1984).

58 *Beeman v. State*, 86 S.W.3d 613 (Tex. Crim. App. 2002).

59 See *Clay v. State*, 391 S.W.3d 94 (Tex. Crim. App. 2013); Tex. Code Crim. Proc. art. 18.01(b-1)(1)–(5).

60 See Tex. Code Crim. Proc. art. 18.01(i). A county must have no licensed attorneys serving as a judge other than a district judge with multiple county districts for any magistrate to sign evidentiary search warrants. This means no county courts at law and a non-attorney constitutional county judge in that county.

61 Tex. Code Crim. Proc. art. 18.01(d).

62 Tex. Code Crim. Proc. art. 18.01(c).

63 See also *Ashcraft v. State*, No. 03-12-00660-CR (Tex. App. — Austin, Aug. 20, 2013, no pet.) (not for publication) (mere fact that a blood search warrant affidavit fails to note time or date or stop is not necessarily fatal).

64 *Welder v. State*, No. 04-12-00706-CR (Tex. App. — San Antonio Aug. 30, 2013, no pet.) (not for publication) (multiple clerical errors need not prove fatal if the affidavit, when read as a whole, reflects collective observations from officers sufficient to establish probable cause).

65 *Lynch v. State*, 687 S.W.2d 76 (Tex. App. — Amarillo 1985, pet. ref'd).

However, it isn't necessary that the person who actually drew or tested the blood testify.[66] An officer's testimony that she witnessed the nurse draw the defendant's blood will be sufficient.[67] The state need not show who drew the blood.[68] Any objections to the state's failure to call the person who drew the blood—or any other gaps in the chain of custody—will go to the weight, but not the admissibility, of the evidence.[69] Evidence of either serum or whole blood tests are admissible.[70] **[See sample predicates for blood evidence in Chapter 8.]**

### BLOOD DRAW VOCABULARY

**Anticoagulant:** Substance that prevents blood from clotting (coagulating).

**Evacuated tube system:** A closed system in which a patient's blood flows through a needle inserted into a vein directly into a collection tube without being exposed to the air or outside contaminants. The system allows numerous tubes to be collected with a single venipuncture.

**Grey-top tube:** Contains sodium fluoride and potassium oxalate (preservative and anti-coagulent). This is the type of tube that should be used for blood draw samples requested by law enforcement that will be tested in a forensic laboratory.

**Potassium oxalate:** Prevents coagulation and should be mixed immediately upon collection to prevent clot formation. Eight inversions of the blood vial are recommended to ensure proper mixing.

**Povidone–iodine:** A traditional non-isopropyl antiseptic used to clean a draw site prior to collection of a sample for blood alcohol testing. (Regular soap and water may also be used.)

**Sodium fluoride:** Preservative powder found in grey-top vacutainer tubes that inhibits microbial growth.

**Vacutainer:** A sterile vacuum tube. The vacuum in the tube is pre-measured by the manufacturer so the tube will draw the precise volume of blood indicated. Tubes do not fill with blood all the way to the stopper. When filled properly there is always a consistent amount of headspace between the level of blood in the tube and the stopper. For most tubes the stopper color identifies a type of additive placed in the tube by the manufacturer for a specific purpose.

**Vacuum:** Negative pressure, or artificially created absence of air, which causes tubes to fill with blood automatically.

**Venipuncture:** Collecting blood by penetrating a vein with a needle and syringe or other collection apparatus.

### BLOOD TESTING VOCABULARY

**Alcohol concentation:** The number of grams of alcohol per 100 milliliters of blood (see Penal Code §49.01(1)(B)). Equivalent units can also be expressed as g/dl (grams per deciliter) or gm% (grams percent).

**Aliquot:** A portion of a specimen used for testing, typically the portion of blood removed from the blood tube via pipet.

**Calibrators:** Materials prepared from a standard containing a known concentration of ethanol. They provide a reference to determine unknown concentrations or to calibrate analytical instruments through the generation of a calibration curve.

**Calibration curve:** The graphical or mathematical relationship between the instrument readings obtained when calibrators are analyzed vs. the known concentration of ethanol in the calibrators. In blood alcohol analysis, this relationship is a straight line rather than a curve.

**Centrifuge:** A machine that spins blood tubes at a high number of RPMs. It causes the cells and plasma or serum in a blood sample to separate.

**Chromatogram:** A picture of the instrument printout or trace produced when compounds are separated by chromatography.

**Controls:** Prepared materials that contain a known amount of ethanol, prepared separately and apart from calibrators. These samples are evaluated against an established calibration curve to assess the accuracy and reliability of the calibration curve and the day to day performance of the test. Typical forensic blood alcohol assays contain both negative controls (no alcohol is added and a negative result is expected) and positive controls. Positive controls may be run at various levels, and will typically include a control at a level of 0.08 gm% as well as an additional control at a higher level. Positive controls for other alcohols are also typically included in a blood alcohol run, and include controls for methanol, isopropanol, and acetone.

**Gas chromatography:** The most commonly utilized method for the forensic analysis of blood alcohol.

**Headspace sampling:** Process by which sample of headspace above liquid in blood vial is tested by gas chromatograph. A sample of the headspace is removed from vial by syringe and injected into gas chromatograph.

**Henry's Law:** At a given temperature and pressure, the concentration of ethanol in the gaseous phase is proportional to the concentration of the ethanol in the liquid phase. Ethanol can be measured by analyzing the gas phase, which is in equilibrium with the blood in the vial.

**Plasma:** The top layer of clear liquid used for testing; the fluid portion of the blood in the living body. Hospital labs typically test serum or plasma that has been separated from the whole blood sample. Plasma is prepared by spinning a blood sample that contains an anticoagulant until the cells fall to the bottom of the tube.

---

66 *Durrett v. State*, 36 S.W.3d 205 (Tex. App. — Houston [14th Dist.] 2001, no pet.) (contradictory testimony about whether the state had shown who actually tested the blood, but testimony about the precautions taken by the hospital to ensure blood samples are properly drawn, labeled, and tested was adequate to link the blood results in the record to the defendant).

67 *Yeary v. State*, 734 S.W.2d 766 (Tex. App. — Fort Worth 1987, no pet.).

68 *Beck v. State*, 651 S.W.2d 827 (Tex. App. — Houston [1st Dist.] 1983, no pet.).

69 *Penley v. State*, 2 S.W.3d 534 (Tex. App. — Texarkana 1999, pet. ref'd); *Burns v. State*, 807 S.W.2d 878 (Tex. App. — Corpus Christi 1991, pet. ref'd); *Gallegos v. State*, 776 S.W.2d 312 (Tex. App. — Houston [14th Dist.] 1989) (orig. proceeding).

70 *Reidweg v. State*, 981 S.W.2d 399 (Tex. App. — San Antonio 1998, pet. ref'd).

**Serum:** Plasma minus clotting elements, obtained after blood is allowed to stand and clot. It is the clearer liquid above the clotted red cellular material.

**Standard:** A purchased reference material of known composition. An ethanol standard is purchased by labs to generate calibrators and a calibration curve.

**Whole blood:** Blood in the same form as when it circulated in the blood stream. This is the blood usually tested by forensic labs.

## Defense Attacks on Blood Evidence

A blood test can be attacked along any of three fronts: the collection of the specimen, the storage of the specimen prior to testing, and the test, itself. The prosecutor must be prepared to defend the integrity of the process at all three points. Effective prosecution requires that preliminary planning and training be done at all levels to ensure that faulty or questionable procedures do not diminish the integrity of the test.

Blood specimens for alcohol determination often are drawn in hospitals by nurses. Generally a nurse will prepare the injection site with an antiseptic swab. It is important that a non-alcoholic swab be used, and it is equally important that this be documented. Most practitioners use Betadine, a non-alcoholic material, when a blood alcohol specimen is to be taken. If an alcohol swab were used, it could be argued that alcohol from the swab contaminated the specimen and caused an erroneously high result. Actually, most alcohol swabs use isopropyl alcohol, which will not interfere with the determination of the concentration of ethyl alcohol by gas chromatographic analysis.

Another important decision is made at the time the specimen is collected: What type of container it will be collected into? This variable will determine the potential problems that could arise during the storage of the specimen prior to analysis. The most favorable scenario is use of a gray-top "Vacutainer" blood tube. The blood passes directly from the subject into a tube that contains an anticoagulant and sodium fluoride preservative. The anticoagulant prevents the blood from clotting, so that a whole-blood analysis can be done. The sodium fluoride prevents the biological activity of yeasts or bacteria that could increase or decrease the amount of alcohol in the specimen. It has been solidly established that blood alcohol concentration is stable in the presence of 1 percent sodium fluoride. It is important that the specimen be refrigerated during storage and that it be analyzed without delay.

Accurate analysis of alcohol in blood requires an acceptable testing protocol. The best methods utilize gas chromatography. A head-space vapor sample is injected onto the chromatographic column, and the resulting ethyl alcohol peak provides data that (1) establish that alcohol is present, instead of some other interfering substance, and (2) determine how much alcohol is present. Because alcohol is a volatile liquid, an equilibrium will be established between the alcohol in the blood and the alcohol in the head space above the blood. Head-space analysis minimizes problems that could arise in injection of whole-blood samples. The alcohol peak for the specimen is compared to the alcohol peaks for standard solutions with known alcohol concentrations. Because injection technique is an unavoidable source of error in chromatographic analysis, it is critical that the procedure use an internal standard. A measured quantity of another volatile liquid is placed into the specimen. The analyst then compares the peak ratio of alcohol: internal standard with the peak ratios of the standard solutions.

### THE BLOOD VIAL

Early in the investigation, prosecutors should locate and personally observe the condition of the vial of blood that was tested. If a blood kit was used, ask your officer for a sample blood kit and examine its contents. Most such kits contain one or two gray-top glass vials, a vacutainer tube and needle, a non-alcohol swab, and labels. If gray-top vials are in the sample kit, look for and note the presence of powder. You may have to tap the top or bottom of the vial to visualize the powder which may be lodged around the rubber cap. Also look to see if the package has an expiration date, and check for the same date on the actual package used. The date relates to the vacuum seal on the vial. This is another detail you can ask the witness about to prove the integrity of your sample.

The vial should have been stored in a refrigerator. Find out how soon after the blood was drawn it was placed in a refrigerator in the property room. The longer the delay, the greater room for defense attacks on the way the blood sample was preserved. The color of the top of the vials is a way of determining what was in the vials. Namely, a gray top vial should signify that it was a vacu-seal container with preservative, anti-coagulating powder, in it. This powder helps maintain the integrity of your blood sample even if it is not refrigerated immediately. Look to see if the label was placed on the vial such that some portion of the top of the vial is covered. This practice provides the chemist with an additional basis for testifying the vial had not been tampered with prior to testing.

### DEFENSE ABILITY TO RETEST BLOOD

Police departments should draw at least two vials of blood, in part so there will be sufficient blood drawn if the defense wants to have the blood retested by another lab. The best practice is to cooperate and sign an agreed order. **[A sample of an agreed order is included below.]** Using this order will facilitate the retesting as well as protect the State's evidence. It limits the release of the evidence only to an accredited lab and gives the laboratory used by the prosecutor control over how the evidence is transferred to the defendant's chosen lab.

Cause No. ____________________-

| | | |
|---|---|---|
| THE STATE OF TEXAS | § | IN THE __________ |
| VS. | § | COURT NO. __________ |
| ____________________ | § | ____________ COUNTY, TEXAS |

**AGREED ORDER**

On the ____ day of __________, 20___, came to be heard a Motion for Defense Analysis of Blood Sample, and said motion is hereby:

GRANTED DENIED

ACCORDINGLY, IT IS ORDERED that the ____________________ provide a sufficient sample of the defendant's blood to a forensic laboratory, accredited under §411.0205 of the Texas Government Code, designated by the defendant for retesting. Any transfers of evidence made under this order shall comply with applicable standards set by the laboratory's national accrediting body as well as the laboratory's internal standard operating procedures.

AGREED AS TO FORM AND SUBSTANCE:

______________________________ ______________________________

Attorney for the State Attorney for the Defendant

SIGNED AND ENTERED this _____ day of ________________, 20___.

______________________________

JUDGE PRESIDING

### THE PAPER CHASE

Don't assume it will be easy to establish a proper chain of custody on hospital-drawn blood. If you intend to rely on this, you may find it difficult to discover who drew the blood and to establish a link between the blood drawn and the result of the hospital tests.

Educate yourself on the policy of your respective police departments and hospitals regarding police-requested blood samples. Try to get your police departments to use the blood withdrawal form included at the end of this chapter. By using this form you will know why, who, when and where the sample was drawn. Where the state shows the beginning and the end of the chain of custody, any gaps in the chain go to the weight of the evidence and not to its admissibility.[71]

Note also that the hospital may use an independent lab to perform the testing. This may require you to call additional witnesses to establish your chain of custody. Hopefully, you will have a distinct identification number that applies to the patient and any and all tests done on the sample drawn from their body. Don't take this fact for granted, however, and make this determination before presenting the case to the grand jury.

### BLOOD WITHDRAWAL FORM

At trial, the two key witnesses you need to be concerned about are the officer who witnessed the blood being drawn and the nurse/ technician who drew it.[72] First, the prosecutor should subpoena hospital records to determine if a hospital draw was conducted, who completed the draw, and any evidence of intoxication the blood analysis showed. One potential problem will be their recollection of what specifically was done at the time the sample was drawn. The officer is at a disadvantage because he will know little about proper medical procedures and will be focused on the suspect in his custody. The

---

71 *Penley v. State*, 2 S.W.3d 534 (Tex. App. — Texarkana 1999, pet. ref'd); *Burns v. State*, 807 S.W.2d 878 (Tex. App. — Corpus Christi 1991, pet. ref'd); *Gallegos v. State*, 776 S.W.2d 312 (Tex. App. — Houston [14th Dist.] 1989) (orig. proceeding).

72 *Krause v. State*, 405 S.W.3d 82 (Tex. Crim. App. 2013) (allowing draw by EMT-1 working in the ER); *Edwards v. State*, No. 11-11-00135-CR (Tex. App. — Eastland, Nov. 12, 2013 (not for publication) (medical technologist is qualified technician for purposes of DWI blood draw).

nurse/technician may have trouble recalling exactly what was done because drawing blood is such a common occurrence for them. The form included in the appendix to this chapter was drafted to deal with this memory problem. If you have the officer and nurse/technician fill out the form at the time the sample is drawn, it will serve as a written record they can use later to refresh memory and assure themselves—and your jury—that the sample was collected and preserved properly.

### HOSPITAL BLOOD COLLECTION AND TESTING

If the suspect was injured in a crash, there is a good chance that the hospital drew a sample of blood in connection with treatment of that suspect. These hospital-ordered blood draw results can be used as evidence against the suspect in trial, but it is important to be familiar with the differences in the way hospital blood is collected and tested. Even in those cases with a police-requested, forensically tested blood sample, it is a good idea to obtain and prepare to prove the results of the hospital testing. Hospital results will often corroborate a forensically tested sample. It is important to note any time difference between the draw of the hospital sample and the blood-requested sample so the time difference can be factored into any later comparison. Prosecutors can subpoena hospital records to see if a hospital draw was conducted, by whom, and if the blood analysis showed any evidence of intoxication. Though HIPAA regulations were written to ensure privacy of medical records, there is no 4th Amendment protection for hospital records containing blood alcohol results during a criminal investigation.[73]

Previously, preference was for forensic blood samples to be drawn in grey-top vacutainers. A hospital will often draw a series of blood samples into vials with a variety of colored tops, which may or may not include the familiar grey-top vial. The color of the vial top chosen for the blood draw is related to the type of testing that will be done on the vial. Do not be concerned, however, about the absence of the powders contained in the grey-top vials, because the hospital samples arrive at the lab and are tested immediately.

Samples drawn for hospital testing are labeled with a unique code tied to that suspect/patient. Once the vials are drawn and labeled, they are typially sent by a chute (similar to those used at a bank drive-in) to the lab, where they are tested by the hospital laboratory. The results are typically sent back to the treating nurse or physician in less than an hour. The method of testing used in the hospital lab will be an enzymatic method. Meet with the hospital lab director to discuss this testing method, and be prepared to call that witness to establish the reliability of this testing method.

Hospital personnel may have used an isopropyl swab to cleanse the area of the draw. You can expect the defense to attack this with the argument that use of isopropyl contaminated the sample drawn. They will suggest that the area was cleansed with alcohol, and then the cleansing alcohol mixed with the blood sample and raised the alcohol level. Studies have shown that use of an isopropyl swab will not impact the blood alcohol result. Make sure you have discussed these studies with your witness, and have them available to use in cross-examination of any defense witness.[74] Case law also supports the proposition that use of isopropanol swabs will go to the weight and not the admissibility of the samples.[75]

Unlike the law enforcement samples submitted for forensic testing, the hospital will not retain the untested blood in the vials, and you can expect that those will have been destroyed a week to 10 days after collection. If you act quickly, you can obtain those hospital-drawn samples for retesting in your forensic lab. Hospitals are often willing to delay the destruction of samples upon request while you arrange for their retrieval. Either a grand jury subpoena or a search warrant may be used to collect the samples from the hospital. Remember that the samples may not have preservatives added, so the window of time for retesting is relatively short.

A final point is that hospitals test a serum sample rather than a whole-blood sample, so the hospital result must be translated into whole-blood concentrations. **[See "Translating Hospital Serum to Whole Blood," below.]**

#### *Translating Hospital Serum to Whole Blood*

Prosecution of a DWI case in which a hospital has analyzed the sample is complicated by the fact that a hospital laboratory will typically analyze a serum sample, rather than a whole blood sample. It is well known that serum alcohol content and whole blood alcohol content are not equivalent. Ethanol distributes to a blood compartment in proportion to the water content of that material; serum contains on average 15 percent more water than whole blood.[76] It therefore

---

73 *State v. Hardy*, 963 S.W.2d 516 (Tex. Crim. App. 1997); *Kennemur v. State*, 280 S.W.3d 305 (Tex. App. — Amarillo 2008, pet. ref'd).

74 Goldfinger and Schaber, "A comparison of blood alcohol concentrations using non-alcohol and alcohol containing skin antiseptics," ANNALS OF EMERGENCY MEDICINE Vol. 1, No. 11 (Dec. 1982) (use of ADH and enzymatic oxidation to look for ethanol when isopropanol pads were used did not impact the blood alcohol result). **[See a copy of this and other studies on blood evidence on the CD-Rom.]**

75 *Kennemur*, 280 S.W.3d 305; *Kaufman v. State*, 632 S.W.2d 685 (Tex. App. — Eastland 1982, pet. ref'd).

76 A.W. Jones. *Disposition and Fate of Ethanol in the Body*. In *Medical-Legal Aspects of Alcohol*, 4th ed., J.C. Garriott, Ed., Lawyers and Judges Publishing, Tucson, AZ, 2003, pp. 62.

stands to reason that ethanol concentrations in serum will be higher than the corresponding whole blood value due to the increase in the relative water content of serum in comparison to whole blood.

The predicted increases in serum alcohol levels have been confirmed in a number of scientific studies.[77] A serum/whole blood ethanol distribution ratio of 1.16:1 was reported in a study encompassing a large number of subjects.[78] This study is supported by a comprehensive review of many previous studies (3), in which the overall mean was also found to be 1.16 to 1. Realizing that the exact serum/whole blood ethanol ratio is variable from person to person and even within the same person from day to day, a conservative estimate of a ratio of 1.2 has been recommended by at least one author.[79]

Consult with your toxicologist about testimony surrounding serum/blood alcohol conversion ratios. Published mean ratios are not designed for use as scientific absolutes, but rather as working values that may be subject to individual variation. To appropriately convert and interpret a serum ethanol level, one should be aware of the range of possible whole blood concentrations in light of a given serum concentration. A recent study[80] addressed this issue. At a confidence level of 95 percent, a serum ethanol concentration of 103 mg/dL corresponded to a blood ethanol concentration of at least 0.08 g/dL (in only 5 cases out of 100 would the blood ethanol value be expected to be less than 0.08). Similarly, at a confidence level of 99 percent, a serum ethanol concentration of 107 mg/dL corresponded to a blood ethanol concentration of at least 0.08 g/dL (in only 1 case out of 100 would you expect the blood ethanol to be less than 0.08). Your toxicologist will be a valuable resource in providing guidance on these predictive values.

### Additional Defense Attacks on Blood Evidence and Responses

While the expansion of the category of cases where mandatory blood samples can be drawn and the increased use of blood search warrants has provided the State with an abundance of new evidence of intoxication, it has also created a need for the prosecutor to be familiar with defense attacks on that evidence. What follows is a short review of the most common attacks made against blood evidence. In each case, the response to overcome the attack and, where applicable, a study that supports the response is cited. A copy of those studies will be found on the CD contained in this publication.

**Attack:** The grey-top vial was not rotated the requisite 8 times after collection.

This attack focuses on the fact that the literature on blood alcohol collection in grey-top vials recommends that the vial be rotated 8 times after collection to ensure that the blood is mised with the anti-coagulant and preservative powders contained in the vials. You will notice that this recommendation has been memorialized on the "Blood Withdrawal Form," so if the form was used, that should put an end to this attack. If it was not used or witnesses are unsure of the number of rotations, you still should have no problem.

**Response:** It does not make a difference.

In spite of the fact that this number of rotations is mentioned both in the literature and on the paperwork that comes with the grey vacutainer packaging, there is no scientific study cited in support of the number 8. In fact, calls by the author to the manufacturer of the vials disclosed that the manufacturer could not explain where they got that number. The lab technician who did the testing will have done a visual examination of the blood vial and its contents before testing to ensure that it is not coagulated or spoiled, and that is probably the best evidence that the number of rotations was adequate. One private laboratory, Integrated Forensic Laboratories, Inc., showed that less than the 8 rotations did not impact the testing results.

**Attack:** The vacutainer tube was expired.

When you examine the vials and/or packaging of the forensic blood draw kits that contain the grey-top vacutainers, you will note that they include an expiration date. The date does not apply to the powders but to the vacuum, which is the mechanism by which the tube draws the blood from the suspect into the tube. the defense argument is that if an expired tube is used, the vacuum is compromised and contamination will occur, or an insufficient amount of blood will be drawn into the tube.

**Response:** This does not impact the result.

From a logical standpoint, if you see a tube of blood, then the vacuum was obviously sufficient to draw the blood into the tube, whether before or after the expiration date. A study was done to compare the results obtained from expired and unexpired grey-top tubes. The results were that the ethanol concentration of expired and unexpired tubes were statistically identical for up to 74 months after collection. Zitel and Hardin, "Comparison of Blood Ethanol Concentrations Simultaneously Collected into Expired and Unexpired Venipuncture Tubes," ANALYTICAL TOXICOLOGY (2006).

---

77 P.M. Rainey. *Relation between Serum and Whole-Blood Ethanol Concentrations.* CLINICAL CHEMISTRY 39(11): 2288-2292, 1993; Iffland, R. et al. *Zur Zuverlässigkeit der Blutalkoholbestimmung Das Verteilungsverhältnis des Wassers zwischen Serum and Vollblut.* RECHTSMEDIZIN 9: 123-130, 1999; R.C. Charlebois, M.R. Corbett, and J.G. Wigmore. *Comparison of Ethanol Concentrations in Blood, Serum, and Blood Cells for Forensic Application.* J. ANALYTICAL TOXICOLOGY 20: 171-178, 1996.

78 Rainey.

79 A.W. Jones. *Disposition and Fate of Ethanol in the Body. In Medical-Legal Aspects of Alcohol,* 4th ed., J.C. Garriott, Ed., Lawyers and Judges Publishing, Tucson, AZ, 2003, pp. 63.

80 M.T. Barnhill, Jr., D. Herbert, and D.J. Wells, Jr. *Comparison of Hospital Laboratory Serum Alcohol Levels Obtained by an Enzymatic Method with Whole Blood Levels Forensically Determined by Gas Chromatography.* J. ANALYTICAL TOXICOLOGY 31: 23-30, 2007. **[See a copy of this and other studies on blood evidence on the CD-Rom.]**

**Attack:** The blood vial was not refrigerated after the blood was drawn.

It is recommended that blood samples be refrigerated after the draw. The argument here is that failure to do so impacted the integrity of the blood draw sample.

**Response:** This does not make a difference over a short period of time.

In a study involving blood drawn from living humans to see if the failure to refrigerate impacted the sample, the finding was that in the short term, it did not. The study found that alcohol analysis could be delayed as long as 14 days without significant change in alcohol content whether those samples were refrigerated or not and without preservative added to the sample. Winek and Paul, "Effect of short-term storage conditions on alcohol concentrations in blood from living human subject," CLINICAL CHEMISTRY (1983).

Two things that are significant about this study are that the blood was drawn from live humans. One area of inquiry you should make of any study used to attack the way your blood was drawn and stored is the origin of the blood. Blood draws from someone who is deceased or from a blood bank will have different results than those drawn from a live subject. The other important point is that the result discussed in the Winek and Paul study was identical whether there was preservative powder in the vial or not.

The majority of the blood samples you deal with will be collected in grey-top tubes and vials that have preservative powders in them. If those samples are tested by a DPS laboratory, it is likely they traveled through the mail and were unrefrigerated during that trip. Your DPS chemist will certainly testify that the lack of refrigeration during that journey did not impact the test result due to the presence of those powders. another study found that no alcohol was generated in blood samples over a 42-day storage period with or without preservative powder in the vials and with or without refrigeration. Anderson, et al., "The effects of storage on the accuracy of blood alcohol readings," Int'l Conf. on Alcohol, Drugs & Traffic Safety (2004). Another study on the ipact of heat on blood samples found no alcohol gain in blood collected in EDTA/Fluoride tubes even if stored in the passenger compartment or trunk of a car and exposed to temperatures ranging from 63° F to 116° F for up to 78 days. Some decrease in alcohol concentration was noted. Paul Glover, "The Effect of Heat on Blood Samples Containing Alcohol," Int'l Conf. on Alcohol, Drugs & Traffic Safety (2002).

**Attack:** Microbes or yeast got into the blood sample and created alcohol.

This attack, which is alluded to in some of the studies cited above, argues that if blood is improperly drawn or stored, microbes or yeast that interact with the sample will actually cause the sample to generate additional alcohol.

**Response:** This is not supported by studies or samples properly stored and drawn from living subjects.

The studies that speak of this phenomenon almost exclusively deal with blood samples drawn from deceased individuals. Assuming the person you are prosecuting is not deceased, this is not an issue and the risk of this happening in your samples is negligible. In one study, blood samples containing preservatives that were purposely inoculated with Candida Albicans (one of the most commonly cited contaminants) and refrigerated showed no alcohol production for up to 182 days. There was some alcohol production found in samples that weren't refrigerated, but note that these samples came from blood banks and were exposed to non-forensic conditions. The study noted no reference to this causing alcohol increase in samples taken from living subjects. Chang and Kollman, "The Effect of Temperature on the Formation of Ethanol by Candida Albicans in Blood," *Forensic Sciences* 1989.

Beyond reading and sharing these studies, be prepared to deal with any studies presented by the defense by asking the following questions about those studies:

- Did collection, testing, and storage procedures follow accepted forensic practices?
- Did the vials used in the studies contain anticoagulant and preservative powders?
- Was the source of the blood used in the studies: live subjects, dead subjects (more prone to decomposition and microbial contamination), or blood banks (whose samples contain additives like glucose)?

Other important areas of inquiry that could minimize the impact of the defense-cited studies include:

- When was the study done?
- How many subjects were used in the study?
- What instrumentation was used to test the blood sample?
- Where was the study published?
- Was it peer-reviewed?
- What other studies does it cite?

# Value of Blood & Breath Evidence

### OBJECTIVE EVIDENCE

There are certain things that a breath test will and won't tell. The advantage of a breath or blood test is that it presents objective evidence, a scientific means of measuring alcohol concentration. The disadvantage is that it provides this measure only as of the time the test was administered—not the time of driving. The legislature clearly contemplated this discrepancy, because Chapter 724 of the Transportation Code provides that the sample will be admissible with no requirement that the specimen be obtained near the time of driving.[81] And obviously, it would be impossible to obtain a breath

[81] See, e.g., *Annis v. State*, 578 S.W.2d 406 (Tex. Crim. App. 1979) (breath test taken one hour and 20 minutes after stop may be sufficient to prove intoxication at the time of the stop when coupled with arresting officer's testimony); *Dorsche v. State*, 514 S.W.2d 755 (Tex. Crim. App. 1974).

or blood sample at the time the defendant is driving. So if a breath or blood sample can only show alcohol concentration at the time of the test, how can a prosecutor use this information?

First, there are only two conclusions to draw for alcohol concentration at the time of driving: The defendant's alcohol concentration was either on the way up on or on the way down. If prosecutors have enough information to do retrograde extrapolation, it would be easier to figure out whether the defendant's BAC was higher or lower at the time of driving. [**Retrograde extrapolation is covered in more detail later in this chapter.**]

But without this science, prosecutors should keep in mind details that help pinpoint where the defendant was at the time of driving. For instance, on the video at the scene, the defendant might look terrible, but he might perform and appear better later. What does common sense tell us about where his blood alcohol concentration was at the time of driving? Higher than at the time of the breath test.

Another conclusion you can draw from a sample given by the defendant—even without extrapolation—is evidence of how much alcohol the defendant actually consumed. Prosecutors should be able to determine the defendant's weight and the period of time during which they were not drinking (at the very least, from the time the officer pulled the driver over to the time he gave a sample). With this much information, you can determine how many drinks it would have taken the defendant to get to the level of intoxication reflected by the breath test.

Third, the breath or blood test instrument is the only objective "observer" in the equation. While a defense attorney might argue that the officer had some motivation for believing the defendant was intoxicated, the instrument has no such motive. The instrument has the same ability to free a person as to convict a person.

Finally, whether you have breath or blood test evidence or not, prosecutors must remind the jury there are two separate definitions of intoxication—BAC of .08 or higher, and loss of mental and physical faculties. Every person has his or her own unique tolerance of alcohol. Our law contains two separate definitions of intoxication because it wouldn't make sense to have a law that favors people who can hold liquor over people who can't. If one or two drinks causes a driver to have diminished reaction time and reflexes, even if a breath sample shows their BAC was below .08, that driver is still legally intoxicated.

## RETROGRADE EXTRAPOLATION

Retrograde extrapolation is the computation back in time of the blood-alcohol level, or the estimation of the defendant's BAC at the time of driving based on a test result from some later time.[82] The Court of Criminal Appeals' decision on retrograde extrapolation in *Mata v. State*[83] sent broad ripples through the state. Some trial judges began requiring retrograde extrapolation evidence; others ruled that it could never be admitted. In truth, *Mata* stands for neither proposition but merely sets out guidelines for when retrograde extrapolation evidence may be admitted. The Court of Criminal Appeals later ruled that breath test results are admissible without retrograde extrapolation as long as the probative value of the results outweighs the prejudicial effect.[84]

Extrapolation testimony is admissible under T.R.EVID. 702 and the *Kelly* test.[85]

### SAMPLE RETROGRADE EXTRAPOLATION PROBLEMS

The following calculations may help you formulate information for experts to do retrograde extrapolation.

For instance, say you have a defendant who said at the scene he had only two beers to drink that night. The test result was a .15. If you give the witness the weight of the defendant (this information should be in book-in records) you can try asking the following:

---

82 *Mata v. State*, 46 S.W.3d 902, 908-09 (Tex. Crim. App. 2001), citing Lawrence Taylor, DRUNK DRIVING DEFENSE §5.2 (5th ed. 2000).

83 *Mata*, 46 S.W.3d 902.

84 *Stewart v. State*, 129 S.W.3d 93 (Tex. Crim. App. 2004); *Wyatt v. State*, No. 06-12-00150-CR (Tex. App. — Texarkana 2013, pet. ref'd) (not for publication) (BAC of .10 taken 90 minutes after driving was probative and supported by accompanying evidence of impairment observed at time of arrest).

85 *Fulenwider v. State*, 176 S.W.3d 290 (Tex. App. — Houston [1st Dist.] 2004, pet. ref'd); *Peden v. State*, 2004 WL 2538274, No. 01-03-522-CR (Tex. App. — Houston [1st Dist.] 2004, pet. ref'd); *Hartman v. State*, 2 S.W.3d 490 (Tex. App. — San Antonio 1999, pet. ref'd). The dissent in this case is worth reading because it constitutes something of a defense-oriented treatise on the problems with retrograde extrapolation.

1. If you have an adult male weighing 180 pounds, how many 12-ounce beers would he have to drink before he would reach a blood alcohol level of .15?

   **Note: It helps to know if the person has eaten but if the number of drinks is this low it doesn't matter as it is physically impossible to reach that level with two drinks.**

Another way to go about it if you have enough details (and you may only have them if the defendant has testified and been cross-examined) is as follows:

2. Consider the following hypothetical:

   An adult male weighing 180 lbs had his first beer at 6:00 p.m. He had a hamburger and fries for dinner at 5:30 and that was all he ate before he was stopped by police. Over the next four hours he says he drank four more beers, taking approximately a half an hour to finish each beer. He finished his last beer at 9:00 p.m.

   What would you predict his alcohol level would be when he was stopped at 10:30 p.m. that night?

   **Your expert will always have to qualify his estimates as they relate to the average person but don't let that deter you.**

Another way you can do it is to ask:

If an adult male blew a .15 at 11:00 p.m. and he had his last drink at 9:00 p.m. what would you expect his alcohol level to be at 10:30 p.m.?

The degree to which you can extrapolate will depend on the number of facts available about a defendant's drinking habits on the offense date and on what your expert is comfortable doing. Explore this area with your expert before he takes the stand.

## REFUSALS AS EVIDENCE

It is common sense for each of us to assume the worst of those who purposely and visibly seek to hide something. How many times is an arrest for possession of weapons or drugs preceded by a defendant's refusal to show what is in his hand or take that hand out of his pocket? Texas courts have held that intoxication is a legitimate deduction from a defendant's refusal to take a breath test.[86]

Remember to explain to the jury in voir dire (and come back to the concept while questioning witnesses) that the law contains no general right not to incriminate yourself. What the law prohibits is compelled self-incrimination, and even that is limited to verbal communications. There is no right not to take a breath test, and a defendant's actions or inactions—as opposed to a defendant's statements—can always be used to incriminate her.

Compare a breath test refusal to the crime of fleeing from a police officer. If a suspect flees from police, their flight is evidence that a jury can hear about at trial, one of the few extraneous offenses that a jury can always hear about during guilt/innocence. Refusing to submit to a breath test is like respiratory "flight." The defendant is refusing to do something—give evidence—and this refusal can be used against them the same way evidence of flight can be used against a fleeing defendant in a trial for an underlying offense.

### BLOOD EVIDENCE RETENTION RULES

The rules regarding disposal of blood evidence drawn under Penal Code Chapter 49 can be found in Code of Criminal Procedure Article 38.50, enacted effective Sept. 1, 2015. These rules apply to prosecutor offices, law enforcement agencies, and crime labs. All toxicological evidence must be retained and preserved for two years from the offense date for a misdemeanor and three years for a felony if there is no charge. If convicted,the evidence must be retained for the duration of the incarceration or term of probation, or until the defendant is acquitted, an indictment or information is dismissed with prejudice, or in a juvenile case, until the court determines by way of a hearing that the child has not engaged in delinquent conduct or is not in need of supervision.

---

86 *Standefer v. State*, 59 S.W.3d 177 (Tex. Crim. App. 2001); *Gaddis v. State*, 753 S.W.2d 396 (Tex. Crim. App. 1988); *Thomas v. State*, 990 S.W.2d 858 (Tex. App. — Dallas 1999, no pet.).

## Sample Forms

### BLOOD WITHDRAWAL PROCEDURE FORM

❒ 1) Officer placed suspect under arrest for a Chapter 49 offense involving operation of a motor vehicle.

❒ 2) Officer read DIC-24 to suspect and did provide suspect with written copy.

❒ 3) Suspect did ❒ consent / ❒ refuse to give blood sample / ❒ unconscious or incapable of refusal.

❒ 4) Officer did remove vial from blood collection kit.

❒ 5) Expiration date on blood kit/vial is ______________________________.

❒ 6) Officer did fill out label that came with kit completely except for the time blood was drawn.

❒ 7) Vial was closed when handed to the nurse.

❒ 8) Preservative/anti-coagulant powder was seen in vial.

❒ 9) Nurse/technician did the following in withdrawing blood from subject:

❒ Used betadine (or other:_____________) solution to disinfect arm.

❒ Officer should save swab packaging.

❒ Rotated vial as directions indicated 8 times so as to mix blood with preservative anti-coagulant.

❒ 10) Vial (top never having been opened) was then delivered to officer and officer finished completing label by adding time blood was drawn and officer and nurse/technician initialed label, which was used to seal vial top closed.

Signed by:

______________________________
Arresting Officer/PD Dept.

______________________________
Nurse/Medical Technician

SUSPECT NAME______________________________ DATE: ____________

OFFENSE NO.________________ TIME OF BLOOD DRAW: ____________

## STATUTORY WARNING

DIC-24 (Rev. 9/11)

SUBJECT'S NAME ______ DL NO./STATE ______ DOB ______

PHYSICAL DESCRIPTION (if unlicensed) Race:______ Sex:______ Height:______ Weight:______ Eyes:______ Hair:______

DATE OF ARREST: ______ TIME OF ARREST: ______ COUNTY OF ARREST: ______

You are under arrest for an offense arising out of acts alleged to have been committed while you were operating a motor vehicle in a public place, or a watercraft, while intoxicated, or an offense under Section 106.041, Alcoholic Beverage Code. You will be asked to give a specimen of your breath and/or blood. The specimen will be analyzed to determine the alcohol concentration or the presence of a controlled substance, drug, dangerous drug or other substance in your body.

If you refuse to give the specimen, that refusal may be admissible in a subsequent prosecution. Your license, permit or privilege to operate a motor vehicle will be suspended or denied for not less than 180 days, whether or not you are subsequently prosecuted for this offense.

If you refuse to submit to the taking of a specimen, the officer may apply for a warrant authorizing a specimen to be taken from you.

If you are 21 years of age or older and submit to the taking of a specimen and an analysis of the specimen shows that you have an alcohol concentration of 0.08 or more, your license, permit or privilege to operate a motor vehicle will be suspended or denied for not less than 90 days, whether or not you are subsequently prosecuted for this offense.

If you are younger than 21 years of age and have any detectable amount of alcohol in your system, your license, permit or privilege to operate a motor vehicle will be suspended or denied for not less than 60 days. However, if you submit to the taking of a specimen and an analysis of the specimen shows that you have an alcohol concentration of less than 0.08, you may be subject to criminal penalties less severe than those provided for under Chapter 49, Penal Code.

If you were operating a motor vehicle and you refuse to give the specimen or provide a specimen that shows you have an alcohol concentration of 0.08 or more, you may be disqualified from driving a commercial motor vehicle for a period of not less than one year.

You may request a hearing on the suspension or denial. This request must be received by the Texas Department of Public Safety at its headquarters in Austin, Texas, no later than 15 days after you receive or are presumed to have received notice of suspension or denial. The request can be made by written demand, fax, or other form prescribed by the Department.

I certify that I have informed you both orally and in writing of the consequences of refusing to submit to the taking of a specimen or providing a specimen. I have provided you with a complete and true copy of this statutory warning.

I am now requesting a specimen of your ☐ **Breath** ☐ **Blood**

☐ Subject refused to allow the taking of a specimen and further refused to sign below as requested by this officer.

OR

☐ Subject refused to allow the taking of a specimen as evidenced by his/her signature below.

______
Subject's Signature

☐ I further certify that because you are a child as defined in Section 51.02, Family Code, the above request for a specimen and your response have been videotaped.

______
Officer's Signature

______
Officer's Printed Name

______
Agency

______
Telephone No.

**FOR DEPARTMENT USE ONLY**

**DPS Copy—White** **Driver's Copy—Yellow**

## Form 3-2: INSTRUCTIONS FOR BLOOD SEARCH WARRANT

Attached to these instructions are all the forms needed to get a search warrant for a blood sample.

You are going to need this search warrant and your affidavit signed by a judge. Note: This must be a judge from a court of record, district court, municipal court of record, or county court.

Each fill-in-the-blank has a brief explanation below the line requiring information.

If you have prepared search warrants before, you will note there is nothing different or special about this warrant. It just may help you obtain the warrant in a shorter amount of time.

The Court of Criminal Appeals has upheld obtaining this search warrant even if the defendant has refused your request for a breath or blood test after reading the statutory warnings.

## SAMPLE SEARCH WARRANT DOCUMENTS FOR BLOOD

THE STATE OF TEXAS §
COUNTY OF TARRANT §

### AFFIDAVIT FOR SEARCH WARRANT AND MAGISTRATION

**I. AFFIANT**

The undersigned Affiant, a peace officer under the laws of the State of Texas, and after first being duly sworn, on oath makes the following statements and accusations:

My name is ______________________. I am a peace officer employed by ________________________. I have successfully completed the State-mandated requirements to become a peace officer. Additionally, I have successfully completed courses and/or training in the field of alcohol detection and intoxication-related offenses. I have seen intoxicated persons in the past and, during the course of my employment, I have observed numerous people who are under the influence of alcohol or other substances and:

☐ I am certified and/or trained in the detection of impaired or intoxicated drivers through the use of three standardized field sobriety tests [SFSTs], namely: Horizontal Gaze Nystagmus [HGN], One-Leg Stand [OLS], and Walk and Turn [WAT].

☐ I have formed opinions on intoxication on many occasions and have had my suspicions confirmed by breath, blood, or urine samples that were administered after I performed my law enforcement duties relating to the detection of intoxicated drivers.

**II. SUSPECT & CRIME**

A. The suspected person ["suspect"] is described as follows:

Name: ________________________________________ TX DL/ID # ____________________

Race: ____________________ Sex: ____________ DOB: ____________________________

Height: ____________________ Weight: ____________ Hair Color: ____________________

B. The suspect is presently in custody of a law enforcement agency here in Tarrant County, Texas, namely the ________________________________, which will present the suspect to execute the warrant requested herein;

C. The suspect has possession of and is concealing human blood, which constitutes evidence that the suspect committed the offense described in paragraph D below;

D. I have good reason to believe that on the _____ day of _________, 20___, the suspect did then and there operate a motor vehicle in a public place in Tarrant County, Texas, while intoxicated by not having the normal use of mental or physical faculties by reason of the introduction of alcohol, a controlled substance, a drug, a dangerous drug, or a combination thereof, into the suspect's body.

**III. REASON FOR CONTACT / EVIDENCE OF OPERATING**

A. My belief that the suspect committed the offense described in paragraph D above is based on the following facts:

1. On the date specified in paragraph D above, at approximately ______ o'clock, ___.M., the suspect was operating a motor vehicle in a public place in Tarrant County, Texas, namely at the following location ______________________________
______________________________________________________________________;

2. Additionally, the following information influenced my reasonable-suspicion consideration (any that apply are checked):

☐ TRAFFIC STOP: I stopped the vehicle at the above time and location for the following reason(s):
______________________________________________________________________
______________________________________________________________________
______________ and, at the time of the stop, I believed that these facts, among others, possibly indicated that the suspect was committing the following Transportation Code violations: ______________________________
______________________________________________ and/or the offense of driving while intoxicated;

☐ ENCOUNTER: The suspect's vehicle was already stopped and I believed that the suspect had been driving and/or operating the vehicle because: ______________________________________________
______________________________________________________ and, at the time of the contact, I believed that these facts, among others, possibly indicated that the suspect was committing the following traffic and/or criminal violations: ______________________________________
______________________________________________ and/or the offense of driving while intoxicated.

☐ WITNESSES: One or more witnesses, ______________________________________, conveyed information to me about observing the suspect's actions and/or motor-vehicle operation. The details of the conveyed information included, but were not limited to: ______________________________________

________________________________________

________________________________________

**B. ORAL ADMISSION RE: OPERATION:** The suspect admitted to me that the suspect had been operating a motor vehicle in a public place in Tarrant County, Texas just a short time prior to my arrival: YES / NO

**C. INTOXICATION EVIDENCE:**

1. GENERAL OBSERVATIONS: During my contact with the suspect, I made the following observations about the suspect:

ODOR OF ALCOHOL: Strong Moderate Faint None

Other: ________________________________________

SPEECH: Slurred Confused Stuttered Accented Fair Good

Other: ________________________________________

ATTITUDE: Cooperative Combative Indifferent Hilarious
Talkative Carefree Excited Insulting
Cocky Sleepy Profane Polite

Other: ________________________________________

BALANCE: Falling Staggering Hesitant Swaying Unsure Sure

Other: ________________________________________

WALKING: Falling Staggering Hesitant Swaying Unsure Sure

Other: ________________________________________

TURNING: Falling Staggering Hesitant Swaying Unsure Sure

Other: ________________________________________

2. EVIDENCE OF POSSIBLE DRUG/CONTROLLED SUBSTANCE USE:

☐ Drug paraphernalia found

☐ Describe drug paraphernalia found ____________________

☐ Odor of marijuana detected (describe) ____________________

☐ Statements made by the suspect or others indicating possible drug usage:

________________________________________

________________________________________

☐ Other: ________________________________________

3. FIELD SOBRIETY TESTS IN GENERAL:

☐ During my contact with the suspect, I requested performance of field sobriety tests by the suspect and recorded the results and my observations of the suspect's performance of field sobriety tests and signs of intoxication which include the following:

☐ The suspect refused to perform (ALL / SOME) of the requested field sobriety tests, and this refusal indicated to me that the suspect was attempting to hide intoxication evidence: YES / NO

4. SPECIFIC FIELD SOBRIETY TESTS:

☐ NYSTAGMUS:

The suspect was first qualified as a candidate by checking the suspect's eyes for equal tracking, no resting nystagmus, and equal pupil size. The suspect was also qualified as a candidate by questions which revealed that he had not suffered from a head injury, did not have any medical problems, and was not currently on any medications. Additional comments: ____________________

HGN: Total number of observed clues ______

Circle observed clues:

L R 1. Lack of smooth pursuit

L R 2. Distinct and sustained nystagmus at maximum deviation

L R 3. Onset of nystagmus prior to 45 degrees

Vertical nystagmus: YES / NO

Other comments: ________________________________________

☐ WALK AND TURN:

WAT: Total number of observed clues ______

Check appropriate clues:

_____ 1. Cannot keep balance while listening to instructions

_____ 2. Starts before instructions are finished

_____ 3. Stops while walking to steady self

_____ 4. Does not touch heel to toe

_____ 5. Loses balance while walking (i.e., steps off line)

_____ 6. Uses arms for balance (raises arms over six inches)

_____ 7. Loses balance while turning/turns incorrectly

_____ 8. Incorrect number of steps

Other comments: ______________________________

☐ ONE LEG STAND:

OLS: Total number of observed clues ______

_____ 1. Sways while balancing

_____ 2. Hops

_____ 3. Puts foot down

_____ 4. Uses arms for balance (raises arms over six inches)

Other comments: ______________________________

5. ADDITIONAL OBSERVATIONS/FACTORS: Additional facts leading me to believe that the suspect was intoxicated while operating a motor vehicle in a public place include: ______________________________
______________________________
______________________________

6. SUSPECT'S ORAL STATEMENTS: The suspect made the following statements: ______________________________
______________________________
______________________________

7. OPEN CONTAINER EVIDENCE:
Open container found: YES / NO
List type of open container(s) found: ______________________________
Describe location of open container(s) found ______________________________

8. SUMMARY: Based upon my experiences, my training in intoxication-related offenses, and my observations of the suspect during my contact with him/her, I believe that the suspect is intoxicated by reason of the introduction of alcohol, a controlled substance, a dangerous drug, or a combination thereof, and that the suspect lost the normal use of his/her mental or physical faculties by reason of the introduction of alcohol or one of the other aforementioned substances, or a combination thereof, into his/her body.

9. REFUSAL EVIDENCE: After placing the suspect under arrest for Driving While Intoxicated, I requested a sample of the suspect's breath and/or blood, which the suspect refused to provide a sample in violation of the Texas Implied Consent law. This is an indication to me that suspect is attempting to hide evidence of his/her intoxication. Other relevant statements made by the suspect when refusing include: ______________________________
______________________________
______________________________

10. I know from my training and experience that alcohol and other intoxicating substances are absorbed into the bloodstream of an intoxicated person and that the blood of such person can be analyzed for the presence of alcohol and other intoxicating substances.

WHEREFORE, based upon this affidavit and *Beeman v. State*, 86 S.W.3d 613 (Tex. Crim. App. 2002), Affiant asks for a search warrant that will authorize Affiant or Affiant's agent to search the person of the suspect for the blood evidence described above and seize the same as evidence that the offense described was committed and that the suspect committed the said offense.

Further Affiant asks for issuance of an order to appropriate third parties directing them to assist Affiant in the execution of said warrant.

____________________________________

Affiant

Subscribed and sworn to before me on this _____ day of _________, 20___, by an official authorized to administer and authorize this oath pursuant to TEX. GOV'T CODE §602.002.

____________________________________

Judge / Peace Officer / Notary

____________________________________

Official's Printed Name & Title

---

THE STATE OF TEXAS §<br>
COUNTY OF TARRANT §

**SEARCH WARRANT**

The State Of Texas: To any Sheriff or any Peace Officer of Tarrant County, Texas, or any Peace Officer of the State of Texas:

Whereas, the Affiant, whose name appears on the Affidavit attached hereto is a peace officer under the laws of Texas and did heretofore this day subscribe and swear to said affidavit before me, which said Affidavit is here now made a part hereof for all purposes and incorporated herein as if written verbatim within the confines of this warrant and whereas I find that the verified facts stated by Affiant in said Affidavit show that Affiant has probable cause for the belief Affiant expresses herein and establishes the existence of proper grounds for the issuance of this Warrant:

Now, therefore, you are commanded to take custody of the suspect and transport the suspect to a physician, registered nurse, qualified technician, phlebotomist or medical laboratory technician skilled in the taking of blood from the human body, in Tarrant County, Texas, where the said physician, registered nurse, qualified technician or medical laboratory technician shall, in the presence of a law enforcement officer, take samples of the Blood from the body of the following described individual:

Name: ____________________________________________ TX DL/ID # __________________

Race: ____________________ Sex: ____________ DOB: __________________________

Height: ____________________ Weight: __________ Hair Color: __________________________

Law enforcement officers are authorized to use all reasonable force necessary to assist the physician, registered nurse, qualified technician, phlebotomist or medical laboratory technician to take the samples from the body suspect. After obtaining the samples of Blood, the physician, registered nurse, qualified technician, phlebotomist or medical laboratory technician shall deliver the said samples to the said law enforcement officer.

Herein fail not, but have you then and there this warrant within three days, exclusive of the day of its issuance, with your return thereon, showing how you have executed the same.

Issued on this the _____ day of _________, 20___, at ______ o'clock, ___.M., to certify which witness my hand this day.

____________________________________

Judge, Tarrant County, Texas

THE STATE OF TEXAS §
COUNTY OF TARRANT §

**RETURN AND INVENTORY**

The undersigned Affiant, being a Peace Officer under the laws of Texas and being duly sworn, on oath certifies that the foregoing Warrant came to hand on the day it was issued and that it was executed on the _____ day of _________, 20___, by making the search directed therein and seizing during such search the following described property:

Specimens of the suspect's blood.

_______________________________
Affiant

SUBSCRIBED AND SWORN to before me, the undersigned authority on this _____ day of _________, 20___.

_______________________________
Judge, Tarrant County, Texas

---

THE STATE OF TEXAS §
COUNTY OF TARRANT §

**ORDER FOR ASSISTANCE IN EXECUTION OF SEARCH WARRANT**

To any physician, registered nurse, qualified technician, phlebotomist or medical laboratory technician skilled in the taking of blood from the human body, in Tarrant County, Texas:

Whereas, the affiant whose name appears on the affidavit attached hereto is a peace officer under the laws of Texas and did heretofore this day subscribe and swear to said affidavit before me which said affidavit is here now made a part hereof for all purposes and incorporated herein as if written verbatim within the confines of this Order, and whereas I find that the verified facts stated by affiant in said Affidavit show that affiant has probable cause for the belief he/she expresses herein and establishes existence of proper grounds for issuance of a search warrant;

And whereas, this court has issued a warrant to search for and seize blood from the suspect named and described in the Affidavit, to-wit:

Name: _______________________________ TX DL/ID # _______________

Race: _______________ Sex: __________ DOB: _______________

Height: _______________ Weight: __________ Hair Color: _______________

THEREFORE, you are hereby ordered and commanded to cooperate with any peace officer requesting your professional assistance in the execution of this warrant. This order is directed to any individual whose aid and assistance is requested by the officer bearing the accompanying search warrant and is authorized by the full authority of this Court to issue warrants and orders to enforce the laws of the State of Texas, and Article 18.08 of the Texas Code of Criminal Procedure. Any individual who fails to comply with this Order when requested shall be liable for contempt of this Court and subject to all penalties authorized by law.

Ordered this the _____ day of __________, 20___ at ______ o'clock, ___.M. to certify which witness my hand this day.

_______________________________
Judge, Tarrant County, Texas

CHAPTER

# 4

# Pretrial Motions & Hearings

Prosecutors will face a number of issues before the DWI trial ever begins. Chapter 4 deals with the most common of these motions and hearings, including drivers license suspensions, discovery motions, conditions for bond, motions to suppress, and discovery of expert witnesses.

# Drivers License Suspensions

Although there are a number of reasons why a driver's license can be suspended in Texas, the world of DWI revolves around three of them. Transportation Code chapter 724 contains the suspension for failing to take a breath test, chapter 524 includes an administrative suspension when a defendant fails to pass a test due to intoxication, and chapter 521 contains a license suspension for being convicted for DWI. A license suspension can last from 90 days to two years (180 days to two years for a chapter 724 suspension), and it is possible to suspend a license both for a DWI conviction and for a blood/breath test refusal or failure arising from the same event.

Drivers younger than 21 who are convicted of an alcohol offense (namely, purchasing or attempting to purchase alcohol by a minor, consumption or possession of alcohol by a minor, or misrepresentation of age) face an additional license suspension of 30 to 180 days. Drivers younger than 21 who are convicted of DWI face an additional license suspension of 60 to 180 days.

## ALR

Once a person has been arrested for DWI, he automatically has his license suspended. Subchapter D of Chapter 724 of the Transportation Code contains the procedures for an administrative license revocation (ALR) hearing, which will be conducted through DPS. The only issues at the ALR hearing are whether:

1. officers had reasonable suspicion or probable cause to make the stop;
2. officers had probable cause to believe the person was driving a motor vehicle or operating a watercraft in a public place while intoxicated;
3. the person was placed under arrest by the officer and was asked to give a blood or breath specimen; and
4. the person refused to give a specimen.[1]

If the administrative judge finds in the affirmative on all four issues, the driver's license is suspended. If not, the license is returned or reinstated.[2]

**Transportation Code §724.041. Hearing on Suspension or Denial**

(a) If, not later than the 15th day after the date on which the person receives notice of suspension or denial under Section 724.032(a) or is considered to have received notice under Section 724.033, the department received at its headquarters in Austin, in writing, including a facsimile transmission, or by another manner prescribed by the department, a request that a hearing be held, the State Office of Administrative Hearings shall hold a hearing.

(b) A hearing shall be held not earlier than the 11th day after the date the person is notified, unless the parties agree to waive this requirement, but before the effective date of the notice of suspension or denial.

(c) A request for a hearing stays the suspension or denial until the date of the final decision of the administrative law judge. If the person's license was taken by a peace officer under Section 724.032(a), the department shall notify the person of the effect of the request on the suspension of the person's license before the expiration of any temporary driving permit issued to the person, if the person is otherwise eligible, in a manner that will permit the person to establish to a peace officer that the person's license is not suspended.

(d) A hearing shall be held by an administrative law judge employed by the State Office of Administrative Hearings....

---

1 Tex. Trans. Code §724.042.

2 Tex. Trans. Code §724.043.

## TABLE 4-1: Driver's License Suspensions

| Offense | Suspension of driver's license |
|---|---|
| Alcohol awareness courses, failure to attend by minor (ABC §106.115) | One year (FC §54.042(c); TC §521.345) |
| Alcoholic Beverage Code violation (must be (conviction and not deferred. CCP 45.051) | 1st offense: 30 days; 2nd offense: 60 days; 3rd offense: 180 days (ABC §106.071) |
| Breath/blood test failure | 90 days if no alcohol-related contact w/in 10 years of arrest date (TC §524.022(a)(1))<br>One year if previous alcohol-related contact w/in 10 years (TC §524.022(a)(2)) |
| Breath/blood failure for offenders under 21 | 1st alcohol-related contact: 60 days; 2nd: 120 days; 3rd: 180 days (TC §524.022(b)(1-3)) |
| Breath/blood test refusal | 180 days; two years if previous alcohol-related contact w/in 10 yrs (TC §724.035(a)(2) & (b)) |
| Controlled Substances Act violation | 180 days after the date of final conviction (§521.372 & .374) |
| Criminally negligent homicide (§19.05) | One year (TC §§521.341(1) & .343) |
| Dangerous drug manuf, delivery, possession transport by D <21 (TC §521.342(a)(4)) | One year (TC §521.342(a)(4) & .343) |
| Driver's license fraud | 90 days to one year (TC §§521.341(7), .451, .& 453) |
| Driving while license invalid or suspended | 90 days to one year (TC §§521.292 & .293) |
| DWI (first offense) (§49.04) | Not probated: 90 days to one year (TC §521.341(3) & .344)<br>Offender under 21 and not probated: one year (TC §521.342(a)(1) & .344)<br>Offender under 21 and probated: 90 days if ignition interlock made condition of CS; (TC §521.342(b)); one year if interlock not condition of CS (CCP 42.12, §13(n)) |
| DWI (second or greater offense) (§49.09) | 180 days to two years (TC §521.341(3) & .344)<br>(1-2 years if offense committed w/in 5 years of previous offense) (TC §521.251(d)) |
| DWI w/child passenger (§49.045) | Not probated: 90 days to one year (TC §521.344)<br>Offender under 21 and not probated: one year (TC §521.342(a)(1) & .344)<br>Offender under 21 and probated: 90 days if ignition interlock made condition of CS; (TC §521.342(b)); one year if interlock not condition of CS (CCP 42.12, §13(n)) |
| Driving with suspended license | One year or same as prev. suspension (TC §§521.343(c), .292, .& 293(b)) |
| Evading arrest using vehicle (§38.04) | One year (TC §§521.341(2) & .343) |
| Failure to pay fine in JP or muni court by juvenile (CCP art. 49.050(c)(2)) | Period juvenile remains in contempt of court for failure to pay (TC §521.3451(b)) |
| Fictitious plates, registration, inspection | 180 days (TC §521.3465) |
| Fleeing/eluding (TC §545.421) | 90 days (TC §§521.292(a)(9) & .293) |
| Failure to stop & render aid (TC §550.021) | One year (TC §§521.341(6) & .343) |
| Graffiti (§28.08) | One year (TC §521.320) (discretionary with the court)<br>Juvenile offenders: up to one year for first offense; one year for subsequent offense (FC §54.042(d), TC §521.345(a)(1)) |
| Habitual violator of license regulations (4+ convictions in 12 months or 7+ in 24) | 90 days to one year (TC §§521.292 & .293) |
| Human trafficking by juvenile (FC §54.042(a)(1)(B)) | One year (FC §54.042(c); TC §521.345) |
| Intoxication assault using vehicle (§49.07) | 1st offense: 90 days to one year (TC §§521.341(4) & .344(a)(2)(A))<br>2nd or subsequent offense w/in 5 years: one year (TC §521.344(a))<br>Offender under 21 and not probated: one year (TC §521.342(b) & .344)<br>Offender under 21 and probated: 90 days if ignition interlock made condition of CS; (TC §521.342(b)); one year if interlock not condition of CS (CCP 42.12, §13(n)) |
| Intoxication manslaughter (§49.08) | 180 days to two years (TC §521.341(3) & .344(b))<br>Offender under 21 and not probated: one year (TC §521.342(b) & .344)<br>Offender under 21 and probated: 90 days if ignition interlock made condition of CS; (TC §521.342(b)); one year if interlock not condition of CS (CCP 42.12, §13(n)) |
| Manslaughter (§19.04) | One year (TC §§521.341(8) & .343) |
| Marijuana/cont. sub. possession | 180 days (TC §521.372) |
| Motor vehicle felonies | One year (TC §§521.341(5) & .343) |
| Purchasing alcohol for or furnishing alcohol to minor (ABC §106.06) | 180 days or one year (TC §521.351) |
| Racing (TC §545.420(a)) | One year plus 10 hours of community service<br>Offenders under 18: one year plus 10 hours of community service (TC §521.350(d)) |
| Registered sex offenders who fail to apply for DL (CCP art. 62.060) | One year (TC §§521.348 & .343) |
| Tampering with gov't records (§37.10) | One year (TC §§521.3466 & .343) |
| Theft of motor fuel (§31.03) | 180 days or one year (TC §521.349; finding required under CCP art. 42.019) |

## CONSEQUENCES OF ALR HEARINGS[3]

Because of events that take place during ALR hearings, prosecutors often face claims of double jeopardy and collateral estoppel in their later DWI prosecutions. These claims will fail, for reasons detailed in the cases discussed in this chapter. The larger significance of ALR hearings is that the defendant gets free discovery of the facts of the case, and your officer will probably testify at the hearing. The prosecutor *must* get audio tape of the hearing or a copy of the transcript from the ALR hearing to make sure the officer's testimony at the hearing and his later testimony at the DWI trial will be consistent.

**TIP**

Always get audio tape of the hearing or a copy of the transcript from an ALR hearing. The defense will.

## DOUBLE JEOPARDY

ALR hearings and any suspensions or other consequences that arise from them do not constitute punishment, and similarly, any finding in the defendant's favor at an ALR proceeding will not bar the State under double jeopardy from trying the defendant for DWI.[4]

**Transportation Code §724.048. Relationship of Administrative Proceeding to Criminal Proceeding**

(a) The determination of the department or administrative law judge:

(1) is a civil matter;

(2) is independent of and is not an estoppel as to any matter in issue in an adjudication of a criminal charge arising from the occurrence that is the basis for the suspension or denial; and

(3) does not preclude litigation of the same or similar facts in a criminal prosecution....

In *Tharp*, the defendant agreed to a breath test at the time of his arrest. The test showed an alcohol concentration level of at least 0.10. After his license was suspended by DPS, the defendant filed a pretrial application for writ of habeas corpus, arguing that prosecuting him for DWI violated double jeopardy because that would subject him to two punishments. The Court of Criminal Appeals rejected that contention, holding that whether a consequence is a "punishment" can't be considered from the defendant's perspective alone. The *Tharp* court ruled that the deterrent effect a license revocation may have on the impaired driver is "merely incidental to the overriding purpose of protecting the public's safety."[5]

> The primary purpose of the administrative license suspension statute is not to deter the licensee or seek retribution, but is to protect the public from the carnage on the public roads of Texas caused by drunk drivers. This primary purpose is clearly remedial, although it also has a secondary deterrent effect on motorists who realize that an arrest for driving while intoxicated may well result in suspension of their licenses.[6]

Whether the defendant agreed to a breath test (as was the case in *Tharp*) or not will not impact the double jeopardy analysis.[7] The courts reason that when the ALR sus-

---

3 For more information on license suspensions and reinstatement requirements, see the Department of Public Safety's website at **www.txdps.state.tx.us.**

4 TEX. TRANS. CODE §724.048; *Tharp v. State*, 935 S.W.2d 157 (Tex. Crim. App. 1996).

5 *Tharp*, 935 S.W.2d at 161.

6 *Tharp*, 935 S.W.2d at 159.

7 *Ex parte Anthony*, 931 S.W.2d 664 (Tex. App. — Dallas 1996, pet. ref'd); *Ex parte Williamson*, 924 S.W.2d 414 (Tex. App. — San Antonio 1996, pet. ref'd); *Ex parte Vasquez*, 918 S.W.2d 73 (Tex. App. — Fort Worth 1996, no pet.).

pension is based on a breath test refusal, the "same elements" test from *Blockburger*[8] is not met, so double jeopardy does not bar a later DWI prosecution. At an ALR hearing, the government must prove that the defendant had the opportunity to submit to a breath test and refused. This is different than the elements of DWI, where the State must prove that the defendant drove a motor vehicle while intoxicated.[9] Texas courts have also held that DWI is not a lesser-included offense of having your license suspended, eliminating this argument as a potential bar for subsequent prosecution.[10]

## COLLATERAL ESTOPPEL

A district or county attorney and the Department of Public Safety are not the same party for purposes of collateral estoppel, so a prosecutor is not precluded from litigating the issue of probable cause even after an administrative judge finds no probable cause for a stop.[11] "The legislature did not intend that a decision made in a civil, administrative, remedial license suspension hearing could be used to bar the state from prosecuting drunk drivers."[12]

Courts have found that ALR judges' denials of license suspensions based on the following reasons do not bar later DWI prosecutions:

- No reasonable suspicion.[13]
- No "operating a motor vehicle."[14]
- No probable cause.[15]

One other reason collateral estoppel does not bar prosecution following an ALR ruling is that probable cause determinations at ALR hearings are made on the basis of the information available at the time of arrest and often don't consider facts that come to light after arrest, including whether the defendant refused to give a specimen at the police station.[16]

---

8 *Blockburger v. U.S.*, 284 U.S. 299, 52 S.Ct. 180, 76 L.Ed.2d 306 (1932) (when the same act violates two statutes, courts must determine whether there are two separate offenses by evaluating whether each requires proof of a fact that the other does not).

9 See *Johnson v. State*, 920 S.W.2d 692 (Tex. App. — Houston [1st Dist.] 1996, pet. ref'd).

10 *Ex parte Gee*, 926 S.W.2d 615 (Tex. App. — Houston [1st Dist.] 1996, pet. ref'd).

11 *Reynolds v. State*, 4 S.W.3d 13 (Tex. Crim. App. 1999) (decided under current version of ALR statute); *State v. Brabson*, 966 S.W.2d 493 (Tex. Crim. App. 1998) (decided under former version of ALR statute); *Ex parte Dunlap*, 963 S.W.2d 954 (Tex. App. — Fort Worth 1998, no pet.); *State v. Anderson*, 974 S.W.2d 193 (Tex. App. — San Antonio 1998, no pet.); *Ex parte Richards*, 968 S.W.2d 567 (Tex. App. — Corpus Christi 1998, pet. ref'd).

12 *Ex parte Serna*, 957 S.W.2d 598 (Tex. App. — Fort Worth 1997, pet. ref'd).

13 *Headrick v. State*, 988 S.W.2d 226 (Tex. Crim. App. 1999); *Ex parte McFall*, 939 S.W.2d 799 (Tex. App. — Fort Worth 1997, no pet.) (no bar—either on collateral estoppel or double jeopardy grounds—from later prosecuting the defendant).

14 *Church v. State*, 942 S.W.2d 139 (Tex. App. — Houston [1st Dist.] 1997, pet. ref'd).

15 *Todd v. State*, 956 S.W.2d 777 (Tex. App. — Waco 1997, pet. ref'd) (license suspension is not "punishment").

16 *Ex parte Ayers*, 921 S.W.2d 438 (Tex. App. — Houston [1st Dist.] 1996, no pet.), citing *Neaves v. State*, 767 S.W.2d 784 (Tex. Crim. App. 1989); see also *Holmberg v. State*, 931 S.W.2d 3 (Tex. App. — Houston [1st Dist.] 1996, pet. ref'd).

## OCCUPATIONAL LICENSE[17]

Any discussion of ALR necessarily leads to a discussion of occupational licenses. Whenever a driver has her license suspended, a natural next step is for the driver to try to find some other legal way to drive. An occupational license is a special restricted license issued to people whose drivers licenses have been suspended or revoked for offenses including DWI. An occupational license authorizes the driver to operate a non-commercial motor vehicle in connection with his job, for educational purposes, or in performing essential household duties. Requests for the licenses must be made to the county or district court in the county of the licensee's residence or to the court of original jurisdiction where the offense occurred.[18] **[See Table 4-3 for sample pleadings and orders relating to occupational licenses through bond conditions.]**

A court order granting an occupational license is not the same thing as the occupational license itself. The driver must submit the court order and all other required items to DPS so that it can issue an occupational license. The court order may be used as a license for 30 days from the date of the judge's signature while DPS processes the occupational license. There are no occupational or essential needs licenses available to operate a commercial motor vehicle.[19]

The requirements for an occupational license are:

- a certified copy of the petition and court order granting the occupational license;
- an original pink SR-22 certificate of insurance;
- a $10 license fee for a one-year license or less (the maximum length of issuance is a two-year license for $20, provided the court order grants this length of time);
- a $100 statutory reinstatement fee for the safety responsibility suspension, if required;
- a $100 statutory reinstatement fee for the driver improvement suspension, if required;
- a $125 statutory reinstatement fee for the administrative license revocation, if required; and
- an SR-37 form to type the occupational license.[20]

---

17 See **www.txdps.state.tx.us/administration/driver_licensing_control/faq/faq.htm** for more information from DPS's official website about restricted licenses.

18 TEX. TRANS. CODE §521.242; 37 TEX. ADMIN. CODE 15.7.

19 TEX. TRANS. CODE §§522.086, 522.089.

20 See **www.txdps.state.tx.us/administration/driver_licensing_control/faq/faq.htm**

All required reinstatement fees must be paid before DPS can issue the occupational license.[21] **Table 4-2** (on the next page) depicts when a defendant is eligible to apply for and receive an occupational drivers license following a conviction for DWI. The flow charts are divided between defendants under 21 years of age and over 21 at the time they commit the offense.

The flow chart is set up to be used in conjunction with a Texas drivers license printout or drivers license "certified packet" from DPS in Austin. By answering a few preliminary questions about the case, you can follow the appropriate path to determine whether the defendant can apply for an occupational license. The relevant sections of the Transportation Code and Code of Criminal Procedure are provided.

---

21 37 Tex. Admin. Code 15.7.

## Eligibility for Occupational Driver's Licenses Over 21

**Looking at the Δ's Driving Record, is this the Δ's FIRST contact with ALR/DWI activity?**

YES

Δ can get an occupational license without waiting, following the effective date of suspension. §521.251(a). The suspension time from the current ALR period can be applied to the current DWI post-conviction suspension. §521.344(c)

NO

From the arrest date on the current case, go back 5years. Does Δ have any alcohol / drug-related contacts OR any final convictions for DWI?

NO

Δ can get an occupational license without waiting, following the effective date of suspension. §521.251(a). BUT, if Δ has a prior conviction for DWI at any time in their history, then the suspension time from the current ALR suspension cannot be applied to the current DWI post conviction suspension. §521.344(c)(1).

YES

If the jury did not recommend to suspend the driver's license as part of the final conviction, you have to treat the conviction as an alcohol / drug related contact for occupational license purposes.

Not Suspended

Prior ALR Suspension &/ DWI Final Conviction where DL not Suspended

The occupational is allowed on the 91st day following the effective date of suspension. §521.251(b). If the Δ does not have a DWI at any time in their history, then the current ALR period can be applied to the current DWI post-conviction suspension. §521.344(c). If the Δ has a prior DWI conviction, then the current ALR suspension cannot be applied to the current post-conviction suspension. §521.344(c)(1).

Suspended

Final DWI Conviction where DL Suspended

The occupational is allowed on the 181st day following the effective date of suspension. §521.251(c). The suspension time from the current ALR suspension cannot be applied to the current DWI post-conviction suspension. §521.344(c)(1). BUT, if the current suspension is for a second conviction for DWI, Intox. Assault, or Intox. Manslaughter, then the effective date for the occupational is 1 year from date of suspension. §521.251(d).

**Key Terms to Know**

"Alcohol or Drug Related Contact"

- DWI conviction from any state
- a Breath/Blood refusal
- being over the legal alcohol concentration. §524.001.

"Effective Date of Suspension"

- can be anywhere between date of conviction until 30 days thereafter. §521.344(a)(1)
- driver's license suspension

### Eligibility for Occupational License Under 21

Defendant cannot get an occupational license for the first 30 days of a suspension for failure of a breath test. Section 524.022(d)(1). If they fail a breath test and they've had one prior conviction of an offense under Section 106.041 ABC code or an offense under Section 49.04, 49.07 or 49.08, Penal Code, they cannot get an **occupational for the first 90 days of the suspension. Section 524.022(d)(2). If they fail a breath test and they've had two or more prior convictions for offenses listed above, the maximum suspension is 180 days and they cannot get an occupational for the entire suspension period. Section 524.022(d)(3).**

## Pretrial Discovery[22]

In 2013, for the first time in decades, the Texas Legislature made significant changes to criminal discovery in Code of Criminal Procedure Article 39.14 via SB 1611, also known as the Michael Morton Act. These changes apply to the prosecution of every criminal offense committed on or after January 1, 2014. Some of the highlights of the changes include:

- mandatory open-file discovery in subsection (a);
- duties for the defense team in subsection (f); and
- codification of *Brady* duties.

In Article 39.14(a), the State must permit "the electronic duplication, copying, and photographing" of evidence and information in its possession, including offense reports, written or recorded witness statements, and pretty much anything else not privileged or considered work product of the State. On paper, the big change is mandatory open-file discovery of offense reports and witness statements (subject to some restrictions discussed in greater detail below). That has long been the practice in most jurisdictions, but now it is mandated.

Note that on its face, subsection (a) mandates three different types of disclosure—electronic duplication, copying, and photographing—which is rather absurd if taken literally. It is also inconsistent with other provisions of the amended statute, including another sentence of this amended subsection that expressly states, "The state may provide to the defendant electronic duplicates of any documents or other information described by this article" That qualifier is unnecessary if the discovery-in-triplicate language is mandatory. How this conflict will be resolved if a defendant insists upon discovery in a particular format—or in all three formats—remains to be seen.

Article 39.14(f) authorizes the attorney for the defendant, or an investigator, expert, consulting legal counsel, or agent of that attorney—but not the defendant—to allow a defendant, witness, or prospective witness to view information provided by the state under this article, but it does not allow that defendant or witness to have a copy of the information (unless it is that person's own statement). Before allowing any viewing, a member of the defense team must redact the listed identifying information, including addresses and phone numbers. How this is to be accomplished, regulated, or enforced is left to the courts.

---

22 This section adapted from materials previously published in *Legislative Update 2013–2015* and *Legislative Update 2015–2017* by Shannon Edmonds (TDCAA © 2013, 2015).

Articl 39.14(g) codifies a *Brady*-derived rule requiring the state to disclose to the defense "any exculpatory, impeachment, or mitigating document, item, or information in the possession, custody, or control of the state that tends to negate the guilt of the defendant or would tend to reduce the punishment for the offense charged." Note that neither materiality nor admissibility are involved in the determination of what should be turned over to the defense.

Under Article 39.14(j), before accepting a plea of guilty or no contest, or at some point before trial, both the state and the defense must acknowledge in writing or on the record in open court the disclosure and receipt of all documents, items, and information provided by the state to the defense under this article.

In the Michael Morton Act, the legislature left the provisions of the law relating to expert witnesses relatively unchanged. This left those reciprocal discovery rules on experts out of step with many other provisions of this article, so in 2015, HB 510 updated Article 39.14(b) on expert witness discovery. These changes apply to the discovery of experts in the trial of an offense committed on or after September 1, 2015; the offense date, not the date of the proceeding, is the trigger for this procedural change. **[See more on discovery of expert witnesses later in this chapter.]**

**CCP art. 39.14(b). Discovery**

*amended effective Sept. 1, 2015 (HB 510, §1)*

(b) On [~~motion of~~] a party's request made not later than the 30th day before the date that jury selection in the trial is scheduled to begin or, in a trial without a jury, the presentation of evidence is scheduled to begin, the party receiving the request shall [~~party and on notice to the other parties, the court in which an action is pending may order one or more of the other parties to~~] disclose to the requesting party [~~making the motion~~] the name and address of each person the disclosing [~~other~~] party may use at trial to present evidence under Rules 702, 703, and 705, Texas Rules of Evidence. Except as otherwise provided by this subsection, the disclosure must be made in writing in hard copy form or by electronic means [~~The court shall specify in the order the time and manner in which the other party must make the disclosure to the moving party, but in specifying the time in which the other party shall make disclosure the court shall require the other party to make the disclosure~~] not later than the 20th day before the date that jury selection in the trial is scheduled to begin or, in a trial without a jury, the presentation of evidence is scheduled to begin. On motion of a party and on notice to the other parties, the court may order an earlier time at which one or more of the other parties must make the disclosure to the requesting party [~~begins~~].

## OPEN RECORDS/PUBLIC INFORMATION ACT

Texas' Open Records Act (now called the "Public Information Act") is sometimes used as a potential discovery tool by the defense bar. In *Holmes v. Morales*,[23] the Texas Supreme Court held that Tex. Gov't Code §552.108, which deals with prosecution and law enforcement files, excepted virtually all of a prosecutor's files from open records request. However, in 1997, the Texas Legislature amended §552.108 to open those files except for: (1) information that would interfere with the "detection, investigation, or prosecution of crime," (2) information relating to cases that did not result in a conviction or deferred adjudication, and (3) work product. The Legislature did

23 *Holmes v. Morales*, 924 S.W.2d 920, 925 (Tex. 1996).

not, however, amend §552.103, which excepts information relating to criminal litigation and defines the timeframe in a criminal case as "until the applicable statute of limitations has expired or until the defendant has exhausted all appellate and post-conviction remedies in state and federal court." **[For further information on information that is excepted from disclosure under the Public Information Act, see TEX. GOV'T CODE ch. 552 and *Public Information Handbook*, published by the Attorney General's Office.]**

A governmental entity has 10 days to request an Attorney General's opinion concerning a Public Information Act (PIA) request or all records are considered "open."[24] The most common reason a prosecutor will not have to disclose information under the PIA is that it is work product. Further, an agency does not have to turn over records not maintained by its office.

### DUE PROCESS AND *BRADY*

Despite the limited nature of discovery in Texas, the due process of the Fourteenth Amendment of the U.S. Constitution absolutely requires disclosure of material evidence favorable to the defendant even without a request.[25] Exculpatory evidence and impeachment evidence are both considered evidence "favorable" to the defendant.[26] Note, however, that a defendant's right to discovery is broader under Article 39.14(g), under which neither materiality nor admissibility are involved in the determination of what should be turned over to the defense.

**[For more information on *Brady* evidence required to be disclosed, see *Brady Duties & the Pretrial Disclosure of Evidence* by Edward Wilkinson (TDCAA © 2009).]**

## Special Bond Conditions

A hearing at which pretrial bond conditions will be set presents prosecutors a critical opportunity to have a role in protecting the community from repeat incidents by a defendant charged with DWI. With appellate courts and the legislature giving trial judges more flexibility to tailor bond conditions to the defendant's circumstances—and to take the community's safety into consideration—prosecutors should not miss the opportunity to be a part of these pretrial proceedings.

In 1998, the Fort Worth court of appeals ruled that a trial judge only had discretion to impose conditions on a defendant's pretrial bond that were specifically authorized by statute.[27] The following year, the Legislature "vetoed" this ruling by enacting Article 17.40, which allows a judge to impose conditions that protect the victim or community. **[See Table 4-3 for sample pleadings and orders relating to special conditions while a defendant is on bond charged with DWI.]**

---

24 TEX. GOV'T CODE §§552.302(a), 552.302.

25 See *Kyles v. Whitley*, 514 U.S. 419, 115 S.Ct. 1555, 131 L.Ed.2d 490 (1995); *U.S. v. Bagley*, 473 U.S. 667, 680, 105 S.Ct. 3375, 87 L.Ed.2d 481 (1985); *Ex parte Mowbray*, 943 S.W.2d 461, 466 (Tex. Crim. App. 1996) (holding State has affirmative duty to disclose favorable evidence).

26 *Bagley*, 473 U.S. at 676.

27 *Ex parte Tucker*, 977 S.W.2d 713 (Tex. App. — Fort Worth 1998), *pet. ref'd*, 3 S.W.3d 576 (Tex. Crim. App. 1999).

Apart from the authority in Article 17.40, however, the Legislature has enacted statutes that allow judges to impose bond conditions unique to intoxication crimes, including mandatory interlock devices and restrictions on drivers licenses.

**CCP Art. 17.40. Conditions Related to Victim or Community Safety**

(a) To secure a defendant's attendance at trial, a magistrate may impose any reasonable condition of bond related to the safety of a victim of the alleged offense or to the safety of the community.

(b) At a hearing limited to determining whether the defendant violated a condition of bond imposed under Subsection (a), the magistrate may revoke the defendant's bond only if the magistrate finds by a preponderance of the evidence that the violation occurred. If the magistrate finds that the violation occurred, the magistrate shall revoke the defendant's bond and order that the defendant be immediately returned to custody. Once the defendant is placed in custody, the revocation of the defendant's bond discharges the sureties on the bond, if any, from any future liability on the bond. A discharge under this subsection from any future liability on the bond does not discharge any surety from liability for previous forfeitures on the bond.

## INTERLOCK DEVICES

Code of Criminal Procedure Article 17.441 allows courts to require as a pretrial bond condition that a defendant charged with a subsequent DWI offense have an ignition interlock device placed on her car. The constitutionality of this statute was upheld in *Ex parte Elliott*.[28]

An ignition interlock device is a breath alcohol analyzer that is connected to a motor vehicle ignition. In order to start the car, the driver must blow a breath sample into the analyzer, which measures alcohol concentration. If the alcohol concentration exceeds the startup set point on the interlock device, the engine will not start.[29]

A restricted interlock license from DPS authorizes the person to operate only a motor vehicle equipped with an ignition interlock device. Once DPS receives notice from a court that a person must drive with an interlock device, DPS sends notice that the drivers license expires on the 30th day after the date of the notice.[30] The interlock is required until DPS receives a court order removing the restriction.[31]

Effective Sept. 1, 2015, the Texas legislature made changes relating to the ability of a defendant convicted under §49.04 to obtain an occupational license. What was once a discretionary provision that the offender have an interlock device as a condition to getting an occupational license is now mandatory under Transportation Code §521.251. Under §521.244, a person who is restricted to operating a motor vehicle equipped with an ignition interlock device is entitled to receive an occupational license without a finding that that person has an essential need, as long as the person shows: (1) evidence of financial responsibility under Transportation Code Chapter 601; and (2) proof that the person has had an ignition interlock device installed on each vehicle the person owns or operates. The SR-22 requirement for a post-conviction occupational license has also been dropped in the amended version of §521.248 of the Transportation Code, along with the requirement that the occupational license contain time, purpose, and location restrictions.

**CCP Art. 17.441. Conditions Requiring Motor Vehicle Ignition Interlock**

(a) Except as provided by Subsection (b), a magistrate shall require on release that a defendant charged with a subsequent offense under Sections 49.04-49.06, Penal Code, or an offense under Section 49.07 or 49.08 of that code:

(1) have installed on the motor vehicle owned by the defendant or on the vehicle most regularly driven by the defendant, a device that uses a deep-lung breath analysis mechanism to make impractical the operation of a motor vehicle if ethyl alcohol is detected in the breath of the operator; and

(2) not operate any motor vehicle unless the vehicle is equipped with that device.

(b) The magistrate may not require the installation of the device if the magistrate finds that to require the device would not be in the best interest of justice.

(c) If the defendant is required to have the device installed, the magistrate shall require that the defendant have the device installed on the appropriate motor vehicle, at the defendant's expense, before the 30th day after the date the defendant is released on bond.

---

28 *Ex parte Elliott*, 950 S.W.2d 714 (Tex. App. — Fort Worth 1997, pet. ref'd).

29 37 Tex. Admin. Code 15.7.

30 Tex. Trans. Code §521.2465.

31 Tex. Trans. Code §521.2465.

(d) The magistrate may designate an appropriate agency to verify the installation of the device and to monitor the device. If the magistrate designates an agency under this subsection, in each month during which the agency verifies the installation of the device or provides a monitoring service the defendant shall pay a fee to the designated agency in the amount set by the magistrate. The defendant shall pay the initial fee at the time the agency verifies the installation of the device. In each subsequent month during which the defendant is required to pay a fee the defendant shall pay the fee on the first occasion in that month that the agency provides a monitoring service. The magistrate shall set the fee in an amount not to exceed $10 as determined by the county auditor, or by the commissioners court of the county if the county does not have a county auditor, to be sufficient to cover the cost incurred by the designated agency in conducting the verification or providing the monitoring service, as applicable in that county.

### Tex. Trans. Code §521.244. Hearing; Order; Determination of Essential Need

(a) The judge who hears the petition shall sign an order finding whether an essential need exists.

(b) In determining whether an essential need exists, the judge shall consider:

(1) the petitioner's driving record; and

(2) any evidence presented by a person under Section 521.243(b).

(c) If the judge finds that there is an essential need, the judge also, as part of the order, shall:

(1) determine the actual need of the petitioner to operate a motor vehicle; and

(2) require the petitioner to provide evidence of financial responsibility in accordance with Chapter 601.

(d) Except as provided by Section 521.243(b), the hearing on the petition may be ex parte.

(e) A person convicted of an offense under Sections 49.04-49.08, Penal Code, who is restricted to the operation of a motor vehicle equipped with an ignition interlock device is entitled to receive an occupational license without a finding that an essential need exists for that person, provided that the person shows:

(1) evidence of financial responsibility under Chapter 601; and

(2) proof the person has had an ignition interlock device installed on each motor vehicle owned or operated by the person.

Amended effective Sept. 1, 2015 (HB 2246, §5). Section 10 of HB 2246 provides: "The change in law made by this Act applies only to a person whose driver's license is suspended on or after the effective date of this Act, regardless of whether the underlying incident giving rise to the suspension occurred before, on, or after that date."

### Tex. Trans. Code §521.246. Ignition Interlock Device Requirement

(a) If the person's license has been suspended after a conviction of an offense under Sections 49.04-49.08 [~~Section 49.04, 49.07, or 49.08~~], Penal Code, the judge[~~, before signing an order,~~] shall [~~determine from the criminal history record information maintained by the department whether the person has any previous conviction under those laws.~~]

[~~(b) As part of the order the judge may~~] restrict the person to the operation of a motor vehicle equipped with an ignition interlock device [~~if the judge determines that the person's license has been suspended following a conviction under Section 49.04, 49.07, or 49.08, Penal Code. As part of the order, the judge shall restrict the person to the operation of a motor vehicle equipped with an ignition interlock device if the judge determines that:~~]

[~~(1) the person has two or more convictions under any combination of Section 49.04, 49.07, or 49.08, Penal Code; or~~]

[~~(2) the person's license has been suspended after a conviction under Section 49.04, Penal Code, for which the person has been punished under Section 49.09, Penal Code~~].

(c) The person shall obtain the ignition interlock device at the person's own expense unless the court finds that to do so is not in the best interest of justice and enters that finding in the record. If the court determines that the person is unable to pay for the device, the court may impose a reasonable payment schedule for a term not to exceed twice the period of the court's order.

(d) The court shall order the ignition interlock device to remain installed for the duration of the period of suspension [~~at least half of the period of supervision~~].

(e) A person to whom this section applies may operate a motor vehicle without the installation of an approved ignition interlock device if:

(1) the person is required to operate a motor vehicle in the course and scope of the person's employment;

(2) the vehicle is owned by the person's employer;

(3) the employer is not owned or controlled by the person whose driving privilege is restricted;

(4) the employer is notified of the driving privilege restriction; and

(5) proof of that notification is with the vehicle.

(f) A previous conviction may not be used for purposes of restricting a person to the operation of a motor vehicle equipped with an interlock ignition device under this section if:

(1) the previous conviction was a final conviction for an offense under Sections 49.04-49.08 [~~Section 49.04, 49.07, or 49.08~~], Penal Code, and was for an offense committed more than 10 years before the instant offense for which the person was convicted; and

(2) the person has not been convicted of an offense under Sections 49.04-49.08 [~~Section 49.04, 49.07, or 49.08~~] of that code committed within 10 years before the date on which the instant offense for which the person was convicted.

Amended effective Sept. 1, 2015 (HB 2246, §6). See effective note following §521.244.

### Tex. Trans. Code §521.248. Order Requirements

(a) An order granting an occupational license must specify:

(1) the hours of the day and days of the week during which the person may operate a motor vehicle;

(2) the reasons for which the person may operate a motor vehicle;

(3) areas or routes of travel permitted;

(4) that the person is restricted to the operation of a motor vehicle equipped with an ignition interlock device, if applicable; and

(5) that the person must submit to periodic testing for alcohol or controlled substances, if applicable.

(b) The person may not operate a motor vehicle for more than four hours in any 24-hour period, except that on a showing of necessity the court may allow the person to drive for any period determined by the court that does not exceed 12 hours in any 24-hour period.

(c) An order granting an occupational license remains valid until the end of the period of suspension of the person's regular driver's license.

(d) A person who is restricted to the operation of a motor vehicle equipped with an ignition interlock device may not be subject to any time of travel, reason for travel, or location of travel restrictions described by Subsection (a)(1), (2), or (3) or (b).

Amended effective Sept. 1, 2015 (HB 2246, §8). See effective note following §521.244.

---

### Tex. Trans. Code §521.251. Effective Date of Occupational License

(a) If a person's license is suspended under Chapter 524 or 724 and the person has not had a prior suspension arising from an alcohol-related or drug-related enforcement contact in the five years preceding the date of the person's arrest, an order under this subchapter granting the person an occupational license takes effect immediately. However, the court shall order the person to comply with the counseling and rehabilitation program required under Section 521.245.

(b) If the person's driver's license has been suspended as a result of an alcohol-related or drug-related enforcement contact during the five years preceding the date of the person's arrest, the order may not take effect before the 91st day after the effective date of the suspension.

(c) If the person's driver's license has been suspended as a result of a conviction of an offense under Sections 49.04-49.08 [~~Section 49.04, 49.07, or 49.08~~], Penal Code, during the five years preceding the date of the person's arrest, the order may not take effect before the 181st day after the effective date of the suspension.

(d) Notwithstanding any other provision in this section, if the person's driver's license has been suspended as a result of a second or subsequent conviction under Sections 49.04-49.08 [~~Section 49.04, 49.07, or 49.08~~], Penal Code, committed within five years of the date on which the most recent preceding offense was committed, an order granting the person an occupational license may not take effect before the first anniversary of the effective date of the suspension.

(d-1) Notwithstanding Subsections (b), (c), and (d), the court may issue an occupational license to a person if the person submits proof the person has an ignition interlock device installed on each motor vehicle owned or operated by the person. If a person issued an occupational license under this subsection fails to maintain an installed ignition interlock device on each motor vehicle owned or operated by the person, the court shall revoke the occupational license under Section 521.252 and reinstate the suspension of the person's driver's license. A person granted an occupational license under this subsection may not be ordered to submit to the supervision of the local community supervision and corrections department under Section 521.2462, unless the order is entered by a court of record.

(e) For the purposes of this section, "alcohol-related or drug-related enforcement contact" has the meaning assigned by Section 524.001.

Amended effective Sept. 1, 2015 (HB 2246, §9). See effective note following §521.244.

**TABLE 4-3: Bond Condition Pleadings & Order**

Cause No. ____________________

| | | |
|---|---|---|
| THE STATE OF TEXAS | § | IN THE ______________ |
| VS. | § | COURT ______________ |
| ____________________ | § | ______ COUNTY, TEXAS |

**STATE'S MOTION TO RAISE AND/OR SET SPECIAL CONDITIONS ON BOND**

NOW COMES THE STATE OF TEXAS by and through ____________, her Criminal District Attorney, and moves this Court to order that the Defendant's bond be raised to $____________ or that in the alternative the following conditions be attached to any bond set on the above referenced Defendant's case:

**I.**

1) That the Defendant not consume any alcoholic beverage.

2) That the Defendant not be allowed to drive or operate any motor vehicle

**OR**

That the Defendant not be allowed to drive or operate any motor-vehicle unless said vehicle is equipped with a device that uses a deep-lung breath analysis mechanism to make impractical the operation of a motor vehicle if ethyl alcohol is detected in the breath of the operator.

That the Defendant's driving, if any is allowed, be restricted to that which is necessary to get him to and from work and that under no condition is he/she allowed to drive between the hours of _________p.m. and ________ a.m.

3) That the Defendant be ordered to undergo Voice Alcohol Radio Frequency Electronic Monitoring to ensure that he is not consuming alcohol in violation of his bond conditions.

4) That the Defendant is ordered to wear a SCRAM device.*

Any other conditions that the Court deems appropriate and necessary to ensure the safety of our community.

In support thereof the State would show the following:

**II.**

*(List all aggravating details of this defendant of this case, including any prior offenses. If no priors refer to the aggravating facts of the case, at a minimum someone was killed, mention B.A.C. level if known, etc....)*

**III.**

Pursuant to Article 17.15, §5, of the Texas Code of Criminal Procedure the amount of bond set should take into account "[t]he future safety ... of the community." The State would contend that the release of this Defendant without said conditions would create a serious risk of harm to other members of the Community.

WHEREFORE PREMISES CONSIDERED the State would respectfully pray that this Honorable Court set each of the above noted conditions on each and every bond concerning this Defendant and any charges pending on this Defendant.

Respectfully Submitted,

______________________________

CRIMINAL DISTRICT ATTORNEY

______________________________

Assistant Criminal District Attorney

* The Secure Continuous Remote Alcohol Monitor (SCRAM) is worn around the ankle and has sensors that are set to measure perspiration for traces of alcohol every hour or every 30 minutes. Test results can be downloaded to a modem each day and the results are then provided to the court or to the probation officers to view.

Cause No. ____________________

| | | |
|---|---|---|
| THE STATE OF TEXAS | § | IN THE ______________ |
| VS. | § | COURT ______________ |
| ____________________ | § | ______ COUNTY, TEXAS |

**ORDER**

The State's Motion to Raise and/or Set Special Conditions on Bond is hereby:

_____ Granted as to Condition 1.

_____ Granted as to Condition 2.

_____ Granted as to Condition 3.

_____ Granted as to Condition 4.

_____ And I further add the following additional Bond Conditions:

______________________________________________________________________

______________________________________________________________________

______________________________________________________________________

______________________________________________________________________

______________________________________________________________________

______________________________________________________________________

____________________________________

Judge Presiding

**TABLE 4-4: Interlock Bond Pleadings & Order**

Cause No. ____________________

| | | |
|---|---|---|
| THE STATE OF TEXAS | § | IN THE ______________ |
| VS. | § | COURT ______________ |
| ____________________ | § | ______ COUNTY, TEXAS |

**STATE'S MOTION TO SET MANDATORY INTERLOCK BOND CONDITIONS**

NOW COMES THE STATE OF TEXAS by and through her Criminal District Attorney, and moves this Court to order that a condition of the Defendant's bond be that:

**I.**

He/she have installed on the motor vehicle owned by said Defendant or on the vehicle most regularly driven by said Defendant, a device that uses a deep-lung breath analysis mechanism to make impractical the operation of a motor vehicle if ethyl alcohol is detected in the breath of the operator, and

**II.**

That said Defendant not operate any motor vehicle unless the vehicle is equipped with a device that uses a deep-lung breath analysis mechanism to make impractical the operation of a motor vehicle if ethyl alcohol is detected in the breath of the operator.

In support thereof the State would show the following:

**III.**

This Defendant is currently charged with a subsequent offense under Sections 49.04–49.06 or with an offense under Section (49.07/49.08) of the Texas Penal Code. See Appendix A. (A copy of the felony information/indictment)

**IV.**

Pursuant to Article 17.441 of the Texas Code of Criminal Procedure condition "I" above is required unless a magistrate finds that to require the device would not be in the best interest of justice and condition "II" is required without exception.

**V.**

The above mentioned device is to be installed before the 30th day after the date the Defendant is released on bond. It has been 30 days since the Defendant was released and no verification that said device was installed has been provided to the Court.

**VI.**

The State would further request that the (Place the name of the monitoring Agency used in your County here, i.e. Probation Department, Pre-Trial Release,....) be ordered to monitor the installation and use of said device.

WHEREFORE PREMISES CONSIDERED the State would respectfully pray that this Honorable Court set each of the above noted conditions on this Defendant Bond.

Respectfully Submitted,

____________________________

CRIMINAL DISTRICT ATTORNEY

____________________________

Assistant Criminal District Attorney

Cause No. ____________________

| | | |
|---|---|---|
| THE STATE OF TEXAS | § | IN THE ______________ |
| VS. | § | COURT _____________ |
| ___________________ | § | ______ COUNTY, TEXAS |

**ORDER**

*The State's Motion to Set Mandatory Interlock Bond Conditions* is hereby:

_____ Granted as to Condition I, and I further order that verification that said device has been installed be delivered to the______________________________ no later than 30 days from the date this order is signed.

_____ Denied as to Condition I, and I further find that to require said device would not be in the "best interest of justice."

_____ Granted as to Condition II.

_____ Denied as to Condition II.

________________________
Judge Presiding

# Pretrial Hearings & Motions to Suppress[32]

Article 28.01 of the Code of Criminal Procedure sets out the proper way to conduct pretrial hearings in state court. Although the trial court may choose to hold a pretrial hearing on any issue raised under Article 28.01 after giving notice to both sides, holding a hearing is not mandatory.[33] The defendant is entitled to 10 days notice after arrest and 10 days after an indictment is served to file any written motions.[34] Attorneys for the defense and the State must be present at the pretrial hearing.[35]

### CCP Art. 28.01. Pre-Trial

**Sec. 1.** The court may set any criminal case for a pre-trial hearing before it is set for trial upon its merits, and direct the defendant and his attorney, if any of record, and the State's attorney, to appear before the court at the time and place stated in the court's order for a conference and hearing. The defendant must be present at the arraignment, and his presence is required during any pre-trial proceeding. The pre-trial hearing shall be to determine any of the following matters:

(1) Arraignment of the defendant, if such be necessary; and appointment of counsel to represent the defendant, if such be necessary;
(2) Pleadings of the defendant;
(3) Special pleas, if any;
(4) Exceptions to the form or substance of the indictment or information;
(5) Motions for continuance either by the State or defendant; provided that grounds for continuance not existing or not known at the time may be presented and considered at any time before the defendant announces ready for trial;
(6) Motions to suppress evidence — When a hearing on the motion to suppress evidence is granted, the court may determine the merits of said motion on the motions themselves, or upon opposing affidavits, or upon oral testimony, subject to the discretion of the court;
(7) Motions for change of venue by the State or the defendant; provided, however, that such motions for change of venue, if overruled at the pre-trial hearing, may be renewed by the State or the defendant during the voir dire examination of the jury;
(8) Discovery;
(9) Entrapment; and
(10) Motion for appointment of interpreter.

**Sec. 2.** When a criminal case is set for such pre-trial hearing, any such preliminary matters not raised or filed seven days before the hearing will not thereafter be allowed to be raised or filed, except by permission of the court for good cause shown; provided that the defendant shall have sufficient notice of such hearing to allow him not less than 10 days in which to raise or file such preliminary matters. The record made at such pre-trial hearing, the rulings of the court and the exceptions and objections thereto shall become a part of the trial record of the case upon its merits.

**Sec. 3.** The notice mentioned in Section 2 above shall be sufficient if given in any one of the following ways:

(1) By announcement made by the court in open court in the presence of the defendant or his attorney of record;
(2) By personal service upon the defendant or his attorney of record;
(3) By mail to either the defendant or his attorney of record deposited by the clerk in the mail at least six days prior to the date set for hearing. If the defendant has no attorney of record

---

32 This section is taken from *Warrantless Search & Seizure* by Diane Beckham (TDCAA © 2015). Pretrial hearings on other matters, including *Jackson v. Denno* hearings on the voluntariness of a defendant's statement, are covered in another TDCAA publication, *The Prosecutor Trial Notebook* by Diane Beckham (TDCAA © 2014).

33 *Bell v. State*, 442 S.W.2d 716 (Tex. Crim. App. 1969).

34 Tex. Code Crim. Proc. arts. 27.11–.12.

35 *Riggall v. State*, 590 S.W.2d 460 (Tex. Crim. App. 1979).

such notice shall be addressed to defendant at the address shown on his bond, if the bond shows such an address, and if not, it may be addressed to one of the sureties on his bond. If the envelope containing the notice is properly addressed, stamped and mailed, the state will not be required to show that it was received.

All pretrial motions to suppress must be filed seven days before the hearing.[36] No motions filed after that can be raised or heard by a court unless the judge gives permission based on a showing of good cause.

Any issues presented in a motion to suppress can also be made at trial, if the judge decides not to hold a pretrial hearing.[37] Section 3 of Article 28.01 provides three different methods for giving notice to the defendant: (1) announcement in open court with the defendant and his attorney present; (2) personal service on the defendant or his attorney; or (3) by mail at least six days before the hearing date. Actual notice of a hearing will also be sufficient under Article 28.01.[38]

## PREPARING FOR MOTIONS TO SUPPRESS

### *Analyze the Motion*

Naturally, a suppression pretrial issue begins with the defendant's motion. A motion to suppress may be boilerplate and generic, or the defense may file a more specific motion setting out the exact state or federal constitutional violation they will allege. In a boilerplate motion, the State will not necessarily be able to identify the defendant's specific legal argument. A boilerplate motion to suppress might argue:

1. the defendant was arrested without a warrant and without probable cause in violation of the Fourth and Fourteenth Amendments;
2. the search in question was therefore illegal and all fruits of the search must be suppressed;
3. if the arrest or search was made through a search or arrest warrant, the affidavit did not allege sufficient facts to establish probable cause; and
4. all written or oral statements made after the defendant's arrest are fruits of the illegal arrest and search and therefore are inadmissible.[39]

If the motion to suppress is generic, the prosecutor should talk to the officer to try to figure out what the specific defense issue might be.

### *State Response*

Once a case appears headed toward trial or a hearing, the prosecutor should make sure she understands the chain of custody on evidence and has certified copies of any search and arrest warrants.

A prosecutor may, of course, file a written response to a motion to suppress, but this is not mandatory. If the prosecutor intends to rely on information developed at the suppression hearing instead, she should bring copies of any cases she will rely on for the defense and the judge.

---

36 TEX. CODE CRIM. PROC. art. 28.01, §2.

37 *Bosley v. State*, 414 S.W.2d 468 (Tex. Crim. App. 1967).

38 *Graham v. State*, 769 S.W.2d 594 (Tex. App. — Corpus Christi 1989, no pet.).

39 See, e.g., sample motion to suppress from McCormick, Blackwell & Blackwell, TEXAS PRACTICE, ch. 54 (West © 2005).

#### *Prepare Officers*

Once a hearing date is set, the prosecutor should subpoena all officers needed to testify at the hearing. Even more important, the prosecutor should talk to any testifying officers beforehand. Figure out the facts and circumstances of the detention, arrest and seizure of any evidence.

Listen carefully to the officers' descriptions of the events and verify their legal theory backing up the search or seizure. Explore with them any other potential exceptions to the warrant requirement that might justify their actions, because the reasonableness of their actions will be viewed under an objective standard in almost all circumstances.

Be sure to familiarize the officer with the legal terms of art used in the relevant area of Fourth Amendment law. Make sure the officer understands concepts such as the difference between a detention and arrest; that a detention is based on reasonable suspicion and not a "hunch;" that a search of a motor vehicle following an informant's tip is a probable cause search and not an inventory.

#### *Beginning the Hearing*

When a defendant seeks to suppress evidence, he initially has the burden of proof to produce evidence that defeats the presumption of proper police conduct.[40] The defendant can meet this burden by showing that police did not have a warrant,[41] but mere allegations in a motion to suppress are not evidence. Prosecutors should be very careful before agreeing to stipulate to facts in the defense motion to suppress.

Once the defendant has met his burden, the burden then shifts to the State to show the search or seizure was reasonable.[42]

### STANDING

Before evidence must be excluded based on a violation of the defendant's constitutional rights, the defendant must show that the challenged search or seizure violated his constitutional rights.[43] To be entitled to challenge a search or seizure, the defendant must show a reasonable expectation of privacy in the area or thing searched, also called "standing." Unless the defendant establishes standing, he cannot challenge the admissibility of evidence under Code of Criminal Procedure Article 38.23.[44] A defendant cannot claim standing based on the legitimacy of another person's position.[45] Article 38.23 does not confer automatic third party standing upon all persons accused of crimes. The right to complain belongs only to the wronged person or injured party.[46]

The State can raise a defendant's failure to show standing for the first time on appeal.[47]

---

40 *Handy v. State*, 189 S.W.3d 296 (Tex. Crim. App. 2006) (defendant seeking to suppress evidence always has the burden of proving standing to complain of the search).

41 *Hogan v. State*, 954 S.W.2d 875 (Tex. App. — Houston [14th Dist.] 1997, pet. ref'd).

42 *Russell*, 717 S.W.2d at 10.

43 *Rakas v. Illinois*, 439 U.S. 128, 99 S.Ct. 421, 58 L.Ed.2d 387 (1978).

44 *Fuller v. State*, 829 S.W.2d 191 (Tex. Crim. App. 1992).

45 *U.S. v. Padilla*, 508 U.S. 77, 113 S.Ct. 1936, 123 L.Ed.2d 635 (1993) (no such doctrine as co-conspirator standing); see *Alderman v. U.S.*, 394 U.S. 165, 89 S.Ct. 961, 22 L.Ed.2d 176 (1969).

46 *Fuller*, 829 S.W.2d at 201.

47 *Wilson v. State*, 692 S.W.2d 661 (Tex. Crim. App. 1984); *State v. Klima*, 934 S.W.2d 109 (Tex. Crim. App. 1996).

#### WHICH PARTY STARTS?

Different counties have different practices on how a suppression hearing proceeds. In some counties, the judge looks to the defense to open the hearing, carry the initial burden of production and persuasion, and establish legal requirements like standing. In other counties, judges tend to look to the State to begin the suppression hearing and do the initial questioning of the officers.

Although the defendant may open a motion to suppress as the author of the motion, the State should shoulder that responsibility unless there clearly is no standing for the defendant to proceed.

#### EVIDENCE

The State must prove the legality of a warrantless search or arrest by "clear and convincing evidence" in a pretrial hearing. When the trial court submits the issue of the legality of a warrantless arrest to the jury, the State must prove facts establishing the arrest's or search's legality beyond a reasonable doubt.[48]

The State should argue as many theories as could justify the officers' actions. If the State loses the motion before the trial court, any theories not raised at the suppression hearing will be waived on appeal.[49] If the State wins at the pretrial hearing, then the ruling can be upheld on any theory supported by the facts (perhaps limited if the trial judge makes specific findings). In some cases, the State may be allowed to present additional evidence after the trial judge rules on the motion to suppress.[50]

The rules of evidence don't apply to a pretrial hearing on a motion to suppress.[51] The Court of Criminal Appeals' 2002 ruling in *Granados* could lead to admission of more statements that ordinarily would be kept out—for instance, hearsay—of suppression hearings, but no reported cases have yet tested the limits of this ruling.

##### *Defendant Testimony*

At some point, the defendant will have to decide whether to testify at the hearing. The defendant can testify for the limited purpose of the issues raised at the suppression hearing. The State cannot cross-examine the defendant on issues beyond these, and if the defendant does not testify at trial, the State cannot use the defendant's testimony from the suppression hearing. If the defendant does testify at trial, the State can use the defendant's testimony at the suppression hearing as a prior inconsistent statement to impeach his testimony at trial.[52]

##### *Judges' Ruling*

Appellate courts should give almost total deference to trial courts' rulings on application of law to fact questions, or mixed questions of law and fact, if resolving these ultimate questions turns on evaluating credibility and demeanor. Appellate courts may review de novo mixed questions of law and fact falling within this category, and the Court of Criminal Appeals may review de novo decisions by intermediate appellate courts.[53]

---

48 Tex. Code Crim. Proc. art. 38.23(a); *Pierce v. State*, 32 S.W.3d 247 (Tex. Crim. App. 2000); *Lalande v. State*, 676 S.W.2d 115, 118 n. 5 (Tex. Crim. App. 1984); *Johnson v. State*, 885 S.W.2d 578, 480 (Tex. App. — Dallas 1994, no pet.); *Peterson v. State*, 727 S.W.2d 125, 126 (Tex. App. — San Antonio 1987, no pet.).

49 *State v. Mercado*, 972 S.W.2d 75 (Tex. Crim. App. 1998).

50 *Montalvo v. State*, 846 S.W.2d 133 (Tex. App. — Austin 1993, no pet.).

51 T.R.Evid. 101(d)(1)(A); *Granados v. State*, 85 S.W.3d 217 (Tex. Crim. App. 2002), *overruling McVickers v. State*, 874 S.W.2d 662 (Tex. Crim. App. 1993).

52 *Simmons v. U.S.*, 390 U.S. 377, 88 S.Ct. 967, 19 L.Ed.2d 1247 (1968); see also T.R.Evid. 104(d).

53 *Guzman v. State*, 955 S.W.2d 85 (Tex. Crim. App. 1997).

A judge can rule on the motion to suppress based just on the written motion and reply,[54] on affidavits, or on oral testimony.[55] Because the judge can rule based only on motion and reply, prosecutors must be cautious in agreeing to stipulate to any facts in the defendant's suppression motion. Most Texas judges hear live testimony at suppression hearings, but a few prefer to rule on suppression motions via affidavits. At least one court of appeals has indicated, however, that it will give less deference to a trial court's ruling on a motion to suppress if the ruling was decided by affidavit alone.[56]

In ruling on the motion, the judge can either just announce her decision or she can make findings of fact and conclusions of law. The findings and conclusions can be dictated to the court reporter in the record, or the judge can rule through a proposed order prepared by the State.

There is no requirement that the judge make written findings,[57] and depending on the circumstances, the State may not want the judge to make written findings. Written findings by the judge may have the undesired effect of later limiting the State to the stated particular legal theory of the case (one theory justifying the officers' actions, in other words). But the State would definitely want the judge to make findings that support the officer's credibility. For instance, if the judge rules against the State because the facts did not establish an exception to the warrant requirement but the judge finds that the officer's testimony was credible, the State will want to have the officer's credibility documented for appellate review.[58]

If a trial court fails to enter findings of fact or conclusions of law on a motion to suppress, the appeals court will assume that the trial court made implicit findings that supported the ruling, as long as the ruling is supported by evidence in the record.[59] There is no consensus among prosecutors—and no uniform practice in the state— as to whether it is preferable for a judge to enter formal findings or not.

## APPEAL

The State can appeal a trial court's adverse ruling on any suppression of evidence under CCP Article 44.01(a)(5).[60] Before this, the State could only appeal suppression orders based on findings that the evidence was illegally obtained. Now, the State can appeal any ruling suppressing evidence (including identification of witnesses) under Article 44.01.[61]

If the prosecutor anticipates appealing the suppression ruling, make sure the judge formally rules on the motion to suppress before the jury is sworn and jeopardy attaches. Code of Criminal Procedure Article 44.01(a)(5) requires that the prosecutor certify that the evidence suppressed is "of substantial importance to the case."

---

54 *State v. Brunner*, 917 S.W.2d 103 (Tex. App. — San Antonio 1996, pet. ref'd); *Rodriguez v. State*, 844 S.W.2d 744 (Tex. Crim. App. 1992) (relying upon TEX. CODE CRIM. PROC. art. 28.01(6)).

55 *Manzi v. State*, 56 S.W.3d 710, 715 (Tex. App. — Houston [14th Dist.] 2001), *aff'd*, 88 S.W.3d 240 (Tex. Crim. App. 2002); *State v. Brunner*, 917 S.W.2d 103 (Tex. App. — San Antonio 1996, pet. ref'd), citing *Rodriguez v. State*, 844 S.W.2d 744 (Tex. Crim. App. 1992); TEX. CODE CRIM. PROC. art. 28.01(6).

56 *Manzi*, 56 S.W.3d at 715 ("In cases where the parties are in substantial agreement on the underlying facts, the use of affidavits may be an efficient means of presenting legal issues to a court for determination prior to trial. Where critical facts are in dispute, however, such disputes are poorly resolved by the use of affidavits. The procedure permits no confrontation, no opportunity to observe, no testing by cross-examination, no inadvertent slips of the tongue, no retraction or recantation of testimony, no clarification of terms, etc.").

57 *State v. Guo*, 64 S.W.3d 662 (Tex. App. — Houston [1st Dist.] 2001, no pet.).

58 See, e.g., *State v. Ross*, 32 S.W.3d 853 (Tex. Crim. App. 2000) (appellate court will give almost total deference to trial court's ruling if only evidence presented is testimony of officer and trial court grants motion to suppress without explanation).

59 *Bass v. State*, 64 S.W.3d 646 (Tex. App. — Texarkana 2001, pet. ref'd); *State v. Ross*, 32 S.W.3d 853, 856 (Tex. Crim. App. 2000).

60 *State v. Medrano*, 67 S.W.3d 892 (Tex. Crim. App. 2002), *overruling State v. Roberts*, 940 S.W.2d 655 (Tex. Crim. App. 1996); see also *State v. Martinez*, 70 S.W.3d 894 (Tex. Crim. App. 2002).

61 See *Guzman v. State*, 955 S.W.2d 85 (Tex. Crim. App. 1997) (standard for state appeal).

# Notice & Hearing on Defense Experts

The prosecution is entitled to notice of defense experts under Code of Criminal Procedure Article 39.14(b). Make sure to schedule a pretrial hearing in your DWI case at which names of experts are due.

Once you have the names of defense experts, find out everything you can about that witness.

1. Check the TDCAA website to see whether any other member has posted information in a user forum about the expert. If not, post a question on the user forum, asking for information any other prosecutor has about that expert.
2. Call the author of this book (Richard Alpert: 817/884-1649; or e-mail to **Rba7289@gmail.com**) or the TDCAA offices (512/474-2436).
3. Type in the expert's name on a search engine on the Internet (such as www.google.com). Pull up any papers they've written or agendas for seminars at which they've spoken. This information might give you insight into the direction from which the expert will be coming.
4. Get transcripts of any previous trials.
5. Run the name of the expert in a Westlaw or LEXIS search.

## RULE 705(B) HEARINGS

A hearing under Rule 705(b) is a final means of getting discovery on any expert before you have the chance to cross-examine them. This hearing is also an opportunity for the prosecutor to make the judge rule on whether the person is qualified to give an opinion.

**Rule 705. Disclosure the Underlying Facts or Data and Examining an Expert About Them**

**(a) Stating an Opinion Without Disclosing the Underlying Facts or Data.** Unless the court orders otherwise, an expert may state an opinion—and give the reasons for it— without first testifying to the underlying facts or data. But the expert may be required to disclose those facts or data on cross-examination.

**(b) Voir Dire Examination of an Expert About the Underlying Facts or Data.** Before an expert states an opinion or discloses the underlying facts or data, an adverse party in a civil case may—or in a criminal case must—be permitted to examine the expert about the underlying facts or data. This examination must take place outside the jury's hearing.

**(c) Admissibility of Opinion.** An expert's opinion is inadmissible if the underlying facts or data do not provide a sufficient basis for the opinion.

**(d) When Otherwise Inadmissible Underlying Facts or Data May Be Disclosed; Instructing the Jury.** If the underlying facts or data would otherwise be inadmissible, the proponent of the opinion may not disclose them to the jury if their probative value in helping the jury evaluate the opinion is outweighed by their prejudicial effect. If the court allows the proponent to disclose those facts or data the court must, upon timely request, restrict the evidence to its proper scope and instruct the jury accordingly.

Explore the expert's qualifications during the hearing. Ask them about any reports or documents they've reviewed in preparation for their testimony, then ask to see those documents, reports, or other materials. If they give you the materials, ask the judge for time to review them. Many times, however, defense experts will not bring these written materials when they testify. At the very least, ask the judge to order them to bring materials. Or you could refuse to release them from recall until they bring the materials back.

### *The Paper Chase*

Experts often will indicate that they have written papers on the subject in question. Find out what they've written, when they wrote, where the papers appeared, and ask for copies of those papers. Remember that it's one thing to write a paper, but another thing to write a peer review paper. Peer review is very important when it comes to evaluating the credibility of a paper. Having others in the field review your work is critical for acceptance in the field. Not only does the author believe the results of her study are accurate, but peer review ensures that the author has the stamp of approval from the scientific community. Be sure to stress any lack of peer review for any papers written by the expert. Defense experts have a tendency to publish papers in periodicals like trial magazines for defense attorneys, which basically just serve as advertisements.

CHAPTER

5

# Charging the Defendant

Setting out the charge against any criminal defendant—including a DWI defendant—involves deciding what to allege specifically and what to allege broadly. Chapter 5 discusses the law regarding DWI jury charges and provides sample forms and suggested charging language.

## DWI Charge Basics

As in any criminal case, crafting an indictment or information for DWI requires a combination of general language, statutory definitions, and specific information about what the defendant did in that particular case.

A defendant has a right to notice of the charges brought against her but the amount of detail required varies from charge to charge. Texas courts have generated as much case law on DWI charging instruments as on any other type of crime. Beware of writing your indictment too specifically: You will be bound to prove everything you allege. Given that most charging decisions are based upon a cursory review of written documents, beware the danger of pleading something you later find you cannot prove. In any criminal charge, a good rule of thumb is to track the statute.

**Penal Code §49.04(a)**

A person commits an offense if the person is intoxicated while operating a motor vehicle in a public place....

### GENERAL STATUTORY ELEMENTS

In every case, the State must name the defendant. The Code of Criminal Procedure also requires the charging instrument to allege a date, and DWI prosecutors should always allege the date in the broadest way. "On or about" a specific date is all that is ever required. Allege the county of the offense, and note that this item is jurisdictional. Your office only has jurisdiction if the offense occurred in your county.[1] Other boilerplate language for the charging instrument is included in Appendix 4-1.

So in our hypothetical example, the information or indictment begins:

**Draft 1**

Joe Drunk, hereinafter called the Defendant, in the County of Tarrant and State of Texas on or about the 4th day of July 2002 did then and there...

### SPECIFIC ALLEGATIONS

#### *Motor Vehicle*

Your charging instrument should track the language of the DWI statute and allege that what the defendant did was "operate a motor vehicle." The Penal Code defines "motor vehicle," and there is no requirement that the State list the model and year of the vehicle the defendant drove.[2]

1 See, e.g. *Barton v. State*, 948 S.W.2d 364 (Tex. App. — Fort Worth 1997, no pet.) (State proved offense occurred in Texas when it proved it occurred in Denton County. Judge could take judicial notice of the fact that Denton County is in Texas).

2 *Turner v. State*, 877 S.W.2d 513 (Tex. App. — Fort Worth 1994, no pet.) (reference by officer to vehicle as "car" sufficient to establish that the vehicle involved in the DWI was a motor vehicle).

### *"Operating"*

Nor does the State have to allege the manner and means by which the defendant exercised physical control of the vehicle. This is an evidentiary matter not required for notice.[3] To find that the defendant operated a motor vehicle, the totality of the circumstances must demonstrate that he took action to affect the functioning of his vehicle, enabling him to use the vehicle. Starting the ignition and revving the accelerator is sufficient.[4] The courts have not required the State to prove actual movement.[5] For instance, the Dallas court of appeals held there was sufficient evidence of operating a motor vehicle when officers found the defendant asleep with the car engine running and his feet on the clutch and brake. "We do not accept the contention that to operate a vehicle within the meaning of the statute, the driver's personal effort must cause the automobile to either move or not move."[6]

### *Public Place*

The DWI statute also requires that the defendant commit the offense in a public place. Alleging that the offense occurred in a "public place" will be sufficient—the prosecutor need not allege the specific city or street where the offense occurred.[7] Courts have ruled that military bases can be considered a public place.[8] Parks are also considered public places, regardless of whether the park is closed (i.e., its hours of operation are over).[9] In ruling that a marina where the defendant drove his vehicle was a public place, the Fort Worth court of appeals focused on evidence that the entire marina area appeared to be accessible to anyone who wanted to use it.[10] This reasoning is consistent with the Amarillo court of appeals' holding that an unpaved driveway of a rural residence located 1/4 mile from a county road in an isolated area could not be considered a public place.[11]

### *Intoxication*

Finally the State must allege that the defendant was "intoxicated." Under previous case law, the prosecutor had to allege which definition of intoxication applied, leading many to opt for the option of alleging all of the ways listed under Penal Code §49.01(2)(A) & (B). The Court of Criminal Appeals made the charging decision much easier when it ruled that the two definitions of intoxication only provide alternative means by which the State can prove intoxication and therefore are not required to be alleged in the charging instrument.[12] There is no longer any need to specify in the charging instrument whether the State intends to prove the loss of "normal use" of faculties or driving with a blood alcohol level of .08 or above. Simply use the word "intoxicated" and you have covered all the alternatives listed in §49.01(2)(A) & (B).

There are many advantages to the State's ability to allege the offense in the broadest sense. For one, this eliminates the need to ask for a synergistic charge when the evidence at trial shows the likely cause of intoxication was the interaction of alcohol with another substance. [**See further information about synergistic charges in Chapter 9, "Jury Charges."**]

## MENTAL STATE

An information charging DWI does not need to allege a culpable mental state.[13] [**See a further discussion of the defendant's mental state in Chapter 7, "Jury Selection."**]

---

3 *Dahl v. State,* 707 S.W.2d 694 (Tex. App. — Austin 1986, pet. ref'd).

4 *Denton v. State,* 911 S.W.2d 388 (Tex. Crim. App. 1995).

5 *Denton* 911 S.W.2d 388; *Hearne v. State,* 80 S.W.3d 677 (Tex. App. — Houston [1st Dist.] 2002, no pet.); *Barton v. State,* 882 S.W.2d 456 (Tex. App. — Dallas 1994, no pet.).

6 *Barton v. State,* 882 S.W.2d 456, 459 (Tex. App. — Dallas 1994, no pet.).

7 *King v. State,* 732 S.W.2d 796 (Tex. App. — Fort Worth 1987, pet. ref'd).

8 *Tracey v. State,* 350 S.W.2d 563 (Tex. Crim. App. 1961); *Woodruff v. State,* 899 S.W.2d 443 (Tex. App. — Austin 1995, pet. ref'd).

9 *Perry v. State,* 991 S.W.2d 50 (Tex. App. — Fort Worth 1998, pet. ref'd).

10 *Shaub v. State,* 99 S.W.3d 253 (Tex. App. — Fort Worth 2003, no pet.).

11 *Fowler v. State,* 65 S.W.3d 116 (Tex. App. — Amarillo 2001, no pet.).

12 *State v. Barbernell,* 257 S.W.3d 248 (Tex. Crim. App. 2008).

13 Tex. Penal Code §49.11; *Hardie v. State,* 588 S.W.2d 936 (Tex. Crim. App. 1979); *Lewis v. State,* 951 S.W.2d 235 (Tex. App. — Beaumont 1997, no pet.); *Reed v. State,* 916 S.W.2d 591 (Tex. App. — Amarillo 1996, pet. ref'd); *Chunn v. State,* 923 S.W.2d 728 (Tex. App. — Houston [1st Dist.] 1996, pet. ref'd); *Sanders v. State,* 936 S.W.2d 436 (Tex. App. — Austin 1996, pet. ref'd); *Burke v. State,* 930 S.W.2d 230 (Tex. App. — Houston [14th Dist.] 1996, pet. ref'd).

## OPEN CONTAINER

For a first offense DWI with evidence that the defendant was driving while he had an open container of alcohol,[14] add an additional paragraph specifying the open container as an enhancement paragraph as follows:

**Enhancement Paragraph 1**

And it is further presented in and to said Court that at the time of the above alleged offense, the defendant who was operating the motor vehicle, knowingly had an open container of an alcoholic beverage, to-wit: **describe container** (i.e., a can of beer) in his immediate possession.

Some prosecutors do not specify the type of container—alleging only "an open container of an alcoholic beverage." Generally, you can specify the type of container without danger, because the presence and contents of the container are generally capable of objective detection and description, and therefore, easy enough to prove.

No case law says that an officer must be able to specify the type of alcohol involved, and if the open container is a cup containing some mixed drink, determining exactly what type of alcohol is in the drink may be impossible. In this case, the safest course seems to be describing the open container in the enhancement paragraph as "a cup containing an alcoholic beverage."

## DEADLY WEAPONS

A motor vehicle can be capable of causing serious bodily injury or death and therefore can be considered a deadly weapon.[15] When the state intends to seek a deadly weapon finding, the better practice is to plead it in the indictment, or at a minimum, give the defendant specific notice of the state's intent to seek a deadly weapon finding. If the allegation is not included in the indictment, the State can give notice by any means, including by motion. However, the courts have held that an allegation in the indictment charging the defendant with causing his own car to collide with the victim's vehicle gives the defendant sufficient notice that the State will attempt to prove the defendant's vehicle was used as a deadly weapon and that the State will seek an affirmative deadly weapon finding.[16] Note that a deadly weapon finding has no effect on misdemeanor DWI cases.

## DWI WITH CHILD PASSENGER

Created in 2003, this offense has all of the elements of DWI and the additional element that the vehicle was operated while occupied by a passenger younger than 15 years of age.[17] The offense is a state jail felony that may not be used to enhance later DWI offenses if committed before Sept. 1, 2005.[18] When it first became law, this offense was not listed in CCP art. 42.12, §5, dealing with deferred adjudication. This omission was corrected in the 2007 legislative session. As a result, if the offense was committed before Sept. 1, 2007, the defendant may receive deferred adjudication and if committed after that date, he may not.[19] Because DWI is obviously an included offense, double jeopardy bars prosecution of both DWI with child passenger and the underlying DWI.

---

14 TEX. PENAL CODE §49.04(c).

15 *Mann v. State*, 58 S.W.3d 132 (Tex. Crim. App. 2001); *Ex parte McKithan*, 838 S.W.2d 560 (Tex. Crim. App. 1992); *Davis v. State*, 964 S.W.2d 352 (Tex. App. — Fort Worth 1998, no pet.); *Roberts v. State*, 766 S.W.2d 578 (Tex. App. — Austin 1989, no pet.); but see *Cates v. State*, 102 S.W.3d 735 (Tex. Crim. App. 2003) (no evidence anyone actually endangered, even though victim was hit and killed in FSRA case); *Williams v. State*, 946 S.W.2d 432 (Tex. App. — Fort Worth 1997), *aff'd in part, rev'd in part*, 970 S.W.2d 566 (Tex. Crim. App. 1998) (deadly weapon finding impermissible without evidence that another motorist was on the highway at the time and place the defendant drove in an intoxicated condition).

16 *Ex parte McKithan*, 838 S.W.2d 560, 561 (Tex. Crim. App. 1992); *Martinez v. State*, 883 S.W.2d 771 (Tex. App. — Fort Worth 1994, pet. ref'd).

17 TEX. PENAL CODE §49.045.

18 HB 51 added this offense to the list in TEX. PENAL CODE §49.09(d), making it an offense that can be used to enhance later DWI offenses, but that change will be effective only for offenses committed after its effective date, Sept. 1, 2005.

19 TEX. CODE CRIM. PROC. art. 42.12, §5(d)(1)(A).

### DWI W/BAC .15 OR ABOVE

If the State shows on the trial of an offense under §49.04 that an analysis of blood, breath, or urine shows an alcohol concentration level of 0.15 or more *at the time of the analysis* of the specimen, the offense is a Class A misdemeanor.

There are several unique aspects of this law change that are worth noting, and that would speak to a decision of whether to pursue the option. First, note that the relevant time is BAC at the time of the analysis, not the time of driving. So unlike the element of intoxication, which is tied to the time of driving, this enhancement is not, and therefore, there is no need for extrapolation formulas to prove it applies.

Second, unlike a first-offense DWI or a DWI subsequent offense, there is no minimum jail sentence that must be served. This is likely an oversight on the part of the drafters, but the impact is that it is the only DWI charge in which no minimum jail time is required. Other than raising the range of punishment from a Class B to a Class A for a first offense DWI, there are no *new* mandatory conditions of probation that come with this charge. A finding of true to the enhancement will trigger a mandatory interlock requirement under CCP Art. 42.12, §13(i), but this is not a new requirement, as it existed prior to this law change.

When this law was first passed, there was a great deal of debate as to whether the allegation of 0.15 at the time of the test constituted an enhancement or was an element of the offense. The Houston court of appeals has ruled that it is an element of a separate type of DWI offense.[20] The practical impact is that the allegation is therefore something the State must prove and the jury must receive an instruction on in the guilt/innocence phase of trial.

## Appendix 5-1: DWI Suggested Charging Language[21]

### (1) ALCOHOL
### (2) DRUGS
### (3) COMBINATION OF INTOXICATING SUBSTANCES

then and there operate a motor vehicle in a public place while the defendant was intoxicated.

### (4) SERIOUS BODILY INJURY

And it is further presented that as a direct result of this offense, another person, namely, #1 [injured party], suffered serious bodily injury.

### (5) OPEN CONTAINER

And it is further presented that at the time of the above offense, the defendant, who was operating the motor vehicle, knowingly had an open container of an alcoholic beverage, to-wit: #1 [describe container and beverage], in #2 ["his" **OR** "her"] immediate possession.

---

20 *Navarro v. State*, No. 14-13-00706-CR (Tex. App. — Houston [14th Dist.] July 7, 2015, no pet. h.).

21 Adapted from *TDCAA Charging Manual* by Alan Curry (TDCAA © 2015).

### (6) ALCOHOL CONCENTRATION LEVEL OF 0.15 OR MORE

And it is further presented that at the time of performing an analysis of a specimen of the defendant's #1 ["blood" OR "breath" OR "urine"], the analysis showed an alcohol concentration level of 0.15 or more.

### (7) ONE PRIOR CONVICTION

#### (A) DRIVING WHILE INTOXICATED

And it is further presented that prior to the commission of the charged offense, on the #1 [date of conviction], in cause number #2 [cause number] in the #3 [name of court] of #4 [county of court] County, Texas, the defendant was convicted of an offense relating to the operating of a motor vehicle while intoxicated.

#### (B) FLYING, BOATING, OR AMUSEMENT RIDE WHILE INTOXICATED

And it is further presented that prior to the commission of the charged offense, on the #1 [date of conviction], in cause number #2 [cause number] in the #3 [name of court] of #4 [county of court] County, Texas, the defendant was convicted of an offense relating to the #5 ["operating" OR "operating or assembling"] #6 ["an aircraft" OR "a watercraft" OR "an amusement ride"] while intoxicated.

#### (C) INTOXICATION MANSLAUGHTER

***(1) Texas Conviction***

And it is further presented that before the commission of the charged offense, the defendant had theretofore been convicted of an offense under Section 49.08 of the Texas Penal Code, in that on the #1 [date of conviction], in the #2 [name of court] of #3 [county of court] County, Texas, in cause number #4 [cause number], the defendant was convicted of the offense of #5 [charge convicted].

***(2) Foreign Conviction***

And it is further presented that before the commission of the charged offense, on the #1 [date of conviction], in the #2 [name of court] of #3 [jurisdiction of court] in cause number #4 [cause number], the defendant was convicted of the offense of #5 [charge convicted], and the offense contained elements that are substantially similar to the elements of an offense under Section 49.08 of the Texas Penal Code.

### (8) TWO PRIOR CONVICTIONS

#### (A) BOTH FOR DRIVING WHILE INTOXICATED

And it is further presented that prior to the commission of the charged offense (hereafter styled the primary offense), on the #1 [date of first conviction], in cause number #2 [cause number of first conviction] in the #3 [name of court of first conviction] of #4 [county of court of first conviction] County, Texas, the defendant was convicted of an offense relating to the operating of a motor vehicle while intoxicated; and on the #5 [date of second conviction], in cause number #6 [cause number of second conviction] in the #7 [name of court of second conviction] of #8 [county of court of second conviction] County, Texas, the defendant was convicted of an offense relating to the operating of a motor vehicle while intoxicated.

#### (B) OTHER

And it is further presented that prior to the commission of the charged offense (hereafter styled the primary offense), on the #1 [date of first conviction], in cause number #2 [cause number of first conviction] in the #3 [name of court of first conviction] of #4 [county of court of first conviction] County, Texas, the defendant was convicted of an offense relating to the #5 ["operating" OR "operating or assembling"] #6 ["a motor vehicle" OR "an aircraft" OR "a watercraft" OR "an amusement ride"] while intoxicated; and on the #7 [date of second conviction], in cause number #8 [cause number of second conviction] in the #9 [name of court of second conviction] of #10 [county of court of second conviction] County, Texas, the defendant was convicted of an offense relating to the #11 ["operating" OR "operating or assembling"] #12 ["a motor vehicle" OR "an aircraft" OR "a watercraft" OR "an amusement ride"] while intoxicated.

CHAPTER

6

# Trial Preparation

Chapter 6 describes the process of getting yourself and your key witnesses ready to go to court. Checklists are included so prosecutors can compile the necessary documents and materials and help educate officers on what to expect when they're on the witness stand.

## Preparing Yourself & Your Officer

Before your first meeting with an officer, you should have a detailed understanding of your case—more specifically, your case file. As you break down the offense report, be sure to look for mistakes, misspelled words, times listed that do not follow, or gaps in details—all of which you should cover with your officer witness at the first meeting.

***Reorganize the facts in the offense report***

Break down the facts in the order and manner you intend to elicit them at trial. The first portion of the report breakdown should set out the scene at the time of the stop, including date, time, city, and specific location of the officer. The notes from which I will formulate my questions look something like this:

July 4, 2011
Officer Dave Walker
Fort Worth Police Department—10 years
Training Certification:
FST instructor—HGN certified
Describe test history and administration
Geographic sector patrolled that night
Fort Worth, Tarrant County, Texas
2:03 a.m.
Weather clear
Marked patrol unit—in uniform
Alone
Late shift: 8 p.m. to 6 a.m.

Get a detailed understanding of the officer, his training, years with the department, schools attended, certifications, and knowledge about FSTs. Our office developed a questionnaire that officers routinely complete when they arrive at the DA's office for an interview with a prosecutor. All responses are kept alphabetically in notebooks in the office, and usually, a prosecutor can pull a previously completed questionnaire and then simply verify that the information in it is still accurate. [**This questionnaire is reproduced as Table 6-1.**]

***Describe the officer's first visual or audio contact***

Whether the first contact came from a radio broadcast arising from a concerned citizen's call, hearing the sound of screeching tires, or observing erratic driving, every reason for the stop should be documented next. Your goal is to try to transport the jury to the scene through your description of it.

First notice of defendant/vehicle
300 block of West Belknap
Green pickup truck
Passed high rate of speed
Radar gun—tested earlier
60 in 40 mph zone
Pursuit—3 blocks w/siren lights
Stopped 600 block of West Belknap
Albertson's parking lot

**TABLE 6-1: Law Enforcement Interview Form**

## LAW ENFORCEMENT WITNESS INFORMATION FORM

NAME: ______________________ DATE: ____________

PHONE #S: HOME: ____________
WORK: ____________
CELL: ____________
EMAIL: ____________

EDUCATIONAL BACKGROUND:
*(LIST ALL SCHOOLS ATTENDED AND YEAR ATTENDED)*

______________________________
______________________________
______________________________
____________

LAW ENFORCEMENT BACKGROUND:
*(STARTING WITH CURRENT AGENCY, LIST RANK AND START DATE & LIST ALL OTHER LAW ENFORCEMENT POSITIONS/EMPLOYMENT DATES)*

______________________________
______________________________
______________________________
______________________________
______________________________

LIST ALL SCHOOLS OR SPECIALIZED TRAINING/CERTIFICATION ATTENDED/RECEIVED RELATING TO LAW ENFORCEMENT:

______________________________
______________________________
______________________________
______________________________
______________________________

*Are you currently certified in Standardized Field Sobriety Testing/HGN? (Yes/No)*
*If Yes, were you so certified on ____________?*
*(Offense Date)*

OTHER SPECIALIZED TRAINING OR CERTIFICATIONS:

______________________________
______________________________
______________________________
______________________________

#### *Document reasons for suspecting intoxication*

Break down where and when the observations and statements were made to ensure that the officer had a legal basis for continuing the detention. You will also want to verify the facts to allow admission of any statements made before the officer asked the suspect to step out of the vehicle to attempt FSTs. My notes would look something like this:

> **TIP**
>
> Officers should be familiar with the legal definitions of reasonable suspicion, probable cause, legal definitions of "intoxicated," and the requirements for SFSTs and keep these in mind when documenting reasons for stopping the defendant.

| | |
|---|---|
| FSTs | Step away from vehicle |
| Suspect asked officer to "give [him] a break" | Requested FSTs |
| Suspect faced away from patrol vehicle lights | HGN—Clues: 6 |
| Marked line in parking lot—7 clues (list them) | Walk & turn |
| Arrested defendant: basis (list all factors) | OLS—Clues: 4 (list) |
| Suspect stated, "I couldn't do those tests if I was sober" | |

While talking to the officer, other things I'd like to know—to put the events during the stop in context,diffuse defense arguments that there's no way even a sober person could have performed SFSTs, and help me convey to the jury that administration of the SFSTs was safe and fair—include:

| | |
|---|---|
| Safety conditions | Other officers present |
| Line/no line on road | Flat/smooth surface |
| Any distractions | Crowd? |
| Passengers? | Traffic conditions |
| Well lit—paved | |

#### *Detail transportation to the station*

Be sure to note any comments the defendant made during the trip. My goal in this stage is to show the detection, stop, and arrest of the suspect is not a rush to judgment, but rather a cautious examination of the circumstances. I want to help the jury see that the decision to move from investigation to arrest was based on articulable observations. I will later use that breakdown in jury argument. After each stage is covered, I ask the jury rhetorically, "What would you have the officer do at this point?" Their logical response should be, "Proceed to the next stage."

## PREPARING OFFICERS FOR CROSS-EXAMINATION

#### *Questions about the stop*

Talk with your officers about all possible reasons for the stop. Remind officers that their subjective reason for the stop is not critical, as long as objective reasons legally justified the stop.[1] Make sure officers understand the difference between reasonable suspicion and probable cause and any other legal terms. Other legal terms the officers must be able to articulate are the different definitions of intoxication.

Whether the officer pulled the defendant's vehicle over immediately after seeing him driving or waited a mile or so before pulling him over, the defense attorney will try to make the officer sound like he handled the situation incorrectly. The defense will suggest either that the officer overreacted and pulled the defendant over without

---

1 See, e.g., *Arkansas v. Sullivan,* 532 U.S. 769, 121 S.Ct. 1876, 149 L.Ed.2d 994 (2001); *Whren v. U.S.,* 517 U.S. 806, 116 S.Ct. 1769, 135 L.Ed.2d 89 (1996); *Ohio v. Robinette,* 519 U.S. 33, 117 S.Ct. 417, 136 L.Ed.2d 347 (1996); *O'Hara v. State,* 27 S.W.3d 548 (Tex. Crim. App. 2000).

having sufficient basis to do so, or the officer waited too long and therefore couldn't have been that concerned about the defendant's potential threat to public safety. Officers might feel like they lose no matter how they answer the defense question. The important thing will be for the officer to maintain his composure.

Make sure your officer understands there's nothing wrong with admitting things the defendant did well. Defense counsel may want to emphasize that the defendant managed to pull over without driving over the curb, stopped immediately when he saw the officer's flashing lights, or seemed to understand the officer's instructions on the field sobriety tests. None of these things are necessarily contradictory to the state's contention that the defendant was driving while intoxicated.

### DISCIPLINARY RECORDS & IMPEACHMENT

Prosecutors should find out from the officer whether the defense (or any other person) has made any open records requests or subpoenas for their disciplinary reports. File a motion in limine on any of these disciplinary matters. There are a large number of restrictions on the extent to which these records can be used for impeachment. For instance, specific instances of conduct cannot be used, because their potential for prejudice outweighs the probative value.[2]

If you get the sense that the defense may attempt to attack your officer's employment record, seek a motion in limine before trial to keep the jury from hearing this information until the judge has ruled it is admissible. If you don't have this opportunity and this line of questioning comes up in the middle of trial, quickly ask to have the jury excused for a hearing outside jurors' presence.

Financial motive might be a permissible area for defense inquiry.[3] In *Castillo v. State*, defense counsel wanted to offer into evidence the aggregate, annual overtime income earned by the arresting officer testifying in court. The Houston court of appeals ruled that although the information might be relevant, the trial court properly excluded it in that case because the "decision to make allegedly 'marginal' arrests is too attenuated from any potential financial gains to overcome the risk of confusion of the issues, embarrassment, harassment, and undue delay." The court of appeals did, however, allow the defense to ask about the amount the officer earned for testifying in that case and his per-hour wage.

Courts have also allowed defense counsel to ask about any departmental quotas for DWI arrests that were in place at the time of the defendant's arrest.[4]

#### *Prior Testimony*

Find out whether the officer has given any prior testimony in related proceedings, such as at the ALR hearing. If the officer has, there is a good chance the defense attorney has access to the transcript or a tape recording of the proceeding. The prosecutor must get a copy of the tape and be familiar with the basis of the officer's testimony at the ALR hearing.

#### *SFST Questions*

Make sure your officers understand how SFSTs work. [**For more information on SFSTs, see Chapter 2. For sample questions on SFSTs, see Chapter 8.**] Verify that if more than one officer administered SFSTs (for instance, one at the roadside and one at the station), the officers administered the tests the same way. If not, find out why not and prepare the officers to explain any discrepancies. Also prepare the officers for

---

2 See, e.g., *Carpenter v. State*, 979 S.W.2d 633 (Tex. Crim. App. 1998).

3 *Castillo v. State*, 939 S.W.2d 754 (Tex. App. — Houston [14th Dist.] 1997, pet. ref'd).

4 *Alexander v. State*, 949 S.W.2d 772 (Tex. App. — Dallas 1997, pet. ref'd).

defense tactics that question whether the SFSTs are an accurate measure of how well the defendant could drive that night. Remember that SFSTs do not test driving, but they do test intoxication.

Can your officer demonstrate how to perform SFSTs correctly? Verify this *before* the officer appears in court. Nothing would be more embarrassing and potentially devastating to an officer's credibility than his inability to perform SFSTs when sober.

### TABLE 6-2: Do's and Don'ts for Officer Testimony

**Be sure to:**

- Watch the videotape carefully before testifying.
- Read over your offense report and look for typos or errors; point them out to the prosecutor.
- Understand and be able to relate the details of any and all professional training that relates to your actions during the arrest
- Understand the difference between the legal basis for an investigative stop and probable cause to arrest.
- Be familiar with the proper way to administer FSTs.
- Avoid legalese or police talk. Don't say, for instance, "The suspect was operating a motor vehicle." Instead say, "The defendant was driving his pickup truck."
- Speak loudly and clearly.
- Keep in mind the following principles of effective testimony: honesty, brevity, clarity, objectivity, emotional control.
- Be courteous to defense counsel even when the same courtesy is not extended to you.
- Have a full copy of your report with you and feel free to refer to it when necessary after you take the stand.
- Listen to each question carefully and be sure you understand the question before you answer it.
- Ask to have a question repeated if you don't understand it, or just say that you didn't understand the question.
- Be aware of two-part questions, and make sure you answer both parts separately.
- Give a simple "yes" or "no" answer without elaboration when this is an adequate response.
- Feel free to explain your answer when a "yes" or "no" will not suffice.
- Stop testifying, in mid-sentence if necessary, if you hear either side make an objection.
- Make sure to tell the prosecutor if you have previously given sworn testimony in this case (at a motion to suppress, ALR hearing, or civil deposition, for instance).

**Don't**

- Be afraid to admit you made a mistake.
- Be fooled by defense attorneys purporting to read from some official document or publication. If they say they are reading from an official document, ask to see it.
- Discuss the case with other officer witnesses once you are placed under the Rule.
- Answer a question in court until the meaning of the question is clear.
- Guess. If you don't know, just say you don't know.
- Apologize for basing an arrest on your "opinion."
- Lose your temper.
- Be afraid to admit the defendant did some things well.
- Volunteer information that goes beyond the scope of the question.
- Argue with the defense lawyer.
- Make sarcastic remarks in response to questions.
- Tense up before cross-examination.
- Be afraid to give answers that help the defense.
- Be late for pretrial meetings.
- Be afraid to ask the prosecutor questions at the pretrial meeting.
- Volunteer testimony that exceeds the scope of your duties or experience.

## Gathering Necessary Reports & Materials

**Table 6-3** is a checklist that can be used to gather all reports and records needed to make a charging decision or to go to trial. In Tarrant County, the criminal district attorney's office sent this list to each police department so they would have an idea of what information was needed to make a filing and indictment decision. Items with an asterisk (*) should be in the file before intake accepts the case. Although not all of this information will be available in every instance, the checklist provides a good guide of what a complete report should contain. Besides providing a means of ensuring proper evidence collection, these items will also help ensure you have addressed any "causation" issues pre-indictment.

**Table 6-4** is a list of reports and materials that a prosecutor will need before trial.

## TABLE 6-3: Reports Checklist

❐ **Medical Records**
Get any of the suspect's medical records if there was a visit to or extended stay at a hospital, any medical examiner's report, the M.E. investigator notes, and the developed photos.

❐ ***Accident Report**

❐ ***Accident Reconstruction Report**
This need not be in final form but should include speed calculations and an opinion on all causation factors. A diagram of how accident occurred should be completed by traffic investigation unit and submitted as early as possible.

❐ **Photographs**
Any autopsy/crime scene photos should be developed and in the file before GJ indictment. These should be developed as early in the process as is possible so photos can be retaken if photo is not clear or if there were areas missed.

❐ **Police Report**
Including the name of the ambulance service and fire department that came to the scene, any other non-police witnesses that had contact with the suspect or the victims, and a list of all officers at the scene or involved in any aspect of the investigation together with a description of the nature of their involvement.

❐ **Blood Test Documentation**
* DIC warning sheets
* Blood test checklist
* Clear chain of custody (beginning and end)
* Name of nurse/technician who drew the blood

(We must be able to clearly identify that person and intake should not accept the case without said identity being very clear. GJ attorney should contact this witness by phone or letter and get all necessary address and phone number information.
* Name of testing agency and name of technician/criminalist who did the testing
* Result of test (lab report) and current location of remaining blood sample
* Test for presence of drugs in all cases and make sure it is a comprehensive screen plus all necessary documentation previously mentioned if said test is done by different agency

❐ **Videotape/Audiotapes**
DWI Videotape should be reviewed by GJ attorney. If it is clear from the file that news agencies were at the scene, GJ subpoenas need to be issued to those agencies pre-indictment as said footage is often valuable at trial and is not kept forever. Check to see if there were any calls by civilians who had made contact with the driver or who came upon the crash site and order copies of those tapes.

❐ ***Civilian Witnesses**
Names, addresses and phone numbers for all non-law enforcement witnesses and a description of the nature of their involvement. These are often critical and these people are often transient. At GJ level, these witnesses need to be contacted by phone or letter to ensure we have all necessary contact information.

❐ **Criminal History**
Run TCIC and NCIC, and all in-state or out-of-state priors should be ordered pre-indictment. A certified D.L. record should be ordered in every case. D.L. record must be in the file pre-indictment.

❐ **Insurance Company Records**
If the defendant or injured party are insured, a contact must be made with that company for two reasons:
1. We need to make sure we know where the vehicles are (if released by the police) and see to it that they are not released or destroyed until police have fully examined them.
2, These records, especially those that belong to defendants often contain statements that in a criminal case are fully discoverable and GJ subpoenas should be issued for same pre-indictment.

❐ **Victim Contacts**
Notes about any such contacts that have been made, including name and relationship of contact person to injured party.

## TABLE 6-4: Jury Trial Checklist

- ❒ **Review Indictment/Information**
- ❒ **Run criminal history on D (TCIC/NCIC)**
- ❒ **Run criminal history on CW**
- ❒ **Meet with officer and copy entire case file**
  - [ ] Copies of all reports & supplements
  - [ ] Copies of all witness statements
  - [ ] Copies of all photographs
  - [ ] Copy of defendant's written statement
  - [ ] Copy of all investigative notes
  - [ ] Copy of all videotape(s)
  - [ ] Copy of all 911 tape
  - [ ] Copy of arrest warrant
  - [ ] Certified copy of search warrant
  - [ ] Copy of consent to search
- ❒ **Obtain medical records (D & CW)**
- ❒ **Obtain EMS reports—locate paramedics**
- ❒ **Copy of D's booking photo (arrest date: ______________)**
- ❒ **Check D's property inventory at time of arrest**
- ❒ **Copies of all jail or prison records—medical & disciplinary**
- ❒ **Jail visitation list**
- ❒ **Current address & phone number for all witnesses**
- ❒ **Run criminal history on all witnesses**
  1. ______________________________
  2. ______________________________
  3. ______________________________
- ❒ **Obtain certified copies of misdemeanor convictions**

  ______________________________

  ______________________________
- ❒ **Jail card request**
- ❒ **Copies of all offense reports for misdemeanor convictions**
- ❒ **Obtain certified copies of felony convictions/pen packets**

  ______________________________

  ______________________________
- ❒ **Copies of all offense reports for felony convictions**
- ❒ **Juvenile records**
  - [ ] Certified copies of adjudications
  - [ ] Copy of offense reports & State's file
  - [ ] Social history & psychological evaluation
  - [ ] TYC records
- ❒ **Obtain certified copies of alias warrants**
- ❒ **Grand jury transcript**
- ❒ **Examining trial transcript**
- ❒ **ALR hearing transcript**
- ❒ **Check file for D's subpoenas & letters to court**
- ❒ **Discovery to defense attorney**
- ❒ **Motion for discovery of expert's witnesses (CCP 39.14(b))**
- ❒ **Rule 404(b) notice: Served on defense attorney __________**
- ❒ **Rule 609 notice: Served on defense attorney __________**
- ❒ **Article 37.07, §3(g) notice: Served on defense attorney __________**
- ❒ **Notice of intent to seek deadly weapon finding (if not in indictment) Served on defense attorney ________**
- ❒ **File business records with affidavit (14 days before trial)**
- ❒ **Motions in limine**
- ❒ **Witness list Given to defense attorney ____________**

### BLOOD TEST DOCUMENTATION

The state cannot rely solely on medical records to prove a blood test result. The state must further show: (1) a proper chain of custody, and (2) that the blood tested was the same as blood drawn from the defendant. Without this evidence, medical records may be inadmissible.[5] But neither the person who drew the blood[6] nor the person who tested the blood needs to testify in every case.[7] If an officer testifies that she witnessed the blood drawn by the nurse, any objections to the failure to call the nurse will go to the weight and not the admissibility of the evidence.[8]

The Court of Criminal Appeals has rejected a court of appeals' ruling that taking a blood sample by hospital personnel constituted assault.[9] In *Hailey v. State*, the evidence at the time of the defendant's arrest showed: (1) the defendant had bounced his car off the guardrail; (2) crossed into oncoming traffic; (3) a PBT administered at the scene showed an alcohol concentration of .337. The officer, fearing that the defendant might be suffering from alcohol poisoning, took the defendant to the hospital. The defendant was read the DIC-24 warnings and refused to give a sample. Hospital personnel drew a medical sample that showed a BAC of .454.

The court of appeals reversed, ruling that the blood was illegally taken via assault by hospital personnel. One problem (and possible explanation for the court's ruling) was that no witness from the hospital was called to say why the blood was taken. The Court of Criminal Appeals ruled that the court of appeals improperly reversed the case based on a theory not presented to the trial court and affirmed the trial court's ruling that the blood sample was admissible.

### PRIVACY & MEDICAL RECORDS

A defendant has no right to privacy in hospital blood test records, and the state can introduce evidence of records obtained by grand jury subpoena.[10] Since the defendant has no constitutional or statutory reasonable expectation of privacy in these hospital records, he also has no standing to complain about alleged defects in the grand jury subpoena process.[11]

---

5 *Lynch v. State*, 687 S.W.2d 76 (Tex. App. — Amarillo 1985, pet. ref'd).

6 *Yeary v. State*, 734 S.W.2d 766 (Tex. App. — Fort Worth 1987, no pet.); *Beck v. State*, 651 S.W.2d 827 (Tex. App. — Houston [1st Dist.] 1983, no pet.) (proper chain of custody was shown in admission of hospital-drawn blood sample even though physician witness could not testify who actually drew the blood sample).

7 *Durrett v. State*, 36 S.W.3d 205 (Tex. App. — Houston [14th Dist.] 2001, no pet.) (testimony about the precautions taken by the hospital to ensure blood samples are properly drawn, labeled, and tested was adequate to link the blood result in the records to the defendant).

8 *Penley v. State*, 2 S.W.3d 534 (Tex. App. — Texarkana 1999, pet. ref'd); *Burns v. State*, 807 S.W.2d 878 (Tex. App. — Corpus Christi 1991, pet. ref'd); *Gallegos v. State*, 776 S.W.2d 312 (Tex. App. — Houston [14th Dist.] 1989) (orig. proceeding).

9 *Hailey v. State*, 87 S.W.3d 118 (Tex. Crim. App. 2002).

10 TEX. R. EVID. 509 (no physician–patient privilege); *Dickerson v. State*, 986 S.W.2d 618 (Tex. Crim. App. 1999); *State v. Hardy*, 963 S.W.2d 516 (Tex. Crim. App. 1997); *Blunt v. State*, 724 S.W.2d 79 (Tex. Crim. App. 1987); *State v. Liendo*, 980 S.W.2d 809 (Tex. App. — San Antonio 1998, no pet.); *Knapp v. State*, 942 S.W.2d 176 (Tex. App. — Beaumont 1997, pet. ref'd); *Clark v. State*, 933 S.W.2d 332 (Tex. App. — Corpus Christi 1996, no pet.); *Corpus v. State*, 931 S.W.2d 30 (Tex. App. — Austin 1996), *pet. dism'd*, 962 S.W.2d 590 (Tex. Crim. App. 1998); *State v. Hurd*, 865 S.W.2d 605 (Tex. App. — Fort Worth 1993, no pet.); *Thurman v. State*, 861 S.W.2d 96 (Tex. App. — Houston [1st Dist.] 1993, no pet.).

11 *Garcia v. State*, 95 S.W.3d 522 (Tex. App. — Houston [1st Dist.] 2002, no pet.).

One new weapon in the defense arsenal is to cite the "Health Insurance Portability and Accountability Act (HIPAA) as a basis for suppressing medical records or statements made to law enforcement about victims' or suspects' medical conditions. One federal law, however, 45 C.F.R. §164.512(f)(1)(ii)(a), provides that the covered medical provider entities can disclose protected health information without patient authorization through a court order exception (which also includes court-ordered warrant, subpoena, summons, or grand jury subpoena). Information released for law enforcement purposes falls under this exception, which specifically provides that medical information may be released to law enforcement about a victim or suspected victim of a crime, to identify or locate a suspect, or as required by law. To download the new HIPAA regulations, see **http:///www.os.dhhs.gov/ocr/index.html.**

## VIDEO/AUDIOTAPES

Before trial, prosecutors should physically examine the room in the stationhouse where the video of the defendant was made. Camera angles can affect the ability of an officer to observe some things, such as a suspect weaving while standing up. An overhead camera might not be able to catch this. The prosecutor needs to be aware of this and be able to explain this phenomenon to a jury, as well as prepare the officer to explain this.

When watching a stationhouse or in-car video with your officer before trial, keep in mind the following things:

- **FST method:** Is the officer asking the defendant to perform tests the same way the officer at the scene did? Either verify that officers followed the same procedure or make them aware that the procedure they used was different, and prepare officers to explain any discrepancies.
- **Time factor:** Verify the amount of time between any FSTs performed on the scene and those performed on video at the station. The same test performed hours later will likely result in a better performance for the defendant.
- **Uncooperative suspects:** Discuss with the officer the suspect's nonverbal behavior, particularly if the defendant refused to cooperate with requests to perform FSTs. Nonverbal behavior can show signs of intoxication—for instance, if a defendant anchored his feet widely apart to help balance himself or put his hand on something (like his car) to stabilize himself.
- **Thought processes:** Discuss with your officer whether the defendant appeared to follow along with instructions as they were given. For instance, did the defendant read along with the written warnings as the officer read them aloud? What was the defendant's facial expression as he was reading along? Did he seem to be following what the officer was saying?
- **Hostile officers:** A stationhouse videotape may show a defendant who appears from the start to be friendly and treat the officer with respect, yet the officer's demeanor makes it clear that he's upset with the defendant. If any previous exchanges were not documented by the officer, he needs to document and explain this. For instance, the defendant may have hit the officer with a stream of racial slurs all the way driving to the stationhouse but then turned into a polite and professional-sounding Eddie Haskell once the videotape was turned on.
- **"Why am I here?"** Many times, a defendant will feign ignorance as to why he's been arrested. If you take these defendants at their word, you can't get much better evidence of intoxication than someone who doesn't understand what

they've been arrested for after being told multiple times by officer what's going on. Discuss this with your officer pretrial. While the officer is testifying, stop the tape and let the officer explain how many times he told the defendant what he was being arrested for and what made him pull the defendant over in the first place.

- **Delays:** If a defendant was stopped at midnight, arrested at 12:20 a.m., but didn't make it to the stationhouse on video until 2:30 a.m., talk with the officer about the reason for the delay. An in-car video will explain any delay. But if there's no video available, check the officer's log to see if it reflects the reasons for delay—for instance, waiting on a tow truck, or waiting in a long line to use the intoxilyzer instrument. (A delay at the intoxilyzer will also subtly remind the jury what a big problem DWI is.)

The bottom line is to do everything you can to educate yourself about the issues at trial so that you, in turn, can educate your officers—and ultimately, your jury— to handle these often difficult cases. Some helpful resources and websites are listed in **Table 6-5**. [**A videotape review form can be found in Chapter 8.**]

**TABLE 6-5: Helpful Websites**

TDCAA: **www.tdcaa.com**
National Highway Traffic Safety Administration: **www.nhtsa.dot.gov**
National College of DUI Defense: **www.ncdd.com**
Gary Trichter's office: **www.texasdwilaw.com**
Texas Criminal Defense Lawyers Association: **www.tcdla.com**
**www.drunkdrivingdefense.com**
**www.duiseminars.com/index.htm**
Texas Accident Reconstructionists: **www.taars.org**
National Traffic Law Center: **www.ndaa.org/ntlc_home.html**
Accreditation Commission for Traffic Accident Reconstruction (ACTAR): **www.actar.org**
U.S. Naval Observatory: **http://aa.usno.navy.mil** (for sunrise/sunset and phases of the moon information)
Insurance Institute for Highway Safety: **www.iihs.org/**
Traffic Accident Reconstruction Origin: **www.tarorigin.com**
Society of Automotive Engineers: **www.sae.org/**
American Society of Mechanical Engineers: **www.asme.org/**
Accident Reconstruction Network: **www.accidentreconstruction.com**
New York Prosecutors Training Institute: **https://login.nypti.org**

## OTHER RESOURCES

1. "Medicolegal Aspects of Alcohol," by James Garriott
2. DWI Journal: Law & Science
3. "Between the Lines" from the National Traffic Law Center
4. "Crash Reconstruction Basics for Prosecutors" (free download from NTLC at APRI) by John Kwasnoski
5. "Investigation & Prosecution of DWI & Vehicular Homicide" by Kwasnoski, Partridge & Stephen
6. "Trial Preparation Manual: Establishing Liability in Vehicular Accidents," by Chieco & Kwasnoski
7. "Handbook of Forensic Pathology," by Vincent DiMaio & Suzanna Dana
8. "Horizontal Gaze Nystagmus: The Science and the Law," published by APRI and available online.

CHAPTER

7

# Jury Selection

A prosecutor's goals during voir dire can be divided into four categories:

1. getting acquainted with the panel;
2. exposing those jurors who should be challenged or rehabilitated;
3. educating them about the law;
4. indoctrinating them towards your theory of the case.

## Voir Dire Goals

Which topics and to what extent you cover them will depend on how much time you have. Because DWI is a misdemeanor charge, you could have as much as two hours or as little as 25 minutes. How much you cover and on which categories you focus should depend on the strengths and weaknesses of your case. And no matter what you focus on, how you do it is as important as what you do. As the old saying goes, "No one gets a second chance to make a first impression."

### CASE EVALUATION

Before voir dire, make a list of the strengths and weaknesses of your case. When you put pen to paper and think about this, it will help you decide which topics are most important to cover during jury selection. Decide which of these strengths and weaknesses need to be addressed in your voir dire. Hit the weaknesses head on. Talk to your jury panel about them and find the people who can deal with the issues.

Evaluate the types of witnesses you have in your case. Do you have only one witness? Do your witnesses have priors? Will you be dealing with any expert witnesses? Decide which of these areas must be covered in voir dire as it relates to your specific case.

### READING VS. SPEAKING

Whether you are picking a jury, giving an opening statement, or delivering your closing argument, you will always be more persuasive without notes. Do not abandon the use of notes completely. For instance, you need to have the names of the members of your jury panel available so you can get their names into the record as you speak to them directly. To accomplish this, you may want to use a seating chart outline. Make some short notes or marks next to the panel members' names as a guide. At the very least, consider using a highlighter to mark those you believe you want to keep and those you don't. This provides you with a handy reference point so you can tell in an instant whether the juror that has just made a ridiculous comment should be saved or allowed to fall into the chasm of unacceptability.

Never read your voir dire questions to the panel. All you really need is an outline of words or very short phrases to remind you of what to cover. If you use an outline, it should be clear and concise enough so that you need only glance at it.

## Getting Acquainted with your Panel

### WRITTEN QUESTIONNAIRE

The process of getting acquainted with your panelists should begin before asking your first question. To this end, a written questionnaire filled out in advance is essential. The more you know about the prospective juror at the beginning, the less time you need to ask background questions and the more focused your individual questions.

Many judges will be skeptical of their use in a misdemeanor case. Work with the defense attorney and the judge to develop a mutually beneficial questionnaire that will make efficient use of time in voir dire.

Besides saving time, another advantage of the written question is that people are more open and candid in their responses than if speaking publicly in front of a group of strangers. Your written questions must be carefully drafted or they may do little more than raise other questions. For instance, asking if a juror has ever been convicted of a crime without further asking them what, when, and where is not productive use of a written questionnaire.

## VISUAL OBSERVATIONS

Judging a book—or a juror—by its cover is a risky venture, but there are some obvious and relevant things you should look for. The way a person is dressed and what book they brought with them into the courtroom can tell you something about them. Racial or ethnic background is something one can easily observe. While it is illegal to base peremptory challenges on a juror's race, it is still important to note a juror's race. What *Batson* has done is require the State to be prepared to explain its reason for excusing all minority group members on a jury panel.[1] That holding extends to gender as well.[2]

You might also note who is speaking with whom as they are waiting for voir dire to begin or during breaks. Also note individuals who appear to have health problems if those problems could affect their ability to observe evidence, follow the proceedings, and be available for the entire trial.

## BEGINNING OF VOIR DIRE

How you begin your voir dire may vary, but don't put venire panelists to sleep with your opening comments. Though many prosecutors begin by introducing themselves, there may be no need to do this if the judge has already introduced you to the panel. You might consider introducing other participants (clerk, court reporter, your investigator, the bailiffs) who are in the courtroom if the judge has not done so. This goes to reinforce the idea that this is your courtroom. The jurors are visiting, helping you take on the role of host.

If you can make the jurors smile in your opening comments, that will ease their tension and make them more likely to open up to you during voir dire. No matter what words you use to begin your voir dire presentation, do so from a position of confidence and strength.

Never read your opening comments from notes. Make eye contact with the potential jurors and try to put them at ease. Explain to them how you will structure your voir dire. If they need to stand when they speak, let them know this in advance.

In the early part of your voir dire examination, go over your witness list with jurors to see if they recognize anyone. If the judge has not done so, ask them if they know the defendant, his attorney, or anyone else in the courtroom.[3]

It is also important to ask if they know other members of their jury panel. Jurors commonly know other panel members from work, church, or other community functions. If you find panel members know each other, explore that relationship briefly, by asking something like: "Mr. Jones, would the fact that you and Mr. Smith work at the same factory make it difficult for you to reach an independent verdict if you were to both end up on this jury?"

---

1 *Batson v. Kentucky*, 476 U.S. 79, 106 S.Ct. 1712, 90 L.Ed.2d 69 (1986). For more information on *Batson* challenges, see Diane Beckham, *Prosecutor Trial Notebook* (TDCAA © 2008).

2 *JEB v. Alabama*, 511 U.S. 127, 114 S.Ct. 1419, 128 L.Ed.2d 89 (1994); *Fritz v. State*, 946 S.W.2d 844 (Tex. Crim. App. 1997).

3 *Noah v. State*, 495 S.W.2d 260 (Tex. Crim. App. 1973) (a prospective juror may be excused for cause when he has a personal acquaintance with the defendant that would make it difficult to be fair and impartial); *Mize v. State*, 754 S.W.2d 732 (Tex. App. — Corpus Christi 1988, pet. ref'd).

Many people like to describe to the jury how the voir dire process works, pointing out that they are on the jury at the end not because they were *selected* but because they were not struck. Though this is the truth, I don't understand the logic of telling the panel this. What benefit does an attorney gain from telling a panel member that their making the jury is an indication that they did not strongly impress either side?

Which, if any, of the topics you go into at the start of voir dire examination will depend on the amount of time you are given. Whatever you discuss in the first five to 10 minutes, the topic should put you in a confident and positive professional light. What kind of impression you make on the jury with your appearance, your comfort level, your confidence, and the rapport you establish with the panelists will control how they view and accept other matters you present during voir dire and throughout the trial of your case.

## Challenging or Rehabilitating Jurors

The prosecutor has dual goals in voir dire. From the time she begins voir dire to the time the panel is passed to the defense, she must firm up those jurors she wants and challenge or expose those who must be eliminated. Both goals demand that the prosecutor put the panel at ease so that jurors feel comfortable admitting their biases. As you ask questions, both you and any prosecutor partner should scan the panel for reactions.

### EXPOSING FOR CHALLENGE

Some jurors may be reluctant to raise their hands to voice dissent with an issue you have raised, but they may not be able to mask their displeasure in their facial expression or body language. If a juror is brave enough to say openly something that would make them a bad state's juror, it is important to mask your disapproval.

For instance, if a potential juror says, "I could not convict upon the opinion testimony of a police officer because I believe most officers are corrupt and will lie on the stand." Let the potential juror know very quickly that she is entitled to her opinion and that it is all right to feel that way. What isn't all right is to hide those feelings. If she bases her negative feelings on a bad experience, you should not explore that in front of the rest of the panel but rather at the bench. Get the juror to agree that her feelings constitute a bias against the state. Before you move on from that juror's statement, survey the rest of the panel to see if anyone agrees with the juror.

### REHABILITATING

Jurors who will probably favor the state are usually easier to spot than those who are defense-oriented. Many times state's-oriented jurors have relatives in law enforcement, and people are more willing to admit to having those relatives than family members who have criminal histories.

You can't just ignore these good state's jurors and assume they will make it by the defense attorney's scrutiny. You need to prepare them for defense voir dire. One way to firm them up is to communicate to them what answers will enable them to stay on the panel. Let them know it is possible to be pro-law enforcement and still be fair. It is possible to believe in stricter DWI laws and still be able to afford the accused his right to a fair trial.

### DEALING WITH OBJECTIONS

If you draw an objection to your description of the law and the judge overrules it, repeat what you said. This will make it clear, in case panelists didn't catch or understand the court's ruling, that your description was accurate. If you make a response, direct that response to the judge. Do not argue with defense counsel. Simply state your response. Get the court's ruling and move on if the objection is sustained.

## BIAS & PREJUDICE

Go over the terminology you will be using during the voir dire examination. "Bias" and "prejudice" are two very harsh words that provide the necessary basis for a successful challenge for cause. You can make it much easier for a panel member to admit they are biased or prejudiced if you make this type of admission more acceptable. One way to approach it is as follows:

> Each of us have certain life experiences that have shaped our views and beliefs. Sometimes those experiences have had such an effect on us that we can no longer view certain matters objectively. For instance, if your were the victim of a burglary last night, you might have trouble sitting on a jury in a burglary case this morning. That doesn't mean that you couldn't be a good juror in another type of case.

Advise potential jurors that you don't intend to embarrass anyone with your questioning. Let them know that if a question calls for information that is too personal for them to discuss in front of the panel, you can discuss it with them outside of the presence of the rest of the panel. You should find out your judge's preference for the timing of these situations. Some judges like to deal with these matters as they come up while others would prefer to reserve them until a break or until the end of the voir dire process.

Avoid the questions "Can you be fair?" or "Can you follow the law?" No one wants to admit outright in front of a crowd of people that he cannot be fair. Moreover, the most unfair people think they are very fair and therefore would never admit to being unable to follow the law. Lead these jurors down a path to get them to admit their biases. Jurors must believe it is acceptable to hold certain views before they will admit to them. Sometimes you can accomplish this either by: (1) admitting one of your own weaknesses or biases, or (2) flushing out at least one juror who will admit a weakness and then asking the other panelists if they agree or disagree with that juror.

## POLICE OFFICER WITNESSES

Many people have a definite bias for or against police officers. Most of the DWI cases you try will rely primarily on the "opinion" testimony of a police officer. This is especially true if there is no videotape at the scene or the station house. Either on the questionnaire or verbally, ask jurors about any bad experiences they may have had with police officers. Firm up the pro-law enforcement jurors by pre-empting the defense's claims that they would automatically give an officer's testimony more weight. Get them to commit to you that they will judge an officer's credibility just like any other witness.

Don't let jurors confuse giving an officer credit for her experience with giving her more credibility because she wears a uniform and a badge. If a juror says he would tend to believe what an officer says just because that person is a police officer, he is demonstrating a bias in favor of law enforcement.[4] This is distinguishable from giv-

**TIP**

A statement by a potential juror that the testimony of one witness would not be enough for him to convict, even if that testimony proved all elements beyond a reasonable doubt, may make that juror challengeable for cause. The juror won't be subject to challenge simply for saying that one witness alone would create reasonable doubt for her. To be challengeable for cause, the juror must state that even after she was convinced of the defendant's guilt beyond a reasonable doubt after the testimony of one witness, she would still require more witnesses. See *Zinger v. State,* 932 S.W.2d 511 (Tex. Crim. App. 1996).

4 See, e.g., *Lane v. State,* 822 S.W.2d 35 (Tex. Crim. App. 1991); *Harris v. State,* 784 S.W.2d 5 (Tex. Crim. App. 1989); *Sawyers v. State,* 724 S.W.2d 24 (Tex. Crim. App. 1986); *Hernandez v. State,* 563 S.W.2d 947 (Tex. Crim. App. 1978).

ing the officer's opinion more weight than a civilian's as a result of the officer's training and experience.

**Practice Pointer**

One way to demonstrate the concept that a person's training can make him a better observer is to ask how many people on the panel have bought a house. Did they hire an inspector to look over the house before they bought it? Did the inspector notice problems that the potential buyers had missed? How was the inspector able to do that? The point you are making is that a person's training can make him aware of certain things that are not obvious to the untrained eye.

## Educating Jurors about the Law

Jurors will enter the voir dire arena with their own definitions and beliefs about the law. Part of your job is to educate them about what the law actually is. Too many times prosecutors put the proverbial cart before the horse and ask a potential juror what they think about the law before discussing that law with them. Let them know early on that the law is often confusing, and it is natural to have questions about it. Use charts so that they have a chance to read the law for themselves. If you just recite it to them, they might miss something that could later cause them concern.

### VISUAL AIDS

As you go over the law applicable to your case, visual aids can be helpful. Most people understand and retain what they read better than what they hear. If you use a chart, make sure it is large, legible, and that all words are properly spelled. When you recite a portion of the law, do so correctly. If you have any doubts about your ability to do this, read it right out of the Penal Code. (One exception to the general rule that does not favor reading during voir dire.) [**See Appendix 7-1 for an example of an elements chart and Appendix 7-2, showing the different definitions of intoxication.**]

### LEGAL ISSUES

#### *"Beyond a Reasonable Doubt"*

Emphasize first of all that "beyond a reasonable doubt" does not mean "beyond all doubt." Stress that the state has this burden only as to the elements of the offense. Point out that the law does not require the evidence to convince jurors immediately but anticipates that jurors may arrive at verdicts after they have heard the views of other jurors. That is why six (or 12) jurors are sent to one room together rather than having each juror alone in her own room.

#### *Elements*

Go over each of the elements that you have to prove. Even though most of these cases come down to a dispute only about one element—whether a suspect was intoxicated—it is still worth explaining to the jury that you have to prove that the offense occurred in a particular county and state and on a public street so they can understand why you ask certain very basic, seemingly obvious questions of your witnesses.

**TIP**

Jurors are properly challengeable for cause when they are unable to base a conviction on one of the three legal definitions of intoxication. See *Fierro v. State,* 969 S.W.2d 51 (Tex. App. — Austin 1998, no pet.); *Hamlin v. State,* 902 S.W.2d 613 (Tex. App. — Houston [1st Dist.] 1995, no pet.).

#### *Intoxication*

Texas has three separate definitions of intoxication. The first two mean not having the normal use of one's mental or physical faculties due to the introduction of alcohol into the body. Stress you need only prove the defendant did not have the normal use of physical or mental faculties. Phrase it as just having to prove "any loss of the normal use..." If the defense objects, you can counter that the law does not require a total loss of faculties.

The third definition requires proving that a person had a blood alcohol content of .08 or greater. You should stress that these are separate and independent definitions of intoxication. Demonstrate to them that the first two are quantitative and the third is qualitative. A person can give a breath sample showing an alcohol content of .05 and still be legally intoxicated if the state can show that she did not have the normal use of her mental or physical faculties. To illustrate this idea, discuss the issue of tolerance with them. Ask the members of the panel if any of them knows someone who appears tipsy after as little as one or two drinks. Ask them if they know anyone who can drink a couple of six packs and still appear to have control of their faculties. Tie those examples into your explanation of why two definitions are necessary.

**Practice Pointer**

One way you can help the panel understand why we need two different definitions is to talk about two hypothetical people the law wants to protect the public from: Bubba and Billy. Bubba is a big guy (200 pounds) has been drinking since he started shaving (at age 16), can put away two to three pitchers of beer without slurring his speech or stumbling. Ask whether anyone on the panel has Bubba's tolerance for alcohol. Does anyone on the panel know a Bubba? Despite Bubba's seeming tolerance for alcohol, however, his BAC would still be over the legal limit.

Consider Billy, on the other hand. Billy weighs 99 pounds and never had a drop of alcohol in his life until his wedding day. Billy has a couple of glasses of champagne, and his balance is affected. His speech is slightly slurred. He is making inappropriate comments to his in-laws. His mental and physical faculties are clearly not normal. Does anyone on the panel have Billy's tolerance for alcohol? Does anyone on the panel know someone like Billy? Despite an under-0.08 BAC, however, Billy doesn't have the normal use of his faculties.

The law says neither Bubba nor Billy should be operating a motor vehicle.

You might also want to follow this up with a question to test the jurors' knowledge and ability to follow the law:

**Sample Question**

If we prove to you that a defendant's alcohol concentration was .08 or greater at the time he was driving, but you believe he had the normal use of his mental or physical faculties, would you be able to find from the evidence that the defendant was legally intoxicated?

A "no" answer qualifies them for a challenge for cause as they have a bias against the law regarding intoxication. Jurors must understand that the definitions are independent and distinct. And they don't have to agree on which mode of intoxication was proven: Two jurors can believe a loss of mental faculties; two can believe a loss of physical faculties; and two can believe the defendant's BAC was .08 or more, and the verdict must be guilty.

**Practice Pointer**

One way to demonstrate that the two definitions are separate and independent ways of proving the same thing is to offer the following example. Tell them to consider the word "sick" and the ways we can determine if a person is sick. Say your child has no obvious signs of being ill, but your instinct tells you that something is wrong. When you take the child's temperature with a thermometer, it reads 103 degrees. Can we all agree that the child is sick? Now let's say your other child is vomiting, lethargic, and has diarrhea, so you take the child's temperature but he has no fever. Can we all agree that despite what the thermometer says, that child is also sick?

You need to get the jurors thinking about why the law has such definitions. Remind them of the complexity of driving or operating a motor vehicle. Get your panel talking about the mental faculties that alcohol might affect. Two that are crucial are judgment and reaction time. Help your jurors see that these and other faculties can be diminished in a person and yet that person may still be able to walk and touch their nose.

The point you want to make is that the law is protecting us from both the intoxicated driver who drives all over the road *and* from the intoxicated driver who appears to be driving just fine until he has to react to an emergency situation.

**Practice Pointer**

One way to get jurors thinking about the importance of having all of our faculties about us is to ask the following question of the entire panel: "If you were on an airplane and the pilot told you over the intercom that he had just left a bar and was not drunk but may not have the 'normal use of his mental and physical faculties,' how would you react? Why?"

**TIP**

A prospective juror who states that he would be unable to convict without a breath test is challengeable for cause because he had a bias against a portion of the law on which the state was entitled to rely. See *Fierro v. State,* 969 S.W.2d 51 (Tex. App. — Austin 1998, no pet.).

***Breath Test***

Typically in voir dire, I only mention the intoxilyzer instrument to ask whether anyone on the panel has heard of it, saving more detailed discussion for how the instrument works for the trial itself. I mention the instrument to remind them that they can use their common sense to determine if the test result obtained after the suspect was driving is proof of how intoxicated the driver was at the time they were operating a vehicle.

***"Normal Use of Faculties"***

The state does not have to show what the defendant's normal faculties are to prove that she did not have them at the time of the offense.[5] Become familiar with the cases cited for this proposition in order to rebut any suggestion the defense may make about the defendant's normal abilities. Because the "normal faculties" cases are based upon the opinion of a police officer, this point might be made through the following question:

**Sample Question**

As I have told you, the law does not require that the state prove what a defendant's normal faculties are to prove intoxication. If an officer could obtain probable cause to arrest individuals for intoxication only when they knew what the person's normal faculties were like, whom could they arrest? (Answer is other officers and the officer's family and friends.)

You can also point out that the members of the jury panel form opinions about whether a person is intoxicated all the time. You can demonstrate this by asking them if they have ever seen a stranger in public whom they believed was intoxicated. Those who say they have should be asked what they saw, heard, and smelled that led them to form that opinion.

The Amarillo court of appeals has ruled that the question, "Do you believe a person is the best judge of whether or not they are intoxicated?" is proper and does not amount to a comment on the defendant's right not to testify.[6]

---

5 *Hernandez v. State*, 107 S.W.3d 41 (Tex. App. — San Antonio 2003, pet. ref'd); *Railsback v. State*, 95 S.W.3d 473 (Tex. App. — Houston [1st Dist.] 2002, pet. ref'd); *Fogle v. State*, 988 S.W.2d 891 (Tex. App. — Fort Worth 1999, pet. ref'd); *Reagan v. State*, 968 S.W.2d 571 (Tex. App. — Texarkana 1998, pet. ref'd); *Massie v. State*, 744 S.W.2d 314 (Tex. App. — Dallas 1988, pet. ref'd).

6 *Kirkham v. State*, 632 S.W.2d 682 (Tex. App. — Amarillo 1982, no pet.).

### TV MYTHS

Television has done so many things to make prosecutors' jobs harder, and justice sometimes suffers at the hands of the media and the entertainment industry. Explain to the panel that real-life trials are not like TV. If a nurse or doctor is on the panel, ask them if everything on the show "ER" is realistic and accurate. Of course, they will say no. You can then make the same comparison to law shows. They are unrealistic and generally inaccurate. Explain that trials are much longer and generally more boring than TV. Explain that TV witnesses are not the same in real life. There are no commercial breaks, no makeup artists, no wardrobe people, etc.

### WHAT YOU DON'T HAVE TO PROVE

Remind the panel members that the state has to prove only the elements of the offense. Point out to them there are things they might want to know on which the state has no burden of proof. For example, the state need not prove that the defendant intended to get intoxicated, that the defendant knew she was intoxicated, what brand or how much alcohol the defendant was drinking, or that the defendant was driving really badly.

Just telling the panel you don't have to prove one of the above may not be enough. I suggest you get them thinking about why those things are not part of our burden. For instance on the issue of not having to prove the defendant intended to drive while intoxicated or even knew that she was intoxicated, you might ask the following question:

**Sample Question**

Could a person who is legally intoxicated not be aware that they have lost the normal use of the their mental faculties? What you hope the panel will see is that if a person's mental faculties are not normal, their ability to perceive the effect of the intoxication on those faculties might likewise be impaired.

### BREATH TEST REFUSAL

Once you've described the different definitions of intoxication, go on to explain the law regarding breath test refusals (if this is a case where there was a refusal). Tell the panel the law contains an implied consent that every person gives upon getting behind the wheel and on the road. This law means that every driver agrees to give a breath or blood sample upon an officer's request after arrest for suspicion of driving while intoxicated.

Explain that the law will not physically compel a person to give a sample, but that the officer warns the driver that if he refuses to give a sample as requested, he could lose his license for 90 days to a year (one year suspension if the person was under the age of 21 at the time of the refusal).

Further advise panelists that a driver is told that his refusal to give a sample is evidence that a jury will hear about and can be considered on the issue of his guilt. See if there are members of your panel who think this is unfair and determine whether they might be subject to a challenge for cause.

The main point you want to get across to them here is that if the state is only relying on the "loss of normal use" definition of intoxication, it is because the defendant refused to provide the jury with the opportunity to consider the ".08" definition.

I like to ask the panel if anyone sees this as a violation of a suspect's right against self-incrimination. Some people will be disturbed by this and will not hold the refusal against the defendant. This question has allowed me to obtain more challenges for cause than any other question in voir dire.

I also ask the panel if anyone is concerned about convicting the defendant without a scientific test. I remind them that the decision to provide them with that evidence is totally in the defendant's hands. I also remind them that the legislature has said that the jury can use that refusal as some evidence of guilt. If any juror still insists he would need a breath or blood test, he is challengeable for cause.[7]

A defense attorney asking a member of a jury panel whether "they could think of a reason why anyone would not take such a [breath] test" was held to be improper in its form.[8] The Court of Criminal Appeals has also ruled that the question, "If someone refused a breath test, would you presume him guilty on their refusal alone?" was improper, because it constituted an attempt to commit the juror.[9] Note that this case also reaffirms that a juror may permissibly presume guilt from evidence of a refusal to submit to a breath or blood test.

## VIDEOTAPES

If you have a videotape that shows the defendant at the scene of the stop, it will presumably be a good tape. A prosecutor can tell jurors that in some cases, the jury might get to see a videotape, and the prosecutor can ask jurors whether they think a tape might be helpful. Other than this brief mention, however, I don't recommend further discussion. Instead, get jurors to think about what they won't be able to tell from a videotape, such as a strong odor of an alcoholic beverage or red, bloodshot eyes. If the tape is of poor quality, it may be difficult to judge whether the defendant had slurred speech.

### *Time*

The main disadvantage of the station house videotape typically involves time. Anywhere from 10 minutes to two hours may have elapsed between the time of the stop and the time of the videotaping. Explore with the panel what difference that time might make by asking the following series of questions:

---

**Practice Pointer**

Ask the panelists if any of them think a tape that shows a defendant five minutes after the stop would be helpful evidence as to whether or not that defendant was intoxicated while driving. Then ask the same question, but make it 15 minutes after the stop, and then 40 minutes after the stop, and so on. You should not inquire into any more of a delay than you have in your case.

---

### *Masking*

You should also discuss the issue of a defendant's ability to hide or mask their loss of mental or physical faculties from officers. See if they believe "masking" is possible over a short period of time by asking questions similar to the following:

---

7 *Fierro v. State*, 969 S.W.2d 51 (Tex. App. — Austin 1995, no pet.); *Hamlin v. State*, 902 S.W.2d 613 (Tex. App. — Houston [1st Dist.] 1995, no pet.).

8 *Harkey v. State*, 785 S.W.2d 876 (Tex. App. — Austin 1990, no pet.).

9 *Standefer v. State*, 59 S.W.3d 177 (Tex. Crim. App. 2001).

**Practice Pointer**

Ask panelists if any of them ever had to sneak by their parents or their spouse after having too much to drink. Were they able to appear to be normal while they were in their parents' presence? What was their motivation for trying to cover their condition? (Probable answer: Fear of punishment.)

## OPERATING A MOTOR VEHICLE IS COMPLICATED

Another very basic line of questioning is to explore with panelists whether a person's ability to walk a straight line and touch her nose means that she can safely operate a motor vehicle. Driving a car is something most of us do without thinking about it. It is such a regular occurrence that we are not even aware of everything we are doing at the same time. Times when a person is reminded how complicated driving a car can be are:

1. When they were learning to drive for the first time; and
2. When they are teaching someone else how to drive.

A good way to explore this is to ask if anyone on the panel thinks driving is a complicated, difficult thing to do. Ask panelists how many things one must focus on at the same time while driving down a street. Make note of those jurors young enough that the learning-to-drive experience is fresh and ask them to recount something about that process. Find a parent who has taught a child to drive, and ask her if it made her appreciate how difficult driving can be. These are good people to ask why it is important to have all of our mental and physical faculties when driving a car.

## RANGE OF PUNISHMENT

If the jury will be assessing punishment, discuss the punishment range with them and qualify panelists on their ability to consider the full range. The law requires that a person be able to do this before he has heard any of the facts in the case. Many times you will hear defense counsel remind the jurors in closing argument that they all promised to consider probation. This is misleading because jurors' obligation to consider the full range of punishment does not extend to the time after they have heard the facts of the case. The process of qualifying them on the range of punishment has two parts:

1. **Expose the weak jurors.** Ask if there is anyone who could not consider jail time for someone charged with DWI. Ask them if they could fairly consider the maximum incarceration period.
2. **Firm up the status of your strong panel members.** You may want to further explain what "fairly consider" means. It doesn't mean that they must commit to give or not give any particular punishment. The law merely asks that jurors keep an open mind until they have heard all of the facts.

One way a prosecutor can determine an undesirable juror is to ask a question like:

**Sample Question**

Have you ever been in the presence of someone who has just read something about a case on trial, and that person says that if he was ever on a jury, he would always give the maximum? Any person who feels that way and cannot wait until the trial evidence has been fully presented—who cannot base their punishment verdict on the facts of that particular case—should not be serving on a jury. Do any of you feel the same way as the person I just described? Can each of you give fair consideration to the full range of punishment and wait until you hear the facts before you determine what that means?

**TIP**

A prospective juror is not challengeable for cause based on inability to consider the full range of punishment as long as she can consider the full range of punishment for the offense as defined by law. A prospective juror may not be challenged for cause simply because he will use facts to determine punishment. The proper question to determine bias against the law regarding punishment is whether in a proper case as defined by statute, where the facts justify it, the venire person could fully and fairly consider the entire range of punishment, including the minimum and maximum. See *Fuller v. State*, 829 S.W.2d 191 (Tex. Crim. App. 1992); *Glauser v. State*, 66 S.W.3d 307 (Tex. App. — Houston [1st Dist.] 2000, pet. ref'd).

### NOT YOUR TYPICAL DEFENDANT

DWI defendants are not like your typical criminal. A DWI defendant likely will remind many of the jurors of themselves. Jurors may remember times when they have gotten behind the wheel of the car after having too much to drink, and they will identify with the defendant and think, "There but for the grace of God go I."

Use part of your voir dire to explore this potential sympathy for the defendant. Ferret out jurors who would be unable to judge the defendant fairly, and remind them that the defendant is not a bad person—he's a person who made a very bad choice.

## Indoctrinating Jurors toward the Theory of your Case

This task is best handled by using examples. For instance, it is not enough to say that the State doesn't have to prove someone is "drunk" but merely that they are "intoxicated." You need to help them see *why* the definition is broader, and arguably more lenient, in a driving while intoxicated case.

**Practice Pointer**

One way to make this point is to discuss another more stringent definition of "intoxication" such as in a public intoxication case. Tell the jury that public intoxication carries a stricter definition in that the state must prove the accused was intoxicated "to the degree that the person may endanger that person or another." Ask the panel if anyone can think of a reason why this more stringent definition is not applied to DWI cases.

Get the panel thinking about the reasons why the legislature said that less than "normal use of faculties" is the standard. Try to get jurors to see driving an automobile for what it is: a complicated, multi-faceted process. Get them focused on how dangerous it can be for a person to operate a vehicle with less than full use of their faculties. One way to make this point is to ask if any of them have ever been in a situation where they were barely able to avoid an accident. If you get a "yes" (and you will find most people have had this experience), ask them if they are sure they would have been able to avoid the accident if their mental or physical faculties had been diminished even slightly.

## Conclusion

Don't worry about covering everything in voir dire. All the suggestions in this chapter would likely take two hours or more to cover effectively. Instead, focus on what is most important for that particular case. For instance, if you are fortunate enough to have a tape of a DWI suspect in which the defendant appears to be clearly intoxicated, you can skip the lengthy explanation of the sometimes-subtle signs of intoxication.

Remember the most important message during voir dire: that you are in control and deserve jurors' trust.

**TABLE 7-1: Voir Dire Do's and Don'ts[10]**

**DOs**

- Pay attention. Listen. Write it down. Believe them. Don't try to talk them out of their position. Just listen.
- Persuade. Sell yourself and sell your case. Appear fair, honest, and real. To do this, you must make certain concessions. We look fair only when we admit and concede the obvious.
- Pay attention to your time. You don't want to be abruptly cut off mid-sentence, as some judges love to do. Make sure you budget your time so you cover the most important topics first. Also, don't be afraid to ask the judge for more time. If the judge says no, then he looks like the bad guy (if you are using your time properly).
- Get jurors talking. A silent juror is a scary juror. Jurors never really believe that they will be selected. They think they won't be chosen, so why bother bearing their souls? Make everyone talk a little bit, and assure them that they have a chance of getting on the jury.
- Ask at least one question of every person so you can see their face and hear their voice, even if just for a short answer.
- Shore up the State's jurors. Anticipate areas where the defense will attack your good jurors. Good State's jurors will always be much too honest and get themselves struck unless you subtly educate them on avoiding it. Explain to them that justice requires jurors to follow certain rules (e.g., defendant's right not to testify, presumption of innocence, etc.) to be fair and impartial.
- Get rid of TV myths. Explain that trials are much longer, less dramatic, and generally more boring than TV.
- Explain under what circumstances you will have certain evidence (e.g., breath test, fingerprints, or DNA). For example, explain that unless a defendant consents to giving a breath sample, there will be no breath test evidence. We are not in the business of forcing someone's face on an Intoxilyzer and making him blow into it. The common theme is that if the defendant leaves the evidence (blood, semen, fingerprints, breath), then the State will have it. But the defendant decides how much evidence is left at the scene. You must explain any lack of evidence as it applies to your case. Jurors expect too much, and they want an explanation for its absence.
- Explain the applicable law without over-lecturing. Pick out the most significant legal concepts and explain them as succinctly and easily as possible. One common mistake is to spend too much time explaining every word in the indictment. Discuss only the pertinent parts in plain language.
- Make the jurors feel at ease about not liking a law or admitting they cannot follow it. Explain that there are laws that even you might disagree with, or even some cases for which you would not be a good juror. ("And that's OK, because some people feel strongly about certain issues and might not be the best juror on this type of case. But you would be a good juror on a different type of case, right, Mr. Smith?" or "Thank you for your honesty. Who feels the same way as Mr. Smith, that this just might not be the right kind of case for you to be on?")
- Find out who has had a prior dealing in the criminal justice system. ("Have you ever visited anyone in TDC or county jail? Who was this person?" and "In your opinion was that person treated fairly?")
- Find out if someone cannot sit in judgment of another for strong moral or philosophical reasons. Note that members of some religious denominations have strong views regarding this issue. Find these people and determine if their feelings are so strong that they will be unable to sit as a fair and impartial juror in this case. Question whether these jurors would be unable to take the required oath. Challenge them for cause.

---

10 Thanks to former Assistant District Attorney Casey Garrett (Harris County), from whose written materials and presentation at the 2003 TDCAA Prosecutor Trial Skills course this information was taken.

### DON'TS

• Don't ever say, "I take by your silence..." The only thing going on in a silent juror's mind is how happy he is that he doesn't have to speak out loud in front of the panel. If you are desperate for time, you might consider going row by row and requiring at least a head nod or shake from each member of the row. But you must make sure you get some kind of response if you really care about the question, because jurors are not going to volunteer their opinions if they can avoid it.

• Don't be paranoid about a juror tainting the panel with his views. If a juror goes off on a tirade about a particular issue, don't rush to cut him off because you think he might influence other jurors. Use him to ferret out others who share his views but are less vocal. ("Well that's a very interesting idea, Mrs. Smith. Who else feels the way Mrs. Smith does about the war on drugs?")

• Don't wimp out on a question and defer to the judge to answer for you. Be honest and answer as best you can. If you don't know the answer to a random question, consider evading it by saying, "That's a very good question, sir. Is that something that would affect your service as a juror?" or "Would that be important to you to sit as a fair juror in this case?"

• Don't be rude or condescending, but don't be afraid to control the discussion. If someone is consistently and uselessly eating up your time with inane comments, feel free to contain this person firmly and politely. Other jurors will be happy you have done this. However, no matter how annoying a talkative juror is, no one will think it's funny if you are rude or mean to the person. One obvious way to control someone is simply to avoid calling on them when they raise their hand for the 20th time. Another old standby is saying, "Thank you so much for your comments, but I need to move to another topic."

• Don't ignore your gut instinct. If you have a funny feeling about a juror or he gives you bad vibes, get rid of him. If you decide you don't like someone, spend some time asking that person specific questions to get them set up for a challenge for cause so you don't have to burn a strike.

Appendix 7-1: Elements Chart

# Driving While Intoxicated

__ Defendant

__ On or About a Certain Date

__ In Tarrant County, Texas

__ Did Operate

__ A Motor Vehicle

__ In a Public Place

__ While Intoxicated

Texas Penal Code §49.04

## Appendix 7-2: Definitions of Intoxication Chart

# Intoxicated in Texas

1.

Not having the normal use of <u>mental</u> faculties by reason of the introduction of alcohol into the body; or

2.

Not having the normal use of <u>physical</u> faculties by reason of the introduction of alcohol into the body; or

3.

Having an alcohol concentration of <u>0.08</u> or higher.

Texas Penal Code §49.01

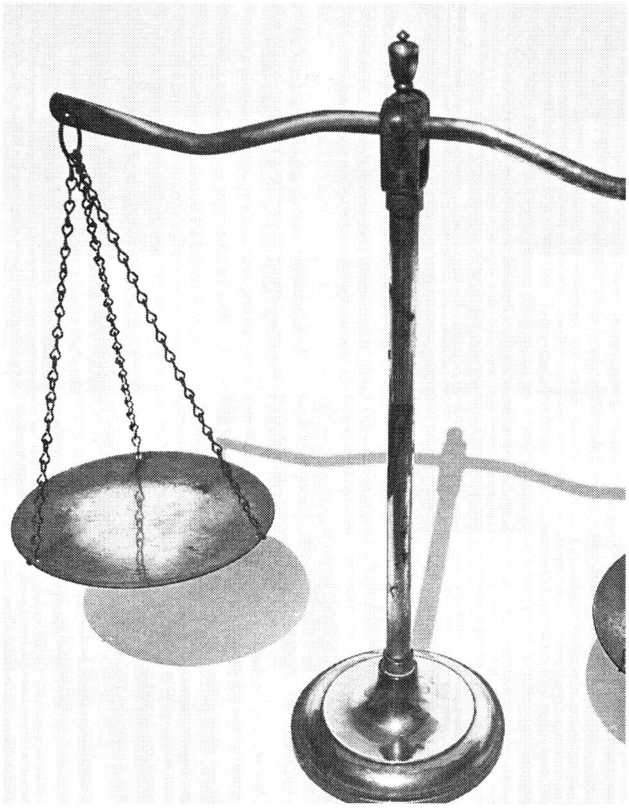



CHAPTER 8

# Evidence

Having the evidence to convict a defendant is one thing—getting the evidence admitted is another. Chapter 8 guides prosecutors through the process of getting your blood, breath, SFST, and video evidence introduced, as well as how to get the most out of your witnesses, rebut defense witnesses, and put together a compelling closing argument.

# Officers

The goal in having your officer testify about the roadside stop is to establish the legality of the stop and everything that happened after it. The officer should first talk about his education, training, and experience, then begin telling the jury what happened when she encountered the defendant; moving to the field sobriety tests, any verbal exchanges, and all signs that support the officer's testimony that the defendant was intoxicated.

The testimony of the arresting officer alone is sufficient evidence to convict a defendant for DWI.[1] An officer can testify about a defendant's pre-arrest, non-custodial statements.[2] **[For more information on custodial interrogation, see Chapter 1.]** Statements made in response to custodial interrogation will be inadmissible without warnings and the defendant's waiver of his rights under *Miranda*.[3] Transportation Code §550.021 and §550.023, which require a driver to give information "to any person injured or the operator or occupant of or person attending a vehicle involved in [a] collision," have no effect on the admissibility of officers' testimony about a driver's oral statements at the scene of an accident.[4]

**TIP**

Chapter 8 contains two different predicates for SFSTs. The first, which begins on page 133, contains more general questions designed to elicit information about the defendant's performance on the SFSTs. The second, which come from APRI, ask more specifically about the administration and evaluating the performance of SFSTs. These questions begin on page 136.

### *Predicates*

The next 13 pages are sample predicates that are helpful in guiding your direct examination of your officers on the traffic stop, the SFSTs, and their opinion as to the defendant's intoxication. While these are intended to be helpful, they're certainly not absolute. Prosecutors must adapt the questions to their own fact scenarios. Remember that the best direct examination feels more like a conversation than simply reading a predicate and waiting for the witness' answer. Your goal should be to make this interesting, interactive, and ultimately persuasive for the judge or jury. **[For more information on preparing officers to testify at trial, see Chapter 6. See also the charts beginning at Table 8-3, which are visual aids for prosecutors to use while officers testify about SFSTs.]**

---

1 *Dumas v. State*, 812 S.W.2d 611 (Tex. App. — Dallas 1991, pet. ref'd); *Valles v. State*, 817 S.W.2d 138 (Tex. App. — El Paso 1991, no pet.); *Irion v. State*, 703 S.W.2d 362 (Tex. App. — Austin 1986, no pet.).

2 *State v. Stevenson*, 958 S.W.2d 824 (Tex. Crim. App. 1997) (controversy over whether defendant or his wife was driving); *Loar v. State*, 627 S.W.2d 399 (Tex. Crim. App. [panel op.] 1981) (statements by defendant that he had "one glass of wine" made during traffic stop and not product of custodial interrogation were admissible); *Hernandez v. State*, 107 S.W.3d 41 (Tex. App. — San Antonio 2003, pet. ref'd); *Lewis v. State*, 72 S.W.3d 704 (Tex. App. — Fort Worth 2002, pet. ref'd); *State v. Waldrop*, 7 S.W.3d 836 (Tex. App. — Austin 1999, no pet.) (roadside stop alone does not place the driver in custody to the degree that he needs to be given *Miranda* warnings; reversing an order suppressing statements about where and when the defendant was drinking and his comment that he was drunk when all the statements were made after the stop but before field sobriety tests were conducted); *Abernathy v. State*, 963 S.W.2d 822 (Tex. App. — San Antonio 1998, pet. ref'd).

3 See, e.g. *Gonzales v. State*, 581 S.W.2d 690 (Tex. Crim. App. 1979) (officer asked defendant if "he had been in trouble before" after asking him to sit in patrol car and telling him he was not free to go); *Alford v. State*, 22 S.W.3d 669 (Tex. App. — Fort Worth 2000, pet. ref'd) (after defendant handcuffed, officer asked him whether he had been drinking; defendant's answer that he had six beers was inadmissible and called for reversal of his conviction).

4 *State v. Stevenson*, 958 S.W.2d 824 (Tex. Crim. App. 1997); *State v. Reyna*, 89 S.W.3d 128 (Tex. App. — Corpus Christi 2002, no pet.); *Spradling v. State*, 628 S.W.2d 123 (Tex. App. — Beaumont 1981, pet. ref'd).

## Sample Questions for Officers

1. State your name for the jury, please.
2. How are you presently employed?
3. Are you a certified peace officer?
4. How long have you been a peace officer with the ___________ Police Department?

 **If the officer has prior employment experience in law enforcement inquire as to when, where, duties... as to each prior job held. It may also be worthwhile to have the officer explain other non-law enforcement training if it adds to credibility or expertise, .i.e. military background, employment as a bartender (chance to observe many intoxicated individuals).**

5. What are your duties in your present position with the ____________ Police Department?

 **If different from his duties on the date of the offense, you would of course have the officer explain those duties as well.**

6. Describe your educational background (high school/college).
7. Have you had any special training pertaining to your duties as a police officer? (Describe/list.)

 **Note: If your arresting officer teaches other officers at the academy or in the field don't neglect to tell the jury about this. If your officer has military background, cover that as well.**

8. Have you had any special training pertaining to detecting signs that a person is intoxicated? (Describe/List).

 **What you are looking for is a description of any and all course training and certifications in FST'S and/or DRE as well as any hands on training in the field.**

9. Were you employed as a police officer with the ___________ Police Department on (offense date)?
10. What hours were you working on that date?
11. Were you in uniform? Were you in a marked patrol unit?
12. Were you working alone or did you have a partner on that date?
13. At about (time first spotted defendant's car) did you observe anything out of the ordinary?
14. What first drew your attention to that car?
15. What type of car was it?

 **Once you identify the type of car, cease calling it a car and call it the "white car, green Honda, blue truck,...".**

16. Is that a "motor vehicle?"
17. Do you see the driver of that car in the courtroom at this time?

 **It is best to get the ID of the defendant done early so you can phrase your driving questions in terms of what the "defendant" did.**

18. Would you point to where the person you recognize as the driver is sitting and identify an article of clothing he/she is wearing for the record?

 Your Honor, may the record reflect that this witness has identified the defendant?

19. When your first observed the defendant's car, what street/highway was it traveling on?
20. Is that a "public place?" Is that located in ___________ County ,Texas?
21. Describe the condition of that road/highway (paved, unpaved, concrete, two lanes, etc.).
22. What were the weather conditions on that date?
23. Where was your car in relation to the defendant's when you first observed it?

**At this point your questioning should focus on the driving behavior of the Defendant and you should take care to describe each and every example of erratic driving behavior the officer observed prior to initiating the stop. What follows will of course vary from case to case.**

***Questions if the Defendant Was Speeding***

1. What is the speed limit on _________ street/highway where the defendant was driving?
2. Is that speed limit posted?

**Have officer note where the last posting is in relation to where the defendant was observed speeding if he/she knows.**

3. What speed was the defendant's car traveling?
4. How did you determine that the defendant was speeding?

**At this point have the officer describe how he determined the defendant's speed. If with radar, have the officer describe how he tested his radar equipment to determine it was working properly. If the determination of speed was done without the help of radar, have the officer describe how he/she arrived at that estimate. It could be important to show that the officer formed the opinion that the defendant was speeding first and merely used radar to confirm the speed.**

5. Was defendant's speed constant?

**Point out fluctuations in speed or the lack thereof. If an officer is right behind a defendant and he/she is not aware of that, this can go to show his/her lack of attention.**

6. Was other traffic present?

**If the defendant was weaving in or out of his lane in heavy traffic you can emphasize the danger the defendant posed to others. If there is testimony that the defendant's car was weaving, ask the officer if there were any obstructions in the road that would account for the defendant's driving behavior.**

7. Over what distance did you follow the defendant's car before you decided to stop him/her?

**If the officer can say, inquire as to the amount of time that passed from the first sighting to the traffic stop.**

8. Describe the driving behavior you observed prior to deciding to stop the defendant's car?

**You want to break this part of the testimony down as much as possible. Don't settle for having the officer say he saw the defendant's car cross over the line. Ask "How many times did he cross the line?" Have the officer be as specific as possible about all the bad driving he/she observed.**

9. What did you do to indicate to the defendant that he should pull over? (activated overhead lights, siren...)
10. Did the defendant pull over immediately?
11. Did the defendant stop in a safe manner and place?

**Don't be afraid to concede that the defendant did some things well. By doing so you pre-empt the defense argument that "All the State wants to tell you about is what the defendant did wrong."**

## DIAGRAMMING THE DEFENDANT'S DRIVING

It is always good to give the jury a visual aid. I feel it is more effective to first have the officer describe the entire spotting, following, stopping sequence to the jury without the use of a diagram. Once that is done, have the officer step down and demonstrate by sketching on a blank sheet of paper on an easel or on a previously prepared diagram that lays out the streets traveled which the officer has described.

***Predicate for the Pre-Drawn Diagram***

1. Officer, I am showing you what has been marked as State's exhibit #_______.
2. Do you recognize this?
3. What is this?

4. Did you create (or help to create) this diagram?
5. Does it fairly and accurately depict the area where you have described seeing this Defendant drive on (date of offense)?
6. Would it aid you in describing what you saw to this jury to be able to refer to and mark on this diagram?

**At this point you can ask the court's permission to have the officer step down and mark on the diagram. I would not offer it at this point unless there is an objection. If there is an objection that it has not been offered into evidence, you may offer it at this time. If the officer marks on it you should re-offer it after he has finished marking it.**

**How the officer marks on it and the type and number of drawings needed will of course vary from case to case. Be sure that you have the officer/witness speak up if they step away from the microphone and see to it that neither you nor the officer blocks the jurors' view as he is using the diagram.**

**WARNING: Before you have the officer demonstrate with the pre-drawn diagram or draw the diagram in front of the jury, you MUST have previously gone over this with the officer. In the jury's presence is not an appropriate time to discover that the officer can't draw or doesn't come across well on his feet. For this reason, I strongly favor the pre-drawn diagram.**

***Making Contact with the Defendant***

1. Once the defendant's car came to a stop, did you make contact with the defendant?
2. When you first made contact with the defendant, was he still in the car?
3. Did you request that the defendant produce his license or other documents?

**If he had difficulty finding his license or registration or said or did anything out of the ordinary, pursue that line of questioning.**

4. Did you ask the defendant any questions at this point?
5. Did you ask the defendant where he had been/was heading?
6. Did you ask the defendant if he had been drinking? Where? What? How many?
7. Did you ask the defendant if he was under a doctor's care or taking any medications?
8. Did you ask the defendant to step out of his car at this time?

**If the defendant had trouble exiting his car, have officer explain/describe.**

9. Did you note any odor on or about the defendant's person?
10. When did you first notice it? (While defendant was in car or when he stepped out of the car)
11. Where did the odor appear to be coming from? (his mouth/breath)
12. How would you characterize the strength of the odor?
13. Could you identify the odor? (alcoholic beverage)
14. Did you observe any alcoholic beverage containers in the defendant's car? If yes, did you observe whether there was any liquid in the container? Was the can/bottle cold to the touch?
15. Did you have an occasion to speak with the defendant?
16. Describe his speech? (slurred, loud, angry, soft)
17. As the Defendant spoke, did you note any odor of an alcoholic beverage?
18. Did you notice anything else about the defendant's appearance? (eyes red/bloodshot, clothing, balance)

***SFSTs (For additional questions on SFSTs, see the predicates suggested by APRI starting on page 136.)***

19. Did you ask the defendant to perform field sobriety *evaluations at the scene?

***Many officers are trained not to call them "tests" and prefer the term "evaluations." It is good to advise them not to be too adamant about this terminology as it can make them appear overly picky and argumentative.**

20. Did the defendant appear to be injured or physically handicapped?

21. Did the defendant tell you that he had any handicaps or disabilities that would interfere with his/her ability to perform physical evaluations?
22. What tests did you have him perform?
23. Explain to the jury what field sobriety evaluations are?

    **This is an area that will depend on the officer's background and experience. Preferably he or she will know that the tests are "Standardized Field Sobriety tests" that were designed and approved by the National Traffic Safety Counsel. If the officer can, have him/her explain that these tests are designed to detect problems with "divided attention." If the officer has a great deal of knowledge or training as to the origin of the tests, have the officer explain that to the jury as well.**

24. What was the first field sobriety test you asked the defendant to perform?
25. Did you demonstrate the test/evaluation first?
26. Did you orally explain how the test was to be performed?
27. Did the defendant indicate he understood your instructions prior to attempting to perform the field sobriety evaluation?
28. Did the defendant attempt to perform the test?
29. Did the defendant successfully complete the test?
30. In what way did the defendant fail to perform the test properly?

    **Have the officer clearly explain what "clues" he/she is looking for in each field sobriety test and the reason behind the significance of these "clues" (If the officer knows enough about the tests to explain it).**

    **The HGN test requires a more detailed explanation of the "clues" the officer is looking for and the underlying theory behind the test. It can be an effective device to have the officer demonstrate how he told the Defendant to do the test and to perform them in front of the jury. Before you have the officer do this in front of the jury, preview his or her performance. If the officer doesn't appear comfortable doing the demonstration, skip it.**

    **A good visual aid for showing the jury what is meant by "jerking" or "nystagmus" is to have the officer use a ping pong ball with a pupil-size black dot on it. Another option is to offer video that shows nystagmus as a visual aid.**

31. In your opinion does it diminish the reliability of the field evaluation result that the defendant was nervous or had not practiced the test? (No)

**GO THROUGH EACH OF THE TESTS PERFORMED IN THE MANNER DESCRIBED ABOVE**

***Conclusion***

32. Have you had an occasion to stop and arrest people for DWI in the past? On few or many occasions?
33. Have you had an occasion to make a determination as to whether an individual was intoxicated before? On few or many occasions?
34. Based upon your training, experience and observations of the defendant's driving and behavior at the scene of the stop, did you form an opinion as to whether the defendant had lost the "normal use of his mental or physical faculties?"

    **Before you ask this question make sure that the officer is aware that "loss of normal use of mental or physical faculties" is the definition of intoxication.**

35. And what was your opinion?
36. On what did you base that opinion?

    **Presumably upon everything the officer observed from first sighting to the point of arrest. The main point here is to let the jury know that no "one" factor led to this determination, but rather it was all of the factors combined.**

37. Do you have an opinion regarding what caused the defendant's intoxication?
38. What caused it? (introduction of alcohol into his system)
39. Once you determined he was intoxicated, what did you do next? (placed him under arrest for DWI)
    * Did you advise the defendant of his rights? What rights? (*Miranda*)

* Did you ask the defendant if he understood his rights?
* Did the defendant indicate he understood his rights?
* Did you ask him if he wanted to waive his rights and make any statements?

***There is no reason for the officer to have given the Miranda warnings at the scene unless that is where the custodial interrogation was going to be conducted. If the officer did not do so you would of course save these questions for later.**

40. Did the defendant volunteer any statements after he was placed under arrest?
41. Where was the defendant transported to? (the jail)
42. Did the defendant volunteer any statements during the trip to the station?

**Only ask this if he did make statements because if he did not, you might be objected to for commenting on his/her exercising his right to remain silent. At this point, if he is videotaped you can go into that or if he was offered a breath test you can go into that as well as long as this witness was present at that time. The questions relating to warnings about the taking of the breath test are contained on the Intoxilyzer operator section.**

**If the same officer was present or had an opportunity to view the videotape made of the defendant (if one was made), you might want to ask the officer if the defendant's performance on the tape was the same as that out at the scene or whether it was better or worse. If you pursue this line of questioning, be sure and point out how much time has elapsed from the time of the stop to the time of the taping.**

## PREDICATE FOR ADMITTING DIC-24 BREATH TEST REFUSAL FORM

1. Officer, when you got the defendant into the videotape room/to the station house did you read any warnings to him/her regarding the giving of a sample of his/her breath?
2. I'm handing you what has been marked as State's Exhibit #____. Do you recognize this? (Yes, it is the DWI statutory warnings sheet.)
3. Is this a true and correct copy of the same warning sheet that you read to this defendant? (Yes)
4. Was a copy of this warning sheet provided to the Defendant so that he/she could read it? (Yes)
5. There appears to be handwriting on this sheet. Whose handwriting is that? (Mine)
6. There is a place for the defendant's signature on this form. Did he/she sign it? (Yes/No)
7. Did the defendant agree to give a sample of his/her breath? (Yes/No)
8. Your Honor, at this time we would offer State's Exhibit #______ into evidence.

**If there is a videotape and you can clearly hear the warning read, I don't think you need to orally publish this to the jury at this time. If that is not the case, you or the officer should read the form to the jury. It is also more effective to publish a written exhibit by reading it than it is to hand it to the jurors and let them each read it separately.**

9. Officer, did you write a report concerning the stop and arrest of this defendant? When did you write this report?
10. Do you have a copy of that report with you?
11. Did you refer to that report prior to testifying?
12. Your Honor, at this time I tender a copy of the report to the defense counsel and pass the witness for cross-examination.

**I go through these last three questions to demonstrate to the jury in a subtle way that the officer is not relying strictly on his memory of what happened a year ago.**

## HORIZONTAL GAZE NYSTAGMUS

| *Direct Examination* | *Expected Officer Response* |
|---|---|
| 1. Which of the SFSTs did you have the defendant perform first? | 1. The horizontal gaze nystagmus (HGN) tests. |
| 2. From your training and experience, could you explain to the jury what HGN is? | 2. HGN refers to an involuntary jerking of the eyes as they gaze to the side. |
| 3. Officer, did you make any observations of the defendant's eyes before he performed the HGN test? | 3. Yes. I observed the defendant's tracking of his eyes and observed that they tracked (or moved side-to-side) the same. I also observed that the defendant's pupils were the same size. |
| 4. Why did you do that? | 4. I wanted to rule out the possibility of any neurological dysfunction. If the eyes did not track the same or if the pupils were noticeably different in size, this would have alarmed me to look at the possibility that the impairment I was seeing would be medically related. |
| 5. Was the tracking of the defendant's eyes different or pupil size unequal? | 5. (Answer should be no.) |
| 6. After checking the tracking ability of the defendant's eyes and seeing that his pupils were the same size, what did you do next? | 6. I had the defendant perform the HGN test. |
| 7. Officer, please explain to the jury exactly how you administered the HGN test to the defendant. | 7. First, I asked the defendant if he wore glasses or contacts. (Glasses taken off for this test; contacts noted.) I also asked the defendant if he was taking any medication. I then held a stimulus (pen, penlight, etc.) approximately 12 to 15 inches in front of the defendant's face, slightly above eye level. I asked the defendant to follow the movement of my stimulus with his eyes and to not move his head. I then moved my stimulus in front of the defendant looking at his right eye. First, I checked for a lack of smooth pursuit (whether or not his eyes moved smoothly from side to side). |
| 8. And what was the next thing that you looked for? | 8. Next, I checked for a distinct jerking at maximum deviation (when the eyes gaze all the way to the side). |
| 9. Did you check for anything else? | 9. Finally, I checked for an angle of onset that began before an estimated 45 degree angle. |
| 10. How did you estimate a 45 degree angle? | 10. A 45-degree angle is approximately halfway between the nose and the ear at the point of the shoulder. I did not estimate the exact angle of onset, only that the onset of nystagmus was prior to 45 degrees. |
| 11. Officer, what did you observe when the defendant performed this test? | 11. I observed a lack of smooth pursuit, a distinct jerking at maximum deviation, and an angle of onset of nystagmus that was estimated to begin prior to a 45-degree angle. |
| 12. Is nystagmus a naturally occurring phenomenon? | 12. Yes, but it cannot normally be seen with the naked eye. |
| 13. Will alcohol, or for that matter, any other drug cause nystagmus? | 13. No. Since nystagmus is a naturally occurring phenomenon, alcohol and certain other drugs will only enhance nystagmus so that it can be seen with the naked eye. |
| 14. Officer, is there a scoring procedure with the HGN tests? | 14. Yes. Since there are three clues that I look for (smooth pursuit, maximum deviation, onset prior to 45 degrees) and I look for these clues independently in each eye. There is a maximum score of six clues (three per eye). |

| | |
|---|---|
| 15. And what do these clues tell you? | 15. Four or more clues indicate a 77 percent likelihood that the blood alcohol concentration (BAC) is greater than 0.10. This percentage is based on a study sponsored by National Highway Traffic Safety Administration and conducted by Southern California Research Institute. |
| 16. And how many clues did you find in the defendant? | 16. (List number of and describe clues.) |
| 17. Do you know whether the HGN test has been accepted in the scientific community as a reliable method of evaluating intoxication? | 17. Yes. These tests have met the Frye standard, which means that they have been accepted by the scientific community as a reliable method of evaluation. |
| 18. In your personal experience, have you found the test to provide results consistent with other field sobriety tests taken at the same time? | 18. (Personal experience.) |
| 19. Officer, are there other types of nystagmus? | 19. Yes. |
| 20. What are the other types of nystagmus? | 20. There are certain types of vestibular nystagmus that are caused by movement or action to the vestibular system. Those types of nystagmus are rotational and post-rotational nystagmus, which require a person to be spun around rapidly, disturbing the fluid in the inner ear. There is also caloric nystagmus, which requires cold water to be put in the other ear, stimulating the inner ear fluids. Nystagmus can also result from neural activity. Optokinetic nystagmus occurs when the eyes fixate on an object that suddenly moves out of sight, or when the eyes watch sharply contrasting moving images. |
| 21. How do you know that these other types of nystagmus did not occur? | 21. Vestibular and caloric nystagmus require a controlled environment. Optokinetic nystagmus can be induced in the field if the subject watched the revolving lights on top of the squad car or watched the traffic headlights as they moved rapidly by. In each of the latter two, the defendant was positioned so that the defendant could not see the revolving lights or the headlights of any oncoming cars. |
| 22. Officer, since you found (number) clues in the defendant when the HGN test was performed, what, if anything, does this mean to you? | 22. It means that this is not normal, that alcohol or certain other types of drugs might be involved, and other field sobriety tests should be performed. |

### *HGN*

An officer's testimony about HGN test results is admissible.[5] The officer need not be an opthamologist or have a "practitioner certification" before his testimony will be admissible.[6] Certification from a training course will suffice.[7]

5 *Emerson v. State*, 880 S.W.2d 759 (Tex. Crim. App. 1994); *Quinney v. State*, 99 S.W.3d 853 (Tex. App. — Houston [14th Dist.] 2003, no pet.); *Gullatt v. State*, 74 S.W.3d 880 (Tex. App. — Waco 2002, no pet.).

6 *Emerson v. State*, 880 S.W.2d 759 (Tex. Crim. App. 1994); see also *Kerr v. State*, 921 S.W.2d 498 (Tex. App. — Fort Worth 1996, no pet.) (T.R.Evid. 702 requirements must be met).

7 *Ellis v. State,* 86 S.W.3d 759 (Tex. App. — Waco 2002, no pet.); *Smith v. State*, 65 S.W.3d 332 (Tex. App. — Waco 2001, no pet.).

## WALK & TURN

| *Direct Examination* | *Expected Officer Response* |
|---|---|
| 1. What was the next Standard Field Sobriety Test you gave after the HGN tests? | 1. The second SFST is the walk & turn test. |
| 2. Would you please explain to the jury what the walk & turn test is? | 2. The walk & turn test is a divided attention psychophysical test. |
| 3. What do you mean by "divided attention psychophysical test"? | 3. Divided attention means concentrating on more than one thing at a time. Psychophysical means using the mind and body at the same time. So with these tasks, a person has to use his mind to process information that is being given to him, and his body to execute the instructions. Thus, the subject would have to concentrate on more than one thing while executing the tests. |
| 4. Is driving a car a divided attention psychophysical test in and of itself? | 4. Yes. A person has to concentrate on more than one thing at a time while driving a car. Information is being processed all the time when a person operates a car. |
| 5. And how were the instructions for the walk & turn test administered to the defendant? | 5. The instruction phase went as follows: The defendant was told to place his left foot on the line (or imaginary line if necessary) and then place the right foot on the line, in front of the left foot, with the heel of the right foot against the toe of the left foot. I then demonstrated this heel-to-toe stance.<br><br>I told the defendant to put his arms down against his sides and to keep them there throughout the entire test. The defendant was instructed to maintain this position while given instructions.<br><br>I emphasized that the defendant must not start walking until I said, "Begin." I asked the defendant if he understood.<br><br>I then told the defendant that when I said "begin," he must take nine heel-to-toe steps down the line, turn around, and then take nine heel-to-toe steps up the line. I told the defendant that every time he took a step, the heel must be placed against the toe of the other foot. I then demonstrated several heel-to-toe steps.<br><br>I told the defendant that when the ninth step was taken, he must leave the front foot on the line and turn around using a series of small steps with the other foot. I then demonstrated a proper turn.<br><br>I reminded the defendant that he must watch his feet at all times, must count the steps out loud, and must keep his arms down at his sides. I instructed the defendant that once he started walking, he must not stop walking until the test had been completed.<br><br>I asked the defendant if he understood those instructions, and then told the defendant to begin the test. |
| 6. What clues did you look for in the walk & turn test? | 6. There are eight validated clues of impairment for the walk & turn test. Two clues apply while the suspect is standing heel-to-toe and listening to the instructions:<br><br>(1) cannot keep balance<br><br>(2) starts too soon<br><br>The other six validated clues apply during the walking stage of the test:<br><br>(3) stops walking<br><br>(4) misses heel-to-toe |

(5) steps off the line

(6) raises the arms while walking

(7) takes the wrong number of steps

(8) turns improperly

Four or more clues indicate a 68 percent likelihood that the blood alcohol concentration (BAC) is greater than 0.10. (This percentage is based on a study sponsored by National Highway Traffic Safety Administration and conducted by Southern California Research Institute.)

7. And how did the defendant perform on this test?

7. (Observations of validated and other clues. For example, could not keep balance during instructions, missed heel-to-toe, turned improperly, stepped off line, etc.)

## ONE-LEG STAND

| *Direct Examination* | *Expected Officer Response* |
|---|---|
| 1. Officer, what was the next field sobriety test that the defendant performed? | 1. The one-leg stand test, which is another divided attention psychophysical test. |
| 2. Please tell the jury what the one-leg stand is. | 2. This test requires the defendant to stand on one leg. The other leg is to be extended in front of the defendant in a stiff-legged manner, with the foot held approximately six inches above the ground and with the toe pointed forward. The defendant is to stare at the elevated foot and count out loud in this fashion: "1001, 1002, 1003..." until told to stop. |
| 3. And how was this test administered? | 3. The defendant was told to stand with his feet together and arms down at his sides. I told the defendant to maintain that position while I gave instructions, emphasizing that he should not try to perform the test until I said, "begin." I asked the defendant if he understood.<br><br>I told the defendant that when I said to "begin," he must raise one leg in a stiff-legged manner and hold his foot approximately six inches off the ground, with the toe pointed forward. I demonstrated this proper one-legged stance.<br><br>I told the defendant that he must keep his arms at his sides and must keep looking directly at his elevated foot while counting in the following fashion: "1001, 1002, 1003..." and so on until told to stop. I asked the defendant if he understood. I then told the defendant to begin. |
| 4. And what are the clues you were looking for with this test? | 4. There are four validated clues of impairment that have been identified for the one-leg stand test: (1) sways while balancing; (2) uses arms to balance; (3) hopping; (4) puts foot down. |
| 5. And what is the accuracy of this test? | 5. Two or more clues indicate a 68 percent likelihood that the blood alcohol concentration (BAC) is greater than 0.10. (This percentage is based on a study sponsored by National Highway Traffic Safety Administration and conducted by Southern California Research Institute.) |
| 6. And how did the defendant perform on this test? | 6. (Observations of validated and other clues. For example, swayed while balancing, etc.) |

## CONCLUSION

| *Direct Examination* | *Expected Officer Response* |
|---|---|
| 1. Did you form an opinion as to the defendant's condition? | 1. I believe that the defendant was intoxicated. |
| 2. And what was that intoxication due to? | 2. It was due to the introduction of alcohol, drugs, or a combination of the two into the body. |
| 3. Did you form your opinion on one factor or on the totality of the information gathered? | 3. I formed it on the totality of the information gathered. |
| 4. Would you please tell the jury what factors you took into consideration in forming the opinion that the defendant was intoxicated? | 4. (Response, e.g., driving; statements; observations of defendant's eyes, speech, breath; performance on SFSTs.) |
| 5. Did you have the defendant perform any other field sobriety tests? | 5. (Other tests if applicable.) |

**TABLE 8-1: Visual Aids for SFST Testimony**

Use the following three visual aids during direct examination and closing argument to explain to the jury how the SFST results are relevant to the officer's determination that the defendant was intoxicated.

# WALK AND TURN

**(Check as many as you observe)**

- ________ **Refused/unable to perform**
- ________ **Cannot keep balance during instructions**
- ________ **Starts too soon**
- ________ **Stops while walking**
- ________ **Does not touch heel to toe**
- ________ **Steps off line**
- ________ **Uses arms for balance (raises arms over six inches)**
- ________ **Improper turn (or loses balance on turn)**
- ________ **Wrong number of steps**

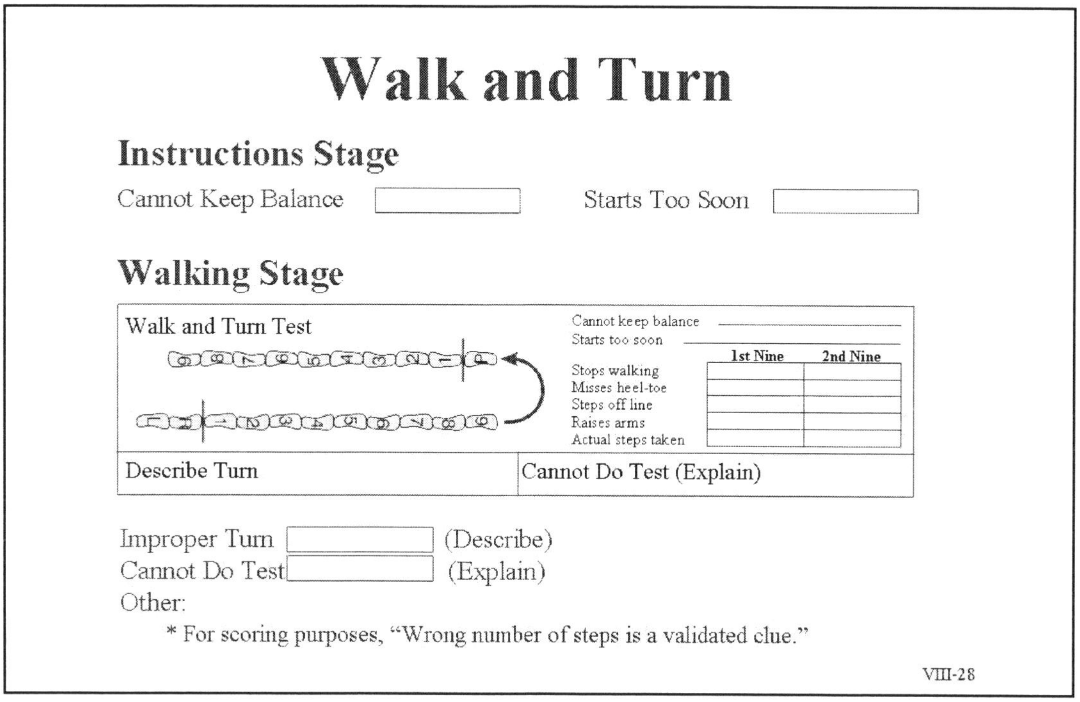

# ONE LEG STAND

**(Check as many as you observe)**

________ **Refused/unable to perform**

________ **Sways while balancing**

________ **Uses arms for balance**

________ **Hops**

________ **Puts foot down**

## One-Leg Stand

**One-Leg Stand:**

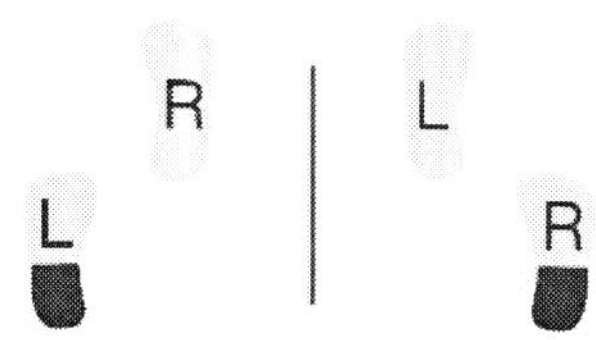


| L | R | |
|---|---|---|
| ☐ | ☐ | Sways while balancing |
| ☐ | ☐ | Uses arms to balance |
| ☐ | ☐ | Hopping |
| ☐ | ☐ | Puts foot down |

# HORIZONTAL GAZE NYSTAGMUS

**(Check as many as you observe)**

**Refused?** Yes_______ No_______

**Contact lenses worn?** Yes_______ No_______

| Left | Right | |
|---|---|---|
| ____ | ____ | Eye does not pursue smoothly. |
| ____ | ____ | Nystagmus in eye is moderate or distinct when eye is moved as far as possible to the left/right. |
| ____ | ____ | Onset of Nystagmus in eye occurs before 45 degrees. Some white is visible. |

**Vertical Nystagmus?** Yes____ No____

## Horizontal Gaze Nystagmus

| | Left | Right |
|---|---|---|
| • Lack of smooth pursuit | | |
| • Distinct nystagmus at max. deviation | | |
| • Onset of nystagmus prior to 45 degrees | | |

Other:

VIII-27

# Videotape Evidence

> **TIP**
>
> For more information about proving the elements of the offense of DWI, see **Chapter 4.** For more information about the types of evidence that place the defendant behind the wheel of the car, see **Chapter 2.**

## EVALUATING THE TAPE

Although it might seem to go against conventional wisdom, videotape can be the State's weakest link in proving a DWI case. There is nothing you can do to make your bad tapes better. The purpose of **Table 8-2** (DWI Videotape Review Form) is to help make the best of bad tapes.

Nothing happens in a vacuum, and videotaping DWI suspects is no exception. To evaluate the videotape, a prosecutor must understand the context in which it was created.

## FILLING OUT THE VIDEOTAPE REVIEW FORM

Complete all the information in the first section (before "warnings given") on the form before reviewing the videotape.

### *Total Elapsed Time*

This is perhaps the most crucial piece of information. It tells you how much time the defendant has had to sober up from the time of the stop to the time she appears on the videotape.

### *Accidents, Injuries, Open Containers*

The offense report is a good source of information for presence of an accident, injuries, or an open container. If the offense report contains no mention of any physical disabilities, check your jail book-in records. These will usually contain a medical history form.

### *Warnings*

All of the necessary warnings that must be given to get the video and/or audio portion of the tape into evidence have been provided for you to check off.

### *Incorrect Warnings*

If your officer has incorrectly told the defendant about the consequences of refusing to give a breath sample, the court will consider the totality of the circumstances in determining whether an extra-statutory warning or statement influenced a driver's decision to provide a specimen.[8]

---

8 *Fienen v. State*, 390 S.W.3d 328 (Tex. Crim. App. 2012) (overruling *Erdman v. State*, 861 S.W.2d 890 (Tex. Crim. App. 1993), and concluding that officer's statements outside the statutory warnings were not coercive because officer was merely responding to the defendant's questions and did not provide any untrue information).

***Prior DWIs***

The main point about noting prior DWIs is to help differentiate the novice from the practiced drunk driver who has been through the taping and field sobriety tests before.

***Attorney Request***

If the attorney request blank is checked, be aware that upon objection from the defense, the invocation of the right to counsel and any subsequent interview will probably be inadmissible.

***Field Sobriety Tests***

The number and type of field sobriety tests will vary from department to department. Hopefully the tests shown on the video are the same tests performed out in the field. It is equally important that the officer demonstrate the test before asking the suspect to perform it. Although this is not an admissibility issue, it is a matter of good police officer practice to show a suspect how you expect them to perform a test before you note that they failed to do it properly.

***Interview***

Even if you determine that the interview portion will be inadmissible, note what the defendant says in case he testifies at trial and changes his story.

***Appearance, Speech, Balance, Tape Rating***

The last items concerning the suspect's appearance, speech, balance, and tape rating are very subjective. If you must err in how you rate the tape, err in favor of the defendant. The more of these tapes you watch, the more critical of the defendant's performance you will become. Try to view these tapes from the perspective of a juror who is expecting to see the same "drunk" the officer described in his report.

## ADMISSIBLE PORTIONS OF VIDEO

In evaluating which portions of the defendant's video will be admissible, one should: (1) note any invocation of the right to counsel; and (2) be able to distinguish testimonial versus non-testimonial acts. In general, constitutional rights (e.g., not to incriminate yourself) do not attach to non-testimonial acts (such as performing field sobriety tests), but it does attach to verbal utterances. All non-testimonial acts on a video, therefore, may come in. But once a defendant has invoked his right to counsel, anything he says on the videotape must be excluded. Remember also that mentions of convictions, arrest, or other extraneous matters may be inadmissible. Identify them for possible objection and extraction.

The following portions of a DWI defendant's videotape may be admitted:

1. visual depictions of field sobriety tests;[9]
2. verbal field sobriety tests-like reciting parts of the alphabet or counting;[10]
3. audio portion of video when police questioning is the type normally incident to arrest and custody and is not reasonably likely to elicit testimony;[11]

> **TIP**
>
> The timing of stationhouse taping and giving defendants their warnings under CCP Art. 38.22 may be critical to getting defendants to perform field sobriety tests. In some jurisdictions, officers ask the defendant to perform field sobriety tests (a request that carries no right to counsel) before they begin custodial interrogation. Reading the Art. 38.22 warnings halts cooperation with law enforcement in many instances and keeps officers from getting valuable non-interrogation evidence on video.

---

9 *Townsend v. State*, 813 S.W.2d 181 (Tex. App. — Houston [14th Dist.] 1991, pet. ref'd) (visual depictions of a sobriety test are not testimonial).

10 *Gassaway v. State*, 957 S.W.2d 48 (Tex. Crim. App. 1997) (reciting and counting are not testimonial).

11 *Jones v. State*, 795 S.W.2d 171 (Tex. Crim. App. 1990); *Dawkins v. State*, 822 S.W.2d 668 (Tex. App. — Waco 1991), *pet. ref'd*, 825 S.W.2d 709 (Tex. Crim. App. 1992); *Pennsylvania v. Muniz*, 496 U.S. 582 (1990).

## TABLE 8-2: Videotape Review Form

TAPE # ____________________ DATE REVIEWED: ____________________
OFFENSE DATE: ____________________ BY: ____________________

DEFENDANT: ____________________ CAUSE #: ____________

POLICE DEPT: ____________________

INTOXILYZER OPERATOR: ____________________ ARRESTING OFFICER: ____________________

DWI: ( ) PRIORS: ____________ ( ) BREATH / BLOOD TEST: ________ ( ) **REFUSAL**
( ) OPEN CONTAINER ( ) SERIOUS BODILY INJURY
( ) ACCIDENT ( ) PHYSICAL DISABILITIES:
____________________
____________________

TIME OF : STOP: ________ TAPE : ________ = TOTAL ELAPSED: ____________

**WARNINGS GIVEN:**

( ) VIDEO
( ) DIC 24: ( ) ORAL ( ) WRITING
( ) POSSIBLE *ERDMAN* PROBLEM: ____________________
____________________

MIRANDA WARNINGS: ( ) GIVEN ( ) WAIVED ATTORNEY REQUESTED: (YES) (NO)

**SOBRIETY TESTS GIVEN:** (YES) (NO)

TEST 1: ____________ ( ) DEMONSTRATED ( ) ATTEMPTED
PERFORMANCE: ( ) GOOD ( ) BAD
COMMENTS: ____________________
____________________

TEST 2: ____________ ( ) DEMONSTRATED ( ) ATTEMPTED
PERFORMANCE: ( ) GOOD ( ) BAD
COMMENTS: ____________________
____________________

TEST 3: ____________ ( ) DEMONSTRATED ( ) ATTEMPTED
PERFORMANCE: ( ) GOOD ( ) BAD
COMMENTS: ____________________
____________________

TEST 4: ____________ ( ) DEMONSTRATED ( ) ATTEMPTED
PERFORMANCE: ( ) GOOD ( ) BAD
COMMENTS: ____________________
____________________

DEFENDANT INTERVIEWED: (YES) (NO)

**INCRIMINATING STATEMENTS:** ____________________
____________________
____________________

GENERAL APPEARANCE ( ) GOOD ( ) FAIR ( ) POOR
COMMENTS: ____________________
____________________

SPEECH: ( ) GOOD ( ) FAIR ( ) POOR
COMMENTS: ____________________
____________________

BALANCE: ( ) GOOD ( ) FAIR ( ) POOR
COMMENTS: ____________________
____________________

**TAPE IS: ( ) GOOD FOR STATE ( ) GOOD FOR DEFENSE ( ) ?**

4. refusal to perform field sobriety tests;[12]
5. the video portions after the audio is suppressed;[13]
6. a defendant's invocation of the right to counsel during a refusal to take a breath test;[14]
7. video portions even if the audio did not record;[15] and
8. the audio portion of field sobriety tests after *Miranda* is invoked.[16]

The following parts of a DWI defendant's videotape can be suppressed:

1. invocation of the right to counsel;[17]
2. invocation of the right to terminate the interview;[18]
3. objected-to extraneous offenses.[19]

## PREDICATE FOR ADMISSION

The goal when putting a videotape into evidence is to get the officer to vouch for its authenticity and accuracy. The officer will testify that the video machine was working properly that night; there was no alteration made to the tape; the appropriate warnings were given, and the defendant seemed to understand the warnings; he waived his rights and agreed to participate in the tests. The video operator will also testify that she had the opportunity to review the tape before trial.

T.R.EVID. 901 controls on the issue of the proper predicate for admission of DWI videotapes.[20] That the machine was operating properly can be inferred from the evidence, and testimony supporting the predicate can come from someone other than the operator of the video.[21] An operator need not have had any special training on the use of video equipment to testify, as long as the operator has some basic knowledge of operating procedures or instructions.[22] **[See sample predicate questions at the end of this section.]**

---

12 *Rafaelli v. State*, 881 S.W.2d 714 (Tex. App. — Texarkana 1994, pet. ref'd); *Dawkins v. State*, 822 S.W.2d 668 (Tex. App. — Waco 1991), *pet. ref'd*, 825 S.W.2d 709 (Tex. Crim. App. 1992); *Barraza v. State*, 733 S.W.2d 379, 381 (Tex. App. — Corpus Christi 1987), *aff'd*, 790 S.W.2d 654 (Tex. Crim. App. 1990).

13 *Huffman v. State*, 746 S.W.2d 212 (Tex. Crim. App. 1988).

14 *Ex parte Jamail*, 904 S.W.2d 862 (Tex. App. — Houston [1st Dist.] 1995, pet. ref'd).

15 *Burke v. State*, 930 S.W.2d 230 (Tex. App. — Houston [14th Dist.] 1996, pet. ref'd); see also *Aguirre v. State*, 948 S.W.2d 377 (Tex. App. — Houston [14th Dist.] 1997, pet. ref'd) (DWI video with no sound is admissible).

16 *Jones v. State*, 795 S.W.2d 171 (Tex. Crim. App. 1990).

17 *Hardie v. State*, 807 S.W.2d 319 (Tex. Crim. App. 1991).

18 *Cooper v. State*, 961 S.W.2d 229 (Tex. App. — Houston [1st Dist.] 1997, no pet.).

19 *Johnson v. State*, 747 S.W.2d 451 (Tex. App. — Houston [14th Dist.] 1988, pet. ref'd) (extraneous offenses mentioned by defendant or police on tape must be objected to at the time the tape is offered or the defendant has not preserved error).

20 *Leos v. State*, 883 S.W.2d 209 (Tex. Crim. App. 1994) (replacing test used in *Edwards v. State*, 551 S.W.2d 731 (Tex. Crim. App. 1977).

21 *Roy v. State*, 608 S.W.2d 645 (Tex. Crim. App. [panel op.] 1980); *Sims v. State*, 735 S.W.2d 913 (Tex. App. — Dallas 1987, pet. ref'd).

22 *Clark v. State*, 728 S.W.2d 484 (Tex. App. — Fort Worth), *vacated and remanded on other grounds*, 753 S.W.2d 371 (Tex. Crim. App. 1987), *on remand*, 781 S.W.2d 954 (Tex. App. — Fort Worth 1989, no pet.); *Holland v. State*, 622 S.W.2d 904 (Tex. App. — Fort Worth 1981, no pet.).

Not every tape will be accompanied by audio, perhaps due to mistake or tape malfunction. Absence of sound on a DWI video will not affect its admissibility.[23] Also, when a tape is in a foreign language, a translation by a sworn interpreter will be necessary.[24]

## ABSENCE OF VIDEOTAPE

In some DWI cases, there is no tape at all. Absence of a videotape in a DWI case is not grounds for acquittal,[25] and the defendant is not entitled to a jury instruction on the state's failure to videotape him.[26] To support a motion to dismiss based on destruction of a video, the defendant must show that the destruction was in bad faith.[27] If the state or police inadvertently destroys their own copy of a DWI video after a copy has been made for the defendant, the state may subpoena the defendant's copy and introduce it into evidence.[28] Losing the videotape between trial and appeal also is not necessarily fatal to the state. An appeals court should only reverse based on the lost tape if the issue on appeal is intoxication and the videotape was made very close in time to the time of driving.[29]

## IN-CAR VIDEO

With the advent of in-car video, DWI cases are beginning to feature more of these types of tapes. The video from a dashboard camera will be admissible.[30] In *Poulos v. State*, the court allowed admission of field sobriety tests videotaped by the officer from a camera mounted on his dashboard. The court ruled that the videotape was not testimonial in nature and therefore did not offend the defendant's Fifth Amendment privilege. The predicate for their admission is the same as for other video: The officer basically must testify that the tape represents a full and accurate depiction of the events in question.

One inventive use by officers is to turn the camera around and tape the defendant as he sits in the back seat of the squad car, which has led to capturing some pretty significant evidence.

---

23 *Aguirre v. State*, 948 S.W.2d 377 (Tex. App. — Houston [14th Dist.] 1997, pet. ref'd).

24 *Leal v. State*, 782 S.W.2d 844 (Tex. Crim. App. 1989).

25 *Williams v. State*, 946 S.W.2d 886 (Tex. App. — Waco 1997, no pet.); *Irion v. State*, 703 S.W.2d 362 (Tex. App. — Austin 1986, no pet.).

26 *Logan v. State*, 757 S.W.2d 160 (Tex. App. — San Antonio 1988, no pet.).

27 *Gamboa v. State*, 774 S.W.2d 111 (Tex. App. — Fort Worth 1989, pet. ref'd).

28 *Adams v. State*, 969 S.W.2d 106 (Tex. App. — Dallas 1998, no pet.).

29 *Yates v. State*, 1 S.W.3d 277 (Tex. App. — Fort Worth 1999, pet. ref'd).

30 *Poulos v. State*, 799 S.W.2d 769 (Tex. App. — Houston [1st Dist.] 1990, no pet.).

# Sample Predicates for Video Admission

### OFFICER QUESTIONS[31]

- Officer, before speaking to the defendant, did you advise him of his constitutional rights in connection with his privilege against self-incrimination?
- Did you advise the defendant of:
  - ❑ His right to an attorney?
  - ❑ His right to remain silent?
  - ❑ That anything he said could be used against him?
  - ❑ His right to have an attorney present prior to and during any questioning?
  - ❑ His right to have an attorney appointed to advise him prior to and during any questioning?
  - ❑ His right to terminate the interview at any time?

### RECORDED CONFESSION

*Texas law (CCP art. 38.22) establishes additional predicate standards for admission of a recorded confession that results from custodial interrogation. Those standards exceed the predicate required by the* Miranda *decision.*

- Officer, I hand to you what has been marked as State's Exhibit Number ___ (tape of defendant's statement) and ask you if you recognize it.
- What is it?
- Was this recording prepared on a device capable of making an accurate recording?
- Did the operator of the device understand how to operate it?
- Is the recording an accurate copy of the statements made by the defendant?
- Has the recording been altered in any manner?
- Would you identify all of the voices on the tape?
- Does the recording reflect the delivery of the defendant's rights to the defendant was done before asking any questions?
- Does the recording reflect that the defendant waived those rights and then agreed to talk to you?

*The State also must present evidence that it "provided" a true, complete and accurate copy of the recording to the defendant at least 20 days before the start of the "criminal proceeding."*

---

[31] For more information, see *Predicates* (TDCAA © 2014).

## Witnesses

### BREATH TEST

The main goal for a prosecutor in questioning an intoxilyzer operator is to show how simple the instrument is to operate. The intoxilyzer operator shouldn't attempt to explain the science behind the breath test instruments, but instead should simply discuss the steps of the process. Analogously, the person who rotates your car's tires doesn't have to understand the nature of hardening rubber—just the proper steps to make sure that the tire stays on the wheel.

The prosecutor should ask the intoxilyzer operator about his experience and background, including DPS certification. The operator should spend most of his time on the stand explaining the process of how the intoxilyzer works and then talking about the defendant's particular breath test slip. [**See sample questions for intoxilyzer operators and technical supervisors at the end of this section.**]

The main goal in questioning a technical supervisor is to set out the safeguards in the intoxilyzer instruments and to vouch for the maintenance records for that particular instrument. A prosecutor should ask the technical supervisor questions about her education and special training, particularly her science background and certification by DPS. The technical supervisor will also be able to give an opinion as to the defendant's intoxication and talk about retrograde extrapolation, if the relevant factors are known about the defendant. [**See a discussion about retrograde extrapolation in Chapter 3.**] A new technical supervisor can lay the predicate for old tests by relying on the previous supervisor's record as a basis for his opinion that the breath test machine was working properly.[32] **Table 8-3** is a visual aid prosecutors can use and have intoxilyzer operators and technical supervisors fill out while they are testifying. Alternatively, prosecutors can simply blow up a copy of the defendant's intoxilyzer slip, which should contain all of the same information. [**See schematic diagrams of the Intoxilyzer 5000 in Chapter 3 on page 43 and following the predicate questions in this chapter.**]

**TABLE 8-3: Intoxilyzer Visual Aid**

**INTOXILYZER 5000 INSTRUMENT**
SN ____________ TS AREA:043
Date____________ ______________ PD
GN01750
SUBJECT: ______________________ OPERATOR: ______________________
SUBJECT DATE OF BIRTH: ________ OPERATOR CERTIFICATE #: ________
OPR AGENCY: ______________________ ARST AGENCY: ______________________
ARST OFFICER: ______________________

REFERENCE PREDICTED 0.080 CIRCUITRY CHECK OK

| **ANALYSIS** | **ALC CONC** | **TIME** |
|---|---|---|
| AIR BLANK | 0.000 | ________ |
| SUBJECT TEST | ________ | ________ |
| AIR BLANK | 0.000 | ________ |
| REFERENCE | 0.080 | ________ |
| AIR BLANK | 0.000 | ________ |
| SUBJECT TEST | ________ | ________ |
| AIR BLANK | 0.000 | ________ |

______________________________
OPERATOR

32 *Henderson v. State,* 14 S.W.3d 409 (Tex. App. — Austin 2000, no pet.).

## Sample Questions for Intoxilyzer Operator[33]

1. State your name for the jury please.
2. How are you presently employed?
3. How long have you been employed as an Intoxilyzer Operator?
4. What do your duties as an Intoxilyzer Operator include?

**If the witness has other duties separate from his/her Intoxilyzer operation, you should let the jury know about those duties as well.**

5. Describe your educational background (high school, college).
6. Have you had any special training/attended any special courses pertaining to your duties as an Intoxilyzer Operator?
7. By whom is the course given?
8. Were you certified as an Intoxilyzer Operator upon completion of that course?
9. Do you presently hold a certificate from the Texas Department of Public Safety as a qualified operator of the Intoxilyzer Instrument?
10. How often must you be certified to maintain your certification as a qualified operator?
11. When were you last certified?
12. Were you certified on (date of test)?
13. What shift were you working?
14. Let me direct your attention to approximately (time of test) on that date, did you have an occasion to administer an Intoxilyzer test to (Defendant)?
15. Do you see that person in the courtroom today?
16. Would you point to where that person is sitting and describe an article of clothing he/she is wearing for the record?

**This is typically the same witness used to get the videotape into evidence, so that predicate is included here.**

**First, have the videotape of the DWI suspect marked for Identification.**

17. Was a videotape made of (Defendant's name) on (offense date)?
18. Is it a common practice of the __________Police Department to make a videotape recording of all persons arrested for DWI?
19. I'm handing you what has been marked as State's Exhibit # ______. Can you identify what this is? (The videotape made of Defendant)
20. Have you had an opportunity to view this tape prior to your testimony?
21. Have any additions or deletions or changes been made to the recording?
22. Can you identify all the persons and voices on this tape? (Have witness say who is on tape.)
23. Were there any warnings given to the defendant that are visible on the tape? Which warnings were given? (*Warned being taped, *Miranda* warning, DWI statutory warning)

***Note: It is not necessary that a defendant be warned he is being videotaped.**

24. Was the machine used to make this tape capable of making accurate video and audio recordings?
25. Was the operator of the equipment trained and competent in the operation of the equipment? Were you the operator of the recording equipment?

---

[33] These questions relate to Intoxilyzer Model 5000. **See sample visual aid at Figure 8-1, diagram of Intoxilyzer Model 5000.**

**Nothing special needed here other than statement that he knows how to work a VCR.**

26. How was this tape preserved?

**NOTE: The above predicate came from *Edwards v. State,* 551 S.W.2d 731 (Tex. Crim. App. 1977). In *Leos v. State,* 883 S.W.2d 209 (Tex. Crim. App. 1994), the court held that the Texas Rules of Criminal Evidence supersede *Edwards* with Rules 803(6), 901(a), and 901(b). These combined rules seem to require the same thing as *Edwards* did. In the *Leos* opinion the tape was ruled inadmissable because all voices were not identified.**

**OFFER THE EXHIBIT INTO EVIDENCE.**

**The question of when to publish the tape exhibit is up to you. My rule of thumb is that if it is a good tape for the State, I will publish it right after the predicate is laid and it has been ruled to be admissible. If it is a bad tape for the State I will wait until I have finished my direct exam.**

27. Prior to administering the test, was the Defendant "continuously in your presence" for at least 15 minutes?

**Note: The DPS regulations no longer require continuous "observation."**

28. For what purpose were you observing the Defendant? (To ensure that he/she did not eat, drink, vomit, regurgitate, place anything in his/her mouth which might have contained alcohol or have interfered with the test.)
29. Did any of the things you were looking for occur during the observation period?
30. Did you check to see if the Defendant had anything in his/her mouth?
31. What Intoxilyzer model did you use to conduct this test?
32. What was the serial number of that Intoxilyzer Instrument?
33. Please tell the jury how the Intoxilyzer test is performed?

**Witness should go through all the steps of checking the instrument and running a test, Namely:**

1. **Observation period**
2. **Air blank — purge**
3. **Subject Sample**
4. **Air blank**
5. **Reference sample**
6. **Air blank — purge**
7. **Subject Sample #2**
8. **Air blank — purge and each step should be explained as it is listed**

34. Did you change the mouthpiece after the Defendant gave his first breath sample?

**Note: As of September 1996, there is no longer a requirement that the mouthpiece be changed between sample 1 and 2 of the same suspect. I do not think you need to point that out in your questioning but make sure the operator is aware of that and check to see if their department does it even though it is not required. It is a better practice, in my opinion, that they do change the mouthpiece even though the regulations do not require it.**

35. Did you check the temperature of the reference sample prior to administering the test on this defendant?
36. Was the temperature 34C +/– 0.2C at the time you checked it?[34]

---

[34] *State v. Garza,* No. 04-0-626-CR 2005 WL 2138082 (Tex. App. — San Antonio 2005) (not desig. for pub.) (no abuse of discretion for trial judge to hold the results of the breath test were inadmissible when the officer failed to note the temperature of the reference sample prior to administering the test and technical supervisor testified that he checked the temperature of the reference sample not one day before or one day after, but rather approximately a week before, and weeks after the subject analysis); *Gamez v. State,* No. 04-02-087-CR 2003 WL 145554 (Tex. App. — San Antonio 2003, no pet.) (not desig. for pub.) (although the arresting officer did not record the actual temperature at the time that he administered the test, the technical supervisor testified that he routinely checks the temperature of the intoxilyzer and that the temperature always remains at 34 degrees centigrade plus or minus two-tenths of a degree centigrade, its "known temperature." Furthermore, he checked the intoxilyzer the day before and the day after the test was administered to the Defendant and both times, the intoxilyzer was at its known temperature. This was found to be sufficient evidence that the technique applied by the police department complied with §19.3(c)(4) of the Texas Breath Alcohol Testing Regulations).

37. What happens after these steps are performed? (a test record is printed)
38. I'm showing you what has been marked for Identification as State's Exhibit #____ (This is the print out slip of the test). Can you identify this?
39. During these inspections, did you verify that the simulator was at the correct temperature?
40. Whose signature is at the bottom of this Intoxilyzer test record?
41. Were you the operator who conducted this test?
42. While conducting this test, did you enter the subject's name and other information into the Intoxilyzer 5000?
43. Was that information printed by the instrument on State's Exhibit # ____ (test record)?
44. Is a test record made each time you conduct a test with the Intoxilyzer instrument?
45. How many parts does each test record? Does the technical supervisor receive one part of the test record?
46. Who was/is the technical supervisor for this instrument?
47. How is the date and time of the test entered on the test record? (automatically entered by the Intoxilyzer 5000)
48. Has the information shown on State's exhibit #______ been altered in any way since the test was conducted?
49. As part of the automatic operation of the Intoxilyzer 5000, does the instrument perform a circuit check before each test?
50. Are the results of that circuit check entered on the test record? What were the results?
51. What was the predicated value for the reference sample? What was the result of the "reference analysis" you conducted?
52. Is there an allowable variance between the predicted value and the actual reference test result? What is the allowable variance?
53. Was the reference test within the allowable range?
54. Using the Intoxilyzer record to refresh your memory, did you make any mistakes when you conducted this test?
55. Did anything unusual happen during the administration of this test?
56. Did you get a test result on the test run on (Defendant's name)?
57. Do you have an opinion as to whether the Intoxilyzer Instrument Model _____________, Serial number__________ was functioning properly when you conducted the test recorded on State's Exhibit #______.
58. What is that opinion?
59. Have you had an occasion to run Intoxilyzer tests on DWI suspects in the past? On approximately how many occasions?

**At this point you may want to get an estimate of how many are run a week. This goes both to show his experience and tells the jury what a serious problem DWI is in their county.**

60. Have you had an opportunity to observe intoxicated individuals in the past?
61. On few or many occasions?
62. Based upon your experience and observations, did you form an opinion as to whether this Defendant was intoxicated when he/she was in your presence?

**At this point, if the operator recalls any other things he or she noted that are not visible on the tape, such as odor of alcoholic beverage, red/bloodshot eyes, ask about them now.**

63. You have testified you are certified as a qualified operator of the Intoxilyzer Instrument #__________. Are you telling this jury that you are qualified to testify about the underlying theory or the electronics of this instrument?

**Answer should be: NO!**

64. Who would be the person qualified to testify on those matter?

**Answer: The technical supervisor (name).**

## Sample Questions for Technical Supervisor[35]

1. State your name for the jury please.
2. How are you presently employed?
3. How long have you been employed as a Technical Supervisor?
4. What are your current duties and responsibilities?

   **If he/she has duties unrelated to the Intoxilyzer Instrument have him/her discuss them here.**
5. How long have you been the Technical Supervisor for _______County?
6. Please tell the jury about your educational background?

   **This question is directed at college and graduate school degrees and not the training required for supervising and maintaining instrument.**
7. What special training have you had regarding the operation and maintenance of the Intoxilyzer Instrument Model # 5000.
8. In the course of your training, have you also learned about the effects of alcohol upon a person's mental and physical faculties?
9. Can the consumption of alcohol affect ones ability to safely operate a car?
10. How does alcohol affect a person's ability to operate a car?

    **You want to break this part down and list all of the mental and physical faculties needed for driving that are affected and why they are affected. Of course you want to emphasize the bad driving/motor skills involved in your case as well. Consider asking hypo's such as "If a person who has consumed alcohol is unable to stay in their lane of traffic, is this consistent with that person's being intoxicated?"**
11. Do you hold memberships in any scientific or professional organizations? Would you please list those for the jury?

**THE FOLLOWING THREE QUESTIONS SHOULD ONLY BE ASKED IF THE ANSWER IS "YES"**

12. Have you written or contributed to any professional publications or articles? Were those articles subject to "peer review?" Would you please list those for the jury?
13. Have you conducted any experiments on your own as to the workings and reliability of the Intoxilyzer Instrument Model Number 5000?
14. Have you yourself conducted any experiments on the effects of alcohol on a person's mental or physical faculties?
15. Are you presently certified by the Texas Department of Public Safety as a Technical Supervisor?
16. What must one do before receiving such certification?
17. Were you certified as a Technical Supervisor of the Intoxilyzer 5000 by the Texas Department of Public Safety on (date of test)?
18. Based upon your studies and your own experience, do you have a personal opinion as to the alcohol concentration at which a person does not have the normal use of his/her mental and physical faculties?

    **The answer to this question is typically .08 though he/she may also be aware of and say that the A.M.A. says the answer is .05**
19. Why do you hold that opinion?

    **This is a good place for a discussion of how intoxication can affect the body when minimal amounts are ingested and how much that can affect ability to operate a motor vehicle. If this is based upon tests and studies performed by this witness elaborate on those tests.**

---

[35] These questions relate to Intoxilyzer Model 5000.

20. Are you familiar with the underlying scientific theory that the Intoxilyzer 5000 Instrument is based upon? (Yes)
21. Could you please explain that theory to the jury?

    **The Intoxilyzer works in accordance with the laws of spectroscopy. The alcohol in a subject's breath absorbs light of specific wave lengths proportional to the alcohol concentration in the breath. The breath sample is taken in such a manner as to minimize the chance of residual mouth alcohol affecting the result.**

22. Is that theory considered valid by the scientific community? (Yes)
23. Can you explain how the Intoxilyzer instrument applies that theory? (i.e. what technique?)

    **The Intoxilyzer measures the light intensity of a beam of light before, during, and after the subject's breath passes through the sample chambers and the decrease in light intensity is read directly as alcohol concentration.**

24. Was that technique properly applied in this case? (Yes)
25. Do you know an Intoxilyzer Operator (name of operator in this case)?
26. Was (operator's name) certified on (date of test) by the Texas Department of Public Safety as an Intoxilyzer Operator?
27. Are you familiar with the Intoxilyzer Instrument Model Number 5000, Serial Number ___________? (The serial number will be noted on the test record & make sure you get it right!)
28. How are you familiar with that instrument? (Answer should incorporate the location of the instrument.)
29. Has the Intoxilyzer Instrument Model 5000 been approved and/or certified by the Scientific Director of the Texas Department of Public Safety?
30. Is the Intoxilyzer Instrument Number 5000, Serial Number __________, certified by the Scientific Director of the Texas Department of Public Safety?
31. Was that particular instrument certified by the Scientific Director of the Texas Department of Public Safety on (date of the test)?
32. Was that instrument operated as part of the Breath Alcohol Testing Program which was certified by the Scientific Director of the Texas Department of Public Safety on that date?
33. As part of your duties are you responsible for the maintenance and monitoring of this particular instrument?
34. Please describe for the jury what the maintenance of this instrument involves and how often these checks are done. (Instruments can be checked by remote computer or personal inspection.)
35. What was the closest date before (date of test) that you checked this particular Intoxilyzer Instrument?
36. What was the operational condition of this particular Intoxilyzer Instrument at that time?
37. What was the closest date after (date of test) that you checked this particular Intoxilyzer Instrument?
38. What was the operational condition of this particular Intoxilyzer Instrument at that time?
39. Did that particular instrument require any repairs between the dates that you checked it?

    **If any other technical supervisor checked the instrument during those periods discussed above, you may need to introduce the records of those checks.**

40. Do you have an opinion, based upon your experience and training, as to the operational condition of Intoxilyzer Instrument Number 5000, Serial # _________, on (date of test)?
41. What is that opinion?
42. I'm showing you what has been previously marked as State Exhibit # ____ (the test record). Do you recognize this exhibit? What is it?
43. As part of the subject test, is the operator required to have the subject continuously in his/her presence for a minimum period of time prior to conducting the test?
44. What is the purpose of that 15-minute requirement?

45. Does the test record indicate that the proper operational methods and testing techniques were followed in administering this test?
46. How can you tell that from observing the test record?
47. What is the reference analysis solution?
48. Who prepares the reference analysis solutions for use with the Intoxilyzer Instruments?
49. How do you prepare these solutions?
50. Are the reference samples periodically checked? How is that done?
51. How and by whom is the predicted value entered into the Intoxilyzer 5000?
52. Does the test record reflect that the result of the reference analysis was within tolerance of the predicted reference sample value?
53. What happens if the reference sample is out of tolerance? (Test is automatically invalidated by the Instrument)
54. The test record says "alcohol concentration." What does "alcohol concentration" mean?
55. Tell the jury what steps the Operator of the Intoxilyzer Instrument should follow if taking a breath sample?

    **This should be the same answer given by the Intoxilyzer Operator!**
56. After the operator has completed these steps what happens? (Instrument automatically performs each step of test.)
57. Please describe for the jury the steps the instrument automatically performs.

    **This is a good place to use an exhibit for demonstrative purposes. What I suggest you use is a blow up of a blank test record. This should be identified as such by this witness and then the witness should stand before the jury and fill in the information from this test read-out on the exhibit. So that the exhibit can be reused, it should be covered with plastic and an erasable marker should be used.**
58. What do you mean when you say the instrument performs the steps automatically?

    **Answer: Without assistance of operator. He/she can't influence the result.**
59. Your Honor, at this time we move to admit State's Exhibit # _____into evidence (the test slip).
60. What were the results of the two breath samples of the subject, in this case as reflected on State's Exhibit # (test record)?

    **This question is not necessary if you used an exhibit or otherwise got that answer before the jury.**
61. Were the results of these two breath samples within the allowed tolerance specified by the Scientific Director of the Texas Department of Public Safety?
62. What is the specified tolerance for breath samples?
63. What happens if two breath samples are not within tolerance? (Instrument automatically invalidates the test)
64. Are the subject's results an expression of the number of grams of alcohol per 210 liters of breath?
65. Are the results of (defendant's name) breath analysis equal to or greater than an alcohol concentration of 0.08?
66. In your opinion, would a person with an alcohol concentration of (test results in this case) have lost the normal use of his or her mental or physical faculties?

**Figure 8-1: Intoxilyzer Diagram for Use During Intoxilyzer Operator's Testimony**

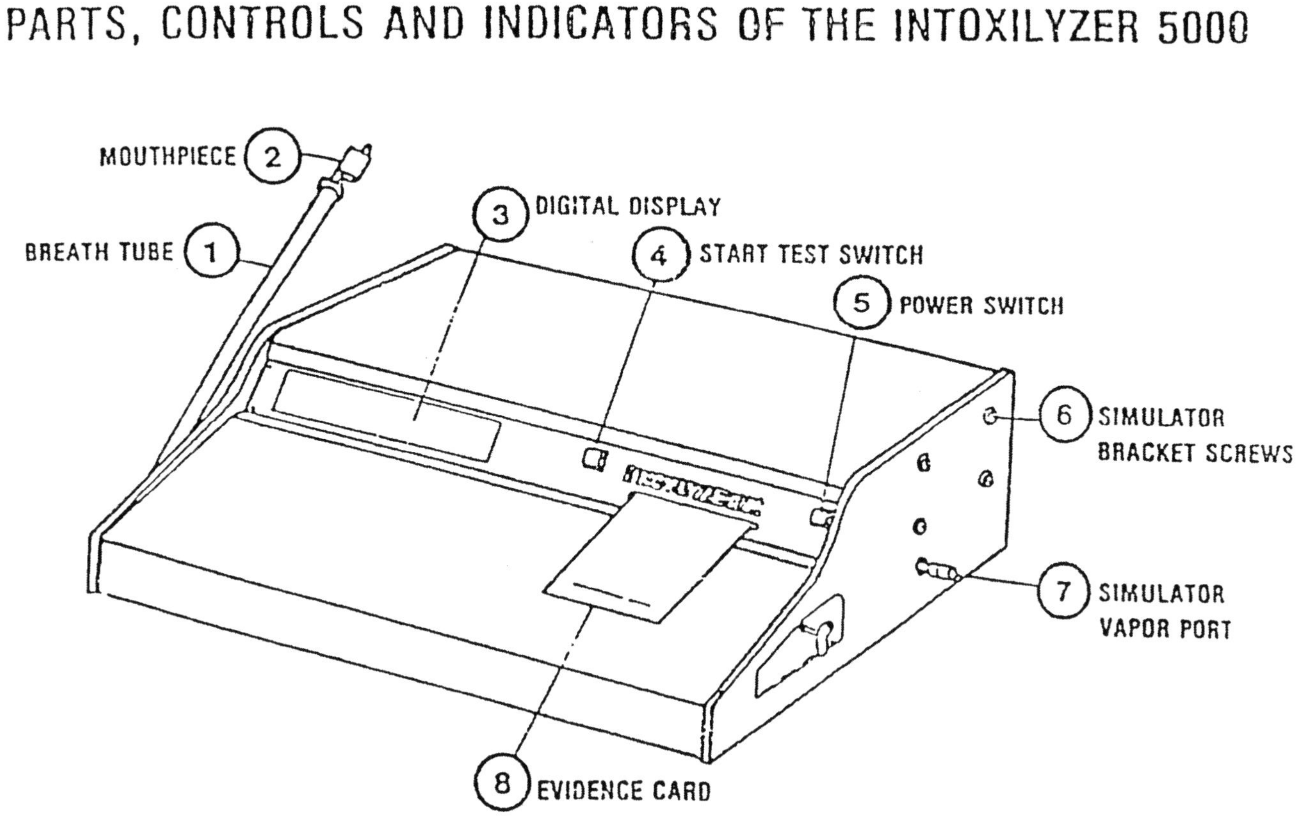


### BLOOD EVIDENCE

To introduce blood results, the state must show: (1) a proper chain of custody, and (2) that the blood tested was the same as the blood drawn from the defendant. The state cannot rely solely on medical records to prove a blood test result.[36] [**For more information about blood evidence, see Chapter 3.**]

Oftentimes, three witnesses will testify in introducing your blood evidence: an officer, a nurse/blood drawer, and a chemist. The goal in the officer's testimony is to show that the defendant consented to the blood draw (or establish circumstances under which the defendant's consent was not required); to talk about where and when the blood was drawn; and to identify the person who drew the blood.

The goal through the nurse's testimony (or testimony of the person who drew the blood) is to describe the blood draw and verify (by memory or paperwork) that the defendant is the person from whom the blood was taken. The prosecutor will also want to establish the nurse's education, experience, and training.

In questioning the chemist who tested the blood, the prosecutor will want to have the witness describe the analysis and protocols used, then testify about the results, and finally, give an opinion as to the defendant's intoxication. [**See sample predicates for blood evidence on the following page.**]

---

[36] *Lynch v. State,* 687 S.W.2d 76 (Tex. App. — Amarillo 1985, pet. ref'd).

## Sample Predicates for Blood Evidence

### OFFICER WHO WITNESSED BLOOD DRAW AND TOOK CUSTODY OF IT

Q. State your name for the jury, please.
A. John Smith.
Q. What rank do you have with the Sheriff's Office?
A. Sergeant.
Q. And how long have you been with the Tarrant County Sheriff's Office?
A. Since May of '91.
Q. Did you have law enforcement experience before coming with the sheriff's department?
A. Yes.
Q. Which department was that and when?
A. I had experience in three other agencies. El Paso Police Department is where I started out.
Q. What year was that?
A. '85 to '86. And then United States Air Force, I was a security policeman from '87 to '90. And then with the Department of Public Safety in New Mexico for two months in 1990.
Q. Have you had any specialized training regarding field sobriety testing?
A. Yes.
Q. Are you a certified practitioner in that?
A. Yes.
Q. Are you also a certified Intoxilyzer operator?
A. Yes.
Q. How were you employed on June 25, 2014?
A. As a patrol deputy.
Q. With the sheriff's department?
A. Yes.
Q. Did you have occasion to be dispatched to assist Officer Fielder on that date?
A. Yes.
Q. Where did you go?
A. From the briefing room, I was instructed to go to John Peter Smith Hospital.
Q. For what purpose?
A. To assist the officer. He didn't have any experience in obtaining a blood specimen.
Q. Did you have such experience?
A. Yes.
Q. On how many prior occasions had you been involved in drawing a blood specimen pursuant to a search warrant?
A. At least five.
Q. Do you know what time you arrived at the hospital?
A. Yes. 7:23 p.m.
Q. Did you bring anything with you?
A. Yes, I brought a blood kit.
Q. Was that blood kit used to draw a blood sample from the defendant Grant Vermin?
A. Yes.
Q. While you were there, did you make contact with a person who was under arrest named Grant Zane Vermin?
A. Yes.

Q. Do you see that person in the courtroom?
A. Yes.
Q. Point to him and describe an article of clothing he's wearing.
A. The gentlemen on the extreme right, wearing the checkered print brown jacket.
**MR. ALPERT:** May the record reflect this witness has identified the defendant?
**THE COURT:** It may.
Q. Did he look like that when you saw him?
A. No, not at all.
Q. Let me show you State's Exhibit 12 (jail book-in photo) now. Does that accurately show how he looked when you saw him at the hospital?
A. Yes.

---

**PRACTICE POINTER**

Criminal defendants commonly clean up considerably before trial. Always order a book-in photo if one was taken around the time of the arrest. Often, the change in their appearance can be dramatic. Asking the officer the above-mentioned questions puts a spotlight on the defendant's in-court charade.

---

Q. Did you notice anything unusual about his condition at the time?
A. Yes, he had a strong odor of an alcoholic beverage coming from his person and his eyes were red and watery.
Q. Was he asked if he wanted medical assistance in your presence?
A. Yes, the nurse asked him if he was injured and whether he wanted to be examined by a doctor and he said no.
Q. Could you describe his attitude for the jury?
A. He was abusive and belligerent.
Q. Did he volunteer any statements in your presence?
A. Yes. When we read him the warning he said, "I'm not going to give you a damn thing."
Q. What was his response when he was informed you had a search warrant?
A. He said we'd have to fight him for the blood.
Q. What did you do in response to that?
A. I called in 3 officers that were at the hospital and he decided to cooperate.
Q. Did the nurse who drew the blood witness this exchange?
A. Yes, she did.
Q. What was the nurse's name?
A. Marsha Mason.
Q. State's Exhibit 13, do you recognize this?
A. Yes.
Q. Is this the warning that you read to the defendant prior to taking the blood sample?
A. Yes.
Q. Looking at State's Exhibit #13, what is this form called?
A. That is the DWI statutory warning.
Q. Was the defendant given a copy of this warning?
A. Yes.
Q. Did you read the contents of this warning to the defendant?
A. Yes.
Q. And down at the bottom, where the name Grant Vermin is written, is that his signature?
A. Yes.
Q. Is the other handwriting on this form yours?
A. Yes.

Q. We offer State's Exhibit #13 into evidence.

ADMITTED

Q. I'm showing you what has been marked for identification as State's Exhibit 16-A (The box that contains the blood testing kit). Do you recognize that?

---

**PRACTICE POINTER**

This witness will have checked out the box/envelope that has the blood kit and the tested vial, which should have been kept together by the laboratory and should be repackaged and sealed before it is released to this officer. This is the first witness to bring the blood test exhibits before the jury. Open the box/envelope in advance and double-check its contents. It is best to do so in the presence of the officer and let him reseal it when you are done.

---

A. Yes.
Q. How are you able to recognize that?
A. It's our standard blood testing kit and on the back I wrote down the date, the serial number and what was inside.
Q. Is this the same boxed kit that you brought with you to the hospital?
A. Yes.
Q. Were the materials in this kit used to draw the blood specimen from this defendant?
A. Yes.
Q. Does this box contain a seal on it?
A. Yes.
Q. Officer, will you take this knife and cut the seal so that the box may be opened and its contents removed?

*(NOTE: All contents are removed and marked by the court reporter at this time for identification purposes.)*

Q. I'm showing you State's Exhibit 16B. Do you recognize that?
A. Yes.
Q. Is that one of the vials that blood was drawn into?
A. One of the two.
Q. There were two that were used, right?
A. Yes.
Q. At the time you drew these items from the kit for the nurse's use, was the vial empty?
A. Yes.
Q. Did you see any powder or anything in it?
A. Yes, the anticoagulant powder was at the bottom of the vial.
Q. But this gray rubber stopper was closed?
A. Yes, it was still on there.
Q. Did it appear that this kit had been tampered with or opened by anyone prior to your giving it to the nurse to use?
A. No.
Q. Did she draw the blood specimen in your presence?
A. Yes.
Q. And were you there when the labels were put on the blood vial?
A. Yes, I assisted in sealing it up.
Q. In fact, this label at the very top here, you can see where it's been torn. Was it completely covering this when you placed this into evidence?
A. Yes.
Q. So that if anyone had looked at this later and they wanted to tell if anyone had opened this, all they'd have to do is examine the label?
A. Right. It would be noticeable if it had been tampered with.
Q. What did you do with the kit after you put it back in the box? Did you seal the box?

A. I sealed the box.

Q. What did you do with the kit once you resealed it?

A. After everything was completed, I took custody of the box and transported it to our patrol office and placed it in the refrigerator in the property room.

Q. And is that property room refrigerator in a secured area?

A. Yes, it is.

Q. Did you later have an occasion to check the blood sample kit out of the property room and deliver it somewhere?

A. Yes, I checked it out on June 26, 2014, and delivered it to the Tarrant County Medical Examiner's Office.

Q. And when you released the blood sample kit to the medical examiner's office, were all the seals in place?

A. Yes.

PASS THE WITNESS.

### DIRECT EXAM OF THE NURSE/TECHNICIAN WHO DREW THE BLOOD SAMPLE

Q. State your name, please.

A. Marsha Mason.

Q. How are you currently employed?

A. I'm employed by John Peter Smith Hospital.

Q. In what capacity?

A. I'm a registered nurse in the emergency department.

Q. Have you had any educational background specifically connected with your being a nurse?

A. Yes, sir. I have a bachelor of science degree with a major in nursing, and I also am certified as an emergency nurse.

Q. How does one become certified as an emergency room nurse?

A. It's a national registry. You have to take an exam that lasts about four hours. And if you pass the exam—it's a very rigorous exam—then you are certified as an emergency nurse.

Q. Are you an RN?

A. Yes, sir.

Q. Are you certified in emergency room nursing, too?

A. Yes, sir.

Q. How long have you been working for John Peter Smith Hospital?

A. Since July of 1997.

Q. How much of that time has been in the emergency room?

A. The whole time.

Q. Do you have any connection or do any work for any other hospitals in your career other than JPS?

A. I worked as a nurse in the emergency room at Cook Fort Worth Children's Medical Center for a short period of time, but that was in conjunction with my job at Peter Smith.

Q. In September of this year, did you take on any other part time employment?

A. Yes, sir. I'm working as a flight nurse for Lifeguard Air Ambulance.

Q. What does that mean?

A. We do transfers of critical patients and patients that are unable to get transportation for long distances without needing medical assistance.

#### PRACTICE POINTER

This last point about working as a flight nurse was not offered so much as proof of her qualifications to draw blood as it was to show she is overqualified and hopefully to impress the jury. Don't be concerned if the blood sample was not drawn by a registered nurse—most of the samples I have dealt with are not. All the law requires is a qualified technician.

Q. In your time working in hospitals as a nurse since 1997, have you had occasions to draw blood samples?
A. Oh, definitely. Every time I go to work, I draw blood.
Q. Could you estimate many times you have done that?
A. No. I have no idea.
Q. Hundreds?
A. More than that—thousands—hundreds of thousands.
Q. Are you familiar with the recognized medical procedure for drawing a blood sample?
A. Yes.
Q. Your duties at JPS, do they, from time to time, involve your drawing a blood specimen from someone in police custody?
A. Yes, sir.
Q. Did you have an occasion to do just that on June 25th, 2014?
A. Yes, sir.
Q. Was that from an individual identified to you as Grant Vermin?
A. Yes, sir, I believe so.
Q. Where were you working on that date?
A. We have our emergency department divided into seven different areas. That day, I was working in the triage area where patients first arrive at our emergency department and they are assessed by a registered nurse and given a priority of care and are assigned.
Q. How did you make contact with the person you were going to draw the blood from?
A. He came into our emergency department in the company of two Tarrant County Sheriff's Department officers.
Q. How would you describe his demeanor when you made contact with him?
A. Originally, I wasn't paying much attention. We get people in custody all the time. But when he first came in, he sat down, we did our initial assessment. I asked him if he wanted to have any doctor look at him for medical injuries and he refused that. But he was rather cooperative at that time.
Q. Did his level of cooperation change at some point?
A. Yes, sir.
Q. When was that?
A. When we went back to the area to draw his blood.
Q. And what did he do then?
A. When they asked him if he wanted to give blood consent using the statutory warnings that they read him, he refused the blood draw. And I was ready to leave because, generally, if a person refuses, then I'm not allowed to draw their blood. But then I was reminded by the Tarrant County officer that there was a search warrant, and that's when he became upset, when I told him I was going to draw his blood.
Q. Did he say anything to you?
A. He told me that he wasn't going to allow me to draw his blood. He stood up, balled up his fist and told me he wasn't going to let me do that.
Q. What did you say to him?
A. I explained to him that I was obliged by law to draw his blood and I was going to draw his blood.

**PRACTICE POINTER**

The details of how a defendant refuses are very important. All "refusals" are not created equal. If a refusal can be considered by a jury as evidence of guilt then a strong refusal is arguably more evidence than a weak one.

Q. Did he calm down at that time?
A. It took a little bit of talking, and the officers talked to him, also, and then he calmed down, sat down, and let me draw his blood.

Q. Where exactly did you take the blood sample?
A. We took him back to a private area in our trauma area.
Q. The area of the hospital where you drew his blood sample, is that a sanitary area?
A. Yes.
Q. And did one of the officers provide you with a blood draw kit?
A. Yes.
Q. I'm going to show you what has been offered into evidence as State's Exhibit 15. Do you recognize that?
A. Yes. That's a request to withdraw blood by a police officer. (See attached copy.)
Q. Is your handwriting on there?
A. Yes, sir.
Q. Did you complete this form at the time the blood was drawn?
A. Yes, sir.
Q. And there is a time indicated on here of 19:52 which, if I'm right, means 7:52 p.m.?
A. Yes.
Q. What does that time indicate?
A. The time that I drew the blood from his arm.
Q. What steps did you do prior to drawing the blood? Tell me the procedure you went through.
A. I collected a tourniquet. Everything else is provided in the kit. I put that on his arm to make the veins pop up, and then used the Betadine swabs.
Q. What is Betadine?
A. It's a cleansing solution that has basically iodine in it.
Q. There is no alcohol in that, is there?
A. No, sir.
Q. Was that swab contained in the kit?
A. Yes, sir. They were individually wrapped.
Q. So the Betadine swab was sealed?
A. Yes, sir. I opened each package.
Q. Is using a Betadine swab a part of the regular procedure you follow when drawing a blood sample?
A. Yes, you are supposed to clean off the area before you draw blood.
Q. And you did that?
A. Yes, sir.
Q. What did you do next?
A. After I cleaned the area with Betadine, I got the vacutainer barrel and needle together.
Q. What is a vacutainer?
A. It has a barrel looking thing with a little needle attached, and then there is another needle that goes into the barrel that has a little rubber stopper on it. When you insert it into a patient's arm, there is no blood that comes out of the barrel until you connect a vacutainer tube, which it has a vacuum seal to it and it pulls the blood out. When you withdraw the tube, then there is no blood that comes out of there. So it keeps you from contaminating yourself losing extra blood. You can draw without getting blood on you.
Q. Does it also keep the blood that's being drawn from being exposed to the air other than what's inside the tube that you've drawn the blood into?
A. Yes.
Q. So it protects it from contamination?
A. Yes.
Q. You did that with two vials?
A. Yes. Two gray top vials.

Q. Does the gray top mean anything?

A. A gray top on the vial means that it has an anticoagulant and a preservative powder in it.

Q. I'm going to show you first what is marked as State's Exhibit 16. Do you know if your handwriting is anywhere on this box? (Note: This is the cardboard box that contained the blood test kit.)

A. Yes.

Q. Where is it? Show me.

A. Right here. It has my initials.

Q. Those initials are there on the seal; is that correct?

A. Yes.

Q. When everything was said and done and drawn, was this box sealed when you put your initials on it?

A. Yes. Both this one here and on this side, also.

Q. So, the seal on this side, which is still sealed, had your initials …

A. Yes.

Q. … and also the seal on this side, which is now open?

A. Yes.

Q. I'm taking out what is marked for identification as 16 B. Is this the packaging that the two vials were in?

A. Yes

Q. Is that you, Marsha Mason?

A. Yes, sir.

Q. And this blood collection report, does that, likewise, contain your signature on it? (Note: The report was placed back into the box before it was sealed by the officer.)

A. Yes, it does.

Q. I'm showing you a single vial marked State's Exhibit 16. Would you look at that and tell me if you can identify that?

**PRACTICE POINTER**

If the two vials were drawn, I recommend you leave the extra vial at the lab rather than bring it into court so that it will be preserved for any later testing by the state or the defense.

A. It has my initials on it and it's a vial of blood.

Q. Based upon your initials & the packaging, are you confident this is the same vial that you drew the blood into from this defendant?

A. Yes, sir.

Q. When you drew the blood, did you turn this over to one of the officers for sealing?

A. No. I sealed it myself.

Q. With this tape over the top of it?

A. Yes.

Q. And it's been moved at this point; is that correct?

A. Yes.

Q. At the time you sealed it, was the tape covering that so that if someone viewed it, they could tell if it had been opened or tampered with?

A. Yes.

Q. That was done on both vials of bloods?

A. Yes.

Q. After sealing the sample, did you do anything else with it?

A. Yes, I turned it over to Officer John Smith.

Q. What did Officer Smith do with the sample?

A. He placed it back into the box the blood and sealed it and then he and I both put our initials over the seal.

Q. Is that the same box as has been identified previously as State's Exhibit 16-A?

A. Yes.

PASS THE WITNESS.

**PRACTICE POINTER**

Sometimes I have offered the blood vial into evidence at this point, but generally I wait and offer it after the chemist who tested it has testified.

## DIRECT EXAM OF THE CRIMINALIST WHO TESTED THE BLOOD SAMPLE

Q. Ms. Patton, if you would, adjust the microphone so we can hear you. Would you tell the jury your name?

A. Carole Patton.

Q. And how are you presently employed?

A. I am employed as a criminalist for the Fort Worth Police Department Crime Laboratory.

Q. What is a criminalist?

A. As a criminalist, I work in the areas of drug identification, blood alcohol, serology, and DNA analysis.

Q. How long have you been employed with the Fort Worth Crime Lab?

A. A little over seven years.

Q. At the time of testing, was your laboratory accredited by the public safety director of the Texas Department of Public Safety? **[See TEX. CODE CRIM. PROC. art. 38.35.]**

A. Yes.

Q. What do your duties include with the Fort Worth Crime Lab?

A. They include analyzing substances for controlled substances; serology, which entails the classical A B O testing and enzyme testing; blood alcohol determination; and DNA analysis.

Q. And you have testified in courts of law as an expert in serology before?

A. Yes, I have.

Q. On few or many occasions?

A. Many.

Q. Can you tell me if you had occasion to examine blood for the purpose of trying to determine its alcohol content?

A. I have.

Q. On few or many occasions?

A. Many.

Q. How were you employed prior to going with the Fort Worth Crime Lab.

A. Senior research scientist in the University of Texas system in San Antonio.

Q. How long were you employed in that capacity?

A. Approximately four years.

Q. Can you tell the jury what your educational background is?

A. I have a Bachelor of Science Degree in chemistry and biology from McMurray University in Abilene, Texas.

Q. When did you receive that degree?

A. 1983.

Q. Have you received any specialized training in connection with the work you do for the Fort Worth Crime Lab?

A. Yes, I have.

Q. Can you list the training and organizations you've been to?

A. I have attended numerous schools in the area of forensics, both in the area of drug identification and serology, which includes schools put on by the Drug Enforcement Administration, FBI at Quantico, in both conventional serology and DNA testing, and also a school sponsored by the Department of Public Safety for breath alcohol determination.
Q. And do you belong to any professional organizations?
A. I do.
Q. Which ones do you belong to?
A. I belong to the Southwestern Association of Forensic Scientists and the American Society of Human Genetics.
Q. Back on June 28, 2014, were you employed as a serologist by the Fort Worth Crime Lab?
A. I was.
Q. Did you have an occasion to collect a sample of blood from the Fort Worth property room on that date?
A. Yes, I did.
Q. And did that blood purport to be from someone named Grant Vermin?
A. Yes, it did.
Q. When did you pick up the blood sample?
A. I received it on June 28, 2014, at 9:10 a.m.
Q. And when you say you received it physically, how did it come into your hands? Where did you go?
A. I received it from the Fort Worth Police property room, from one of the evidence custodians that is employed with the police department.
Q. What was the name of the person you received it from?
A. Mitzi Felts.
Q. And do you know where the sample was when she obtained it?
A. Yes, I do.
Q. Where was it?
A. I saw her retrieve it from the refrigerator located in the police property room.
Q. What physically were you given?
A. I was given a sealed envelope.
Q. Was the envelope cold?
A. Yes, it was.

**PRACTICE POINTER**

You won't always have the benefit of having the criminalist witness the sample being in the refrigerator. If not, it can be very helpful to have the criminalist point out that the sample or its container was cold to the touch. This is a detail that may not be recorded, so contact the criminalist and ask that question as close to the time of testing as possible.

Q. I am showing you what's been marked for identification purposes as State's Exhibit Number 19 A, and ask you if you can identify this.
A. Yes, I can.
Q. What is that?
A. State's Exhibit Number 19 A is an envelope which I had received. I recognize it by the laboratory number and my initials.
Q. At the time you received this envelope—it is now opened—was it open?
A. No, it was not.
Q. Was it in a sealed condition?
A. It was.
Q. Did it have the seal that we see on here—the evidence tape?

A. Yes, it had the yellow evidence tape on it.
Q. When you opened it, did you open it up from the other end?
A. Yes, I did.
Q. Was there any indication at all that the envelope had been opened or tampered with in any way when you received it?
A. No, there was not.
Q. And is your handwriting contained on this envelope?
A. Yes, it is.
Q. Where is your handwriting on it?
A. I put my initials here to show where I received it from Ms. Felts and also beside the laboratory number which I also wrote on the outside of the envelope.
Q. And did you at some point open that envelope?
A. I did.
Q. Where were you when you opened it?
A. In the crime laboratory.
Q. Did you take something out of it?
A. I did.
Q. I want to show you what's been marked as State's Exhibit Number 19, 19 being the plastic bag and the contents therein. I ask you if you recognize that.
A. Yes, I do.
Q. And what is it that's contained in that envelope?
A. State's Exhibit Number 19 is a plastic bag that holds a vial of blood. I recognize it by, again, the same laboratory number and my initials.
Q. Would you take it out of the bag, please?
A. (Witness complies)
Q. The vial of blood, was it in a sealed condition when you received it?
A. Yes, it was.
Q. You will notice in observing it that there is a piece of paper, or sealed piece of paper that seems to cover the top of the screw on vial, which now shows that it has been cut open. At the time you received it, was that top of the vial sealed by that paper to the bottom of the vial?
A. Yes, it was.
Q. Who was it that opened it up?
A. I did.
Q. And do you have any handwriting on this vial?
A. I do.
Q. Where is your handwriting contained on there?
A. My handwriting is contained at the bottom of the label. The laboratory number and my initials are also at the top. I placed a sticker on top of the vial, which contains the same lab number and initials.
Q. Is that the same vial you took from the envelope identified as State's Exhibit Number 19 A?
A. Yes, it is.
Q. When did that envelope and vial leave your custody last?
A. Yesterday morning.
Q. Who did you turn it over to?
A. To Officer John Smith.

**PRACTICE POINTER**

This will be the same officer who witnessed and testified about drawing the blood sample. It simplifies the chain considerably if you can get the criminalist to personally release the sample in its container to the same officer who originally dropped it off. The container and vial and packaging would have already been offered and open for the record by this officer.

MR. ALPERT: Your Honor, at this time the State would offer in evidence State's Exhibit Number 19 A and the vial contained therein, State's Exhibit Number 19.

THE COURT: State's Exhibit Number 19 is admitted into evidence.

MR. ALPERT: Your Honor, may I publish State's Exhibit Number 19-A and 19 to the Jury?

THE COURT: Yes.

(STATE'S EXHIBITS NUMBERS 19 AND 19 A WERE PASSED TO THE JURY)

Q. Ms. Patton, once you received the envelope and the vial, I think you have already testified you took it to the laboratory. Where is your laboratory located?

A. It is located on the fourth floor.

Q. Is that in the same building as the basement floor where you picked up the sample?

A. Yes, it is.

Q. After you opened up the envelope and took the vial out, what did you do?

A. I then placed the laboratory number on the vial and my initials and proceeded with analysis.

Q. Did you do a visual examination of the contents of the vial?

A. Yes, I did a visual examination after I opened the cap, after breaking the seal and opening it.

Q. Did you determine whether there was blood inside the vial?

A. Yes, there was blood inside the vial.

Q. Had the blood coagulated or clotted in any way?

A. No, it had not.

**PRACTICE POINTER**

One basis for defense attacks on the sample is to argue that there was no anticoagulant power in the vial the blood was placed into, or that the powder did not mix with the blood. The criminalist can testify that without powder in the vial before the blood was added, the blood will coagulate very quickly. You can argue this visual examination is circumstantial proof that the powder was in the vial and did mix with the blood sample.

Q. Do you have the ability to take a blood sample and determine, through use of equipment done in your laboratory, the blood alcohol concentration of the person that gave that sample?

A. Yes, I can.

Q. Could you tell the jury what the science or method that one is able to do that is called?

A. The method is called head space analysis.

Q. Could you tell the jury what head space analysis is?

A. In head space analysis, we are able to analyze the vapors above a liquid. What it essentially involves is taking a liquid, capping it off, and analyzing the vapors above it.

Q. What, if any, instruments or equipment are you going to use in doing that?

A. We use what is called a gas chromatograph, or G.C., for short.

Q. Is the use of a gas chromatograph for the analysis of blood for alcohol content, is that accepted by the scientific community?

A. Yes.

Q. Is there any more common method used, to your knowledge, by the scientific community for making an analysis of blood for alcohol?

A. Not to my knowledge, no.

Q. Is this recent technology, or has this been around for a while?

A. It has been around for decades.

Q. And you have had occasion, through employment in the Fort Worth Crime Lab, to do such analysis using a gas chromatograph?

A. Yes, I have.

Q. On few or many occasions?

A. Many.

Q. How many people presently at the crime lab that you work at do that type of work?

A. Just myself.

**PRACTICE POINTER**

At this point, the prosecutor should take the criminalist step by step through the testing procedure. I highly recommend that you witness the testing procedure before trial if possible. Seeing a similar test performed on a blood sample—preferably by the same witness you will call at trial—will help in presenting testimony about the testing procedure to the jury.

Q. What I'd like you to do is I am going to have you go through the procedure you used. I first want you to start with what equipment and materials you have to gather together to do an analysis.

A. First, of course, the gas chromatograph, which is in the laboratory. I first will gather several glass vials. You can think of them as small glass bottles. I will get together a pipe header, which is a small instrument used with the hand in order to transfer liquid from one vessel to another. And also rubber stoppers will be used to cap off the glass vials.

Q. You talked about already opening the vial. Was there any delay from the time you received it until the time you began your testing procedure that you are talking about?

A. No, it was opened immediately.

Q. Once you gathered that equipment together, what is the first thing you are going to do?

A. I first will gather the vials and prepare the standards, the known standards I am going to use.

Q. Would you tell the jury what you mean when you use the phrase "known standard?"

A. In order to determine the alcohol concentration of an unknown sample, we must compare them against a known alcohol concentration. So I will prepare three different samples of known alcohol concentration that I know what that ethanol concentration is.

Q. How do you know the level of ethanol you are going to put in these standards?

A. I weigh them out myself.

Q. And do you use blood in making these standards?

A. I do.

Q. Is it human blood?

A. Yes, it is.

Q. The blood that you are going to put the known amount of alcohol in, where do you get that blood?

A. I have one of our serologists in the lab draw it from myself.

Q. It's your blood?

A. Yes, it is.

Q. How do you know that blood has no alcohol in it?

A. I know, because I don't drink.

Q. And do you always use your own blood as part of the standard when you are doing this testing?

A. Yes, I do.

**PRACTICE POINTER**

I am going to guess that most criminalists don't use their own blood in the standards and if they don't, make sure the witness can tell the jury how she knows the blood samples don't have alcohol in them.

Q. So once you have your blood that's been drawn for the standards and the ethanol, how do you make the standards?
A. I will have three vials. In one of the vials, I am going to make up a .15 percent standard. In another vial, I am going to make up a .25. And in the third vial, I am going to make up a .30. This is so I will have a range of concentrations that I can compare my unknown against. Because the sample that I receive is in blood, my standards also need to be made up in blood. That's why I use blank blood, or blood that essentially has no alcohol in it. In each vial, I will place a control, alcohol free blood. I will place a known amount of alcohol in order to make those standards. I will place a salt, sodium chloride, table salt, in it and I will cap each one of them off with rubber stoppers.
Q. What is the purpose of adding sodium chloride?
A. The sodium chloride is used in order to force the ethanol that is in the blood into the vapor, into the air above it, so now, all the ethanol vapors are trapped above the liquid but still inside that vial. And I have capped it off so that it can't escape.
Q. How do you cap these vials off?
A. I cap them off with a rubber stopper.
Q. Once you have mixed and capped off your three standards in the vials, how many vials do you make using the unknown blood that you have described taken from the envelope?
A. I duplicate two samples.
Q. How do you prepare those duplicate samples?
A. I prepare them in the same way. To each vial, I will add a sample of the blood and an internal standard, which I have also added to the standard, sodium chloride, and I will cap them off, as well.
Q. If I understand you, we now have five vials. Three of them are standards; two of them are the unknown blood?
A. Yes.
Q. What's the next step you do?
A. The next step is to heat them slightly on a warm hot plate. And this will facilitate the ethanol in the blood to rise above the liquid. Ethanol being a volatile substance or substance that evaporates quickly, the heat will help it rise.
Q. How long do you heat these for?
A. Approximately sixty seconds.
Q. Once that time is passed and you take them off the hot plate, do you do anything with them immediately?
A. No, I let them sit to come to room temperature, approximately fifteen to twenty minutes.
Q. And the caps are still on top of the vials?
A. Yes, they are still sealed.
Q. Once they cool to room temperature, are we ready to move to the gas chromatograph?
A. Yes.
Q. Okay. Now, which vials do you use first, and what do you do with them, as relates to the gas chromatograph?
A. I first will analyze the lowest standards, 0.15 percent, and then I will analyze the second two standards, and then I will move to the two samples.
Q. How do you take what was in the vials that you've had stopped off, how does it come in contact with the gas chromatograph? How do the contents get in there?
A. It is done with a syringe, a tuberculin syringe. What I will do is take the syringe and uncap it and depress it through the rubber stopper and withdraw a volume of the vapors itself. Actually, what I am using is just vapors, not the blood.
Q. You are not drawing any liquid into the syringe?
A. No, I am not.
Q. The vapors you say you draw in there, are those generated by the sodium chloride and heating of the substance?
A. Right. It does not create the ethanol, but it forces the ethanol vapors into the vapor base.

Q. Once you do that, how do you get it into the gas chromatograph?
A. It is injected through a piece of rubber into the gas chromatograph
Q. And are you done with that particular vial, then?
A. Yes.
Q. What does the gas chromatograph do with the vapor you have just injected into it?
A. What it is, is essentially a heated oven. What this heated oven contains is a glass column which has packing material, has a solid substance inside of it. What happens is these vapors are injected into the gas chromatograph and flow through this column. And after it flows through the column, it hits a detector, which it elicits an electrical response, which is hooked up to a detector which prints out a hard copy on the paper. Ethanol, as it goes through, because ethanol is a chemical compound, it will travel through the column, hit the detector at a certain time, elicit an electrical response, which causes the detector to tell the printer to print out a response.
Q. And how soon after the first standard is put through do you go to the second vial?
A. One injection takes approximately four minutes.
Q. And do you do the same procedure with the other two standards you have talked about?
A. Yes, I do.
Q. Do printouts come out before you put the nest standard in?
A. Yes, they do.
Q. Is there any danger that the contents of Standard One will be there and affect the contents of Standard Two?
A. No.
Q. How can you say that?
A. Because alcohol is a volatile substance. In other words, it evaporates very quickly. And it's going to evaporate even quicker in a heated situation. If you are injecting alcohol vapors into a heated instrument, it is going to volatize, or evaporate, almost spontaneously. What is actually traveling through the column are the molecules or ionized particles of the chemical compound itself. So there is no danger of carry over from one injection to the next.
Q. Are the unknown samples put through the gas chromatograph in the same way?
A. Yes.
Q. So when you are finished with this, what do you have to tell you whether or not the gas chromatograph is working properly?
A. The standards, when you inject the standards, the printer will give you a peak. It will actually draw a peak. The greater the concentration, the bigger the peak. So Standard Number One, the low standard, will give a small peak. The next standard will give a little bit larger peak. And the third standard will give even a larger peak. So if the instrument is not working correctly, you are going to know it immediately by looking at your standards because the peaks are not going to be the height of the concentration they should be.
Q. So if the standard peaks are not what they are supposed to be, does that tell you the testing of the blood is not going to be accurate?
A. That is correct. It would cause that procedure to be invalid, and it would have to be repeated or stopped at that point.
Q. In your testing of this particular blood sample were the standard peaks accurate?
A. Yes, they were.
Q. And did you get a readout of the unknown blood that came from that vial?
A. Yes.
Q. And as I understand, you are testing it twice.
A. Yes.
Q. How do you compare the peaks that you have on the known blood sample with the unknown blood sample?
A. From the peak values that the detector gives you, you can calculate what we call a standard line. And from this standard line, we can calculate what the concentration of the unknown is. And you can also, looking at the chromatograms, or the printouts, you can look at it visually and look at the peak heights. You can usually look at it

and tell by looking at the peak height from your known sample, you can lay it right against the peak height from your unknown samples, and you can get a feel about where that is going to lie. Of course, that is not accurate enough, so we take the numbers that the detector gives us and actually go through a calculation to determine accurately what the concentration is.

Q. Do you do a mathematical formula?

A. Yes.

Q. Is there anything else that you need to do, other than what you have described in doing the math to determine an alcohol concentration on the unknown blood?

A. No. Once the values are gotten for the unknown you can proceed with the calculations.

Q. And did you do so in this case?

A. I did.

Q. And can you tell the jury what the results was that you obtained on the unknown blood sample?

A. The result was 0.34 grams per hundred milliliters of blood, which is equal to 0.24 percent.

**PRACTICE POINTER**

It can also help the jury to see a diagram or chart that the expert can refer to when describing the testing procedure used in your case.

Q. You've testified that you have tested two samples. Is any variance between the two results acceptable for you to still be able to determine the test results are accurate?

A. The matching criteria that our laboratory uses and most laboratories use is plus or minus 0.01 percent.

Q. Was there any variance at all of these unknown blood samples in this case?

A. No, they both revealed to be the same percent.

Q. .24?

A. .24 percent, yes.

**PRACTICE POINTER**

The results are actually printed out to the fourth decimal point, but only the first two are generally reported. It is worth noting all four points as it may show the variance is much less than it seems when you report only two points. For instance, test results of .1501 and .1487 are much closer than it would appear when reported as .15 and .14.

Q. Once you finished the testing, was there a sufficient amount of the defendant's blood sample left for retesting purposes?

A. Yes.

Q. And where is the remaining sample at this time?

A. It has been recapped and sealed and is being stored in a refrigerator in the laboratory.

Q. So if another scientist wanted to retest the sample, they would be able to do so, correct?

A. Yes.

Q. Have you had occasion to release samples you have tested to other scientists for re-testing purposes in the past?

A. Yes.

Q. Have you received a request or order from anyone to release the remaining sample so that it can be retested and your results verified since the time you did the test you have described to this jury?

A. No.

Q. I pass the witness.

**PRACTICE POINTER**

I believe the last series of questions about the availability of the remaining blood sample for retesting is both relevant and important especially if the defense is challenging the accuracy of the testing procedure. If you are not sure whether they are going to make such an attack, you may want to save those questions for re-direct.

## SAMPLE DIRECT EXAMINATION OF MEDICAL TECHNOLOGIST

Q. Jane Stick, where do you work?

A. I'm employed as a medical technologist at John Peter Smith Hospital.

Q. How long have you been in that position?

A. Nearly two and a half years.

Q. Okay. What is it that your job entails?

A. I am the laboratory medical technologist in an area called the stat lab, which provides rapid turnaround for the E.R. We do testing for chemistry profiles, CBCs, drugs of abuse, alcohol.

Q. What type of training and experience did you have to go through to be qualified for that position?

A. I have a bachelor's degree in science, and then I took an additional year of training in course work rotation through Harris Medical Hospital. I had to take a national exam and keep my certification current.

Q. Where did you go to school to get your bachelor's degree?

A. University of North Carolina.

Q. Okay. Now, back on June 25 of 2014, do you recall if you were asked to do any type of testing regarding a patient named Grant Vermin?

A. Yes.

Q. What type of testing were you asked to do?

A. It was a trauma case that came from the ER, and they were asking for the chemistry profile,alcohol and urine, drugs of abuse.

Q. And are you able to do that testing in your lab?

A. Yes.

Q. Does the training you described qualify you to do that testing?

A. Yes.

Q. As of June 25, 2014, how many of those types of tests had you done in the past?

A. Hundreds probably.

Q. How many would you do on a particular day?

A. Six to 12 during my shift.

Q. You do so many tests, how are you able to be sure that the testing that you do on blood is of the same patient that the blood is brought down for? What type of documentation is there?

A. The specimens come with a paper requisition and the laboratory and hospital policy requires that you match the specimen label. There is a label on the specimen with the patient's name and medical record number, which is unique to that patient. Match that specimen to the paperwork that accompanies it and each specimen must match each piece of paper.

Q. Do you recall on June 25, 2014, if you received some blood from a patient by the name of Grant Vermin?

A. Yes, I did. I received what the hospital calls a rainbow, which is a series of tubes collected in the ER by the nursing staff, for example, and they call it a rainbow because it's four or five different tubes and each tube has a different colored top.

Q. Do you recall any of the color schemes that day?

A. Purple, gold, blue and a green, pale green.

Q. What are the distinctions on the color?

A. The color of the top indicates the type of anticoagulant in the tube. A purple top tube, for example, is used for the complete blood count and it contains EDTA, which is an anticoagulant.
Q. Is there a set of letters that represent "alcohol" in the medical profession?
A. Yes, the shorthand is ETOH.
Q. Let's talk about the physical process of how the blood samples get to you in the lab. It comes to the lab by way of a pneumatic tube?
A. Yes. We call it, the pneumatic tube system. It's like a vacuum system.
Q. The same thing I use at the bank when I take that carrier and put my money in it that winds up in the hands of the teller, right?
A. Yes, sir.
Q. If samples came to you through the pneumatic tube. Would you have been the person that picked them up from the tube?
A. Yes.
Q. Okay. And when you opened it again, you had five vials, and you had paperwork concerning the patient?
A. Yes, sir.
Q. And you compared the labels on the vials to the paperwork; is that correct?
A. Yes, sir.
Q. And which of the vials did you use to determine the amount of alcohol?
A. I used the green top vial. That is the standard tube we use in the stat lab.
Q. Does the green top vial contain an anticoagulent?
A. Yes.
Q. The anticoagulant that is used in the one with the green top, does it contain anything that your instrument could mistake for alcohol?
A. No, sir. At the time we used an anticoagulant called sodium heparin and it does not interfere with the testing on the instrument.
Q. And when you received that blood, did you make sure that you did the correct test on each of the different blood draws?
A. Yes.
Q. And how could you be sure of that?
A. The laboratory has a policy that the instruments need a specific type of blood anticoagulated or not, and it is only run on that particular instrument. The instrument that we used at the time was dedicated solely for alcohol. There were no other specimens run from that tube on that instrument.
Q. And what is the purpose of testing for alcohol for the hospital?
A. Primarily to give the physician an idea of where he stands with reference to treating the patient. If the patient is inebriated, the physician needs to know that so that he or she can make the appropriate determination for that patient's care.
Q. Okay. On the one vial that you did the alcohol testing on, what type of procedure did you go through in order to determine how much alcohol content was in that vial?
A. The instrument, according to laboratory policy, needed to be maintained and that maintenance needed to be documented. In other words, it was cleaned. It was checked each day prior to each shift, actually, to make sure that it was in good working order.
Q. Did you do that?
A. Yes, I did. And we needed to run controls. Controls are known — substances with known substances of alcohol. Those are run on the instrument and you need to reach that known concentration to understand that your instrument is working properly. And that is done each shift, three times every 24 hours. And those two things in tandem indicates that the instrument is working appropriately and you can accept any information off of that instrument.
Q. And were those controls done on June 25, 2014, when testing the blood of Mr. Vermin?

A. Yes.

Q. Do you run a control sample before each test sample, or do you just run one at the beginning of the day?

A. Actually, there are two at the beginning of the shift.

Q. Do you run another control sample at the end of the day?

A. At the beginning of the next shift, which would be at the end of my day, yes.

Q. On that particular night, how did the control samples test after the testing?

A. They were in range, acceptable range.

Q. After you make sure that the standards have been used and the safety procedures and reliability procedures have been followed, what do you do next?

A. I took the specimen to the instrument. Again checked the specimen to make sure it was the correct specimen that I was using and the correct patient. I loaded the instrument with the appropriate plastic parts. You have to add some parts to it. I didn't pop the top until I actually got to the instrument. I took the top off the specimen tube, put a pipette in there, and entered some drops into the instrument, shut the lid, and programmed it.

Q. Are new plastic parts used for each test?

A. That is correct. You use a brand-new one for each specimen or control.

Q. And so those are coming out of a package and presumably have been sealed and are clean; is that correct?

A. That is correct.

Q. Are the procedures that you described the same ones you follow on every test with that instrument?

A. Yes.

Q. What kind of instrument is that?

A. It's made by Abbott and it's called a TBX.

Q. And is that that instrument considered reliable by the scientific and medical community?

A. Yes, it is.

**PRACTICE POINTER**

The witness in this case was aware of and able to explain the scientific method the hospital instrument used to determine alcohol content. In your case, the technician who did the actual testing may not have that knowledge. If not, you may need to call the hospital lab director or supervisor as a witness to cover this issue.

Q. What scientific method does the instrument use for determining the alcohol content?

A. The instrument uses an enzyme called alcohol dehydrogenase. And it mixes with a dye, diaphorase to make a colored dye, which is actually measured by the instrument and applied to a curve and the amount of alcohol is measured off of that internal curve.

Q. So let me see if I put this — see if I can understand this. The chemical reaction between the alcohol and the sample and the substance in the machine creates a color, and the intensity of the color, I assume, varies with the quantity of alcohol?

A. Yes, sir.

Q. And were you able to get any results when you did the testing on June 25, 2014?

A. Yes, I did get results on that patient.

Q. Okay. Would you please tell the jury what those results were?

A. The level was 280 milligrams per deciliter, which is equivalent to 298 milligrams percent.

Q. Okay. And is that over what you would consider the legal limit?

A. Yes.

Q. Would that in fact translate to a 0.28 and 0.29?

A. Yes.

Q. Is there a policy about values that you would need to report to the physician?

A. Yes. If it is a "critical value."

Q. What does that mean?

A. A critical value is 300 milligrams per deciliter. A critical value is something that we have to call to the physician and alert them, so it was close, but it didn't require a call to the physician.

Q. And why would you have to call the physician if it was at that level?

A. That requires immediate intervention. The hospital has determined that that is a value that requires immediate intervention by the patient care staff.

Q. What the value on the testing of Grant Vermin's sample critical?

A. It was what we refer to as nearly critical.

Q. Okay. Now, if you learned that the person who drew the blood in your sample had used alcohol as opposed to Betadine, but allowed the alcohol to dry before the draw was done, would that in any way affect your numbers that you received?

A. No. I would feel very confident if the alcohol was left to dry, I would feel very confident with the results I turned out.

### PRACTICE POINTER

This last question about the use of alcohol swab may or may not apply to your case. With police-requested samples taken by most hospitals, there is a policy that non-alcoholic swabs are used. That precaution may not be followed for medically drawn samples, but common sense says that a hospital relaying on the results of testing to determine treatment is not going to contaminate the sample. The last question and answer speaks to the lack of impact. It would also be worth asking whether or not the instrument can distinguish the difference between isopropyl alcohol and ethyl alcohol.

# Defense Witnesses

## EXPERTS

There are a multitude of resources out there describing how to conduct an effective cross-examination. Proper cross-examination is an art that improves over time, and I certainly continue to find that I have room for improvement. I discovered that it is easier for me to develop an approach to cross- examination by reading the transcripts of the cross-examination done by others. Therefore, I have opted to include some of my cross-examinations of witnesses I have dealt with in cases regarding intoxication crashes in the hopes that you can learn from and improve upon my efforts. These transcripts can be found on the CD that came with this book, and I will reference them in the summaries below.

One skill every cross-examiner must possess is that of critical listening. You must focus on what the defense expert says, how they say it, and what they don't say. Even beyond the benefits I have gained from pre-trial preparation, some of the best points I have made in cross-examination have been the result of my listening critically to what the expert says and turning what started out as a response that hurt me to one that is harmless or even helps my case.

## CASE TRANSCRIPTS

### *State v. Chante Mallard*

This case got a fair amount of publicity as the "Windshield Case." The defendant had struck a pedestrian by the name of Gregory Biggs while driving home after a night of clubbing and some self-reported ingestion of alcohol, marijuana, and ecstasy. The crime was not solved until many months after the collision so there was no conclusive evidence of how the crash occurred or evidence of intoxication beyond the statement of the defendant. The charge in the trial was felony murder.

The defense expert examination I have included is that of Dr. Gary Wimbish. He did not testify until the punishment phase of the trial and the gist of his testimony was that due to the defendant's intoxication by alcohol and drugs, she was not able to make proper decisions that night. The hope was that the jury would view this as mitigation evidence. I had the benefit of having cross-examined Dr. Wimbish in a previous case so I had some idea what to expect. I knew he would be hard to pin down on points and that he was prone to making general statements that sound reasonable but can be discredited with proper questions. My goal in the attached transcript of the 705(b) hearing was to discover the scope and basis of his testimony, and my overall goal in cross- examination was to show the jury that his conclusions were based upon faulty information and were unsupported by hard data.

### *State v. Samuel Hilburn*

This case involved the death of Officer Dwayne Freeto. He was stopped on the shoulder of the roadway assisting a stranded motorist. Officer Freeto was sitting in his squad car on the shoulder with his lights activated when the defendant drove into the back of his vehicle at speeds estimated to be 90+ miles per hour. This resulted in the police vehicle bursting into flames and the death of the police officer. Once again I have included a transcript of my cross-examination of the same Dr. Gary Wimbish mentioned above.

My intoxication evidence was so strong that I really doubted the defense would call an expert as there was little basis for attack other than the civilian friends of the defendant who had described him as drinking much less than his alcohol concentration revealed. My assumption was that any credible expert would have to side with science over lay witness testimony, and I felt good about the results of my efforts to draw favorable testimony from Dr. Wimbish in this case so I used a friendlier and less confrontational cross-examination style.

### *State v. Roy Adams*

This case involved the death of Officer Darren Medlin. He had pulled over a young woman who was speeding and was standing by the driver's window of her car on the shoulder of the road when he was struck by the defendant's vehicle and killed upon impact. This case had a defense new to me in which they claimed that the defendant had a medical condition that explained why he struck the officer. Their argument was that he had a seizure. My pre-trial discovery told me that there was no question that he had suffered some seizures at dates subsequent to the crash, but I still had reason to doubt he had one on the night he killed Officer Medlin.

I contacted a doctor at a local hospital who I had used as a witness in a case a decade before and asked him if he could recommend a colleague who could educate me on the seizures. He put me in touch with a Dr. Hernandez who was kind enough to meet with me, review my evidence including defendant's medical records obtained by subpoena pre-trial and help me focus on areas on which I might want to cross-examine the defense witness. He also made himself available as a rebuttal witness and refused payment for any of these services.

With his help I felt I was able to mount an effective cross of the defense expert. There was no question the defense expert was qualified, but I felt his commitment to the proposition that the defendant had a seizure at the time of our offense was unsupported by science and the facts of the case. I opted to not have a 705(b) hearing because the defense was willing to allow me to speak to their expert in private before he testified. This is an option that you might want to consider using in those cases where you feel you can trust the expert will not change his answers later in court. It is a gamble but it worked well for me in this case.

## IN-COURT DEMONSTRATIONS

A defendant is not entitled to demonstrate his ability (or inability) to perform FSTs in court.[39] Another court of appeals has also disallowed a defendant's attempt to do an experiment where officers had to identify for the jury which cups contained alcoholic and which contained non-alcoholic beer.[40] Similarly, a court did not allow a defense request that jurors smell and taste non-alcoholic mixtures so they could see it is possible for non-alcoholic mixtures to smell and taste like alcoholic beverages.[41]

## FRIENDS AT THE BAR

The defense often calls friends of the defendant who were with him that night to testify. Their testimony generally takes one of two paths:

1. "I was with him, and I know he didn't have too much to drink." or
2. "I looked at the videotape, and he looks normal to me."

### *"Didn't Drink Too Much"*

Explore the friends' statements on this very carefully. Your average person out at a bar with a friend isn't going to be noting how many drinks a companion is having, unless the friend has some reason to be concerned about her companion's consumption of alcohol. Most people only count the number of their friend's drinks if the friend has a drinking problem.

The prosecutor can also point out how unrealistic it would be for a friend to keep an accurate total of the number of drinks the defendant actually consumed. Perhaps there was a gap of time when the friend wasn't around the defendant. The defendant could have consumed alcohol away from the friend's presence.

### *"Seemed Normal to Me"*

This testimony presents a good opportunity to explore the defendant's drinking habits that the friend has observed. If the witness testifies that the defendant seemed normal to him, then either: (1) they have seen the defendant intoxicated before and therefore have a basis of comparison, or (2) they have never seen the defendant intoxicated before and therefore have no basis to make a comparison in court.

If they have seen the defendant intoxicated before, have the witness describe the symptoms of the defendant's typical intoxicated behavior, and see whether they match what the officer saw that day. If the defendant's driving was erratic according to the officers, ask the friend witness whether the defendant is a good driver or not. For instance, does the defendant typically hit a curb when he makes a turn? Does the defendant typically have trouble staying in his lane?

---

39 *Baker v. State,* 879 S.W.2d 218 (Tex. App. — Houston [14th Dist.] 1994, pet. ref'd) (no predicate laid as to reliability or probative value of the demonstration).

40 *Lewis v. State,* 933 S.W.2d 172 (Tex. App. — Corpus Christi 1996, pet. ref'd) (prosecutors impeached defense expert John Castle by pointing out that an in-court experiment with the Intoxilyer 5000 demonstrated that contrary to his expert opinion, certain foods, chewing gum, and medications did not affect the test results).

41 *Kaldis v. State,* 926 S.W.2d 771 (Tex. App. — Houston [1st Dist.] 1996, pet. ref'd).

The tendency of these witnesses is to minimize everything. This defendant normally is a great driver, normally never drinks, this witness might say. This witness, however, can unintentionally make your case better either by overstating his opinions so the jury doesn't believe him, or by drawing a line between the way the defendant normally behaves and the way the officer saw him on that evening.

Explore with this witness the fact that alcohol affects people differently. With some people, you can see visible signs of intoxication, and with others you can't. If the witness has seen the defendant intoxicated before, how many drinks did he have on the occasion when he was intoxicated? Whatever number the witness gives, the prosecutor can use the number to her advantage. If the witness answers 15 drinks, the prosecutor can hammer the fact that this defendant has, on occasion, consumed 15 drinks. If the answer is three, then the prosecutor can establish the defendant as a lightweight who gets drunk and loses control of his mental and physical faculties easily.

Always ask the civilian witness whether she gave a written statement to anyone (including the defense attorney) or wrote down something about the incident. Pursuant to Rule 612, ask the witness for her notes.

### BARTENDERS

Sometimes the defense will call witnesses who don't know the defendant but were working at the bar that night. The bartender or waitress witness typically will testify that they didn't believe the defendant was intoxication. Explore their bias in giving this testimony: The bar's ability to keep its license and the employee's ability to keep his job depends on the witness not having served alcohol to an intoxicated person.

Also explore how the witness remembers—out of all the people he's served—this particular defendant. Is he a regular? What's the employee's frame of reference for knowing the defendant wasn't intoxicated? Has that witness ever had to cut the defendant off before and seen him intoxicated?

### BAR MANAGERS

It is not unusual for the defense to call a bartender, waiter or manager to testify that they have strict policies to ensure that no one is over-served alcohol at their establishment. Though these witnesses may actually believe they do a good job of watching for and cutting off intoxicated individuals, it is not difficult for a well-prepared prosecutor to demonstrate that even the best-intentioned drink-serving policy is not foolproof. Most of the points you can make are simply based on common sense. Here are some sample areas of questioning you might want to consider:

As a preliminary matter, if the defense has not done so in its direct examination, have the witness explain the layout of the bar. This can expose problems with the argument that the defendant was where the manager or waiter could see him the entire time. Obviously if you know where the defendant was drinking, you should visit the establishment in advance of trial so you can see for yourself how the bar operates. Ask about drink prices and size of the drinks, in particular the size of the glasses for serving beer. In my experience, few establishment serve 12-ounce glasses of beer. Many hold as much as 23 or 24 ounces. This may help establish that the three beers the defendant consumed were actually the equivalent of six 12-ounce beers. Even if the defendant was at a table being waited on by a specific waiter or waitress, there is typically nothing that prevents anyone from walking up to the bar and ordering a drink. It is important to establish that the "tab" is not necessarily the only source of accounting for alcohol the defendant consumed at the establishment.

The next point you want to make is that the ability to know when to cut someone off is a purely subjective exercise. The limited training the waiter or manager has had from TABC is far less than the training your officer has received. Get the witness to admit that some people show signs of intoxication after one or two drinks while others who consume alcohol on a daily basis may not show obvious signs of intoxication even after consuming a number of drinks. You also want to point out that the ability to observe poor balance requires you to be in a position to see the person walk, and most people at a bar or restaurant are seated while they are drinking.

Finally you want to discuss their policy of cutting people off. Most will say they have a strict policy that they cut off service to patrons who have had too much to drink. You want to first ask how often they are called upon to cut someone off on a typical work night or week. Once she has answered, ask her, "Would you agree with me that the fact that you ever have to cut someone off is some sign that your efforts to have a strict policy against over-serving are not foolproof?" The witness can't help but agree. You can also point out that if she truly wanted to be sure the establishment didn't over-serve anyone, the establishment could have a strict drink-count policy that limited how many drinks an individual could be served each hour. I have yet to encounter a bar or restaurant that has such a policy.

## CROSS-EXAMINING THE DEFENDANT

The State doesn't always get the opportunity to question the defendant. But once the defendant takes the stand, the prosecutor should be prepared to capitalize on the opportunity to use the defendant to advance the State's case. The following list contains the top 10 rules for effective cross-examination of defendants:

1. Be prepared. Collect all necessary documents (including TCIC/NCIC on the defendant; checking for new charges or arrests; getting copies of all priors, including tickets and DWIs; ordering a copy of DPS drivers license records; ordering and reviewing the defendant's book-in/jail records).
2. Be organized. Make a point-by-point outline of each state witness' testimony.
3. Forget about the rule that you never ask a question if you don't know the answer.
4. Forget about the rule that you only ask leading questions.
5. When you do lead, insist on responsive answers and object if the defendant is non-responsive.
6. Some of the most important questions on cross are the ones you don't ask so you can make your point with your closing argument.
7. Listen to the defendant's direct examination very carefully.
8. Take careful notes only of those areas of the defendant's testimony you intend to cross. Taking down everything that is said leaves you ill-prepared to identify areas you need to address.
9. Look for gaps in the defendant's description of the facts. There is usually a good reason why he has skipped certain areas. Don't be afraid to test the waters.
10. Know when to stop asking questions.

### SAMPLE CROSS-EXAMINATION QUESTIONS

The following list of questions will *usually* be safe to pursue in your cross-examination of the defendant. Of course, if the answers have already come out on direct, don't ask for the information again on cross-examination unless clarification is needed.

1. Where was the alcohol bought/obtained?

If at a commercial establishment, ask the defendant how it was paid for. If by credit card, ask if the defendant has the receipt.

> **Argument point:** If the defendant says he paid by credit card but did not bring a credit card receipt, you can question why he didn't bring documentation to back up his story.

2. Find out what the defendant did earlier in the day, if not discussed during direct examination.

Remember the extrapolation information you need, such as when the defendant last ate; when drinking began and ended; what type of alcohol was consumed; when the defendant last ate; and any over-the-counter or prescription drugs taken.

3. Who was the defendant with on the offense date?

If the defendant was with friends, get their names. Do *not* ask whether the defendant has seen them lately or if they are going to testify.

> **Argument point:** If they don't testify, you can comment on that in argument.

Do find out what the friends had to drink. Did they show any signs of intoxication? In case they do testify, you have begun to impeach their ability to perceive.

4. Work out a time line with the defendant.

> **Argument point:** There is no credible way the defendant could have kept track of that, so you will either succeed in showing that he has no clear memory of times, or he has an overdeveloped recollection of every minute.

5. If the defendant goes through the stop and arrest in some detail, focus on the areas not mentioned and consider asking about them to see how many, "I don't recall," answers you get.

6. If the defendant refused to submit a breath sample, ask if he understood the DIC-24 warning options.

If he says "no," have him read it in court and ask if he understood the options. If he had slurred speech on the tape, you may want to ask the defendant to read them aloud.

> **Argument point:** If the defendant couldn't understand at arrest time but can now, you can attribute that to intoxication.

7. If the defendant insists she only had two or three drinks, you might want to ask why she refused to take the one available test that could have confirmed the amount of alcohol in her body.

8. If she insists she wanted to talk to an attorney before she decided to give a breath sample and lists that as her reason for refusing to give a sample, consider the following arguments: (1) What information could an attorney have given her about her level of intoxication? (2) If the attorney thought she was intoxicated, what breath test advice does the jury think he would have given?

9. Look at the DIC-24 signature if the defendant signed a refusal and compare it to the signature on other court papers. If they look different, show these to the defendant and ask about the difference. Consider offering them into evidence so the jury can see.

10. Focus on all consistencies and conflicts between officers' testimony and defendant's testimony. Give emphasis to: (1) pointing out things that officer saw that the defendant would be in no position to contradict (such as weaving within the lane, which would be difficult to detect from inside a car); and (2) whether the defendant agrees or disagrees with most of what the officer says.

> **Argument point:** If he agrees, then you argue, "How could the officer be right on so many things but wrong on the most important issues?" If he disagrees, you can argue, "Is it logical that the officer would risk his job for the sake of a DWI conviction?" Or, "If the officer were going to lie, couldn't he have invented testimony that was much more damaging to the defendant?"

11. Does the defendant think she was intoxicated at the time of arrest?

12. What does "intoxicated" mean to the defendant?

If you get the legal definition verbatim, ask when she first learned that particular definition. Before she "learned" what the law said, what did the term mean to her? What difference, if any, is there in her mind between "drunk" and "intoxicated"? Can a person be intoxicated but not drunk?

13. Does the defendant believe his actions at the scene and on tape were normal?

Especially if the defendant denies the actions occurred (but even if admitted), go through the objectively *not* normal things the defendant said or did at the scene and on the tape and see if the defendant will concede they aren't normal.

14. Has the defendant ever consumed enough alcohol that she was intoxicated?

This can sometimes draw an objection as an attempt to elicit an extraneous offense. If so, reply that you are not ask the defendant if she's ever broken the law. (Being intoxicated is not against the law.) You're simply testing the defendant's basis for saying she was not intoxicated on the offense date.

a. If yes, how many drinks did it take?

b. If she gives a number of drinks (for instance, six), ask the following:

- Are you saying that after just five drinks you would not be intoxicated?
- Are you saying that after five drinks you would not hesitate to drive a car?
- Would you go to your job and work after five drinks? Would you ever go have four or five drinks at lunch on a work day?
- Would you drive your child to school after five drinks?

If she answers "no" to this question, ask what the maximum number of drinks she would be comfortable consuming if she knew she had to leave and pick up her child as soon as she finished.

- Depending on the response, ask why she would not want to have any or very much alcohol to drink before engaging in some of the above activities.

15. What signs are/were visible when the defendant is/was intoxicated?

Once again, you want to draw on the officer's testimony as a guide. For instance, if the officer said the defendant's balance was unsteady, ask if the defendant's balance is affected when he is (or the last time he was) intoxicated.

Another approach is to take the signs seen by the officer and ask:

- You are not normally unsteady when you walk?
- You are not normally rude and abusive?

16. If he denies ever being intoxicated or knowing what he looks like when intoxicated, consider asking if he has ever seen other people that he thought were intoxicated. What did they look like?

If the "other person" he described was obviously drunk, follow up with questions about whether he has seen people whose intoxication signs were *not* as obvious.

17. Find out how often the defendant consumes alcohol and how much he normally consumes. No matter what he says, you can use it against him.

- Heavy or regular drinker: Likely was drinking heavily in this case, or more likely, his good appearance on the arrest date can be attributed to masking/tolerance.
- Light drinker: Not as familiar with his limits; low tolerance means he would be affected by a small amount of alcohol.

18. Does he agree that a person who has consumed enough alcohol that his mental and physical faculties are affected:

- Might not be aware of his condition?
- Might have his ability to perceive himself and his circumstances affected?
- Might have had his ability to recall details affected?

19. When the defendant was being videotaped, isn't it true:

- You knew you were being taped?
- You knew a judge or jury would see it later?
- You knew you had to do well? Or you knew you couldn't afford to let anyone see how bad your condition was?

20. If the defendant claims that the officer was overly abusive or physical with him, ask if he filed a complaint with the police department.

21. Did he write down the events of that night for anyone? Did he review what he wrote down before testifying?

If the answer is yes, ask for a copy under T.R.EVID. 611. If the answer is no, contrast that in argument with the officer who did write a report.

22. If the defendant looks good on the tape, consider asking questions about whether she was nervous, stressed, or frightened.

**Argument point:** Most people would view arrest as a "sobering" experience. Using this common belief, you can argue that the time delay between the stop and the video, coupled with adrenalin rush brought about by the arrest, account for the defendant's good appearance on the videotape.

## Closing Argument

To constitute proper jury argument, the argument must encompass one (or more) of the following: (1) summation of the evidence presented at trial; (2) a reasonable deduction from the evidence; (3) an answer to opposing counsel's argument; or (4) a plea for law enforcement.[42]

Closing argument is your opportunity focus the jury on your theory of the case, to make sense of the facts and the law, and ultimately to persuade the jurors to your view of the offense and the appropriate outcome of the case. Use your imagination. Any trial attorney can simply stand up and regurgitate the elements of the offense and the evidence presented at trial. If that is all you plan to do, then you have wasted a tremendous opportunity to connect with your jury. As with all stages of trial work, an effective closing argument begins with thorough preparation.

### PREPARING FINAL ARGUMENT

While preparing your final argument, you should keep several things in mind. Most important, always remember the ultimate purpose of closing argument: persuasion. Your objective is to discuss and analyze the law and the evidence to persuade the jury to arrive at the verdict you desire.

It should go without saying, but to be effective, you must know your case inside and out—both the facts and the law. You must know the strengths and weaknesses of your case, and deal with both during your argument. Long before trial has begun, you should have developed a theory or theme of your case that you have built upon from the beginning. Use your theme in closing argument to tie everything together.

At this point, you should also narrow the list of topics you will cover in your closing argument. Acknowledge those issues that are not in dispute, but spend the bulk of your time addressing those areas that are critical to your case. We often overlook the simple truth that our jurors can only be expected to absorb so much information in such a short period of time, yet we bombard them with unnecessary details in closing argument. You—and ultimately your jury—will be well served if you take the time to focus simply on those few issues that are critical to your case.

You must also know yourself—your strengths and weaknesses as an advocate. Never try to be someone you are not. Watching talented and experienced trial lawyers is always recommended, but trying to copy their style exactly is not. You must project honesty and sincerity to your juries, so your closing arguments should be custom-fitted to fit you and your style.

Finally, you must know your jury. By now, you have invested a great deal of effort to learn as much about your jurors as possible. Make use of this effort and all the information you have gathered. Their backgrounds, education, social lives are important in deciding how to present your argument. Remember, they are not all lawyers and are probably not too impressed with those of us who are. More often than not, they will not decide a case strictly on the law, but will base their decision of human tendencies. You must account for this and present your arguments in such a way as to appeal to both their heads and their hearts. Clearly, you should not make the same argument that you would make before a trial judge or a court of appeals.

### DELIVERY

In Texas, the State has the right to both open and close final argument, although opening argument may be waived.[43] If not waived, opening argument typically refers to the court's charge, promises made during jury selection and opening statement, and the facts of the case. This part of the argument should be structured and disciplined. It is extremely important not to mistakenly open up or establish any points of rebuttal for the defense.

Closing argument is less structured. It is at this point that the prosecutor will answer any defense arguments, focus more on those disputed issues that are critical to the outcome of the case, and make a more emotional plea to the jury. The following is a list of simple strategies to apply to all jury arguments:

---

42 *Alejandro v. State,* 493 S.W.2d 230 (Tex. Crim. App. 1973).

43 Tex. Code Crim. Proc. art. 36.08; *Cole v. State,* 125 S.W.2d 575 (Tex. Crim. App. 1939); *Nelson v. State,* 828 S.W.2d 185 (Tex. App. — Houston [14th Dist.] 1992, pet. ref'd).

- Always start strong
- Move away from the podium—if possible
- Never, never read your argument
- Maintain a respectable distance between yourself and the jurors
- Speak loudly enough to be heard while varying the infection, level, and pace of your voice
- Talk to the jury, not at them
- Do not talk like a lawyer
- Use visual aids
- Maintain eye contact with your jurors
- Be fair
- End strong

### ARGUMENT THEMES AND SUGGESTIONS

When you argue a DWI case to the jury, don't forget to spend some time reminding them of the dangers of this offense. The case you are prosecuting may not have involved a crash but the thanks for that goes to the police officer who had the skill and training to recognize the danger this defendant posed before it happened.

The defense will usually focus on the how the jury should not ruin this defendant's life by giving him a conviction. You should be prepared to point out that by finding this defendant guilty you are simply holding him accountable and making him recognize that he has a problem before he kills someone.

The defense is very likely to make light of the fact that his client was arrested for stepping off a line a couple of times. Relate that misstep to driving. If it seems like too much is being made of the fact that this defendant missed the line by an inch, you need to ask yourself what kind of difference it would have made if the he missed the brake by an inch.

If the defendant refused to do SFSTs on the videotape or give a breath sample, remind the jury that the defendant had a chance to have an objective evaluation of his intoxication done by a scientific instrument and he refused because he knew he would fail. Likewise you can point out that the defendant was aware that his performance on the field sobriety tests would one day be viewed by a jury and he decided that he could not afford to let you see how intoxicated he was.

As to the refusal to give a breath test, this defendant made a contract with the state of Texas. He promised that in exchange for the privilege of driving on our streets he would give a sample of his breath if arrested for DWI. Now you know what his word is worth; now you know that that he is more concerned about ensuring that he is able to continue to put his pleasure above the safety and security of the rest of us that must share those streets with him.

Also, never fail to point out that the refusal to give a sample is evidence of guilt. It is human nature to try to hide things that are harmful. This defendant was so sure that the instrument would prove his intoxication that he was willing to sacrifice his ability to drive for 180 days. Don't you know that if this defendant really only had two beers that night that nothing could have kept him from taking advantage any means available to support that statement?

Some areas of argument that have been upheld as proper include:

- prosecution referring to the risk of injury or death imposed by drunk drivers, regardless of lack of evidence in the record that someone was injured or killed by defendant;[44]
- prosecutor's argument that "you hold in your hands the community's welfare. You can make this a safer place. You can help us enforce the laws, because if a six-time DWI doesn't go to prison in Brazos County, the next time somebody comes to my office as a five-time, I can't send him to prison;"[45]
- prosecutor's argument to jury that defendant "did not want jury to know how much alcohol he had in him" was reasonable inference drawn from defendant's refusal to submit breath sample;[46]

---

44 *Waters v. State,* 330 S.W.3d 368 (Tex. App. — Fort Worth 2010, pet. ref'd) (proper plea for law enforcement).

45 *Flores v. State,* 125 S.W.3d 744 (Tex. App. — Houston [1st Dist.] 2003, no pet.).

46 *Talkington v. State,* 2004 WL 102474 (Tex. App. — Fort Worth 2001, no pet.).

- prosecutor's argument that "… defense counsel doesn't have a burden, but once he chooses to, he doesn't get to create reasonable doubt by coming up with unreasonable ideas;"[47]
- prosecutor's argument that the defendant refused to give a sample because he knew he would fail;[48]
- prosecutor's argument that the defendant failed to do FSTs on the video because he knew the jury would see how he did;[49]
- prosecutor's arguments that jurors should not "reward defendant for doing nothing" and that they should not send a message that it was "OK to refuse to do everything;"[50]
- prosecutor's argument that "common sense tells you that when an individual knows [he is] being taped and knows it's important, [he] will straighten up;"[51]
- prosecutor's comment about the defendant's failure to call a designated expert.[52]

In the vast majority of cases, the only contested issue is the defendant's intoxication. Oftentimes, some of the best arguments are simple pleas that the jury use their common sense. An easy way to organize and deliver your argument is using an "All Evidence Points To…" chart as shown in **Appendix 8-1.**

## CONCLUSION

While there may be disagreement among lawyers as to the value of closing argument, all would agree that a good final argument cannot hurt, while a bad one certainly will not help. Whatever your personal opinion may be, it is always to your advantage to know the law and to present the best final argument possible.

---

47 *Id.*

48 *Nunez v. State,* 2007 WL 1299241 (Tex. App. — Fort Worth 2007, no pet.) (not desig. for pub.); *Gaddis v. State,* 753 S.W.2d 396 (Tex. Crim. App. 1988).

49 *Emigh v. State,* 916 S.W.2d 71 (Tex. App. — Houston [1st Dist.] 1996, no pet.).

50 *Castillo v. State,* 939 S.W.2d 754 (Tex. App. — Houston [14th Dist.] 1997, pet. ref'd).

51 *Gomez v. State,* 35 S.W.3d 746 (Tex. App. — Houston [1st Dist.] 2000, pet. ref'd).

52 *Pope v. State,* 207 S.W.3d 352 (Tex. Crim. App. 2006).

## Appendix 8-1: "All Evidence Points To..."

This chart can be blown up and used as a tool during closing argument. List all the factors that point to intoxication on the lines surrounding the circle, and write the word "Intoxication" in the middle when the circle is complete.

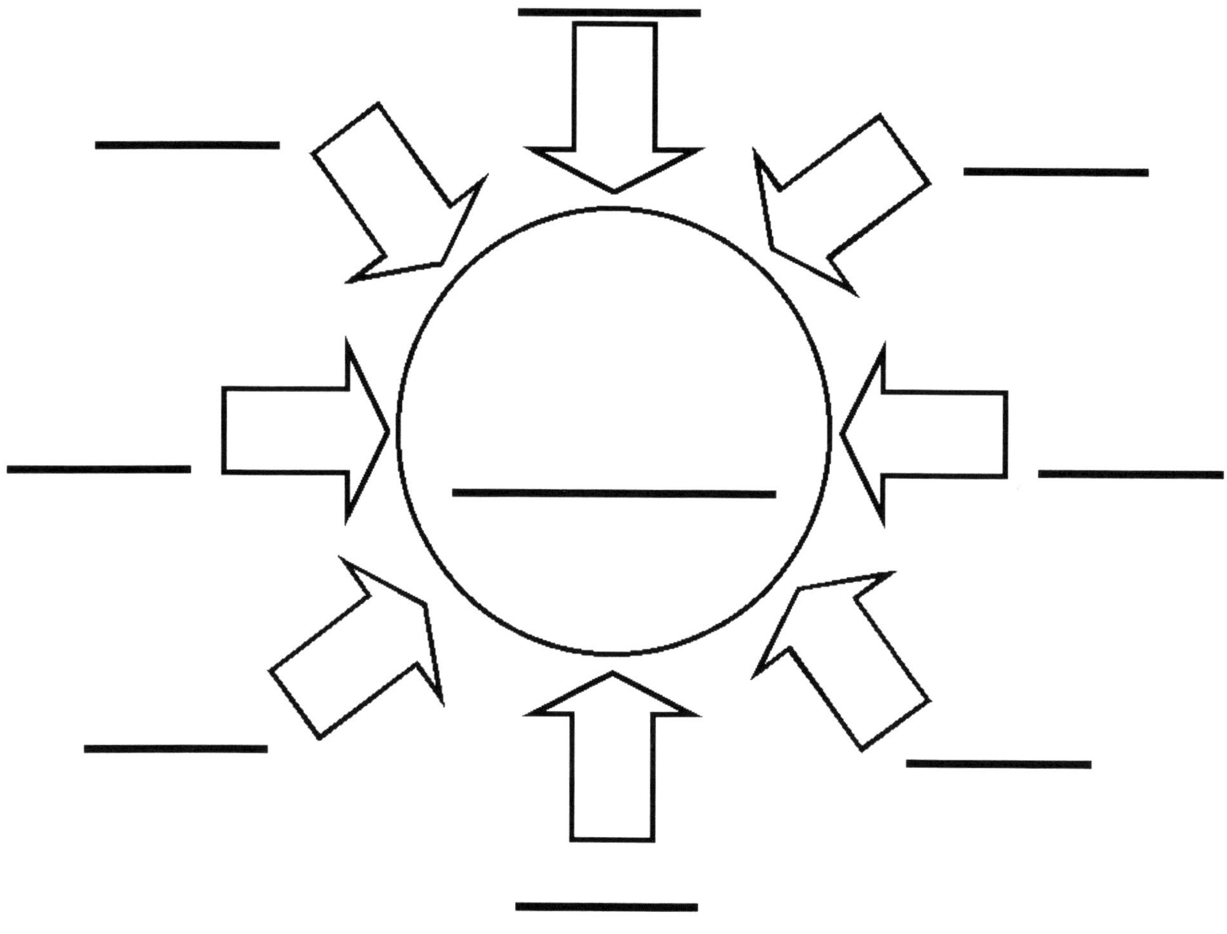

CHAPTER

9

# Jury Charges

One of the last—but most important—steps in a DWI trial is crafting a jury charge that will stand up in appellate court. Chapter 9 discusses the law of jury charges and jury argument and offers up sample forms.

## Charge Basics

A jury charge consists of two parts: the abstract portion (which tells the jury about the law) and application portion (which applies the law to the facts).[1] An abstract charge on a theory of law that does not apply the facts is insufficient to bring the theory before the jury.[2] A jury cannot be instructed on a means of committing the offense that wasn't alleged in the charging instrument.[3]

## Elements

The charge must include all the elements essential to the offense; however, the court must not include any portion of the statute not pleaded in the indictment, because that would authorize conviction for an offense not charged.[4]

### DEFINITIONS

Rather than simply typing out all definitions that might apply from the Penal Code, edit out any options not pleaded or supported by the evidence presented at trial. Words not defined by statute that have a commonly understood meaning need not be defined.[5]

> "Intoxicated" means not having the normal use of one's mental or physical faculties by reason of the introduction of alcohol into the body.
>
> "Public place" means any place to which the public or a substantial group of the public has access and includes, but is not limited to, streets, highways, and the common areas of schools, hospitals, apartment houses, office buildings, transport facilities, and shops.

### GENERAL VERDICT

Even if the state alleges different theories of intoxication, a general verdict form is sufficient if the evidence supports conviction under either theory.[6] The defendant is not entitled to separate verdict forms on whether his guilt is due to: (1) loss of physical faculties or (2) loss of mental faculties.[7]

### REASONABLE DOUBT

An instruction on "reasonable doubt" is no longer required and has even been discouraged.[8] Even if trying a case where the offense was committed prior to *Paulson*, you need not give a definition of "reasonable doubt." The *Paulson* holding applies prospectively because it is procedural in nature.[9] Courts of appeals are split on whether the court errs to charge the jury that the State doesn't have to prove guilt "beyond all doubt."[10]

---

1 *Hutch v. State*, 922 S.W 2d 166 (Tex. Crim. App. 1996).

2 *Campbell v. State*, 910 S.W.2d 475 (Tex. Crim. App. 1995).

3 *Rodriguez v. State*, 18 S.W.3d 228 (Tex. Crim. App. 2000) (reversal where jury charged on intoxication by alcohol or a combination of unknown drugs and alcohol while information only alleged intoxication by alcohol).

4 See, e.g., *Rodriguez v. State*, 31 S.W.3d 736 (Tex. App. — Houston [1st Dist.] 2000, pet. ref'd) (indictment limited to alcohol intoxication, but jury charge allowing conviction for intoxication by controlled substance).

5 See, e.g., *Murphy v. State*, 44 S.W.3d 656 (Tex. App. — Austin 2001, no pet.) (defining "normal use" unnecessarily).

6 *Price v. State*, 59 S.W.3d 297 (Tex. App. — Fort Worth 2001, pet. ref'd); *Blok v. State*, 986 S.W.2d 389 (Tex. App. — Houston [1st Dist.] 1999, pet. ref'd); *Reardon v. State*, 695 S.W.2d 331 (Tex. App. — Houston [1st Dist.] 1985, no pet.); *McGinty v. State*, 740 S.W.2d 475 (Tex. App. — Houston [1st Dist.] 1987, pet. ref'd); *Sims v. State*, 735 S.W.2d 913 (Tex. App. — Dallas 1987, pet. ref'd); *Sullivan v. State*, 807 S.W.2d 342 (Tex. App. — Houston [14th Dist.] 1991), *vacated*, 817 S.W.2d 344 (Tex. Crim. App. 1991).

7 *Chauncey v. State*, 837 S.W.2d 179 (Tex. App.—El Paso 1992), *aff'd*, 877 S.W.2d 305 (Tex. Crim. App. 1994); but see *Reidweg v. State*, 981 S.W.2d 399 (Tex. App. — San Antonio 1998, pet. ref'd).

8 *Paulson v. State*, 28 S.W.3d 570 (Tex. Crim. App. 2000).

9 *Baker v. State*, 94 S.W.3d 684 (Tex. App. — Eastland 2002, no pet.); see also *Wilson v. State*, 473 S.W.2d 532 (Tex. Crim. App. 1971).

10 *Rodriguez v. State*, 96 S.W.3d 398 (Tex. App. — Austin 2002, pet. ref'd); *Phillips v. State*, 72 S.W.3d 719 (Tex. App. — Waco 2002, no pet.); *Carriere v. State*, 84 S.W.3d 753 (Tex. App. — Houston [1st Dist.] 2002, pet. ref'd).

An instruction about the burden of proof would look something like this:

> All persons are presumed to be innocent and no person may be convicted of an offense unless each element of the offense is proved beyond a reasonable doubt. The fact that a person has been arrested, confined, or indicted for, or otherwise charged with the offense gives rise to no inference of guilt at this trial. The law does not require the defendant to prove his innocence or produce any evidence at all. The presumption of innocence alone is sufficient to acquit the defendant, unless the jurors are satisfied beyond a reasonable doubt of the defendant's guilt after careful and impartial consideration of all the evidence in the case.
>
> The prosecution has the burden of proving the defendant guilty, and it must do so by proving each and every element of the offense charged beyond a reasonable doubt, and if it fails to do so, you must acquit the defendant.
>
> It is not required that the prosecution prove guilt beyond all possible doubt; it is required that the prosecution's proof excludes all reasonable doubt concerning the defendant's guilt.
>
> In the event you have a reasonable doubt as to the defendant's guilt after considering all the evidence before you, and these instructions, you will acquit the defendant and say by your verdict Not Guilty."

### ELECTION

The state is not required to elect among different methods of committing one offense; it is entitled to a jury charge on anything the evidence shows.[11] Nor is the State required to elect when it has charged two separate offenses.[12]

## Charges Specific to DWI

Aside from the elements that the jury charge *must* contain, the state and defense typically ask for various additional charges that tend to benefit one side or the other.

### OBSERVATION PERIOD

It is no longer necessary for the defendant to be observed continuously for 15 minutes before the jury can consider the intoxilyzer result. The rules still require the operator of the test to "remain in the presence of the subject at least 15 minutes before the test."[13] Where a fact issue is raised with respect to this requirement, a defendant is entitled to an instruction that the jury disregard the test if it believes or has a reasonable doubt as to whether the 15-minute observation requirement was met.[14] Current regulations have made these cases somewhat obsolete, as it is no longer necessary that the defendant be observed.[15]

Two San Antonio Court of Appeals cases question the admissibility of Intoxilyzer results where the operator failed to check the reference-sample temperature prior to test administration. Based upon fact-bound scenarios, one decision held that the trial court did not abuse its discretion in excluding the test results,[16] and the other upheld the trial court's denial of the suppression request because the technical supervisor had checked and confirmed the correct temperature the prior day.[17]

Two points are worth making about these opinions. First, neither of these unpublished San Antonio decisions explicitly holds that a trial judge must exclude the breath test results if the temperature was not checked. Second and of paramount importance, the current version of the Texas Breath Alcohol Testing Regulations does not require operators check the reference sample temperature.[18] **[See the full version of the rules on the CD-Rom.]**

---

11 *Kitchens v. State,* 823 S.W.2d 256 (Tex. Crim. App. 1991).

12 *O'Neal v. State,* 746 S.W.2d 769 (Tex. Crim. App. 1988).

13 37 TEX. ADMIN. CODE §19.3(c)(1). This provision overrules language from *Gifford v. State,* 793 S.W.2d 489 (Tex. App. — Dallas 1990), *pet. dism'd improv. granted,* 810 S.W.2d 225 (Tex. Crim. App. 1991), citing that continuous observation, for a minimum period of 15 minutes, of an individual prior to initiating a BAC test is required for it to be admissible as evidence of intoxication (citing *State v. Kost,* 785 S.W.2d 936, 939 (Tex. App. — San Antonio 1990, no pet.).

14 *Adams v. State,* 67 S.W.3d 450, 453 (Tex. App. — Fort Worth 2002, pet. ref'd); *Howes v. State,* 120 S.W.3d 903 (Tex. App. — Texarkana 2003, pet. ref'd); *Davis v. State,* 949 S.W.2d 28 (Tex. App. — San Antonio 1997, no pet.); *Garcia v. State,* 874 S.W.2d 688 (Tex. App.. — El Paso 1993, no pet.); *Smithey v. State,* 850 S.W.2d 204 (Tex. App. — Fort Worth 1993, pet. ref'd).

15 37 TEX. ADMIN. CODE §19.4(c)(1).

16 *State v. Garza,* No. 04-02-626-CR, 2005 WL 2138082 (Tex. App. — San Antonio 2006).

17 *Gamez v. State,* No. 04-02-087-CR, 2003 WL 145554 (Tex. App. — San Antonio 2003, no pet.).

18 37 TEX. ADMIN. CODE §19.4(c)(4).

## BREATH TESTS

A judge is not allowed to charge the jury that it should disregard the results of the breath test if it has reasonable doubt whether the instrument was in good working order.[19] However, a defendant is entitled to an instruction on the issue of whether officers and operators complied with DPS regulations regarding breath testing. In *Atkinson v. State*,[20] the Court of Criminal Appeals approved the following jury charge on the working condition of the instrument:

> You are instructed that under our law in order to be considered valid, a chemical test must be performed according to the rules and regulations governing such test by the Department of Public Safety concerning proper techniques and methodology. Included in those regulations are: (1) continuous observation of the person tested for a minimum of fifteen (15) minutes prior to the actual test; ... If you have found beyond a reasonable doubt that each of these regulations were complied with you may consider such test and give it whatever weight you choose. If you do not so find or if you have a reasonable doubt as to whether these regulations were complied with you may not consider said test for any purpose and shall not refer to it further in your deliberations.

The *Atkinson* court set out the following standard for these types of instructions:

> Accordingly, we hold that a jury instruction which identifies evidence requiring special jury consideration under the law, and which sets out the law governing such consideration, does not violate the article 36.14 prohibition against judicial comment so long as it does not intimate that the jury should resolve any fact question in a certain way or that any of the evidence bearing upon such a fact question should be given greater weight or credibility than other evidence bearing on the same question.[21]

Note, however, that the *Atkinson* opinion cites to DPS regulations that were current at the time the case was tried. Those regulations called for "continuous observation of the person tested," but they have since been amended to say only that the operator must "remain in the presence of" the person for at least 15 minutes.[22] Amendments and changes in those regulations continue to occur, so it is a good practice to always check the applicable version of those regulations before taking your case to trial because some requirements set out in past case law based on the older versions of the rules may no longer be relevant. **[See Appendix 9-2 for the most current version of the regulations.]**

## BLOOD, BREATH, URINE

The judge is not required to give an instruction on alcohol concentration as it relates to blood or urine when the evidence shows only that a breath test was given.[23] An instruction that defines intoxication in terms of presence of alcohol in the defendant's body—rather than his breath, blood, or urine—is proper.[24]

## ALTERNATIVE CAUSATION

A defendant is entitled to a jury instruction on another causation factor only when he: (1) denies using alcohol, and (2) can explain his suspect action.[25] A charge that singles out limited parts of the evidence may constitute an improper comment by the judge on the weight of the evidence. In *Neaves v. State*,[26] for instance, the judge was not entitled to charge the jury about the possibility that the defendant received a blow to the head, which the officer could have mistaken for intoxication. A defendant is not entitled to a jury instruction on an alternative cause—like fatigue—that merely negates the existence of an element of the state's case.[27]

---

19 *Stone v. State*, 685 S.W.2d 791 (Tex. App. — Fort Worth 1985), *aff'd*, 703 S.W.2d 652 (Tex. Crim. App. 1986) (hole in breath test tube goes to weight jury should give the evidence).

20 871 S.W.2d 252 (Tex. App. — Fort Worth 1994), *rev'd*, 923 S.W.2d 21 (Tex. Crim. App. 1996), *on remand*, 934 S.W.2d 896 (Tex. App. — Fort Worth 1996).

21 *Atkinson*, 923 S.W.2d at 25.

22 37 Tex. Admin. Code §19.4 (c)(1).

23 *Maddox v. State*, 705 S.W.2d 739 (Tex. App. — Houston [1st Dist.] 1986), *pet. dism'd*, 770 S.W.2d 780 (Tex. Crim. App. 1988).

24 *Reardon v. State*, 695 S.W.2d 331 (Tex. App. — Houston [1st Dist.] 1985, no pet.).

25 *Grissett v. State*, 571 S.W.2d 922 (Tex. Crim. App. 1978).

26 767 S.W.2d 784 (Tex. Crim. App. 1989).

27 *Drapkin v. State*, 781 S.W.2d 710 (Tex. App. — Texarkana 1989), *rev'd*, 175 S.W.3d 795 (Tex. Crim. App. 2005); see also *Moore v. State*, 736 S.W.2d 682 (Tex. Crim. App. 1987) (defense not entitled to instruction contesting his intoxication, because this merely goes to negating an element of the state's case).

## SYNERGISTIC CHARGES

If the evidence shows that the defendant became intoxicated from less alcohol than might ordinarily make a person intoxicated because of other substances in his body, the court can give the jury a charge—known as a "synergistic charge"—on this effect. An example of a synergistic charge is:

> You are further instructed that if a person by the use of medications or drugs renders himself more susceptible to the influence of intoxicating liquor than he otherwise would have been and by reason thereof became intoxicated from the recent use of intoxicating liquor, he would be in the same position as though his intoxication was produced by the use of intoxicating liquor alone.[28]

A charge that includes this principle does not create a new crime nor require a different culpable mental state.[29]

The state is entitled to a synergistic charge on the effect of intoxication from alcohol and drugs when drug use evidence comes out at trial, even if it is not alleged in the indictment.[30] A synergistic charge is not appropriate when fatigue is the aggravating factor.[31] A synergistic charge also may not be used for a theory of intoxication that was not alleged.[32] In *Rodriguez v. State*, the defendant was charged with intoxication via alcohol, but testimony at trial showed that he had not been drinking alcohol at all but had taken cold/flu medication (Contac) that made him drowsy. The Court of Criminal Appeals ruled that *Sutton* and *Heard* only address situations in which another substance makes a defendant more susceptible to alcohol—but the defendant has been drinking *some* alcohol. The State could not expand its theory of the case by allowing conviction of intoxication via a drug, which had not been charged in the indictment. However, *Rodriguez* did not overrule *Sutton* or *Heard*. Further proof of the continued viability of synergistic charges as an option can be found in *Gray v. State*.[33] If you allege in the charging instrument simply that the defendant was "intoxicated," you should not need a synergistic charge, because "intoxicated" encompasses all potential intoxicating substances.

## ARTICLE 38.23 INSTRUCTION ON VALIDITY OF STOP

Often in DWI trials, the defense questions the validity of the traffic stop before the jury even though the issue was already litigated in a pretrial suppression hearing. When such a factual issue is raised before the jury, CCP article 38.23 mandates submission of an exclusionary-rule instruction.[34] The focus of this factual dispute must be on *how* evidence was obtained—ask yourself whether any evidence, from any source, questions the legality of the officer's authority to stop or arrest the defendant.[35]

Temporary stops occur for innumerable reasons that include reasonable suspicion of DWI itself and reasonable suspicion of various traffic code violations.[36] When the judge submits an exclusionary-rule jury instruction applying reasonable suspicion, make sure that its language follows *Terry* law and does not raise your burden of proof on the stop. Some courts have utilized instructions that incorrectly require proof of the underlying traffic offense in the language submitted

---

28 *Booher v. State,* 668 S.W.2d 882 (Tex. App. — Houston [1st Dist.] 1984, pet. ref'd).

29 *Booher,* 668 S.W.2d at 884; see also *Sutton v. State,* 899 S.W.2d 682 (Tex. Crim. App. 1995); *Heard v. State,* 665 S.W.2d 488 (Tex. Crim. App. 1984); *Miller v. State,* 341 S.W.2d 440 (Tex. Crim. App. 1960).

30 *Sutton v. State,* 899 S.W.2d 682 (Tex. Crim. App. 1995); *Heard v. State,* 665 S.W.2d 488 (Tex. Crim. App. 1984); *Miller v. State,* 341 S.W.2d 440 (Tex. Crim. App. 1960); *Booher v. State,* 668 S.W.2d 882 (Tex. App. — Houston [1st Dist.] 1984, pet. ref'd).

31 *Atkins v. State,* 990 S.W.2d 763 (Tex. App. — Austin 1999, pet. ref'd) (harmless error when court gave synergistic charge that spoke to defendant's "allowing his physical condition to deteriorate").

32 *Rodriguez v. State,* 18 S.W.3d 228 (Tex. Crim. App. 2000).

33 *Gray v. State,* 152 S.W.3d 125, 129 (Tex. Crim. App. 2004).

34 *Bell v. State,* 938 S.W.2d 35, 48 (Tex. Crim. App. 1996). A liberal standard applies: Does the evidence contain a factual dispute questioning the legality of the initial stop? The dispute can originate from any evidentiary source (even from a state witness or exhibit) and arises regardless of the evidence's credibility (or lack thereof). *Garza v. State,* 126 S.W.3d 79, 85 (Tex. Crim. App. 2004). When a dispute exists, the instruction is mandatory.

35 The following two cases illustrate instances when no exclusionary-rule instruction is required because no evidence questioned the *legality* of the officer's conduct. For example, where an officer relied on a vehicle's weaving to justify his stop and the defendant agreed she had swerved, but cited an innocuous reason for her poor driving, no factual dispute questioned the officer's legal authority to stop the defendant. See *Beasley v. State,* 810 S.W.2d 838, 842 (Tex. App. — Fort Worth 1991, pet. ref'd). In the second case, two deputies testified that they observed the defendant's unlit tail light from far away. The defense attorney did not attempt to impeach this testimony on cross, and no other witness controverted the state's proof regarding the justification for the stop. Thus, the record contained no factual dispute requiring submission of an article 38.23 instruction even though defense counsel argued that the officers' testimony was unbelievable. *Shpikula v. State,* 68 S.W.3d 212, 217 (Tex. App. — Houston [1st Dist.] 2002, pet. ref'd).

36 See generally **Chapter 1 (Making the Stop).**

pursuant to article 38.23.[37] This is not correct. *Terry* hinges on the officer's *reasonable belief*, which requires a lower evidentiary threshold than proof of a violation. Here's an example showing *Terry* correctly applied:

> You are instructed that, under our law, no evidence obtained by an officer as a result of an unlawful stop and detention shall be admissible against the accused. An officer is lawfully permitted, however, to temporarily detain a motorist if the officer has a reasonable suspicion, based on specific and articulable facts, for believing that some activity out of the ordinary is or has occurred, that the person detained is connected with such activity, and that there is some indication that the activity is related to a criminal offense. The reasonableness of an officer's belief for such a temporary investigative detention is based upon the totality of the circumstances including the officer's training and experience.
>
> Now bearing these instructions in mind, if you believe beyond a reasonable doubt that Officer Obie had a reasonable suspicion that the defendant, Our Hero, drove a vehicle and failed to maintain a single lane of traffic, then you may consider the evidence obtained as a result of the stop. If you have a reasonable doubt that the peace officer lawfully stopped the defendant, then you are instructed to disregard the testimony of Officer Obie and say by your verdict not guilty.

Finally, do not forget to include the statutory definition of the traffic violation which was the basis for the stop in the definitional instructions at the beginning of the court's charge.

### PER SE DEFINITION WITHOUT EXTRAPOLATION

Many times the defense will try to prevent the per se definition being submitted to the jury or seek an instruction limiting the consideration of the BAC evidence under the argument that without extrapolation testimony, the State has not satisfied its burden of proof under that definition. This argument has been rejected by the Court of Criminal Appeals, which held that it was proper for the trial court to instruct the jury it could find the defendant guilty under the per se impairment definition of intoxication, despite the absence of retrograde extrapolation evidence.[38] The defendant's blood showed a BAC of 0.10 at the hospital 80 minutes after he was involved in a car wreck. The Court found these results were evidence from which the jury could find the defendant guilty under the per se impairment definition. The trial court's instruction that the jury could consider the BAC test result "for the limited purpose of showing that the individual tested had ingested alcohol only at some point before the time of the test" was held to be "misleading and an improper comment on the weight of the evidence." Even in cases where the BAC at the time of the test is under .08, it is proper to submit the per se definition to the jury when the submission is supported by the facts of the case.[39]

## Deadly Weapons

A motor vehicle can be considered a deadly weapon in a DWI case if a collision might have occurred under the circumstances present in the defendant's case, and that collision would have been capable of causing death or serious bodily injury.[40] A deadly weapon instruction and finding is not proper without evidence that another motorist was on the highway at the time and place the defendant drove while intoxicated.[41] At least one court of appeals has stated that officers on the road with the defendant may be considered part of the class of persons capable of being endangered.[42] Notice that the state intends to seek a deadly weapon finding must be timely and adequate.[43]

---

37 Problematic language forces the state to prove that the observed misconduct actually occurred, instead of focusing on the officer reasonably believing that conduct relating to a crime took place. After a description of the law pertaining to temporary detentions, an instruction using the following language would not accurately apply *Terry* but, instead, would erroneously require proof of the underlying conduct:

> Now, bearing in mind these instructions, if you find from the evidence that the defendant, Our Hero, did not fail to maintain a single lane of traffic or, if you have a reasonable doubt thereof, you will disregard the testimony of the officer.

38 *Kirsch v. State,* 306 S.W.3d 738 (Tex. Crim. App. 2010).

39 *Williams v. State,* 307 S.W.3d 862 (Tex. App. — Fort Worth 2010, no pet.) (even though BAC was 0.07 90 minutes after defendant's arrest and there was no extrapolation evidence, the trial court properly submitted the per se theory of intoxication as the evidence supported an inference the defendant was intoxicated under both theories).

40 *Mann v. State,* 58 S.W.3d 132 (Tex. Crim. App. 2001) (defendant almost hit another vehicle head-on when he crossed the center line; driver of other car took evasive action and avoided the collision); *Davis v. State,* 964 S.W.2d 352 (Tex. App. — Fort Worth 1998, no pet.).

41 *Williams v. State,* 946 S.W.2d 432 (Tex. App. — Fort Worth 1997), *aff'd in part, rev'd in part,* 970 S.W.2d 566 (Tex. Crim. App. 1998).

42 *Drichas v. State,* 152 S.W.3d 630 (Tex. App. — Texarkana 2004), *rev'd on other grounds,* 175 S.W.3d 795 (Tex. Crim. App. 2005).

43 *Hocutt v. State,* 927 S.W.2d 201 (Tex. App. — Fort Worth 1996, pet. ref'd) (faxed notice three days before voir dire that the state was seeking a deadly weapon finding—but without informing defendant the automobile was the alleged deadly weapon—was neither timely nor adequate).

# Appendix 9-1: Sample Jury Charges

## DWI WITH NO BREATH TEST

**Cause No. __________**

| | | |
|---|---|---|
| THE STATE OF TEXAS | § | IN COUNTY CRIMINAL |
| VS. | § | COURT NUMBER _____ |
| <<DEFENDANT>> | § | _____ COUNTY, TEXAS |

**MEMBERS OF THE JURY:**

The defendant, «Defendant2», stands charged by information with the offense of being intoxicated while operating a motor vehicle in a public place in ________ County, Texas, on or about the «Date» day of «Month», «Year».

To this charge the defendant has entered a plea of "not guilty."

I.

Our law provides that a person commits an offense if that person is intoxicated while operating a motor vehicle in a public place.

II.

"Intoxicated" means not having the normal use of one's mental or physical faculties by reason of the introduction of alcohol into the body.

"Public place" means any place to which the public or a substantial group of the public has access and includes, but is not limited to, streets, highways, and the common areas of schools, hospitals, apartment houses, office buildings, transport facilities, and shops.

III.

Now, if you find from the evidence beyond a reasonable doubt that in ________ County, Texas, on or about the «Date» day of «Month», «Year», the defendant, «Defendant2», did then and there operate a motor vehicle in a public place while the said defendant was intoxicated, then you will find the defendant guilty as charged.

Unless you do so find beyond a reasonable doubt or if you have a reasonable doubt thereof, you will acquit the defendant and say by your verdict, "not guilty."

IV.

All persons are presumed to be innocent and no person may be convicted of an offense unless each element of the offense is proved beyond a reasonable doubt. The fact that a person has been arrested, confined, or indicted for, or otherwise charged with the offense, gives rise to no inference of guilt at this trial. The law does not require the defendant to prove «hisorher» innocence or produce any evidence at all. The presumption of innocence alone is sufficient to acquit the defendant, unless the jurors are satisfied beyond a reasonable doubt of the defendant's guilt after careful and impartial consideration of all the evidence in the case.

The prosecution has the burden of proving the defendant guilty and it must do so by proving each and every element of the offense charged beyond a reasonable doubt and if it fails to do so, you must acquit the defendant.

It is not required that the prosecution prove guilt beyond all possible doubt; it is required that the prosecution's proof excludes all reasonable doubt concerning the defendant's guilt.

In the event that you have a reasonable doubt as to the defendant's guilt after considering all the evidence before you, and these instructions, you will acquit the defendant and say by your verdict "Not Guilty."

V.

The information in this case is no evidence whatsoever of the guilt of the defendant. It is a mere pleading necessary in order to bring this case into court for trial, and you will consider it for no purpose at all.

Your verdict must be by a unanimous vote of all members of the jury. In deliberating on this case, you shall consider these written instructions as a whole and you must not refer to or discuss any matters not in evidence before you.

After you retire to the jury room, you should select one of your number as your presiding juror. It is his or her duty to preside at your deliberations, vote with you, and when you have unanimously agreed upon a verdict, to certify to your verdict by using the attached form and signing the same as your presiding juror.

You are the exclusive judges of the facts proved, of the credibility of the witnesses, and of the weight to be given to their testimony, but you are bound to receive the law from the Court, which is herein given, and be governed thereby.

If the jury wishes to communicate with the Court pertaining to this case, such communication must be in writing and signed by the presiding juror and handed to the bailiff.

______________________________

JUDGE PRESIDING

**VERDICT FORMS**

We, the Jury, find the Defendant, ______________, not guilty.

______________________________

PRESIDING JUROR

**OR**

We, the Jury, find the Defendant, ______________, guilty as charged.

______________________________

PRESIDING JUROR

## DWI CHARGE WITH BLOOD

**Cause No. __________**

| | | |
|---|---|---|
| THE STATE OF TEXAS | § | IN COUNTY CRIMINAI |
| vs. | § | COURT NUMBER _____ |
| <<DEFENDANT>> | § | _____ COUNTY, TEXAS |

**COURT'S CHARGE**

**MEMBERS OF THE JURY:**

The defendant, «Defendant2», stands charged by information with the offense of being intoxicated while operating a motor vehicle in a public place in _________ County, Texas, on or about the «Date» day of «Month», «Year».

To this charge the defendant has entered a plea of "not guilty."

I.

Our law provides that a person commits an offense if that person is intoxicated while driving or operating a motor vehicle in a public place.

II.

"Intoxicated" means not having the normal use of one's mental or physical faculties by reason of the introduction of alcohol into the body or by having an alcohol concentration of 0.08 or more.

The term "alcohol concentration" as used in this charge means the number of grams of alcohol per 100 milliliters of blood.

"Public place" means any place to which the public or a substantial group of the public has access and includes, but is not limited to, streets, highways, and the common areas of schools, hospitals, apartment houses, office buildings, transport facilities and shops.

III.

Now, if you find from the evidence beyond a reasonable doubt that in _________ County, Texas, on or about the «Date» day of «Month», «Year», the defendant, «Defendant2», did then and there operate a motor vehicle in a public place while the said defendant was intoxicated, then you will find the defendant guilty as charged.

Unless you do so find beyond a reasonable doubt or if you have a reasonable doubt thereof, you will acquit the defendant and say by your verdict, "not guilty."

IV.

All persons are presumed to be innocent and no person may be convicted of an offense unless each element of the offense is proved beyond a reasonable doubt. The fact that a person has been arrested, confined, or indicted for, or otherwise charged with the offense, gives rise to no inference of guilt at this trial. The law does not require the defendant to prove his innocence or produce any evidence at all. The presumption of innocence alone is sufficient to acquit the defendant, unless the jurors are satisfied beyond a reasonable doubt of the defendant's guilt after careful and impartial consideration of all the evidence in the case.

The prosecution has the burden of proving the defendant guilty and it must do so by proving each and every element of the offense charged beyond a reasonable doubt and if it fails to do so, you must acquit the defendant.

It is not required that the prosecution prove guilt beyond all possible doubt; it is required that the prosecution's proof excludes all reasonable doubt concerning the defendant's guilt.

In the event that you have a reasonable doubt as to the defendant's guilt after considering all the evidence before you, and these instructions, you will acquit the defendant and say by your verdict "Not Guilty."

V.

The information in this case is no evidence whatsoever of the guilt of the defendant. It is a mere pleading necessary in order to bring this case into court for trial, and you will consider it for no purpose at all.

Your verdict must be by a unanimous vote of all members of the jury. In deliberating on this case, you shall consider these written instructions as a whole and you must not refer to or discuss any matters not in evidence before you.

After you retire to the jury room, you should select one of your number as your presiding juror. It is his or her duty to preside at your deliberations, vote with you, and when you have unanimously agreed upon a verdict, to certify to your verdict by using the attached form and signing the same as your presiding juror.

You are the exclusive judges of the facts proved, of the credibility of the witnesses, and of the weight to be given to their testimony, but you are bound to receive the law from the Court, which is herein given, and be governed thereby.

If the jury wishes to communicate with the Court pertaining to this case, such communication must be in writing and signed by the presiding juror and handed to the bailiff.

______________________________

JUDGE PRESIDING

**VERDICT FORMS**

We, the Jury, find the Defendant, ________________, not guilty.

______________________________

PRESIDING JUROR

**OR**

We, the Jury, find the Defendant, ________________, guilty as charged.

______________________________

PRESIDING JUROR

## DWI CHARGE WITH EVIDENCE OF .08 INTOXICATION

**Cause No. __________**

| THE STATE OF TEXAS | § | IN COUNTY CRIMINAL |
|---|---|---|
| vs. | § | COURT NUMBER _____ |
| <<DEFENDANT>> | § | _____ COUNTY, TEXAS |

**COURT'S CHARGE**

**MEMBERS OF THE JURY:**

The defendant, «Defendant2», stands charged by information with the offense of being intoxicated while operating a motor vehicle in a public place in ________ County, Texas, on or about the «Date» day of «Month», «Year».

To this charge the defendant has entered a plea of "not guilty."

I.

Our law provides that a person commits an offense if that person is intoxicated while driving or operating a motor vehicle in a public place.

II.

"Intoxicated" means not having the normal use of one's mental or physical faculties by reason of the introduction of alcohol into the body or by having an alcohol concentration of 0.08 or more.

The term "alcohol concentration" as used in this charge means the number of grams of alcohol per 210 liters of breath.

"Public place" means any place to which the public or a substantial group of the public has access and includes, but is not limited to, streets, highways, and the common areas of schools, hospitals, apartment houses, office buildings, transport facilities and shops.

III.

Now, if you find from the evidence beyond a reasonable doubt that in ________ County, Texas, on or about the «Date» day of «Month», «Year», the defendant, «Defendant2», did then and there operate a motor vehicle in a public place while the said defendant was intoxicated by not having the normal use of «hisorher» mental or physical faculties by reason of the introduction of alcohol into «hisorher» body, or by having an alcohol concentration of 0.08 or more then you will find the defendant guilty as charged.

Unless you do so find beyond a reasonable doubt or if you have a reasonable doubt thereof, you will acquit the defendant and say by your verdict, "not guilty."

IV.

All persons are presumed to be innocent and no person may be convicted of an offense unless each element of the offense is proved beyond a reasonable doubt. The fact that a person has been arrested, confined, or indicted for, or otherwise charged with the offense, gives rise to no inference of guilt at this trial. The law does not require the defendant to prove «hisorher» innocence or produce any evidence at all. The presumption of innocence alone is sufficient to acquit the defendant, unless the jurors are satisfied beyond a reasonable doubt of the defendant's guilt after careful and impartial consideration of all the evidence in the case.

The prosecution has the burden of proving the defendant guilty and it must do so by proving each and every element of the offense charged beyond a reasonable doubt and if it fails to do so, you must acquit the defendant.

It is not required that the prosecution prove guilt beyond all possible doubt; it is required that the prosecution's proof excludes all reasonable doubt concerning the defendant's guilt.

In the event that you have a reasonable doubt as to the defendant's guilt after considering all the evidence before you, and these instructions, you will acquit the defendant and say by your verdict "Not Guilty."

V.

The information in this case is no evidence whatsoever of the guilt of the defendant. It is a mere pleading necessary in order to bring this case into court for trial, and you will consider it for no purpose at all.

Your verdict must be by a unanimous vote of all members of the jury. In deliberating on this case, you shall consider these written instructions as a whole and you must not refer to or discuss any matters not in evidence before you.

After you retire to the jury room, you should select one of your number as your presiding juror. It is his or her duty to preside at your deliberations, vote with you, and when you have unanimously agreed upon a verdict, to certify to your verdict by using the attached form and signing the same as your presiding juror.

You are the exclusive judges of the facts proved, of the credibility of the witnesses, and of the weight to be given to their testimony, but you are bound to receive the law from the Court, which is herein given, and be governed thereby.

If the jury wishes to communicate with the Court pertaining to this case, such communication must be in writing and signed by the presiding juror and handed to the bailiff.

______________________________

JUDGE PRESIDING

**VERDICT FORMS**

We, the Jury, find the Defendant, ________________, not guilty.

______________________________

PRESIDING JUROR

**OR**

We, the Jury, find the Defendant, ________________, guilty as charged.

______________________________

PRESIDING JUROR

## DWI CHARGE WITH EVIDENCE OF DRUGS

**Cause No. __________**

| | | |
|---|---|---|
| THE STATE OF TEXAS | § | IN COUNTY CRIMINAL |
| vs. | § | COURT NUMBER _____ |
| <<DEFENDANT>> | § | ______ COUNTY, TEXAS |

**COURT'S CHARGE**

**MEMBERS OF THE JURY:**

The defendant, «Defendant2», stands charged by information with the offense of being intoxicated while operating a motor vehicle in a public place in ________ County, Texas, on or about the «Date» day of «Month», «Year».

To this charge the defendant has entered a plea of "not guilty."

I.

Our law provides that a person commits an offense if that person is intoxicated while driving or operating a motor vehicle in a public place.

II.

"Intoxicated" means not having the normal use of one's mental or physical faculties by reason of the introduction of a controlled substance, a dangerous drug or a combination of two or more of those substances or any other substance into the body.

"Public place" means any place to which the public or a substantial group of the public has access and includes, but is not limited to, streets, highways, and the common areas of schools, hospitals, apartment houses, office buildings, transport facilities and shops.

III.

Now, if you find from the evidence beyond a reasonable doubt that in ________ County, Texas, on or about the «Date» day of «Month», «Year», the defendant, «Defendant2», did then and there operate a motor vehicle in a public place while the said defendant was intoxicated by not having the normal use of «hisorher» mental or physical faculties by reason of the introduction of a controlled substance, a dangerous drug, or a combination of two or more of these substances or any other substance into «hisorher» body, then you will find the defendant guilty as charged.

Unless you do so find beyond a reasonable doubt or if you have a reasonable doubt thereof, you will acquit the defendant and say by your verdict, "not guilty."

IV.

All persons are presumed to be innocent and no person may be convicted of an offense unless each element of the offense is proved beyond a reasonable doubt. The fact that a person has been arrested, confined, or indicted for, or otherwise charged with the offense, gives rise to no inference of guilt at this trial. The law does not require the defendant to prove «hisorher» innocence or produce any evidence at all. The presumption of innocence alone is sufficient to acquit the defendant, unless the jurors are satisfied beyond a reasonable doubt of the defendant's guilt after careful and impartial consideration of all the evidence in the case.

The prosecution has the burden of proving the defendant guilty and it must do so by proving each and every element of the offense charged beyond a reasonable doubt and if it fails to do so, you must acquit the defendant.

It is not required that the prosecution prove guilt beyond all possible doubt; it is required that the prosecution's proof excludes all reasonable doubt concerning the defendant's guilt.

In the event that you have a reasonable doubt as to the defendant's guilt after considering all the evidence before you, and these instructions, you will acquit the defendant and say by your verdict "Not Guilty."

V.

The information in this case is no evidence whatsoever of the guilt of the defendant. It is a mere pleading necessary in order to bring this case into court for trial, and you will consider it for no purpose at all.

Your verdict must be by a unanimous vote of all members of the jury. In deliberating on this case, you shall consider these written instructions as a whole and you must not refer to or discuss any matters not in evidence before you.

After you retire to the jury room, you should select one of your number as your presiding juror. It is his or her duty to preside at your deliberations, vote with you, and when you have unanimously agreed upon a verdict, to certify to your verdict by using the attached form and signing the same as your presiding juror.

You are the exclusive judges of the facts proved, of the credibility of the witnesses, and of the weight to be given to their testimony, but you are bound to receive the law from the Court, which is herein given, and be governed thereby.

If the jury wishes to communicate with the Court pertaining to this case, such communication must be in writing and signed by the presiding juror and handed to the bailiff.

____________________________

JUDGE PRESIDING

**VERDICT FORMS**

We, the Jury, find the Defendant, ________________, not guilty.

____________________________

PRESIDING JUROR

**OR**

We, the Jury, find the Defendant, ________________, guilty as charged.

____________________________

PRESIDING JUROR

## DWI WITH EVIDENCE OF 0.15

*Add this language to the preceding sample for DWI Charge with Blood:*

Now bearing in mind the foregoing instructions, if you find from the evidence beyond a reasonable doubt that on or about the ____ day of ________________, 20____, in ____________ County, Texas, the defendant ________________, did then and there operate a motor vehicle in a public place while the said defendant was intoxicated, and that the analysis of a specimen of the defendant's blood showed an alcohol concentration level of 0.15 or more at the time the analysis was performed, then you will find the defendant guilty as charged.

Unless you do so find beyond a reasonable doubt or if you have a reasonable doubt thereof, you will acquit the defendant and say by your verdict not guilty.

### OR IF A LESSER-INCLUDED IS REQUESTED

Unless you do so find beyond a reasonable doubt or if you have a reasonable doubt thereof, you will next consider whether the defendant is guilty of the lesser-included offense of Driving While Intoxicated.

Now bearing in mind the foregoing instructions, if you find from the evidence beyond a reasonable doubt that on or about the ____ day of ________________, 20____, in ____________ County, Texas, the defendant ________________, did then and there operate a motor vehicle in a public place while the said defendant was intoxicated, then you will find the defendant guilty of Driving While Intoxicated.

## PUNISHMENT CHARGE — JAIL TIME ONLY

**Cause No. __________**

| | | |
|---|---|---|
| THE STATE OF TEXAS | § | IN COUNTY CRIMINAL |
| VS. | § | COURT NUMBER _____ |
| <<DEFENDANT>> | § | _____ COUNTY, TEXAS |

### COURT'S CHARGE

**MEMBERS OF THE JURY:**

You have found the defendant, ____________, guilty as charged in the information of driving while intoxicated, and it is now your duty to affix the punishment to be assessed against the defendant.

You are instructed that the punishment for this offense is by confinement in the _________ County Jail for a period from 3 days to 180 days or a fine from $0 dollars to $2,000 dollars, or both such fine and jail time.

You are further instructed that in fixing the defendant's punishment, you may take into consideration all of the facts shown by the evidence submitted before you in the full trial of this case and the law as submitted to you in this charge and the charge heretofore given to you by the Court.

The defendant has elected not to testify in this case. Our law provides that the election of the defendant not to testify shall not be taken as a circumstance against him, and you must not allude to, comment on or discuss in your deliberations the election of the defendant not to testify in this case.

Nor will you refer to or discuss with any other juror during your deliberations anything you might know, or may have heard, concerning the defendant or the case, other than what you have heard from the witness stand during the trial.

Your verdict must be by a unanimous verdict of all members of the jury. In arriving at your verdict, it will not be proper to fix the same by lot, chance, or any other method than by a full, fair, and free exercise of the opinion of the individual jurors under the evidence admitted before you.

You are the exclusive judges of the facts proved, of the credibility of the witnesses and of the weight to be given to the evidence, but you are bound to receive the law from the Court as herein given and be governed thereby.

______________________________

JUDGE PRESIDING

### VERDICT FORM

We, the Jury, having found the defendant, ____________, guilty of the offense of driving while intoxicated as charged in the information, hereby assess his punishment at confinement in the ________ County Jail for __________________ (3 days to 180 days).

In addition thereto, WE DO / WE DO NOT assess a fine in the amount of $________________ (from $0 dollars to $2,000 dollars).

______________________________

PRESIDING JUROR

### DWI PUNISHMENT — PROBATION

**Cause No. __________**

| | | |
|---|---|---|
| THE STATE OF TEXAS | § | IN COUNTY CRIMINAL |
| vs. | § | COURT NUMBER _____ |
| <<DEFENDANT>> | § | _____ COUNTY, TEXAS |

**COURT'S CHARGE**

**MEMBERS OF THE JURY:**

You have found the defendant, ____________________, guilty as charged in the information of driving while intoxicated, and it is now your duty to affix the punishment to be assessed against the defendant.

You are instructed that the punishment for this offense is by confinement in the __________ County Jail for a period from 3 days to 180 days or a fine from $0 dollars to $2,000 dollars, or both such fine and jail time.

You are further instructed that in fixing the defendant's punishment, you may take into consideration all of the facts shown by the evidence submitted before you in the full trial of this case and the law as submitted to you in this charge and the charge heretofore given to you by the Court.

In this case, the defendant has filed, before trial, a motion praying that in the event of a conviction, probation be granted. If you find that the defendant has never been convicted of a felony in this or any other state or the courts of the United States, and if you recommend probation be granted in this case, then let your verdict show the punishment which you assess and show that the defendant has never before been convicted of a felony in this or any other state or the courts of the United States. If you further find and believe that the ends of justice and the best interest of society and of the defendant will be served by granting probation, further show that you will recommend that the sentence be suspended and that the defendant be placed on probation.

If the jury wishes to assess a fine, a recommendation of probation should state whether or not the fine will be paid or be suspended and probated.

Your verdict must be by a unanimous verdict of all members of the jury. In arriving at your verdict, it will not be proper to fix the same by lot, chance, or any other method than by a full, fair, and free exercise of the opinion of the individual jurors under the evidence admitted before you.

You are the exclusive judges of the facts proved, of the credibility of the witnesses and of the weight to be given to the evidence, but you are bound to receive the law from the Court as herein given and be governed thereby.

______________________________

Judge Presiding

**VERDICT FORMS**

We, the Jury, having found the defendant, ________________, guilty of the offense of driving while intoxicated as charged in the information, hereby assess his punishment at confinement in the ________ County Jail for ________________ (3 days to 180 days), and we, the Jury, find that the defendant has never before been convicted of a felony in this state or any other state or the courts of the United States and WE DO RECOMMEND that the imposition of his sentence be suspended.

In addition thereto, WE DO / WE DO NOT assess a fine in the amount of $________________ (from $0 dollars to $2,000 dollars), and WE DO / WE DO NOT recommend that such fine be probated and payment thereof be suspended.

______________________________
Presiding Juror

**OR**

We, the Jury, having found the defendant, ________________, guilty of the offense of driving while intoxicated, as charged in the information, hereby assess his punishment at confinement in the ________ County Jail for ________________ (3 days to 180 days).

In addition thereto, WE DO / WE DO NOT assess a fine in the amount of $________________. ($0 dollars to $2,000 dollars.)

WE DO NOT RECOMMEND probation.

______________________________
Presiding Juror

CHAPTER

10

# Punishment

DWI is unlike other crimes in that it has its own system for enhancement. Although some of the general rules for enhancing punishment and imposing conditions of probation apply to DWI, Chapter 10 discusses punishment issues unique to DWI and other intoxication offenses.

# Prior Convictions

## SOURCES OF PUNISHMENT EVIDENCE

As a starting point, run TCIC and NCIC on all your suspects as soon as the case comes in. Don't wait until you're facing a trial date, because for out-of-state or out-of-county prior convictions, you could have a long wait on getting all the relevant information. If you need documentation on a prior conviction quickly, try going directly to another prosecutor in that county's office rather than relying on the clerk's office. [**See the TDCAA directory for a listing of prosecutors in each office.**] Call the TDCAA offices to find out which prosecutors handle which types of cases in a county.

Along with the judgment and sentence, get a copy of the charging instrument (indictment or information) to see the way it was worded and solve any potential problems before trial. For instance, some old probation cases from Dallas County had judges "vacating" the defendant's probation. This amounts to a void order—one that does not affect the legitimacy of the conviction—but the prosecutor may want to get a judge in Dallas County to sign a nunc pro tunc order.[1]

Always order a certified copy of the defendant's drivers license record. Some of the judgments and sentences for prior convictions will come without fingerprints, and the driving record may provide another way to help tie the defendant to the sentence.[2] The driving records usually will reference a case number and include the conviction, offense, date, and county, along with the fingerprints and a photograph. This, along with the judgment, sentence, and cause number, will give you a provable prior conviction. DPS records alone, without a judgement and sentence, are not sufficient to prove enhanced priors.[3]

If you find the defendant has a prior DWI, order the offense report so you can compare the details of that offense with the current offense. Call the police agency that made the arrest or the prosecutor and ask for a copy of the report.

Look for traffic citations in your county. Some greater offenses might have been bumped down and disposed of as a ticket. Prior DWIs sometimes appear in the form of public intoxication, reckless driving, deadly conduct, or obstructing a highway. Even speeding tickets can be useful. If your theme for your trial is that the defendant is indifferent to the danger he poses to other drivers on the roadway, showing the number of accidents, DWI arrests, or speeding tickets he has had in the past can better demonstrate to a jury that this defendant is a danger.

Many young offenders may have been charged with alcohol offenses in municipal or justice court. Many times these citations never appear on a TCIC or a DL record. Check with those clerks in all the jurisdictions where the offender has resided.

Interlock providers keep records that can shed light on how well a defendant is following the letter and the spirit of that bond condition. For instance, they will be able to tell you the number of times the defendant tried to start his car and the number of times it wouldn't start because he had alcohol on his breath. Also look for long periods of time where the defendant was not driving, as shown by the interlock device. The defendant could have been driving another vehicle without an interlock device during this time. The defendant's inability to adhere to his pretrial bond conditions might be a good sign for jurors that he is not a good candidate for probation.

## ONE USE FOR ENHANCEMENTS

The same prior DWI convictions cannot be used both to enhance the underlying DWI charge and to prove habitual felony offender status.[4] The state can use a prior felony DWI conviction under Penal Code §12.42 for enhancement purposes, as long as that prior is not also used to elevate the alleged offense to a felony.[5] Also note that felony DWI can be

1 See, e.g., *Mosqueda v. State*, 936 S.W.2d 714 (Tex. App. — Fort Worth 1996, no pet.); *Williamson v. State*, 46 S.W.3d 463 (Tex. App. — Dallas 2001, no pet.); *Rizo v. State*, 963 S.W.2d 137 (Tex. App. — Eastland 1998, no pet.).

2 *Gibson v. State*, 952 S.W.2d 569 (Tex. App. — Fort Worth 1997, pet. ref'd); *Williams v. State*, 946 S.W.2d 886 (Tex. App. — Waco 1997, no pet.); *Spaulding v. State*, 896 S.W.2d 587 (Tex. App. — Houston [1st Dist.] 1995, no pet.); *Abbring v. State*, 882 S.W.2d 914 (Tex. App. — Fort Worth 1994, no pet.); *Lopez v. State*, 805 S.W.2d 882 (Tex. App. — Corpus Christi 1991, no pet.).

3 *Gentile v. State*, 848 S.W.2d 359 (Tex. App. — Austin 1993, no pet.).

4 *Rodriguez v. State*, 31 S.W.3d 359 (Tex. App. — San Antonio 2000, pet. ref'd); *Rivera v. State*, 957 S.W.2d 636 (Tex. App. — Corpus Christi 1997, pet. ref'd).

5 *Maibauer v. State*, 968 S.W.2d 502 (Tex. App. — Waco 1998, pet. ref'd).

enhanced with non-DWI prior convictions, so that a person convicted of felony DWI can be a habitual offender.[6]

An underlying misdemeanor conviction can be used to elevate the DWI jurisdictionally even where a prior felony DWI (enhanced by that same misdemeanor conviction) is used to enhance the defendant to habitual status.[7] In *Perez v. State*, a 1994 misdemeanor DWI was used to enhance the charged offense to felony DWI, as it had been used in 1996 to enhance another prior DWI to felony. That 1996 felony conviction was used in the charged DWI to enhance the defendant to habitual offender status. The Fort Worth court of appeals ruled that this was a permissible use of the defendant's priors because no independent proof of the misdemeanor's existence is required under Penal Code §12.42(d) to enhance an offender to habitual status.

## PROVING PRIOR CONVICTIONS

The State must prove the jurisdictional prior offenses for felony DWI at the guilt-innocence stage of trial.[8] The prior DWI convictions are not enhancements to be used at the punishment phase, but are part of the proof at the guilt/innocence stage for felony DWI.[9] That said, a defendant has the ability to stipulate to his prior convictions and keep the jury from hearing evidence about them. [**See a further discussion later in this chapter under the heading "Felony DWI & Stipulations."**]

A faxed copy of judgment and sentence will be admissible to prove prior convictions.[10] Criminal docket sheets and related county court judgments are insufficient to prove the two prior DWI offenses required to raise a prosecution from a misdemeanor to a felony.[11] In *Renshaw v. State*, to prove the defendant had two prior DWIs, the state offered a criminal docket sheet and the related county court judgment as proof of each offense. The court of appeals reformed the sentence to lesser-included Class B DWI. The court found that the evidence failed to show the dates when the offenses were committed, and it rejected the argument that the appearance of the case's filing date in the docket sheets allows the presumption—because of the limitations period in C.C.P. Article 12.02—that the offense occurred no more than two years earlier. Citing *Ex parte Arnold*,[12] the court decided that the date of the commission of the two prior offenses, as an element of the offense, is an evidentiary matter that the State must prove at trial. The holding of this case may be affected by the repeal of the 10-year rule, as described later in this chapter.

In a felony DWI, Penal Code §49.09(b) does not require the State to prove the defendant's prior two DWI convictions occurred sequentially,[13] and the two prior convictions can arise from the same criminal transaction.[14] The *Gibson* court distinguished the enhancement provisions in §12.42(d) from the DWI enhancements by concluding that prior intoxication-related convictions serve the purpose of enhancing the offense in §49.09(b) whereas the prior convictions used in §12.42(d) serve the purpose of enhancing punishment. The court also found that the plain language of §49.09 provides that the prior offenses don't have to occur in a specified order, nor do they have to arise from separate transactions.

Under §49.09(b), the state may offer evidence that a defendant has more than two prior DWI convictions.[15] However, if the state alleges more prior DWIs than it needs, courts of appeals have split on whether the state must prove them all.

---

6 *Jones v. State*, 796 S.W.2d 183 (Tex. Crim. App. 1990); *Phifer v. State*, 787 S.W.2d 395 (Tex. Crim. App. 1990); *Seaton v. State*, 718 S.W.2d 870 (Tex. App. — Austin 1986, no pet.); *Rawlings v. State*, 602 S.W.2d 268 (Tex. Crim. App. 1980).

7 *Perez v. State*, 124 S.W.3d 214 (Tex. App. — Fort Worth 2002, no pet.); *Orona v. State*, 52 S.W.3d 242 (Tex. App. — El Paso 2001, no pet.); *Carroll v. State*, 51 S.W.3d 797 (Tex. App. — Houston [1st Dist.] 2001, pet. ref'd).

8 *Barfield v. State*, 999 S.W.2d 23 (Tex. App. — Houston [14th Dist.] 1999), *pet. dism'd as improv. granted*, 63 S.W.3d 446 (Tex. Crim. App. 2001); see also *Will v. State*, 794 S.W.2d 948 (Tex. App. — Houston [1st Dist.] 1990, pet. ref'd); *Jimenez v. State*, 981 S.W.2d 393 (Tex. App. — San Antonio 1998, pet. ref'd); *Hampton v. State*, 977 S.W.2d 467 (Tex. App. — Texarkana 1998, pet. ref'd); *Williams v. State*, 946 S.W.2d 886 (Tex. App. — Waco 1997, no pet.).

9 See, e.g., *Luedke v. State*, 711 S.W.2d 657 (Tex. Crim. App. 1986).

10 *Englund v. State*, 907 S.W.2d 937 (Tex. App. — Houston [1st Dist.] 1995), *aff'd*, 946 S.W.2d 64 (Tex. Crim. App. 1997) (requirements of T.R.EVID. 1001(3), 1001(4) and 901(a) & (b)(7) met when faxed judgment and sentence offered in lieu of originals).

11 *Renshaw v. State*, 981 S.W.2d 464 (Tex. App. — Texarkana 1998, pet. ref'd).

12 574 S.W.2d 141 (Tex. Crim. App. 1978).

13 *Streff v. State*, 890 S.W.2d 815 (Tex. App. — Eastland 1994, pet. ref'd); *Peck v. State*, 753 S.W.2d 811 (Tex. App. — Austin 1988, pet. ref'd).

14 *Gibson v. State*, 995 S.W.2d 693 (Tex. Crim. App. 1999) (two previous convictions for manslaughter based on two deaths arising out of a single act of DWI both can be used to enhance).

15 *Read v. State*, 955 S.W.2d 435 (Tex. App. — Fort Worth 1997, pet. ref'd).

The San Antonio court of appeals has ruled that by alleging more offenses than required, the state has increased its burden of proof.[16] The Court of Criminal Appeals and three other appeals courts, however, have ruled that the state may allege as many prior DWIs as it wants and still need not prove any more than two of them.[17]

### DOCUMENTATION OF PRIOR CONVICTIONS

It is always important to obtain and review all judgments and sentences you intend to offer into evidence at trial well in advance of the trial date. The documentation provided on these convictions often contains irregularities that may impact their use as evidence at trial. To aid in your review of the documents, the following case law rules should be helpful:

**Defendant not represented by counsel:** If a defendant pleaded guilty and was unrepresented by counsel, the judgment must state that the defendant knowingly, intelligently, and voluntarily waived in writing his right to representation by counsel.[18] If a defendant pleaded guilty and was unrepresented, the judgment also must reflect that the defendant was given *Faretta*[19] warnings; that is, it must show he was advised of the dangers of self-representation, that he knowingly, intelligently, and voluntarily waived in writing the right to representation by counsel and elected to represent himself.

**Jury waivers:** A written judgment must state that the defendant waived a jury in person and in open court, and the State's consent to the waiver must be in writing.[20] If the judgment recites that the defendant has waived jury trial in writing and in open court, the recital is presumed sufficient to establish that the defendant validly waived the right to trial by jury, absent an affirmative showing to the contrary.[21] If the record is silent as to admonishments, the use of the judgment will create reversible error.[22] Once an accused has stated that he understands the nature of his plea and that it was involuntary, he has a heavy burden on appeal to prove that his plea was involuntary.[23]

---

#### Penal Code §49.09. Enhanced Offenses and Penalties

(a) Except as provided by Subsection (b), an offense under Section 49.04, 49.05, 49.06, or 49.065 is a Class A misdemeanor, with a minimum term of confinement of 30 days, if it is shown on the trial of the offense that the person has previously been convicted one time of an offense relating to the operating of a motor vehicle while intoxicated, an offense of operating an aircraft while intoxicated, an offense of operating a watercraft while intoxicated, or an offense of operating or assembling an amusement ride while intoxicated.

(b) An offense under Section 49.04, 49.05, 49.06, or 49.065 is a felony of the third degree if it is shown on the trial of the offense that the person has previously been convicted:

(1) one time of an offense under Section 49.08 or an offense under the laws of another state if the offense contains elements that are substantially similar to the elements of an offense under Section 49.08; or

(2) two times of any other offense relating to the operating of a motor vehicle while intoxicated, operating an aircraft while intoxicated, operating a watercraft while intoxicated, or operating or assembling an amusement ride while intoxicated.

(b-1) An offense under Section 49.07 is a felony of the second degree if it is shown on the trial of the offense that the person caused serious bodily injury to a peace officer, a firefighter, or emergency medical services personnel while in the actual discharge of an official duty.

(b-2) An offense under Section 49.08 is a felony of the first degree if it is shown on the trial of the offense that the person caused the death of a person described by Subsection (b-1).

(b-3) For the purposes of Subsection (b-1):

(1) "Emergency medical services personnel" has the meaning assigned by Section 773.003, Health and Safety Code.

---

16 *Jimenez v. State*, 981 S.W.2d 393 (Tex. App. — San Antonio 1998, pet. ref'd) (alleging three prior DWIs in the charging instrument meant that state had increased its burden of proof; error, however, in jury charge allowing conviction of felony DWI by finding two of the three was found harmless).

17 *May v. State*, 350 S.W.2d 924 (Tex. Crim. App. 1961); *Wesley v. State*, 997 S.W.2d 874 (Tex. App. — Waco 1999, no pet.); *Read v. State*, 955 S.W.2d 435 (Tex. App. — Fort Worth 1997, pet. ref'd); *Biederman v. State*, 724 S.W.2d 436 (Tex. App. — Eastland 1987, pet. ref'd).

18 *Johnson v. State*, 614 S.W.2d 116 (Tex. Crim. App. 1981).

19 *Faretta v. California*, 422 U.S. 806, 95 S.Ct. 2525 (1975).

20 TEX. CODE CRIM. PROC. art. 1.13.

21 *Brazealey v. State*, 683 S.W.2d 446 (Tex. Crim. App. 1984); *Johnson v. State*, 72 S.W.3d 346 (Tex. Crim. App. 2002); *Parke v. Railey*, 506 U.S. 20, 29 (1992).

22 *Goffney v. State*, 843 S.W.2d 583 (Tex. Crim. App. 1992); *Samudio v. State*, 648 S.W.2d 312 (Tex. Crim. App. 1983); *Boykin v. Alabama*, 395 U.S. 238 (1969).

23 *Acosta v. State*, 160 S.W.3d 304 (Tex. App. — Fort Worth 2005, no pet.).

(2) "Firefighter" means:

(A) an individual employed by this state or by a political or legal subdivision of this state who is subject to certification by the Texas Commission on Fire Protection; or

(B) a member of an organized volunteer fire-fighting unit that:

(i) renders fire-fighting services without remuneration; and

(ii) conducts a minimum of two drills each month, each at least two hours long.

(b-4) An offense under Section 49.07 is a felony of the second degree if it is shown on the trial of the offense that the person caused serious bodily injury to another in the nature of a traumatic brain injury that results in a persistent vegetative state.

(c) For the purposes of this section:

(1) "Offense relating to the operating of a motor vehicle while intoxicated" means:

(A) an offense under Section 49.04;

(B) an offense under Section 49.07 or 49.08, if the vehicle operated was a motor vehicle;

(C) an offense under Article 6701l-1, Revised Statutes, as that law existed before September 1, 1994;

(D) an offense under Article 6701l-2, Revised Statutes, as that law existed before January 1, 1984;

(E) an offense under Section 19.05(a)(2), as that law existed before September 1, 1994, if the vehicle operated was a motor vehicle; or

(F) an offense under the laws of another state that prohibit the operation of a motor vehicle while intoxicated.

(2) "Offense of operating an aircraft while intoxicated" means:

(A) an offense under Section 49.05;

(B) an offense under Section 49.07 or 49.08, if the vehicle operated was an aircraft;

(C) an offense under Section 1, Chapter 46, Acts of the 58th Legislature, Regular Session, 1963 (Article 46f-3, Vernon's Texas Civil Statutes), as that law existed before September 1, 1994;

(D) an offense under Section 19.05(a)(2), as that law existed before September 1, 1994, if the vehicle operated was an aircraft; or

(E) an offense under the laws of another state that prohibit the operation of an aircraft while intoxicated.

(3) "Offense of operating a watercraft while intoxicated" means:

(A) an offense under Section 49.06;

(B) an offense under Section 49.07 or 49.08, if the vehicle operated was a watercraft;

(C) an offense under Section 31.097, Parks and Wildlife Code, as that law existed before September 1, 1994;

(D) an offense under Section 19.05(a)(2), as that law existed before September 1, 1994, if the vehicle operated was a watercraft; or

(E) an offense under the laws of another state that prohibit the operation of a watercraft while intoxicated.

(4) "Offense of operating or assembling an amusement ride while intoxicated" means:

(A) an offense under Section 49.065;

(B) an offense under Section 49.07 or 49.08, if the offense involved the operation or assembly of an amusement ride; or

(C) an offense under the law of another state that prohibits the operation of an amusement ride while intoxicated or the assembly of a mobile amusement ride while intoxicated.

(d) For the purposes of this section, a conviction for an offense under Section 49.04, 49.05, 49.06, 49.065, 49.07, or 49.08 that occurs on or after September 1, 1994, is a final conviction, whether the sentence for the conviction is imposed or probated.

(e) & (f) *Repealed effective Sept. 1, 2005.*

(g) A conviction may be used for purposes of enhancement under this section or enhancement under Subchapter D, Chapter 12, but not under both this section and Subchapter D.

(h) This subsection applies only to a person convicted of a second or subsequent offense relating to the operating of a motor vehicle while intoxicated committed within five years of the date on which the most recent preceding offense was committed. The court shall enter an order that requires the defendant to have a device installed, on each motor vehicle owned or operated by the defendant, that uses a deep-lung breath analysis mechanism to make impractical the operation of the motor vehicle if ethyl alcohol is detected in the breath of the operator, and that requires that before the first anniversary of the ending date of the period of license suspension under Section 521.344, Transportation Code, the defendant not operate any motor vehicle that is not equipped with that device. The court shall require the defendant to obtain the device at the defendant's own cost on or before that ending date, require the defendant to provide evidence to the court on or before that ending date that the device has been installed on each appropriate vehicle, and order the device to remain installed on each vehicle until the first anniversary of that ending date. If the court determines the offender is unable to pay for the device, the court may impose a reasonable payment schedule not to extend beyond the first anniversary of the date of installation. The Department of Public Safety shall approve devices for use under this subsection. Section 521.247, Transportation Code, applies to the approval of a device under this subsection and the consequences of that approval. Failure to comply with an order entered under this subsection is punishable by contempt. For the purpose of enforcing this subsection, the court that enters an order under this subsection retains jurisdiction over the defendant until the date on which the device is no longer required to remain installed. To the extent of a conflict between this subsection and Section 13(i), Article 42.12, Code of Criminal Procedure, this subsection controls.

## TABLE 10-1: ENHANCED DWI PUNISHMENTS

| Current offense | Enhanced by these prior convictions or conditions | Enhancing statute | Enhanced penalty range |
|---|---|---|---|
| DWI | 1 intoxication offense | §49.09(a) | Class A misdemeanor |
| DWI | 2 or more intoxication offenses | §49.09(b) | 3rd degree felony |
| DWI | w/BAC 0.15 or higher at the time analysis performed | §49.04(d) | Class A misdemeanor |

1. Prior intoxication convictions are considered "final" whether the sentence is imposed or probated, for crimes committed on or after Jan. 1, 1984.
2. Deferred adjudication is not available for intoxication offenses under Chapter 49.
3. "DWI" also includes flying (§49.05) and boating (§49.06) while intoxicated.
4. Note the repeal of the 10-year rule (former §49.09(e)), which limited use of some prior convictions, as of 9-1-05. See annotation under §49.09.

### ERRORS IN ENHANCEMENT PARAGRAPHS

Mistakes in the wording of enhancement paragraphs will not negate the effect of that enhancement unless the defendant can show surprise or prejudice from the discrepancy. Variances in information as alleged and as proven that have not called for reversal have included:

- conviction dates in DWI enhancements;[24]
- case numbers;[25]
- state where prior conviction occurred;[26]
- using word "indictment" rather than "information."[27]

[24] *Valenti v. State*, 49 S.W.3d 594 (Tex. App. — Fort Worth 2001, no pet.); *Zimmerlee v. State*, 777 S.W.2d 791 (Tex. App. — Beaumont 1989, no pet.).

[25] *Human v. State*, 749 S.W.2d 832 (Tex. Crim. App. 1988); *Cole v. State*, 611 S.W.2d 79 (Tex. Crim. App. 1981).

[26] *Plessinger v. State*, 536 S.W.2d 380 (Tex. Crim. App. 1976).

[27] *Hall v. State*, 619 S.W.2d 156 (Tex. Crim. App. 1980).

## 10-YEAR RULE

The 79th Legislature repealed sections of §49.09, Penal Code, which effectively ends the 10-year rule.[28] Before Sept. 1, 2005, if the defendant had two priors with no more than 10 years between discharge on the first and conviction on the second, the prior convictions could be used to enhance the current offense to a felony.[29] With the repeal of the 10-year rule, after Sept. 1, 2005, the date of an offense, judgment, or discharge of judgment in a prior DWI—or other Chapter 49 offense—need not be proven to enhance DWI to a Class A misdemeanor or felony DWI. This radically simplifies the charging process.

Offenses committed before Sept. 1, 2005, must be enhanced pursuant to the law in effect at the time of the offense. That law remains fairly complicated. The Court of Criminal Appeals resolved the issue of what priors could be used for pre-2005 cases. The Court decided in *Getts v. State* that prior intoxication offenses could be used to enhance a current offense only if there were no more than 10 years between the prior offenses.[30] This is true even if neither prior conviction was discharged within 10 years of the present offense. On the other hand, even if the second prior was discharged within 10 years of the new offense, the first prior offense must have been discharged within 10 years of the second. In other words, the intervening prior will not resurrect all previous prior convictions. Obviously the court anticipated that its ruling would not be easy to apply. The court ended its opinion with a helpful chart:

**Prior Convictions and Availability for Enhancement**

| | |
|---|---|
| A. Discharge date of one prior conviction within 10 years of current offense; other prior conviction also within 10 years of current offense; both prior convictions within 10 years of one another | Both prior convictions available for enhancement |
| B. Discharge date of one prior conviction within 10 years of current offense; other prior conviction more than 10 years before current offense; both prior convictions within 10 years of one another | Both available for enhancement; the less-than-10-years between two makes older one available |
| C. Discharge date of one prior conviction more than 10 years before current offense; other prior conviction also more than 10 years before current offense; both prior convictions within 10 years of one another | Both available for enhancement; the less-than-10-years between two makes both available |
| D. Discharge date of one prior conviction within 10 years of current offense; other prior conviction more than 10 years before current offense; prior convictions more than 10 years apart | Recent conviction available; older one not |
| E. Discharge date of one prior conviction more than 10 years before current offense; other prior conviction also more than 10 years before current offense; prior convictions more than 10 years apart | Neither available; over 10 years between both convictions |

---

28 TEX. PENAL CODE §49.09(e), repealed by HB 51, 79th R.S., effective for offenses committed on or after Sept. 1, 2005.

29 *Getts v. State*, 155 S.W.3d 153 (Tex. Crim. App. 2005).

30 *Getts*, 155 S.W.3d at 155-57.

## PRIOR PROBATIONS

Subsection (d) of §49.09 doesn't mean that only probations after 1994 are considered "final" for enhancement purposes. Look at §49.09(c)(1)(C) & (D), which bring in the provision in former Article 6701*l* that allowed probations since 1984 to be used for enhancement purposes. Probated sentences imposed under the former DWI statute (VTCS Article 6701*l*) can be used to enhance a sentence under the current DWI statute.[31]

An erroneous dismissal of probation by the court won't affect the finality of the conviction for purposes of enhancement.[32] The problem in *Jordy v. State* wasn't with the face of the judgment but with a subsequent order by the sentencing court that discharged the defendant from probation, set aside the verdict, dismissed the complaint, and released the defendant from all penalties and disabilities resulting from commission of the offense. The Fort Worth court of appeals rejected the defense's argument that this order prevents the state from offering the prior as a final conviction. The court pointed out that the judge had issued the order under Code of Criminal Procedure article 42.12, §20, which does not apply to DWI cases. Since the order was therefore void, it had no effect on the finality of the defendant's conviction.

## FELONY DWI & STIPULATIONS

Upon request of the defense, the State is required to stipulate to a defendant's prior convictions used to enhance a DWI to a felony.[33] The State is permitted to read the indictment at the beginning of trial, mentioning the two prior convictions, but if the defendant stipulates, the State may not present evidence of the convictions beyond the details in the stipulation, and those should be limited to only what is necessary to prove the jurisdictional prior.[34] Examples of details the prosecutor should not attempt to bring before the jury would include references to the case being a "felony DWI" or a "DWI rep."

The jury can be informed of the defendant's stipulation, and, in fact, the trial court can admit the stipulation itself into evidence.[35] The prosecutor can also discuss the prior convictions in voir dire, opening statements, and closing argument.[36] Also note that the prior convictions—as elements of the offense that must be found by the fact-finder—*must* be mentioned in the jury charge.[37]

---

31 *Ex parte Serrato,* 3 S.W.3d 41 (Tex. Crim. App. 1999).

32 *Jordy v. State,* 969 S.W.2d 528 (Tex. App. — Fort Worth 1998, no pet.).

33 *Tamez v. State,* 11 S.W.3d 198 (Tex. Crim. App. 2000), citing *Old Chief v. United States,* 519 U.S.172, 117 S.Ct. 644, 136 L.Ed.2d 574 (1997) (federal government prohibited from telling jury what type of prior conviction supported a felon in possession charge); *Hernandez v. State,* 18 S.W.3d 699 (Tex. App. — San Antonio 2000), *aff'd,* 109 S.W.3d 491 (Tex. Crim. App. 2003); *Smith v. State,* 12 S.W.3d 149 (Tex. App. — El Paso 2000, pet. ref'd).

34 *Robles v. State,* 85 S.W.3d 211 (Tex. Crim. App. 2002) (details contained in the priors can be prejudicial to the defendant).

35 *Hollen v. State,* 117 S.W.3d 798, 802 (Tex. Crim. App. 2003); see also *State v. McGuffey,* 69 S.W.3d 654 (Tex. App. — Tyler 2002, no pet.) (same); *Orona v. State,* 52 S.W.3d 242 (Tex. App. — El Paso 2001, no pet.).

36 *Hollen,* 117 S.W.3d at 802.

37 *Martin v. State,* 84 S.W.3d 267 (Tex. App. — Beaumont 2002, pet. ref'd) (trial court may not assume role of fact-finder on the issue of the two prior convictions; priors must be found to be true before a jury can find defendant guilty of felony DWI).

# Probation

## ELIGIBILITY

The defendant has the burden of proof to show by sworn affidavit plus testimony from some source that he is eligible for probation under Code of Criminal Procedure article 42.12, §3.[38]

## DISCRETIONARY CONDITIONS[39]

Under Code of Criminal Procedure article 42.12, §11(a), a judge has the ability to impose any condition of probation that is designed to protect or restore the community, protect or restore the victim, or punish, rehabilitate, or reform the defendant. **[DWI also carries some mandatory conditions of probation, listed in Table 10-4.]**

Creative conditions often arise from a case's unique facts and seek to address a defendant's peculiar criminal misconduct. In general, these creative orders are divided into performance and prohibition conditions.

***Performance***

*A performance condition seeks to require a defendant to perform or accomplish a particular task.* Generally, the task is related in some way to the misconduct and seeks to impress upon the defendant the misconduct's significance or the need for additional work to reform him.

For example, an Orange County prosecutor recently recommended that a defendant sleep in a doghouse outside his home for 30 consecutive nights. The defendant, who had used excessive force against his son and made him sleep in a doghouse, agreed to the condition to avoid spending 30 consecutive days in the county jail.[40] By sleeping in a doghouse, the defendant no doubt experienced the humiliation and discomfort that he had imposed upon his own son and perhaps gained more insight into why his own misconduct was wrong and should not be repeated.

There have been several instances of this type of condition, including a Harris County judge who required a drive-by shooter to observe the autopsy of a gunshot victim. As the judge said at the time, "Young people do not realize the terrible wounds made by knives and guns. When you see someone opened up like that (at an autopsy), the brains removed, you realize that life has ended."[41]

A variation of this type of condition is one that requires the defendant to remind himself and others of his misconduct. For example, a Bexar County prosecutor recommended that a defendant, who had killed an off-duty police officer while driving drunk, carry a photo of the officer at all times in his wallet.[42] Likewise, a Harris County judge has required a defendant to stand at the scene of his crime with a sign notifying passing drivers about the dangers of drunk driving.[43]

---

38 *Baker v. State*, 519 S.W.2d 437 (Tex. Crim. App. 1975); *Tenery v. State*, 680 S.W.2d 629 (Tex. App. — Corpus Christi 1984, pet. ref'd).

39 This section taken from "Creative Conditions of Probation," by John Bradley, *The Texas Prosecutor*, March/April 2003.

40 HOUSTON CHRONICLE, Associated Press, Section A, p. 36 (March 14, 2003).

41 HOUSTON CHRONICLE, Jo Ann Zuniga, Section A, p. 37 (November 15, 1996).

42 HOUSTON CHRONICLE, Section A, p. 22 (January 29, 2003); SAN ANTONIO EXPRESS-NEWS, p. 1B (December 27, 1998).

43 HOUSTON CHRONICLE, Stefanie Asin, Section A, p. 33 (November 22, 1997).

Another option for the prosecutor looking for a creative condition of probation is to require the defendant to make a public apology. Public acceptance of responsibility and the accompanying shame has long been recognized as a legitimate step in the reformation of a defendant. So it is a positive, restorative act for a wife-beater to apologize on the steps of city hall, as a Harris County judge once required.[44] And that was the motive for a Brazos County prosecutor recommending that a college student take out a full-page newspaper ad to apologize for secretly videotaping his sexual encounter with a girlfriend and sharing the tape with his fraternity brothers.

Finally, a growing motive for public acknowledgement of a crime is for the protection of the community. For example, a Nueces County judge amended the conditions of all sex offenders to require them to post a large sign outside their homes, stating: "DANGER: REGISTERED SEX OFFENDER LIVES HERE."[45] The purpose of such notice was to warn neighbors about the risk that one of the defendants might victimize another child.

For a discussion of the legal issues surrounding performance conditions, see the rules, statutes, opinion, and cases listed in the following table:

**TABLE 10-2: Permissible Performance Conditions of Probation**

| Task | Authority |
|---|---|
| Place sign on door of home notifying neighbors of sex offender status | CCP art. 42.12 §11(a)(23); AG Opin. DM-437 (1997) |
| Consent to search of home at any time | *United States v. Knights*, 534 U.S. 112, 122 S.Ct. 587, 151 L.Ed.2d 497 (2001) |
| Submit to polygraph | *Ex parte Renfro*, 999 S.W.2d 557 (Tex. App.—Houston [14th Dist.] 1999, pet. ref'd) |
| Obtain nursing school diploma in one year | *Shipp v. State*, 985 S.W.2d 621 (Tex. App. —Texarkana 1999, no pet.) |
| Resign from job | *United States v. Gerena*, 553 F.2d 723 (1st Cir. 1977) |
| Surrender peace officer license | 37 Tex. Admin. Code §223.13(a)(2) |

44 Houston Chronicle, John Makeig, Section A, p. 11 (July 30, 1996).

45 *Banales v. Court of Appeals*, 93 S.W.3d 33 (Tex. Crim. App. 2002).

To avoid litigation on the imposition of a performance condition, a prosecutor should draft the wording of the condition to specify in detail the task to be performed, establish a deadline for its performance, and provide a means of proof for showing the completion of the task. In addition, the task should have an obvious relationship to the particular misconduct of the defendant and be a reasonable method for accomplishing the goal.

#### *Prohibition*

*A prohibition condition prohibits a defendant from participating in a particular behavior.* For example, several years ago, a Houston judge prohibited a music teacher from playing the piano while on supervision for indecently touching two female students. When he imposed the condition, the judge explained, "You can't have a piano in your house. You can't play the piano. You stole that (pleasure) from these girls, so it is only right that you not have a piano."[46]

For a discussion of the legal issues surrounding prohibition conditions, see cases cited in the following table:

**TABLE 10-3: Permissible Prohibition Conditions of Probation**

| Prohibition | Authority |
| --- | --- |
| Stay out of bars; change jobs to not work at bar | *Lacy v. State*, 875 S.W.2d 3 (Tex. App. — Tyler 1994, no pet.) |
| No access to computer | *United States v. Paul*, 274 F.3d 155 (5th Cir. 2001) |
| Not run for political office or campaign for others | *United States v. Tonry*, 605 F.2d 144 (5th Cir. 1979) |
| Avoid race tracks and not place bets | *United States v. Bishop*, 537 F.2d 1184 (4th Cir. 1976) |
| No employment in law enforcement | *United States v. Brochway*, 769 F.2d 263 (5th Cir. 1985) |

To avoid litigation on the imposition of a prohibition condition, a prosecutor should draft the wording of the condition to specify in detail the behavior to be avoided, any steps the defendant must take in avoiding the behavior (such as resignation from employment or surrender of a license), and provide a means of proof for showing the behavior is being avoided.

#### *Challenges*

Creative conditions of supervision can be controversial, particularly if a defendant believes they infringe on a constitutional right. For example, last year the U.S. Supreme Court decided whether a defendant's Fourth Amendment search and seizure rights were violated by a condition requiring him to submit to a warrantless search by police at any time. The Court concluded that the search was reasonable under the Fourth Amendment, given the defendant's reduced expectation of privacy and the presence of a reasonable suspicion that the defendant was involved in criminal activ-

[46] Houston Chronicle, Rad Sallee, Section A, p. 26 (May 20, 1994).

ity.[47] However, the Court expressly left open the question of whether a search is legal absent any reasonable suspicion, and at least one lower court has already answered in the negative.[48]

In addition, the Legislature has narrowed judicial discretion regarding conditions in two areas: payment of money and a particular surgical procedure. As to money, the Legislature has written its laws to set out the specific circumstances in which a defendant may be ordered to pay money, excluding all financial conditions not expressly authorized by law.[49] As to surgery, in response to a controversial decision made by a Harris County judge (granting probation in exchange for castration), the Legislature has prohibited judges from requiring an orchiectomy (removal of a defendant's testicles) as a condition of supervision.[50]

By far, the simplest method for avoiding a challenge to a condition of supervision is to have the defendant agree to its imposition or waive any right to appeal.[51] Interestingly, according to the Court of Criminal Appeals, even questionable financial and surgical conditions may be imposed if the defendant does not object.[52]

#### Interlock Devices

Code of Criminal Procedure article 42.12 §13(i) provides that judges may require installation of an interlock device on a DWI defendant's car as a condition of probation. The judge may only waive this condition if she makes a finding that the interlock device would not be in the "best interest of justice."[53]

#### Jail Time

Penal Code §49.09(a), which requires three days' jail time as a condition of probation for repeat offenders, is mandatory, and a trial judge has no discretion to fail to enter this order.[54]

#### Probations

A judge does not have authority to terminate or set aside DWI probations early.[55]

---

47 *United States v. Knights*, 534 U.S. 112, 122 S.Ct. 587, 151 L.Ed.2d 497 (2001).

48 See *United States v. Crawford*, 372 F.3d 1048 (9th Cir. 2004) (en banc) (holding that suspicionless search violated parolee's Fourth Amendment, even though condition of parole authorized the search).

49 TEX. CODE CRIM. PROC. art. 42.12 §11(b); *Busby v. State*, 984 S.W.2d 627 (Tex. Crim. App. 1998); Tex. AG Opin. DM-245 (1993).

50 TEX. CODE CRIM. PROC. art. 42.12 §11(f); HOUSTON CHRONICLE, Julie Mason, Section C, p. 1 (March 22, 1992).

51 *Speth v. State*, 6 S.W.3d 530 (Tex. Crim. App. 1999).

52 *Speth*, 6 S.W.3d 530, n. 8.

53 *State v. Lucero*, 979 S.W.2d 400 (Tex. App. — Amarillo 1998, no pet.).

54 *Lucero*, 979 S.W.2d 400.

55 *In re State of Texas ex rel. Hilbig*, 985 S.W.2d 189 (Tex. App. — San Antonio 1998, no pet.) (granting writ of prohibition on judge's unauthorized early termination).

## Table 10-4: Mandatory DWI Punishments & Community Supervision Conditions

| Offense | Punishment range | Community supervision conditions |
|---|---|---|
| 1st DWI | Class B misdemeanor; at least 72 hours jail time [PC §49.04(b)] | Drug/alcohol evaluation/rehabilitation [CCP Art. 42.12 §13(a)(2) & 13(f)] |
| | | Defendant pays costs of rehabilitation program [CCP Art. 42.12 §13(d)] |
| | | Defendant must complete alcohol education program unless the judge waives it for good cause [CCP Art. 42.12 §13(h)] |
| | | Ignition interlock if BAC > 0.15 [CCP Art. 42.12, §13(i)] |
| 1st DWI (offender younger than 21) | | All of the above conditions, plus 90 day drivers license suspension at the beginning of the community supervision period [CCP Art. 42.12 §13(n)(1)] |
| | | Ignition interlock device, regardless of BAC [CCP Art. 42.12 §13(n)(2)] |
| 1st DWI with open container | Class B misdemeanor; at least 6 days jail time [PC §49.04(b)] | Drug/alcohol evaluation/rehabilitation [CCP Art. 42.12 §13(a)(2) & 13(f)] |
| | | Defendant pays for costs of rehabilitation program [CCP Art. 42.12 §13(d)] |
| | | Defendant must complete alcohol education program unless the judge waives it for good cause [CCP Art. 42.12 §13(h)] |
| 2nd DWI | Class A misdemeanor; at least 30 days in jail [§49.09(a)] | At least 72 continuous hours or 5 days in jail [see CCP Art. 42.12 §13(a)(1)] |
| | | Drug/alcohol evaluation/rehabilitation [CCP Art. 42.12 §13(a)(2) & 13(f)] |
| | | Defendant pays for costs of rehabilitation program [CCP Art. 42.12 §13(d)] |
| | | Defendant has ignition interlock device placed on his vehicle [CCP Art. 42.12 §13(i)] |
| | | Defendant must complete a program for repeat alcohol & drug offenders unless the judge waives it for good cause [CCP Art. 42.12 §13(j)] |
| | | Defendant must complete alcohol education program unless the judge waives it for good cause [CCP Art. 42.12 §13(h)] |
| DWI with child | State jail felony [§49.045] | Drug/alcohol evaluation/rehabilitation [CCP Art. 42.12 §13(a)(2) & 13(f)] |
| | | Defendant pays for costs of rehabilitation program [CCP Art. 42.12 §13(d)] |
| | | Defendant must complete alcohol education program [CCP Art. 42.12 §13(h)] |
| 3rd or subsequent DWI | 3rd degree felony [§49.09(b)] | At least 10 days in jail [CCP Art. 42.12 §13(a)(1)] |
| | | Drug/alcohol evaluation/rehabilitation [CCP Art. 42.12 §13(a)(2) & 13(f)] |
| | | Defendant pays costs of rehabilitation program [CCP Art. 42.12 §13(d)] |
| | | Defendant has ignition interlock device placed on his vehicle [CCP Art. 42.12 §13(i)] |
| | | Defendant must complete a program for repeat alcohol & drug offenders [CCP Art. 42.12 §13(j)] |
| | | Defendant completes an alcohol education program unless the judge waives it for good cause [CCP Art. 42.12 §13(h)] |

| Offense | Punishment range | Community supervision conditions |
|---|---|---|
| Intoxication assault | 3rd degree felony [§49.07] | No less than 30 days in jail [CCP Art. 42.12 §13(a)(1)] |
| | | Drug/alcohol evaluation/rehabilitation [CCP Art. 42.12 §13(a)(2) & 13(f)] |
| | | Defendant pays costs of rehabilitation program [CCP Art. 42.12 §13(d)] |
| | | Defendant completes an alcohol education program [CCP Art. 42.12 §13(h)] |
| Intoxication assault (peace officer, firefighter, or EMT personnel as victim) | 2nd degree felony [§49.07(b-1)] | All of the above conditions for intoxication assault/3rd degree |
| Intoxication assault (traumatic brain injury)π | 2nd degree felony [§49.07(b-4)] | All of the above conditions for intoxication assault/3rd degree |
| Intoxication assault (defendant younger than 21) | 3rd degree felony [§49.07] | All of the above conditions, plus 90 day drivers license suspension at the beginning of the community supervision period [CCP Art. 42.12 §13(n)(1)] |
| | | Ignition interlock device [CCP Art. 42.12 §13(n)(2)] |
| 2nd or subsequent intoxication assault | 3rd degree felony [§49.07] | All the above conditions for intoxication assault, plus defendant has ignition interlock device placed on his vehicle [CCP Art. 42.12 §13(i)] |
| Intoxication manslaughter | 2nd degree felony [§49.08] | No less than 120 days confinement [CCP Art. 42.12 §13(b)] |
| | | Drug/alcohol evaluation/rehabilitation [CCP Art. 42.12 §13(a)(2) & 13(f)] |
| | | Defendant pays costs of rehabilitation program [CCP Art. 42.12 §13(d)] |
| | | Defendant completes an alcohol education program [CCP Art. 42.12 §13(h)] |
| Intoxication manslaughter (defendant younger than 21) | 2nd degree felony [§49.08] | All of the above conditions, plus 90 day drivers license suspension at the beginning of the community supervision period [CCP Art. 42.12 §13(n)(1)] |
| | | Ignition interlock device [CCP Art. 42.12 §13(n)(2)] |
| Intoxication manslaughter (peace officer, firefighter, or EMT personnel as victim) | 1st degree felony [§49.08(b-2)] | All of the above conditions |
| 2nd or subsequent intoxication manslaughter | 2nd degree felony [§49.08] | All the above conditions for intoxication manslaughter, plus defendant has ignition interlock device placed on his vehicle [CCP Art. 42.12 §13(i)] |

1. The defendant does not get credit toward time served for the time he serves in jail as a condition of community supervision. CCP Art. 42.12 §13(e).
2. These community supervision conditions do not apply to public intoxication.
3. "DWI" also includes flying and boating while intoxicated.
4. The jury can recommend against a driver's license suspension under CCP Art. 42.12, §13(g).
5. See the license revocations provisions (if the defendant does not complete the alcohol & drug education program or repeat offender program) under CCP Art. 42.12 §13(h) & 13(k).

# Open Containers

Penal Code §49.031 provides a Class C misdemeanor penalty for anyone who possesses an open container of alcohol in the passenger area of a vehicle on the public highway. Penal Code §49.04(c) carries a minimum term of confinement of six days on a Class B DWI if the state shows that the driver had an open container of alcohol in his immediate possession.

The open container enhancement does not require the state to prove that the defendant actually held a beer while driving.[56] Evidence of a half-full beer can lodged between the windshield and dash immediately in front of the steering wheel, when the defendant is alone in the car, is sufficient, even without the state presenting evidence that the can smelled or tasted of alcohol.[57]

**Penal Code §49.031. Possession of Alcoholic Beverage in Motor Vehicle**

(a) In this section:

(1) "Open container" means a bottle, can, or other receptacle that contains any amount of alcoholic beverage and that is open, that has been opened, that has a broken seal, or the contents of which are partially removed.

(2) "Passenger area of a motor vehicle" means the area of a motor vehicle designed for the seating of the operator and passengers of the vehicle. The term does not include:

(A) a glove compartment or similar storage container that is locked;

(B) the trunk of a vehicle; or

(C) the area behind the last upright seat of the vehicle, if the vehicle does not have a trunk.

(3) "Public highway" means the entire width between and immediately adjacent to the boundary lines of any public road, street, highway, interstate, or other publicly maintained way if any part is open for public use for the purpose of motor vehicle travel. The term includes the right-of-way of a public highway.

(b) A person commits an offense if the person knowingly possesses an open container in a passenger area of a motor vehicle that is located on a public highway, regardless of whether the vehicle is being operated or is stopped or parked. Possession by a person of one or more open containers in a single criminal episode is a single offense.

(c) It is an exception to the application of Subsection (b) that at the time of the offense the defendant was a passenger in:

(1) the passenger area of a motor vehicle designed, maintained, or used primarily for the transportation of persons for compensation, including a bus, taxicab, or limousine; or

(2) the living quarters of a motorized house coach or motorized house trailer, including a self-contained camper, a motor home, or a recreational vehicle.

(d) An offense under this section is a Class C misdemeanor.

(e) A peace officer charging a person with an offense under this section, instead of taking the person before a magistrate, shall issue to the person a written citation and notice to appear that contains the time and place the person must appear before a magistrate, the name and address of the person charged, and the offense charged. If the person makes a written promise to appear before the magistrate by signing in duplicate the citation and notice to appear issued by the officer, the officer shall release the person.

---

[56] *Troff v. State*, 882 S.W.2d 905 (Tex. App. — Houston [1st Dist.] 1994, pet. ref'd) (decided under former version of open container law).

[57] *Walters v. State*, 757 S.W.2d 41 (Tex. App. — Houston [14th Dist.] 1988, no pet.).

**Penal Code §49.04. Driving While Intoxicated**

(a) A person commits an offense if the person is intoxicated while operating a motor vehicle in a public place.

(b) Except as provided by Subsections (c) and (d) and Section 49.09, an offense under this section is a Class B misdemeanor, with a minimum term of confinement of 72 hours.

(c) If it is shown on the trial of an offense under this section that at the time of the offense the person operating the motor vehicle had an open container of alcohol in the person's immediate possession, the offense is a Class B misdemeanor, with a minimum term of confinement of six days.

(d) If it is shown on the trial of an offense under this section that an analysis of a specimen of the person's blood, breath, or urine showed an alcohol concentration level of 0.15 or more at the time the analysis was performed, the offense is a Class A misdemeanor.

## Minors & DWI

The "zero-tolerance" law, which prohibits minors from driving with any detectable amount of alcohol, is found in Alcoholic Beverage Code §106.04. Existence of this DUI law does not preclude the state from prosecuting defendants younger than 21 for DWI.[58]

## Appeal Bond Conditions

A trial court has the power to impose conditions on bail that are reasonable.[59] Although pretrial bond conditions must meet three conditions—(1) reasonableness; (2) securing a defendant's attendance at trial; and (3) related to the safety of the victim or community—conditions of bond on appeal do not have the meet all three conditions and only must be reasonable.[60]

Conditions of an appeal bond are subject to review for abuse of discretion by the trial court.[61] Conditions that have been found to be reasonable include not operating a motor vehicle, home confinement, electronic monitoring, random urinalysis, interlock devices, payment for electronic monitoring, payment for probation supervision fees, the safety of the victim, remaining in the county, abstention from drug use, urinalysis and posting the results, paying for urinalysis, and staying away from victims.[62]

---

58 Tex. Att'y Gen. Op. LO 98-027 (1998).

59 *Ex parte Anderer*, 61 S.W.3d 398 (Tex. Crim. App. 2001).

60 *Anderer*, 61 S.W.3d at 402.

61 *Anderer*, 61 S.W.3d at 405 (holding that *Estrada v. State*, 594 S.W.2d 445 (Tex. Crim. App. 1980) provides valuable guidance for conditions on pretrial bond but is misleading as to conditions on bail pending appeal in requiring more conditions than the legislature intended).

62 *Anderer*, 61 S.W.3d at 406; *Grady v. State*, 962 S.W.2d 128 (Tex. App. — Houston [1st Dist.] 1997, pet. ref'd); *Easton v. Rains*, 866 S.W.2d 656, 659 (Tex. App. — Houston [1st Dist.] 1993), *overruled in part by Anderer*, 61 S.W.3d 398; *Ex parte Davila*, 623 S.W.2d 408 (Tex. Crim. App. [Panel Op.] 1981); *Ex parte Sotelo*, 878 S.W.2d 179 (Tex. App. — Fort Worth 1993, pet. ref'd), *overruled in part by Anderer*, 61 S.W.3d 398.

### CCP Art. 44.04. Bond Pending Appeal

(a) Pending the determination of any motion for new trial or the appeal from any misdemeanor conviction, the defendant is entitled to be released on reasonable bail, and if a defendant charged with a misdemeanor is on bail, is convicted, and appeals that conviction, his bond is not discharged until his conviction is final or in the case of an appeal to a court where a trial de novo is held, he files an appeal bond as required by this code for appeal from the conviction.

(b) The defendant may not be released on bail pending the appeal from any felony conviction where the punishment equals or exceeds 10 years confinement or where the defendant has been convicted of an offense listed under Section 3g(a)(1), Article 42.12, but shall immediately be placed in custody and the bail discharged.

(c) Pending the appeal from any felony conviction other than a conviction described in Subsection (b) of this section, the trial court may deny bail and commit the defendant to custody if there then exists good cause to believe that the defendant would not appear when his conviction became final or is likely to commit another offense while on bail, permit the defendant to remain at large on the existing bail, or, if not then on bail, admit him to reasonable bail until his conviction becomes final. The court may impose reasonable conditions on bail pending the finality of his conviction. On a finding by the court on a preponderance of the evidence of a violation of a condition, the court may revoke the bail.

(d) After conviction, either pending determination of any motion for new trial or pending final determination of the appeal, the court in which trial was had may increase or decrease the amount of bail, as it deems proper, either upon its own motion or the motion of the State or of the defendant.

(e) Any bail entered into after conviction and the sureties on the bail must be approved by the court where trial was had. Bail is sufficient if it substantially meets the requirements of this code and may be entered into and given at any term of court.

(f) In no event shall the defendant and the sureties on his bond be released from their liability on such bond or bonds until the defendant is placed in the custody of the sheriff.

(g) The right of appeal to the Court of Appeals of this state is expressly accorded the defendant for a review of any judgment or order made hereunder, and said appeal shall be given preference by the appellate court.

(h) If a conviction is reversed by a decision of a Court of Appeals, the defendant, if in custody, is entitled to release on reasonable bail, regardless of the length of term of imprisonment, pending final determination of an appeal by the state or the defendant on a motion for discretionary review. If the defendant requests bail before a petition for discretionary review has been filed, the Court of Appeals shall determine the amount of bail. If the defendant requests bail after a petition for discretionary review has been filed, the Court of Criminal Appeals shall determine the amount of bail. The sureties on the bail must be approved by the court where the trial was had. The defendant's right to release under this subsection attaches immediately on the issuance of the Court of Appeals' final ruling as defined by Tex. Cr. App. R. 209(c).

---

Chapter 17 of the Code of Criminal Procedure also contains some conditions a judge may place on appeal bonds,[63] including:

- electronic monitoring, home confinement, and random urinalysis;[64] and
- interlock devices.[65]

---

63 Tex. Code Crim. Proc. Art. 17.38.

64 Tex. Code Crim. Proc. Art. 17.44.

65 Tex. Code Crim. Proc. Art. 17.441(a)(1).

CHAPTER

11

# Juvenile Offenders

***by Riley Shaw, Assistant Criminal DA, Tarrant County***

The rules for processing an intoxication offense change when it comes to young drivers. Chapter 11 discusses the differences between the rules and procedures applicable to adults and those applicable to drivers under the age of 17, including "zero tolerance" laws for drivers under 21.

# Defining "Child" and its Importance

For purposes of investigation, prosecution, and sentencing, Texas treats adults and children differently. Therefore, it is important to know who you are dealing with. A "child" is defined as a person who is 10 years of age or older, but younger than 17 at the time of the offense. It also includes persons 17 years of age who are accused of committing offenses between ages 10 and 16.[1]

Note, if the defendant is a 17-year-old who has committed an offense while 17, the adult rules apply.[2] Likewise, once the person turns 18, the adult rules apply regardless of the person's age at the time of the offense.[3]

If a person is a "child" accused of committing an offense covered by the Family Code, that child will in many cases receive greater protection than an adult. Most DWI and related offenses are covered by the Family Code.[4] As such, you must satisfy the child-specific requirements set forth in the Family Code (and elsewhere) when questioning children, taking them into custody, and obtaining breath and blood consent in DWI-related cases.

## CONSTITUTIONAL PROTECTIONS AND EVIDENCE COLLECTION

Adults and juveniles are both protected against compulsory self incrimination by the U.S. and Texas Constitutions. With regard to adults, this essentially means complying with *Miranda*[5] and art. 38.22 of the Texas Code of Criminal Procedure. The procedure for taking a juvenile confession, on the other hand, is not generally covered by CCP art. 38.22; rather, in addition to the protections afforded by *Miranda* and the U.S. and Texas Constitutions, juvenile statements and waivers of rights are primarily governed by the following Texas Family Code sections:

- 54.03 (Adjudication Hearing),
- 51.09 (Waiver of Rights),
- 51.095 (Admissibility of Statement by Child),
- 52.02 (Release or Delivery of Child), and
- 52.025 (Juvenile Processing Office).[6]

---

1 TEX. FAM. CODE §51.02(2).

2 *Ramos v. State*, 961 S.W.2d 637, 639 (Tex. App. — San Antonio 1998, no pet.).

3 See TEX. FAM. CODE §§51.02(2) and 51.095(a); *Texas Juvenile Law*, 7th ed., Robert Dawson (2008), at 388. Persons 18 and older are excluded from the definition of a "child."

4 TEX. FAM. CODE §51.03(a) states: "Delinquent conduct is (1) conduct, other than a traffic offense, that violates a penal law of this state or of the United States punishable by imprisonment or by confinement in jail; … (3) conduct that violates Section 49.04, 49.05, 49.06, 49.07, or 49.08, Penal Code; or (4) conduct that violates Section 106.041, Alcoholic Beverage Code, relating to driving under the influence of alcohol by a minor" (third or subsequent offense). Note, however, that DWI with Child Passenger (PC §49.045) and Assembling or Operating an Amusement Ride While Intoxicated (PC §49.065) are NOT specifically listed. This should not preclude prosecution in juvenile court because these offenses are not "traffic offenses" as defined in Family Code. Also note that there is no "safe harbor" or other prohibition against charging a juvenile offender with violations of PC §§49.045 and 49.065.

5 *Miranda v. Arizona*, 384 U.S. 436 (1966).

6 See also TEX. FAM. CODE §§51.17(c) [Chapter 38, CCP applies in a juvenile proceeding,except as otherwise provided in the Family Code], 53.03(c) [juvenile statements made as part of deferred prosecution are inadmissible], 54.01(g) [juvenile statements made during detention hearings are inadmissible], 54.03(d) [the Rules of Evidence applicable in criminal proceedings and Chapter 38, CCP apply in adjudication hearings].

The mandates of the Family Code are critically important any time you seek to interview a child, obtain evidence from a child, or seek to have that child waive his/her rights. This affects not only misdemeanor DWI cases, but also felony cases such as intoxication manslaughter and intoxication assault.

Family Code §54.03(e) provides the general evidentiary guidelines applicable to juvenile proceedings, essentially stating that:

- children have the same right against self-incrimination as adults;
- a statement of a child obtained without meeting the requirements of the Family Code is inadmissible;
- a child's out of court statement is not enough for conviction without corroboration;
- the accomplice-witness rule applies; and
- illegally seized or obtained evidence is inadmissible.[7]

Family Code §51.09 is the general "waiver of rights" section of the Family Code. It provides the mechanism by which a child can waive his/her rights—it requires participation of the child and the child's attorney, the waiver must be knowing and voluntary, and must be either in writing or in recorded court proceedings.

**Tex. Fam. Code §51.09. Waiver of Rights**

Unless a contrary intent clearly appears elsewhere in this title, any right granted to a child by this title or by the constitution or laws of this state or the United States may be waived in proceedings under this title if:

(1) the waiver is made by the child and the attorney for the child;

(2) the child and the attorney waiving the right are informed of and understand the right and the possible consequences of waiving it;

(3) the waiver is voluntary; and

(4) the waiver is made in writing or in court proceedings that are recorded.

[7] TEX. FAM. CODE §54.03(e) states: "A child alleged to have engaged in delinquent conduct or conduct indicating a need for supervision need not be a witness against nor otherwise incriminate himself. An extrajudicial statement which was obtained without fulfilling the requirements of this title or of the constitution of this state or the United States, may not be used in an adjudication hearing. A statement made by the child out of court is insufficient to support a finding of delinquent conduct or conduct indicating a need for supervision unless it is corroborated in whole or in part by other evidence. An adjudication of delinquent conduct or conduct indicating a need for supervision cannot be had upon the testimony of an accomplice unless corroborated by other evidence tending to connect the child with the alleged delinquent conduct or conduct indicating a need for supervision; and the corroboration is not sufficient if it merely shows the commission of the alleged conduct. Evidence illegally seized or obtained is inadmissible in an adjudication hearing."

## BREATH TESTS

A child who has been arrested for DWI may be taken in for a breath test, but the rules are different than in cases involving adult suspects.

When an officer takes a child into custody for an offense that is a Class B misdemeanor or higher, the officer must follow the requirements of Family Code §52.02(a) and (b). These requirements essentially provide that when a child is taken into custody, the officer must either release the child to an adult, take the child to detention, take the child to the hospital, divert the child and dispose of the case, or take the child to school—and the officer must do so without unnecessary delay and without first taking the child anywhere else except for a juvenile processing office. In addition, the officer has to notify the child's parent (and a person designated by the juvenile board) that he has taken the child into custody and the reason why he has done so.

The legislature crafted an exception to the requirements of §52.02(a) for use in cases involving alcohol and driving (the exception appears limited to driving, as opposed to boating or flying). This exception is found in §52.02(c) and allows the officer to first take the child to a place to get a breath or blood specimen (per Texas' implied consent provisions in Chapter 724 of the Transportation Code). It also allows the performance of intoxylizer processing and videotaping of the child in an adult processing office.[8]

> **TIP**
>
> In general, under Family Code §51.09, a child must consent to provide a sample with his attorney's concurrence. There is an exception to this rule regarding the attorney's consent in Family Code §52.02(d), but only for *breath* specimens. If an officer asks a child for a *blood* sample, the child's response—as well as the blood result—will likely be inadmissible if the officer does not comply with §51.09.

There is also an exception to §51.09, which otherwise would require that the child's waiver/consent with regard to providing a breath sample be *joined by his attorney*. This exception is found in §52.02(d), which specifically provides that a child can submit or refuse to submit to the taking of a breath sample without his attorney's concurrence. Note that this exception is limited to requests for breath specimens (not blood) and requires that the request and the child's response must be videotaped. Without this exception, it would appear that an attorney needs to be present and agree, in writing, with the child's waiver/consent, thus making it likely that if an officer asks a child for a blood instead of a breath sample, the child's response, as well as the blood result, would be inadmissible for lack of compliance with §51.09.

## ASKING QUESTIONS

When and how an officer may ask a child questions depends on whether the child is in custody. As with adults, custody and interrogation are required for constitutional protections to attach. If the child is in custody and there is going to be interrogation, you must follow the requirements of Family Code §§51.095 and 52.02.

Juvenile statements are generally covered by §51.095, which incorporates the guarantees of *Miranda v. Arizona*. As with *Miranda*, the requirements of §51.095 are only triggered when the child is "in custody" and the officer intends to "interrogate." Note that §51.095 acts as a specific exception to the waiver requirements of §51.09.

Further, "custody" has its own unique definition in the juvenile context. Custody occurs when a child is either: confined in detention of some sort; or is in the custody of a police officer; or is in the legal custody of the Department of Family and Protective Services ("DFPS") and is a suspect.[9]

---

8 See TEX. FAM. CODE §52.02(c).

9 TEX. FAM. CODE §51.095(d) states: "Subsections (a)(1) [written statements] and (a)(5) [oral statements] apply to the statement of a child made: (1) while the child is in a detention facility or other place of confinement; (2) while the child is in the custody of an officer; or (3) during or after the interrogation of the child by an officer if the child is in the possession of the Department of Family and Protective Services and is suspected to have engaged in conduct that violates a penal law of this state."

With regard to the second type of custody, a child is considered in an officer's custody only if, based on the objective circumstances, a reasonable child would believe her liberty was restrained to the degree associated with a formal arrest (i.e., that her freedom of movement was significantly restricted).[10] Each case is reviewed on its own merits under the totality of the circumstances test.[11] Factors considered by the courts include: the child's age, maturity, experience, background, intelligence, education, ability to understand, and all of the circumstances surrounding the giving of the statement in question.[12] Circumstances that tend to mitigate against a child being considered in custody include: the officer telling the child that she is not in custody, that she is free to leave at any time, and, when the questioning is finished, the officer actually letting her go.[13]

Of course, if the child is not in custody, her statement will be admissible without need for compliance with §§51.09 and 51.095, as long as the statement is voluntary.[14] Even when the child is in custody, her statement will be admissible if it is not the result of interrogation.[15]

***What is interrogation?***

The definition of interrogation is the same for adults and juveniles: actual questioning of a suspect by an officer or an agent of law enforcement, and any speech or conduct by the officer that is reasonably likely to elicit an incriminating response from the suspect. Questions normally attendant to arrest or custody (e.g., booking questions) are not considered interrogation.[16]

To obtain a custodial statement from a child, you must first comply with §52.02, discussed above. Part of the analysis will involve a determination of whether there was an "unnecessary delay."

***What is a "necessary" as opposed to an "unnecessary" delay?***

Necessary delays are determined on a case-by-case basis. They can include securing the scene, attempting to contact the child's parents, and providing medical attention.[17] Unnecessary delays include taking the child to another location to locate evidence[18] or to a non-juvenile processing office to take a statement.[19]

***What is a Juvenile Processing Office (JPO)?***

A JPO is a room or office designated by the juvenile board for the temporary detention of a child taken into custody. It can be within a police facility or sheriff's office or a school, courthouse, etc.[20] A JPO is a limited purpose facility where, among other

---

10 *In re L.M.*, 993 S.W.2d 276, 287 (Tex. App. — Austin 1999, pet. den.).

11 *Id.; Martinez v. State*, 131 S.W.3d 22, 31 (Tex. App. — San Antonio 2003, no pet.).

12 *In re L.M.*, generally; *Martinez* at 32-33.

13 *Martinez* at 35; *In re M.R.R.*, 2 S.W.3d 319, 324-325 (Tex. App. — San Antonio 1999, no pet.).

14 *Martinez* at 32; *In re R.J.H.,* 79 S.W.3d 1, 6 (Tex. 2002).

15 TEX. FAM. CODE §51.095(b) states: "This section and Section 51.09 do not preclude the admission of a statement made by the child if: (1) the statement does not stem from interrogation of the child under a circumstance described by Subsection (d); or (2) without regard to whether the statement stems from interrogation of the child under a circumstance described by Subsection (d), the statement is voluntary and has a bearing on the credibility of the child as a witness."

16 *Rhode Island v. Innis*, 446 U.S. 291, 301 (1980); *Roquemore v. State*, 60 S.W.3d 862, 868 (Tex. Crim. App. 2001).

17 *Contreras v. State*, 67 S.W.3d 181, 185 (Tex. Crim. App. 2001); *Coffey v. State*, 2002 WL 437110 at 8 (Tex. App. — Austin 2002, pet. ref'd) (not for pub.).

18 *Roquemore v. State*, 60 S.W.3d 862, 870 (Tex. Crim. App. 2001).

19 *Baptist Vie Le v. State*, 993 S.W.2d 650, 656 (Tex. Crim. App. 1999).

20 TEX. FAM. CODE §52.025(a).

things, a child may be detained for issuance of *warnings* to the child (under *Miranda* and §51.095) and receipt of a *statement* from the child.[21]

Further conditions that *must* be satisfied under §52.025: the child may *not* be left unattended in the JPO; is *entitled* to be accompanied by the child's parent/guardian/custodian or by the child's attorney;[22] and may *not* be detained in a JPO for longer than *six hours*.[23]

Texas courts have typically required strict compliance with the mandates of §§52.02 and 52.025; thus, failure to follow them may render important evidence inadmissible.[24]

***What statutory requirements are associated with the interview itself?***

You have taken a child into custody, have taken her to a JPO without unnecessary delay, have not left her unattended, she's been allowed to talk to her parent/attorney (if requested), and it has been less than six hours. Now it's time to conduct your interview. What has to be done? You must conduct your interview in accordance with §51.095.

**Written statements** are covered by §51.095(a)(1), which requires:

1. *before* interviewing the child, the child must be taken to a magistrate (in a JPO), outside the presence of law enforcement (this means the officer must leave the room; there is a limited exception for safety/no weapon), for the appropriate statutory warnings; then
2. the written statement is taken in the JPO, but is *not* signed (note: the interviewer can assist the child by writing or typing the child's statement);[25] then
3. the child is returned to the magistrate (in a JPO), outside the presence of law enforcement, where the magistrate makes a determination regarding voluntariness and waiver of rights; then

---

[21] TEX. FAM. CODE §52.025(b) states: "A child may be detained in a juvenile processing office only for: (1) the return of the child to the custody of a person under Section 52.02(a)(1); (2) the completion of essential forms and records required by the juvenile court or this title; (3) the photographing and fingerprinting of the child if otherwise authorized at the time of temporary detention by this title; (4) the issuance of warnings to the child as required or permitted by this title; or (5) the receipt of a statement by the child under Section 51.095(a)(1), (2), (3), or (5)." **Note:** Performing tasks at a JPO other than those listed above may be considered an "unnecessary delay."

[22] There is conflicting statutory language and caselaw on whether a child must request parental access. See *Hardy v. State*, 1995 WL 634163 at 2, 5 (Tex. App. — Dallas 1995, pet. ref'd) (not for pub.) (no Family Code violation when child told of right to have parent present but did not make a request for his parent); *Glover v. State*, 1996 WL 384932 at 2 (Tex. App. — Houston [14th Dist.] 1996, no pet.) (not for pub.) (no request made by child, no violation: "the Family Code does not require that a child be allowed to speak with a parent or guardian prior to taking a statement"). On September 24, 2009, the above holdings were called into question by *In re D.J.C.*, 312 S.W.3d 704, 718 (Tex. App. — Houston [1st Dist.] 2009) (§52.025(c) violated when request made by guardian, not child, and officer refused to allow guardian to accompany child in room during interview). It is this author's opinion that the holding in *In re D.J.C.* is erroneous because the Family Code expressly states that when it comes to the parents' right to access to their child while the child is in a JPO [see TEX. FAM. CODE §61.103(1)], failure to provide the parents' right of access is not a ground for exclusion of evidence. See TEX. FAM. CODE §61.106(3). In any event, if the child requests to speak to her parent and the interviewing agency actively prevents such communication prior to obtaining a statement, it will likely result in suppression of the statement.

[23] TEX. FAM. CODE §52.025(c) & (d).

[24] *Roquemore* at 869; *Pham v. State*, 36 S.W.3d 199, 201-02 (Tex. App. — Houston [1st Dist.] 2000, no pet.).

[25] *Texas Juvenile Law*, 7th ed., Robert Dawson (2008), at 402.

4. the child *signs* the statement in the magistrate's presence and the magistrate makes the required certifications; and, finally
5. fewer than six hours have elapsed.

**Oral statements** are covered by §51.095(a)(5), (c), and (f): To be admissible, a child's custodial oral statements have to be voluntary, must be audio or audio/video recorded, and must be received in compliance with §51.095(a)(5). This basically means that in addition to complying with §§52.02 and 52.025, discussed above, the child will make a recorded statement where the magistrate's warning and the child's waiver under §51.095 are on the recording *prior* to the statement, and all voices are identified. Note, if the magistrate requests *on the recording* that the officer return the child and the recording to the magistrate at the conclusion of the questioning, the officer's failure to comply with such request will make the statement *inadmissible.* Similarly, if a magistrate makes such a request and, after the child and recording are returned, fails to follow the procedures regarding making the voluntariness determination, the statement may be held inadmissible.[26]

Other types of **custodial** oral statements that may be admissible include statements in which the child makes a statement of facts or circumstances that are found to be true and that tend to establish the child's guilt, such as the finding of secreted or stolen property, or the instrument with which the child states the offense was committed; or res gestae statements; or statements made by the child in open court, or before the grand jury, or during a preliminary hearing (other than a detention hearing).[27]

***Can you turn the camera around in the patrol car and tape the child after she is in custody?***

Yes. If there is no interrogation, this should result in admissible evidence.[28]

***Do Texas' implied consent laws apply to children?***

Yes. Texas' implied consent laws (Transportation Code ch. 724) apply to children accused of DWI, BWI, and DUI-Minor.[29] As discussed above, a child operating a motor vehicle (watercraft, aircraft, and amusement rides are not listed) in a public place may submit or refuse to submit to the taking of a breath specimen without the concurrence of an attorney (despite §51.09), but only if the request and the child's response are videotaped and the video is maintained and made available to the child's attorney.[30] If officers do not comply with this provision, the child's response—as well as the breath test result itself—may be inadmissible under §54.03(e). Remember that a request for a blood specimen will likely require the concurrence of an attorney in compliance with §51.09, so get a warrant if you want a blood specimen.

***Are the mandatory sample provisions the same for children as adults?***

While the mandatory breath and blood sample provisions of Transportation Code §724.012(b)(1) and (2) apply to a "child" operator, the procedure is different. As

26 See *Reta v. State*, 2008 WL 2260726 (Tex. App. — San Antonio 2008) (not for pub.), which deals with a similar issue in the context of written statements and held that failure to examine a child regarding whether the child understands the nature and contents of written statement renders his statement inadmissible.

27 See Tex. Fam. Code §51.095(a)(2)-(4).

28 See Tex. Fam. Code §51.095(b).

29 See Tex. Trans. Code §724.001(2), (4), & (5); Tex. Trans. Code §§724.011-.013.

30 See Tex. Fam. Code §52.02(d).

noted above, a child can submit or refuse to submit to the taking of a *breath* specimen without the concurrence of an attorney, provided that the requirements of Family Code §52.02(d) are satisfied. A child must have the concurrence of an attorney, however, if the request is for blood.

Under §724.012(b), the trigger for a mandatory breath or blood sample is the refusal of a proper request for a "voluntary" breath or blood sample. Because an officer may properly request a breath sample from a child without the need for an attorney, the child's refusal of such request for a breath sample should be sufficient to invoke the mandatory provision of either breath or blood.[31] Nothing appears to limit the officer's choice of type of mandatory specimen to the type of specimen initially requested from the child. Please note that a "child" is likely not covered by the mandatory breath sample provision found at §724.012(b)(3) regarding persons with priors because the Transportation Code does not define the terms "convicted" and "community supervision" to include juvenile adjudications and juvenile probations.

## Blood Warrants

#### *Who can issue a blood warrant?*

Although the Family Code does not directly address search warrants or expressly incorporate Chapter 18 of the CCP, it does incorporate Chapter 38, including CCP art. 38.23, which allows admission of evidence obtained in good faith reliance on a warrant.[32] In addition, because juvenile proceedings are quasi-criminal in nature, it follows that the constitutional protections afforded adults—as well as the mechanisms established for complying with the constitution—should apply to children. Consequently, a validly issued, PC-based blood warrant under CCP Chapter 18, issued by a person approved under CCP Chapter 18, should be sufficient for use in a juvenile proceeding.[33] [**Blood warrants are more fully covered in Chapter 3, "Blood & Breath Evidence."**]

#### *Where can the child be taken for a blood draw under warrant?*

Because a blood specimen obtained by warrant is NOT one obtained pursuant to Chapter 724 of the Transportation Code, the exception found in Family Code §52.02(c)(1) will not apply. Also, seizing blood pursuant to a warrant isn't listed as something that can be done in a JPO under §52.025(b), nor will it justify a detour to a medical facility *unless* the child is believed to suffer from a serious physical condition or illness that requires prompt treatment under §52.02(a)(5).

As a result, before executing a search warrant for blood on a child who is in police custody, the officer will have to:

1. release the child to his parent pursuant to §52.02(a)(1);

---

31 TEX. TRANS. CODE §724.012(b).

32 See TEX. FAM. CODE §51.17: "(a) Except ... when in conflict with a provision of this title, the Texas Rules of Civil Procedure govern proceedings under this title.... (c) Except as otherwise provided by this title, the Texas Rules of Evidence [applicable] in criminal cases and ... Chapter 38, Code of Criminal Procedure, apply in a judicial proceeding under this title." Subsection (a) gives the general rule; subsection (c) gives the specific, controlling rule.

33 See generally *In re L.J.*, 2005 WL 3338302, at 2 (Tex. App. — Austin 2005, no pet.) (not for pub.); *Texas Juvenile Law*, 7th ed., Robert Dawson, at 445 (2008); see TEX. CODE CRIM. PROC. art. 18.01(c), (d), (i) and (j).

2. take the child to detention pursuant to §52.02(a)(2)-(4); or
3. take the child to school pursuant to §52.02(a)(7).

Once the officer has complied with §§52.02(a) and (c) (notification to parent and juvenile board designee), the officer should be able to execute the search warrant. Failure to comply with the above requirements may result in inadmissible blood evidence.

Until the legislature offers further guidance, the best course of action when you have a child in custody and a blood warrant is to take the child to the local juvenile detention center (JDC) before executing the warrant. Many JDCs will refuse to take custody of an intoxicated child until that child has been medically "cleared" at a hospital.

If the JDC does accept the child, you should immediately serve the blood warrant upon transfer of custody and either have qualified medical personnel at the JDC perform the blood draw or "flag" the child back out and take him to an appropriate facility for the blood draw. Either way, whether the JDC accepts or refuses the child, by first taking the child to the JDC in compliance with §§52.02 and 52.025, and then serving the warrant, you will be in the best position to protect the evidence from a legal challenge.

# Trial Considerations

## STATEMENT ADMISSIBILITY

***What if a child's statement was taken as a result of custodial interrogation but fails to satisfy the requirements of the Family Code?***

Because §51.095 acts as an independent exclusionary rule, violations will result in an illegal, inadmissible statement.[34] However, when addressing violations of §§52.02 or 52.025, there must be a causal connection between the violation and the confession.[35] In conducting a causal connection analysis, the burden shifts as follows: The child has the initial burden to show a violation, then it is the State's burden to prove compliance. If a violation is proven, then it becomes the child's burden to show a causal connection. If the child meets her burden, then the burden again shifts to the State to prove attenuation of the taint.[36] If an initial statement is inadmissible for a violation of §51.095, the illegal, inadmissible first statement will not automatically invalidate a subsequent confession.[37]

## VIDEO ADMISSIBILITY

In-car video of a juvenile should generally be admissible the same as for an adult, but any questions/responses after the onset of "custody" will likely be suppressed unless they comply with §§51.09 and 51.095.

---

34 *Gonzales v. State,* 67 S.W.3d 910, 912 (Tex. Crim. App. 2002).

35 *Id.*

36 *Pham v. State,* 175 S.W.3d 767 (Tex. Crim. App 2005); *Roquemore* at 869-870.

37 *In re RJH,* 79 S.W.3d 1, 8 (Tex. 2002).

As noted above, custody will be determined on a case-by-case analysis.

Station video should be admissible on the issue of breath test request/refusal,[38] but any questions beyond name, address, parental contact information and "Will you provide a specimen of your breath?" will likely be suppressed unless there is compliance with §§51.09 and 51.095.

It is an open question regarding whether doing anything in the intoxilyzer room other than the breath test request and actual testing qualifies as an "unnecessary delay." In other words, a court may find it was an "unnecessary delay" to have a child perform field sobriety tests on the station video because §52.02(c)(2) does not specifically provide for performance of FSTs.

## BREATH/BLOOD ADMISSIBILITY

Voluntary breath tests should be admissible as long as officers have complied with §52.02(c)(2) and (d). It does not appear that a child can consent to a voluntary blood draw without the consent of his attorney. Mandatory blood draws under Chapter 724 of the Transportation Code should be admissible under §52.02(c)(1) if the procedures outlined above are followed. Blood obtained by proper warrant should also be admissible.

## ENHANCEMENT BASED ON PRIORS

Because ordinary juvenile delinquency cases result in adjudications for engaging in delinquent conduct rather than criminal convictions, they do not satisfy the requirements for enhancement of DWI-related offenses found in Penal Code §49.09. Unlike offenses under Chapter 49 of the Penal Code, the Alcoholic Beverage Code specifically incorporates juvenile adjudications into its definition of "conviction" for purposes of DUI-Minor.[39]

Of course, a conviction in criminal court for any offense for which a child is "certified" to stand trial as an adult will be available for enhancement purposes in the same way that other adult convictions are available for that purpose. As discussed below, a child can only be "certified" for felony offenses.

Finally, for purposes of repeat offender status under Penal Code §12.42(a), (b), (c)(1), and (e) in an adult/criminal court, any felony juvenile adjudication related to conduct occurring after Jan. 1, 1996, and for which a child went to TYC (either directly or through revocation of probation) will be considered a final felony conviction.[40] Note that habitual felony offender status under Penal Code §12.42(d) is *not* included in the above list, thus excluding the use of a juvenile prior for habitual felon status.

---

38 Tex. Fam. Code §52.02(d).

39 See Tex. Alc. Bev. Code §106.041(h)(1).

40 See Tex. Penal Code §12.42(f); Tex. Fam. Code §§54.03, 54.04(d)(2), (d)(3), & (m), 54.05(f).

# Punishment Options

## PROBATION

The court can impose any "reasonable and lawful terms as the court may determine" for conditions of probation under Family Code §54.04(d)(1).[41]

A term of probation for an intoxication offense cannot extend past the child's 18th birthday, except for intoxication manslaughter which, if approved by a grand jury for a determinate sentence, can be up to 10 years. The same is true for intoxication assault if the new offense qualifies as habitual felony conduct and is approved by a grand jury for a determinate sentence under the Family Code.[42]

## TEXAS YOUTH COMMISSION

Only felony offenders can be committed to TYC; misdemeanor offenders cannot.[43] As a result, TYC:

- is not available for the misdemeanor offenses of DUI-Minor, DWI, boating while intoxicated, flying while intoxicated, and assembling/operating an amusement ride while intoxicated; but
- is available for the felony offenses of DWI with child passenger, intoxication assault, and intoxication manslaughter.

## CERTIFICATION

Certification to stand trial as an adult is not available for misdemeanor offenses, so all the offenses listed above under TYC as misdemeanors are out. However, for offenses committed at age 15-16, certification is available for DWI with child passenger, intoxication assault, and intoxication manslaughter. For offenses committed at age 14-16, certification is available for 1st degree intoxication manslaughter.[44]

## ZERO TOLERANCE LAWS

Alcoholic Beverage Code §106.041 (driving or operating watercraft under the influence of alcohol by a minor)[45] is a Class C misdemeanor. For children (someone who is 10-16 at the time of the offense), the adult criminal courts (JP/municipal, etc.) have original jurisdiction over the child's first two DUI-Minor offenses, although they have discretion to transfer those first two cases to juvenile court for prosecution as CINS offenses under Family Code §51.08(b)(2).

---

[41] Note that TEX. FAM. CODE §54.041 covers orders affecting parents and others; Tex. Fam. Code §54.042 covers license suspensions, more fully discussed below.

[42] See TEX. FAM. CODE §§51.031, 53.045(16), and 54.04(q).

[43] See TEX. FAM. CODE §54.04(d).

[44] See TEX. FAM. CODE §54.02. Note that §54.02 is the general certification statute. There is a secondary certification statute, TEX. FAM. CODE §54.02(j), used in cases that aren't solved prior to the defendant turning 18.

[45] For offenses committed before September 1, 2009, DUI-Minor only covers operation of a motor vehicle in a public place.

A juvenile court has original jurisdiction over third and subsequent driving under the influence of alcohol offenses as delinquent conduct under Family Code §51.03(a)(4). While it is true that a child who is prosecuted for a first or second DUI-Minor offense in JP or municipal court is subject to the "adult" rules related to interrogation and breath testing, it is recommended that the juvenile procedures be followed in DUI-Minor offenses involving a child because the JP or municipal court may elect to transfer the case to juvenile court, in which event compliance with the juvenile rules and procedures is required.

As noted above, unlike a juvenile adjudication for DWI, a juvenile adjudication for DUI-Minor is specifically considered a "conviction" under this statute.

Also note that there is no such concept as "deferred adjudication" or "deferred disposition" in juvenile court;[46] there is, however, a similar concept known as the deferred prosecution ("DPP"),[47] but offenses under Penal Code §§49.04, 49.05, 49.06, 49.07, and 49.08, and §§106.04 and 106.041 are *not* eligible for participation in DPP. Curiously, it appears that both DWI with child passenger (§49.045) and assembling or operating an amusement ride while intoxicated (§49.065)—because they are not specifically mentioned in the list under §54.04—*are* eligible for DPP.

## DRIVERS LICENSE SUSPENSIONS

Under Transportation Code §724.035, if a child refuses to provide a specimen, the refusal will result in a 180-day suspension or denial, which can increase to two years if the child has a prior offense. If a child consents and has any detectible amount of alcohol, the child will receive a 60-day license suspension, which can increase to 180 days if there are priors.[48]

A juvenile court must suspend a child's license for one year upon adjudication for DWI, DWI with child passenger, intoxication assault, or intoxication manslaughter.[49] If the offense adjudicated is DWI, intoxication assault, or intoxication manslaughter, in addition to the above one-year suspension, the court shall also impose the suspensions under Transportation Code chs. 524 or 724, if applicable. The court shall give the child credit toward the one-year total for these additional suspensions unless the child has been previously adjudicated for DWI, intoxication assault, or intoxication manslaughter, in which event no such credit may be given.[50]

---

46 See generally TEX. FAM. CODE §54.04.

47 See generally TEX. FAM. CODE §53.03.

48 See TEX. TRANS. CODE §524.022.

49 TEX. FAM. CODE §54.042(a)(1); TEX. TRANS. CODE §521.342(a).

50 See TEX. FAM. CODE §54.042(h).

# Index

## AAA



## BBB

# CCC

# DDD



# EEE

# FFF



# GGG



# HHH



# III

# JJJ

## LLL



## MMM

# OOO



# PPP

# Index of Cases

## A



## B

# C



# D

# E



# F



# G

# H

# I



# J



# K

# L



# M

## N



## O



## P



## Q



## R

# S

# T

# U



# V



# W

## Y



## Z



# Index of Statutes